The Taxonomy and Ecology
of

The Genus Ferocactus

Explorations in the USA and Mexico

George Lindsay

New Studies of *Ferocactus*
A review of *Ferocactus* Britton & Rose

contributed by J. Hugo Cota

with written additional contributions by

Madelyn Lee: *Ferocactus* Synonyms
Larry Mittich: Biography of George Lindsay
Frank Thrombley: *Ferocactus acanthodes*

with illustrations by

T. M. Bock
Lucretia Breazeale Hamilton
Dallas Hanna
Sandra Reed
Gerhard Marx

Tireless Termites Press
1996

First published in the United States of America in 1996 by Tireless Termites Press, a division of Bayshore Energy Systems.

Library of Congress Cataloging-In-Publication Data 96-061169
Lindsay, George
The Genus *Ferocactus*: Field and Laboratory Explorations
Includes contributed chapters on Taxonomy, Molecular Phylogenetics, Propagation, and Illustrations.

ISBN 0-9654359-0-3

1. Cactus 2. Ferocactus 3. Lindsay, George 4. Cota, J. Hugo

Book Design By Tireless Termites Press
Printed in the United States of America

TABLE OF CONTENTS

List of Figures . . . .
List of Distribution Maps ii
List of Figures by Species ii
Welcome to the Genus *Ferocactus* 1
Acknowledgments 3
The Taxonomy and Ecology of the
Genus *Ferocactus* by George Lindsay
Introduction 5
Characteristics and Evolution 7
Taxonomy 21
Key to the Species 29
Species and Varieties Descriptions . . . . 87 - 336
Imperfectly Known Species 337
Taxa Excluded 341
Bibliography 345
A Review of *Ferocactus* Britton and Rose by J. Hugo Cota
Prelude 35
Introduction 36
Taxonomic Background 37
Reproductive Biology in *Ferocactus* 39
Cytological Studies 43
Current Molecular Phylogenetic Knowledge 46
The Biogeography of *Ferocactus* 51
Conclusions 53
References 55
Glossary 77
Ferocactus Distributions 81
Ferocactus Synonyms 83
Observations on *Ferocactus acanthodes* 290
Illustrated Glossary 353
Illustrators Corner drawings 375
The Hanna Portfolio color photos 383
Growing *Ferocactus* Seedlings 371
George E. Lindsay biography **357**
Editors' Choices photographs 418

Listing of Figures by Species

NO.	SPECIES	VARIETIES	FIGURE #	DIST. MAPS	ILLUS. C'NER.	HANNA FOLIO	EDITORS' CHOICES
23	*acanthodes*	*acanthodes*	115-117,120-121	7	141	148	164
		lecontei	126				
		tortulispinus	123-125				165
		eastwoodiae					
		"rostii"	118-119,122				
7	*alamosanus*	*pottsii*	30-32	2			181
		alamosanus	29				
14	*covillei (emoryi)*		64-68	4	142	149	166
20	*chrysacanthus*		99-100	5			167
25	*diguetii*	*diguetii*	132-134	8		150	
		carmenensis	135-136				
4	*echidne*	*echidne*	19-20,64-68	1		151	see Fig. 6
		victoriensis	21-22				168
		= rafaelensis					
1	*flavovirens*		12	1		152	see Fig. 6
21	*fordii*	*fordii*	101-102	6			169
		grandiflorus	103-104				
19	*gatesii*		97-98	4		153	
3	*glaucescens*		16-17	1		154	170
18	*gracilis*	*gracilis*	90-92	6		154	171, 172, 1
		coloratus	93-98				174
28	*haematacanthus*			7			175
29	*hamatacanthus*	*hamatacanthus*		9	143		
		sinuatus					
13	*herrerae*		62-63	4		156	
8	*histrix*		26-28	2		157	176a
24	*johnstonianus*		129-131	8			177
10	*latispinus*		44-45	3			178
27	*lindsayi*		139	7			
8	*macrodiscus*		33-37	2		158	see Fig. 6
16	*peninsulae*	*peninsulae*	73-74	5		159	
		viscainensis					179
11	*pilosus*		46-49,51-52	3			180
15	*rectispinus*		69-71	4		160	182
9	*recurvus*	*recurvus*	38-41	3			183
		greenwoodii					176b

NO.	SPECIES	VARIETIES	FIGURE #	DIST. MAPS	ILLUS. C'NER.	HANNA FOLIO	EDITORS' CHOICES
26	*reppenhagenii*			1			184
2	*robustus*		15	1		161	
5	*schwarzii*		23-24	2			185
30	*setispinus*			9	144		
17	*townsendianus*	*townsendianus*	80-85	5	145	162	186A, 187A
		santa-maria	86-89				186B, 187B
22	*viridescens*	*viridescens*	105-110	6	146		187B
		littoralis	111				
12	*wislizenii*	*wislizenii*	53-59	3 & 4	147	163	188
		tiburonensis	60-61				

Welcome to The Genus *Ferocactus*

This book has George Lindsay's 1955 doctoral thesis, "The Taxonomy and Ecology of the Genus *Ferocactus*," at its core. To round it out, there are updates and other contributions, all with Dr. Lindsay's blessing. These include a biography, some interesting color photos, botanical illustrations, tips on propagation, an illustrated glossary, a table summarizing *Ferocactus* distributions, a listing of *Ferocactus* synonyms, and a chapter on current taxonomy research involving analyses of DNA to rearrange the taxa tree. The book can serve as a pocketable field guide, be useful to a gardener, and bring one up-to-date on recent laboratory techniques, which when backed with field work can be used to trace what was thought to be untraceable a decade ago.

Cactophiles are attracted to these New World plants for their forms, their hardiness, their floral varieties, their ecologies, and their biological adaptations. Ferocacti are one of the 200 plus cactus genera with about three-dozen species and varieties. George Lindsay's enthusiasm began at an early age, and he elected to leave ranching behind and pursue a life of botanical research and exploration. This is described in the biography by Larry Mittich.

It is generally agreed that *Ferocactus* have evolved from *Echinocactus* and that *Ferocactus* transformations into species and varieties have occurred according to some order. Tracing this order via DNA techniques was selected as a doctoral thesis topic by Hugo Cota, with Professor Robert Wallace at Iowa State University as his advisor. The genus *Ferocactus* was a fortuitous selection for this pioneering work for several reasons: the genus is large enough to find a pattern, but not so large as to be an impenetrable thicket; Lindsay's field work is a reliable guide to morphology and biogeography of the species. Hugo describes these reasons in his own way in his chapter. The techniques developed by the Iowa group will continue to improve and serve others who wish to pursue studies within other plant taxa. At the time of original publication of this book, the *Ferocactus* studies were incomplete and these published results should be considered only as indicative of future findings.

A few updating revisions in italic form have been included within Lindsay's text. They include the addition of two added species; the rearrangement of some species into varieties; and some details on *Ferocactus acanthodes* varieties, provided by Frank Thrombley, who has field collected and studied *Ferocactus* for many years. Since the positions of species and varieties are likely to change following Cota's work, we expect to be forgiven for an occasional disarrangement in our arrangements. These are exciting times!

The editors have supported the text with a few appendices. George Lindsay's thesis, while easy reading, uses botanical terms which may be unfamiliar to some readers. Hence we have provided an illustrated glossary. Madelyn Lee, Manager of the Grigsby Cactus Gardens and a longtime *Ferocactus* enthusiast, provided a list of past and present synonyms. The editors have included a list of *Ferocactus* localities.

It was important to us that this book reflect the beauty of *Ferocactus* and the work of all involved. We have included the remarkable color plates produced by Dr. Dallas Hanna and team several decades ago on ordinary office equipment; the illustrations of Lucretia Breazeale Hamilton, made for George Lindsay's doctoral adviser and friend, Ira Wiggins; the amusing rear cover caricature of George Lindsay and Reid Moran by Gerhard Marx; and the poetic front cover and end papers by Sandra Reed, our Art Director.

Charley Glass wrote us that he has been waiting for the Lindsay book for 35 years. A book is an experience. We predict that this experience will serve for a long time.

Acknowledgments

This book represents the efforts and contributions of many people. The core of the book, Dr. Lindsay's informative PhD thesis, has never before been effectively published, being available only as illustrationless copies, extracted from microfiche. The California Academy of Sciences typed most of the text on a word processor. The balance of text was scanned by OCR (optical character recognition) software and subsequently smoothed into English. The approximately 120 accompanying photos and figures were scanned into the text apart from the captions, which were separately blended in. In areas where there was new information, it was gently inserted as editorial notes or as appendices. The sources of this new information include Frank Thrombley, a frequent Baja California explorer, who wrote on *Ferocactus acanthodes* varieties; Madelyn Lee, Manager of Grigsby Cactus Gardens, who supplied a list of synonyms; and authorities such as Curt Backeburg's Cactus Lexicon; Nigel Taylor's articles on *Ferocactus* in Bradleya Nos. 2/1984 & 5/1987; Lyman Benson's The Cacti of the United States and Canada; and Ira Wiggins' Flora of Baja California.

George Lindsay and the editors were interested in how molecular studies being performed by Hugo Cota at Iowa State University would clarify the phylogenetic relationships of Ferocacti. Despite a heavy field, laboratory, and academic schedule, Hugo made time to write a chapter describing his current work. This work will bring about a rearrangement of the genus and will serve as a model for work on other genera.

Aesthetics were not neglected. The "Illustrators Gallery" appendix shows the botanical illustration skill of Lucretia Breazeale Hamilton. These were reprinted from "The Cacti of the United States and Canada" by Lyman Benson with permission of the publishers, Stanford University Press, (1982). Our Art Director, Sandra Reed, not wishing to duplicate the botanical illustration style of Lucretia Hamilton, created the fanciful and colorful front cover. The rear cover by Gerhard Marx makes us smile. The Hanna Color Plates were made decades ago at George Lindsay's instigation by an ingenious office copying process devised by an ingenious man and his helpers (more about Hanna in the book).

The lucid illustrations of cactus forms, flowers, and spines within the Illustrated Glossary foldout were done by Thor Methven Bock. They appeared in Cactaceae by W. Taylor Marshall and T. M. Bock (1941) and are reprinted with the permission of Charles Glass, publisher of the former Abbey Garden Press.

Galleys of the book were reviewed and edited by George Lindsay and all of the contributors. The editors welcome corrections and suggestions for future printings. The book was assembled by the editors, using a blend of old crafts and the latest in digital processing methods. This book now resides in digital form. It will be printed in small batches as needed, a process called "printing-on-demand." What we have learned during the publication process will be made available to others.

Eventually, the editors expect that publishing-on-demand will become a smooth process. At present there are many speed bumps. We were able to glide over them through the help and ingenuity of our premiere suppliers. They include: Copy Girls for endpaper printing, who made my overlays match up; McKibben Silk Screen Printing who easily handled what others couldn't; and Universal Reprographics for text printing, inputting our files through their system. Special thanks go to Jerry Kiley, Manager of Golden Rule Bindery, for exceptional help and ingenuity. Golden Rule assembles this book from components as needed.

The Editors

Reese Brown Mark Raptis Stan Yalof Fred Fox

The Taxonomy and Ecology of the Genus Ferocactus

Dr. George Lindsay

Introduction

The genus *Ferocactus* belongs to the subtribe Echinocactinae of the tribe Cereeae, in the Cactaceae. Ferocacti are commonly called "barrel cacti" or "visnagas" and inhabit certain arid and semi-arid regions of Mexico and southwestern United States. They are bulky succulent plants, globular or cylindric in shape, with a covering of spines borne on parallel ridges or ribs. True leaves are lacking, and photosynthesis takes place in the superficial layers of the stem.

Ferocactus was one of the more natural segregate genera proposed by Britton and Rose in 1922, when they subdivided the large polyphyletic genus *Echinocactus*. Political unrest in Mexico, as well as the inaccessibility of some of the major cactus territories, prevented adequate field work by Britton and Rose. A number of the 31 species which they assigned to the new genus were imperfectly known, and several have been found to be synonyms or have been transferred to other genera. Recent plant exploration has added new species. A monographic study of the genus *Ferocactus* therefore seemed desirable.

Cacti present unusual problems for the taxonomist, and effectual work with them requires somewhat unorthodox research procedures. Ordinarily taxonomic research involves a review of the literature, the examination of a mass of herbarium material, and, if possible, field investigations of critical taxa or areas. The literature concerning the Cactaceae is fairly abundant but often of inadequate quality. Many species were described from a single, sterile, seedling plant, the geographical origin of which was unknown. Descriptions were often meager and before 1900 the preservation of type material was the exception rather than the rule. Even now cacti are poorly represented in herbaria because their succulence and spininess make field preparation and preservation slow. Those specimens which are available are often unsatisfactory because they consist of only flowers or fruit or fragments of vegetative material. Complete specimens may fail to show the characters of the living plant, these characters having been lost or altered with the drying of succulent tissue. Several species of *Ferocactus* apparently were not represented by a single specimen in any herbarium when this study was undertaken

I used the following investigational procedure. The available literature was reviewed and photocopies of pertinent information were made. The major cactus herbaria and botanical gardens of the United States were visited and critical and type material was studied and photographed. Specimens, photographs, and information were obtained from European herbaria through correspondence. Herbaria visited included those of the New York Botanical Garden, Missouri Botanical Garden, Desert Botanical Garden of Arizona, Biological Institute of the University of Mexico, University of Arizona, University of California, San Diego Natural History Museum, California Academy of Sciences, United States National Herbarium, Allan Hancock Foundation, Rancho Santa Ana Botanic Garden, Pomona College, and Dudley Herbarium of Stanford University. In addition, living plants were studied in the collections of the University of Michigan, New York Botanic Garden, Henry E. Huntington Botanical Garden, Desert Botanical Garden, the Botanic Garden of the University of California, Howard E. Gates Lower California Botanic Garden, and at the Biological Institute of the University of Mexico. I am indebted to the officials of all of those institutions for the assistance they gave me. Special thanks are due Charles Baehni, Director of the Botanical Gardens and Herbarium in Geneva; Sir Edward Salisbury, Director of the Royal Botanical Gardens at Kew; Dr. A. W. Ewell, Deputy Keeper of the Department of Botany of the British Museum; Prof. Guillaumin, Director of the Laboratoire de Culture of the Museum National d'Histoire Naturelle; and Dr. Reed C. Rollins, Director of the Gray Herbarium of Harvard University. All of these gentlemen were most cooperative in searching for critical specimens and supplying photographs, loans, and important information.

The major phase of my research was that conducted in the field. I traveled about 20,000 miles by automobile and truck and 5,000 miles by boat in order to visit the general areas where Ferocacti grow. There the species were studied, photographed, and collected as living and herbarium specimens. The living plants were grown and observed at Stanford and the Desert Botanical Garden of Arizona. The field studies were essential for any understanding of the plants which are poorly represented in herbaria, and for information about the variation within and between taxa. The collections of herbarium material have been adopted in the Dudley Herbarium, with duplicates going to the San Diego Natural History Museum.

Ecological data do not constitute a major portion of this paper, but some of the more obvious ecological factors are discussed. A comprehensive ecological study would have involved methods of field investigation incompatible with the schedule of collecting which was maintained in order to observe all of the species in their native habitats.

I want to thank the many friends who have helped investigate the Ferocacti. My major professor, Dr. Ira L. Wiggins, has been most generous with counsel and suggestions, has evidenced a deep personal interest in the problem, and has been my companion on field trips. Dr. Richard W, Holm has also advised and helped me in many ways. Mr. J. W. Sefton, Jr, sponsored a major expedition, the Sefton Foundation - Stanford University Expedition to the Gulf of California, which allowed me to collect on the inaccessible islands along the west coast of Lower California and the Gulf of California. Dr. Helia Bravo Hollis, noted authority on Mexican cacti, has given me much information about the species in central and southern Mexico, and has arranged trips in that area in order for me to study them in the field. Mr. Howard E. Gates, who discovered and named several Ferocacti in the Lower California region, has been a personal friend for many years and always most generous in supplying information. Dr. Faustino Miranda, of the University of Mexico, accompanied Dr. Wiggins and me on a survey trip through the arid regions of the states of Puebla and Oaxaca. Dr. Miranda's knowledge of the thorn forest and desert flora increased tremendously the value of the trip for us. Mr. Fritz Schwarz, of San Luis Potosi, has been very generous in supplying information about collecting localities of the Mexican mainland species, and has personally shown me where many grow. Dr. Reid Moran has been my companion on several botanical exploration trips and has been very helpful with ideas and information. Mr. Wm. Taylor Marshall, Director of the Desert Botanical Garden of Arizona, has raised and kept records of plants for me, and has also supplied data from his own knowledge of the family. Dr. Lyman Benson of Pomona College not only gave me the use of his splendid cactus herbarium, but also supplied helpful suggestions and ideas concerning various taxonomic problems within the Cactaceae, on which he has actively worked for many years. Mr. Thomas MacDougall, veteran plantsman of southern Mexico, collected with us in Tehuantepec, showed us where unusual species were found, and has made special efforts to procure rare plants for me. Prof. William C. Steere, of Stanford University, has given me friendly encouragement and advice and has been my companion on several collecting trips. Mr. Charles F. Harbison of the San Diego Natural History Museum has given me photographs and specimens of Ferocacti from isolated areas in Lower California which I have not visited. Some of the specimens and information which he obtained cost him considerable effort, and proved to be of great value. This is but a partial list of those to whom I am indebted, and to whom I wish to express sincere appreciation.

Characteristics and Evolution of the Cactaceae

General Characteristics. Cacti are perennial succulent plants, usually leafless, and with greatly thickened cylindrical or flattened stems. The most primitive genera have broad flat leaves, but in only slightly advanced types the leaves are reduced to small, early deciduous terete or scale-like structures. Nearly all cacti bear spines, produced in clusters in specialized and characteristic organs called areoles, which are located in the axils of leaf bearing types. The areoles are homologous to axillary buds or shoots, and the spines are modified bud scales or leaves. Flowers are usually solitary at an areole, perfect, sessile, and produced laterally. The perianth consists of numerous spirally arranged segments which are only weakly differentiated into sepals and petals. The stamens are numerous, spirally inserted at the base of the hypanthium, and bear two-celled anthers. The style is single, with two to many stigma lobes, these probably reflecting the number of carpels. The ovary is typically inferior, polycarpellate and unilocular, with parietal placentation. Ovules are numerous with large funiculi which in some genera persist to envelope the seed. Enlarged funiculi often form the fleshy portion of edible cactus fruit. The fruit is a many-seeded berry, commonly glochidiate, spiny, or bristly, but sometimes naked. Seeds are variable, with a curved or straight embryo and little or no endosperm. In the genus *Rhipsalis* the endosperm is sometimes viscid.

The Cactaceae are an American family, and occur from southern Canada to Patagonia. A few species of *Rhipsalis*, a genus of tropical epiphytes, occur in forests of West Africa, Madagascar, and Ceylon, but are probably not indigenous there. Many Opuntias have become naturalized in various parts of the Old World, particularly in the Mediterranean region, but also throughout the semidesert areas of central and south Africa, as well as Australia and New Zealand. In many areas in which they have become established they are of positive economic value, but some species are aggressive, noxious weeds, and their control is a serious problem.

Derivation of the Cactaceae. The Cactaceae is a remarkably natural family, very distinct from other plant families, and often treated as a separate order. However, their phylogenetic position and derivation are not clear, and they have been variously treated as belonging to the Grossulariodeae, Cucurbitaceae, Loasaceae, Sonneratiaceae, and Centrospermae. The strongest evidence seems to indicate a relationship with the Centrospermae. There are a number of conditions in the Phytolaccaceae which anticipate peculiar characters of cacti, including formation of ribs, appearance of proareoles, spinous first bracts, serial splitting of the axillary product, etc. In the flowers of cacti and *Phytolacca* Buxbaum (1953, *p.* 103) found similar peltate carpels and vascularization, which formed a series from *Phytolacca* through *Pereskia* to other cacti. Buxbaum thinks that tile Cactaceae have developed from the Phytolaccaceae and parallel to *Mesembryanthemum.*

Additional evidence also suggests the Centrospermae kinship. Erdtman (1952, p. 88) found that apertures and sexine details of cactus pollen show the same characters as those of the Centrospermae, and "the grains in the Loasaceae, Saxifragaceae (Ribesoideae), and Sonneratiaceae are more or less different, and so it would appear, are the grains in the Cucurbitaceae." Among the dicots the seed characters of starchy endosperm and peripheral embryos are apparently confined to cacti and the Centrospermae. Mahesnwari (1950, *p.* 363), on the basis of embryological evidence, suggests that the Cactaceae should be regarded as a sort of hybrid between the Aizoaceae and Portulacaceae .

Phylogeny of the Cactaceae. There are no reliable fossil records of cacti, and any system of phylogeny within the family must be based on evidence obtained from living species. Fortunately, the family contains a series of intermediate forms from unspecialized primitive tropical taxa to the highly evolved and modified types, and major evolutionary lines of development can be deduced from comparative morphology. Berger (1926) published a theory of the phylogeny within the Cactaceae, based on morphological studies of present species .

Most authors consider the Cactaceae to comprise three tribes (or subfamilies), the Pereskieae, Opuntieae, and Cereeae. The Pereskieae include the most primitive existing cacti. They are woody shrubs or trees with broad foliage leaves, and look like typical dicots. *Pereskia aculeata* and *P. sacharosa* are the most primitive, with superior flowers born in panicles, and large foliage leaves responsible for the photosynthetic activity of the plants. The genus *Rhodocactus* exhibits the first advance in the Pereskieae with the production of a true seed chamber with parietal placentation, increased succulence of stem, and thicker leaves with reduced surface areas.

The tribe Opuntieae includes the large genus *Opuntia*, the chollas and prickly-pears, and a few smaller genera. The Opuntias show a strong reduction of the surface of the leaf blade, in fact in most cases very minute leaves appear only on new growth and are early deciduous. At the same time there is a great enlargement of the leaf base, or podaria, which results in the formation of a fleshy structure called a tubercle. The tubercles are responsible for a decided increase in the succulence of the stem. In this tribe the tubercles are not fused to form ribs, except in the monotypic genus *Grusonia* and a few other cylindropuntias. The tribe is characterized by the presence of specialized retrorsely barbed spines, called glochids, which are present in all species. The flowers are sessile, diurnal, and produced singly at an areole. The fruit retains many stem features, for example in *Opuntia subulata* the ovary is enclosed in an enlarged terminal portion of the stem. In many species the areoles of the fruit remain meristematic, with other flowers and fruits produced from them, resulting in a series of eighteen or twenty fruits in a chain. The fruit of this type is often sterile and easily detached. When knocked to the ground it strikes root and produces shoots from the areoles.

The genus *Pereskiopsis*, assigned to the Opuntieae, is rather close to the Pereskieae. It has small but persistent leaves and forms woody shrubs or trees, resembling *Pereskia* and other normal dicots. The flowers are similar to those of Opuntia, although the ovary of *Pereskiopsis opuntiaeflorae* is short pedunculate. All of the *Pereskiopsis* species bear glochids.

Berger (1926, p. 9) suggested evidence that the Opuntia tribe is polyphyletic. In any case, they are not an intermediate stage to the third tribe, but are an end product of a separate line. A highly successful and widely distributed group, there are representatives from the cold plains of

Canada and Patagonia to the tropics. Opuntias occur at altitudes of over 14,000 feet in the Andes and 10,000 feet in the Rocky Mountains.

The third tribe, Cereeae, is a polyphyletic complex of over 100 genera and 1000 species. It evolved from a *Pereskia*-like ancestor, as did the Opuntias, but the trail is not so clear. Intermediate forms between the Cereeae and Pereskieae do not exist, at least there are no obvious examples such as *Pereskiopsis* which links *Pereskia* and *Opuntia*. Certainly the Cereeae and the Opuntieae occupy two distinct divergent lines. The Cereeae progress, as did the Opuntias, through forms with much reduced, deciduous leaves and increased body succulence. Leaves are found in young plants of *Rhipsalis*, *Epiphyllum*, *Hylocereus*, *Pfeiffera*, *Acanthocereus*, *Nyctocereus*, and perhaps others. However, the majority of the genera have lost all external evidence of leaves, although vestigial traces are to be seen in microscopic preparations of the apical meristems of the most highly evolved types. Another advance which can be traced through the Cereeae is the decrease in size of the cotyledons, with increased fleshiness of the hypocotyl. In other words, the morphology of the embryo reflects reduction of leaf area, and increased succulence of the plant body, which is found to be the trend in the adult. In the Cereeae the podaria, or enlarged leaf bases, are usually fused to form ribs in columnar species, but a return to the tuberculate condition is found in the most highly evolved cactoid types. The stem or axial nature of the ovary is almost completely lost in some genera and meristematic areoles on the fruit are not found. The fruit gradually lose their areoles with spines and bristles, to finally become quite naked.

The tribe Cereeae has four distinct subtribes, Rhipsalideae, Epiphylleae, Hylocereae, and Cereae. The first three are tropical epiphytic or clambering cacti. The fourth subtribe, Cereae, has a large number of polymorphic subdivisions, of which for this study the most important are the *Trichocereus* complex and *Pachycereus* complex.

The Trichocerei are large columnar South American cacti of the relationship which apparently gave rise to most of the globular cacti of that continent. The *Pachycereus* complex is the North American equivalent of the South American *Trichocereus* group. *Pachycereus* has thick stems, campanulate flowers, and spiny fruit. Several genera of bulky tree cacti apparently developed from it, including *Carnegiea* and *Lemaireocereus*, and nearly all of the North American cactoid (globular) genera seem to have been derived from this relationship. The North American Echinocacti share no close relationship with the South American cactoid genera, which were evolved from the *Trichocereus* complex, and their distributions are entirely distinct. Buxbaum (1951a, P. 193) has proposed a new phylogenetic system for the North American Echinocacti, which Moran (1954, pp. 45-48) recently reviewed. Buxbaum proposed a fifth tribe, Euechinocactineae, which includes nearly all of the North American globular cacti. In his diagnosis of the relationships within his new tribe he considered all of the available morphological data, but placed special emphasis on the inner and outer shape of the seed. The system proposed by Buxbaum has little effect on the former position of *Ferocactus*, deriving it directly from *Echinocactus*, but it does change some concepts of genera formerly considered to be derivatives of *Ferocactus*, e.g. *Echinomastus*, *Sclerocactus*, *Hamatocactus*, etc. More important changes result at the ends of the lines, where some old genera, such as *Mammillaria*, have been split up in accordance with their proposed polyphyletic origins.

Buxbaum indicates the genus *Echinocactus* is the most primitive in his tribe, with four phylogenetic lines diverging from it. He derives *Ferocactus* directly from *Echinocactus* and *Coloradoa* and *Echinofossulocactus* from *Ferocactus*. The position of the flowers, which are produced in a procephalium in *Echinocactus*, might indicate, however, that it is more advanced than *Ferocactus*, and there is reason to believe that such genera as *Sclerocactus*, *Echinomastus*, and *Hamatocactus* are more closely related to *Ferocactus* than Buxbaum indicates.

Morphology. The bulky, globular, leafless character of Ferocacti demonstrates the striking morphological modifications which enable them to grow in environments hostile to most plants. This study is not concerned with *Ferocactus* morphology per se, but some of the more obvious features are worth reviewing. The observations reported here came mostly from a rather superficial study and dissection of specimens of *Ferocactus viridescens*, *F. acanthodes*, and *F. wislizenii*.

The root system of a barrel cactus is in two series. A few short vertical tap roots apparently serve to anchor the plant, while a system of shallow radiating lateral roots are the principal absorptive organs. Preston (1900, p. 348) studied the roots of F. *wislizenii* and found plants about seven dm tall usually had rapidly tapering tap roots which penetrated the ground about 30 cm. The xylem of these was composed largely of fibrous sclerenchyma, and the roots themselves were strong and elastic. The proportion of conducting tissue was small. However, the plants also had three or four long sinuous radiating roots which tapered very slightly but branched frequently and bore many fine rootlets. This absorptive system was not over 10 cm deep, and effectively covered the ground area within a radius of about two and a half meters from the plant. The roots were weak and brittle, with the xylem composed largely of conducting rather than mechanical tissue.

A unique root character was observed in *Ferocactus macrodiscus*, which has thick and well developed tap roots. These had the transverse creases characteristic of contractile roots, such as those of *Taraxacum*. The flattened stem of *F. macrodiscus* is depressed below the surface of the soil during periods of drouth, probably as a result of the loss of some of the turgidity of the plant body and the contractile pull of the tap roots. This species also has a well developed system of lateral absorptive roots.

The stems of Ferocacti are fleshy globular or columnar structures. The woody central cylinder is a siphonostele of small diameter. Stem succulence results from a great development of the cortex, which is composed of parenchymatous storage cells. The stele has numerous gaps and departing vascular bundles which provide the thick succulent cortex with a good vascular supply. The bundles are homologous to leaf traces, but are not usually directly connected with the areoles. The metabolic activity of the areoles ceases after the early production of a flower and fruit, and the function of photosynthesis is carried on in the superficial layers of the stem, which are well supplied with vascular elements. The stele of the barrel cactus thus is primarily an organ of circulation rather than support, and it lacks the mechanical strength of the skeletal systems of the arborescent cacti.

The epidermis of the plant body is protected by a thick cuticle, which not only covers the surface but also extends into and lines the chambers under the stomata. It consists of a single layer of cells with greatly thickened exterior walls. In *Ferocactus viridescens* the thickness of the outer wall may be more than half the diameter of the entire cell. The integument is perforated by numerous small stomata, but these are not located in deep pits or depressions, as is often the case with xerophytes. The epidermis is underlain by a thick hypodermis which is penetrated by the stomatal chambers connecting the deeper assimilative tissue and the guard cells. This internal cuticle-lined chamber is doubtlessly a more effective water vapor trap than would be an external vestibule of the same dimensions. The hypodermal cells are thick-walled, druse-containing sclereids. Brown (1915, p. 317) gave 200 micra as the thickness of the entire integument of *F. wislizenii*. He found that the cuticle was nine micra, the epidermal cells about 40 micra, and the hypodermis 150 micra thick. The outer walls of the epidermal cells of this species were 11 micra thick. The whole integument is highly adapted to prevent water loss.

The photosynthetic portion of the plant is a layer of palisade parenchyma about three mm thick, which lies just under the hypodermis. The cells are barrel-shaped and attached at the ends to form columns. In *F. viridescens* this tissue is quite compact, but Brown (ibid) found the columns of palisade cells in *F. wislizenii* to be free of each other, with few lateral contacts. The columns of palisade cells intergrade imperceptibly into more rounded cells beneath, which also contain chloroplasts. Under this area is the great mass of quite compact, rounded or rectangular parenchyma cells of the storage tissue in the enlarged cortex.

Ribs are characteristic of all Ferocacti, and are thought to represent rows of vertically fused podaria. The number of ribs of a cactus thus reflects its phyllotaxy. The apical meristem produces tuberculate structures bearing the areoles, and these tubercles almost immediately fuse into ribs. The ribs are an advantage because they permit rapid expansion, like the bellows of an accordion, allowing for rapid intake of water when moisture is present.

Spines are produced serially on the abaxial side of the meristem of the areole, thus the flower, though terminal, appears on its upper side. Only one flower is produced by an areole in *Ferocactus*, and in cultivation, at least, not all areoles are floriferous. The spines are rather arbitrarily classified as centrals, radials, or bristles, depending upon their position and character. This is not entirely satisfactory because the position is only relative and subject to varying interpretations, and the character of the radial spines is variable. All spines are produced in the same manner by the activity of a meristematic area at the base. The cells are soft and round when first formed, but elongate and become impregnated with calcium carbonate and pectic substances. The tip of a partially grown spine is hard and horny while the base is still soft. The larger spines of most Ferocacti are transversely striated, with each striation indicating one day's growth.. The long central spines of *Ferocactus rectispinus* may take as long as 150 days to grow.

In a number of cactus genera, particularly *Ferocactus*, certain spines are modified for the production of a sweet secretion, and serve as extra-floral nectaries. These gland-spines are located between the spine fascicle and the point of flower production in the areole. They appear during the blossoming period of the plant and attract large numbers of ants and insects. The gland-spines appear as heavy, blunt protuberances, usually less than five mm long. At the top, the tissues disintegrate and produce nectar, which accumulates and dries into a very sweet sugar. The stumps of the glands harden and persist as dwarf spines.

Flowers of Ferocacti are perfect, solitary, and regular, and are produced by young areoles near the top of the plant. The ovary is inferior, and the carpels covered with a pericarpel tissue which bears scales. The scales intergrade with the outer perianth segments. The perianth consists of many spirally arranged segments which are not clearly differentiated into sepals and petals, although the outer are usually more sepal-like and the inner more petal-like. The very numerous stamens are spirally inserted in the thickened tube between the base of the inner perianth segments and a nectareous pit at the base of the style. The style of *Ferocactus* is rather short and thick, grooved, with the tip divided into several to many stigma-lobes.

The fruit is semifleshy, and bears scales with naked axils. Some species, for example *F. echidne*, *F. histrix*, and *F. flavispinus*, have fleshy pulp composed of enlarged funiculi surrounding the many seeds. In some species the funiculi fill the locule of immature fruit, but deliquesce as the fruit approaches maturity. The walls of the fruit are largely pericarpel tissue, which does not extend over the actual connection between the fruit and the areole. When the fruit is loosened a basal pore is opened, because the thin carpel tissue usually remains on the plant. In some species the basal carpel tissue is retained on the fruit and no pore is formed.

Seeds of the Ferocacti have a pitted or sculptured black or brown testa, and are usually one to three mm long. The hilum and micropyle are not conspicuous. The embryo is slightly curved, with rather small cotyledons and quite succulent hypocotyl. Endosperm is lacking but a small amount of perisperm is present in the chalazal end of the seed.

Ecology. The habitat of Ferocacti is one of low and uneven rainfall, low humidity, high air and surface soil temperatures with great diurnal and seasonal fluctuations, and strong winds. Moisture may be abundant during short periods, but these times are separated by intervals of drouth which are sometimes years in duration. Any life form which is to survive such conditions must be able either to utilize rapidly the moisture when it is present or to secure water which is in such minute supply or accessibility as to be unavailable to unspecialized organisms. All forms must have adaptations and devices which prevent extravagant spending of water when it is not available. A plant must both absorb and transpire water, and it is the ratio or balance between the rates of the two processes which determines its fitness for arid survival. Species prodigal with water are eliminated. Xerophytes have developed means to maintain a satisfactory water balance even under adverse conditions and the ability to resist drouth is one of the important determining factors of plant distribution.

An admittedly overly simplified classification of the plant life forms represented in arid regions would include **ephemerals**, the annual plants which complete their life cycles during the rare intervals of adequate moisture, and exist through the times of drouth in the form of seeds. These are often called "drought escaping." The second type is the **woody perennial**, which exhibits an amazing array of modifications, the most conspicuous of which is the reduction of transpiration surface. The ecological adaptations of these has been studied in some detail, by Cannon (1906), Delf (1912), Maximov (1929), Runyon (1934), Scott (1950), Shields (1950), and Went (1955), to mention but a few. The third form of desert plant, to which *Ferocactus* belongs and which we will briefly consider here, is the **succulent plant**.

All xerophytes have "water proof" integuments of one sort or another, to prevent uncontrolled water loss. There must be gas exchange with the environment, however, and this is through the regulated stomatal openings. In the woody perennials, as in mesic plants, transpiration and gas exchange are greatest during the daylight hours, when light furnishes the energy for photosynthesis and there is a demand for the carbon dioxide from the air. The greatly increased evaporative rate resulting from the higher temperatures and frequent winds during the daylight hours makes this a particularly precarious and unfavorable time for relaxing the barriers between the moist interior of the plant and the evaporative forces of the environment.

Livingston (1907) discovered that cacti transpire heavily during the night, rather than in the day time, as is the case with non-succulent plants. He charted the rates and came to the conclusion that cacti have a mechanism for governing the rate of water loss which is entirely different in its response to the external conditions and periodicity. Edith Shreve (1916) undertook a series of experiments to find the causes of the variation, and discovered the nocturnal transpiration of cacti was at least partially caused by the stomata being open at night and closed during the day. She decided that if it was an increase in the osmotic pressure of the guard cells which, for non-succulent plants, caused the stomata to open by bringing about a greater rate of water entrance to the guard cells, then the increased osmotic pressure may be overbalanced in the plant by increase in the water holding capacity of the tissue within. On the other hand, the decrease in osmotic strength which had generally been postulated to explain stomatal closure at night might be counteracted in the cactus by the nocturnal decrease in the water holding capacity of internal tissues.

Mrs. Shreve observed that there is an appreciable increase in acidity of the protoplasm of cacti through the night, which seemed to be the probable explanation for the decrease in the water retention ability of the protoplasm within the cells. The permeability of the protoplasm to water is decreased under the influence of weak acids. Mrs. Shreve concluded that the changes in the hydrogen ion concentration of the protoplasm were to some extent responsible for the water holding capacity, but not independently responsible for those changes. Rather, the acid content affects transpiration through its effect on the turgidity of the guard cells of the stomata. The water holding power of cactus tissue was also found to be proportional to the temperature during the night.

Mrs. Shreve concluded that there are two complex factors which govern the water loss in plants, aridity of environment as a whole and the transpiring power of the plant itself. In cacti there is a regular diurnal change of water holding capacity in the internal tissues and the theory was offered that these changes are both directly and indirectly responsible for transpiring power and also the secondary absorbing power of the plant. The transpiring power of a cactus is usually greater at night than during the day because the water holding capacity of its tissues is greater by day than by night; i.e., the plant's power of resistance to the aerial aridity factor is greater by day than by night. The probable source of the energy of this resistance lies in the imbibitional forces of the hydrophilic colloids and cell walls, which are affected by the hydrogen ion concentration of the water, and hence the surface tension forces; that is, the mutual attraction of the molecules.

Skene (1924, p. 113) states that succulent plants vary from other plants in their carbon dioxide exchange. Their gas exchange with the external environment is limited. When they respire at night the production of carbon dioxide is small, and organic acids - malic in the Cactaceae, isomalic acid

Figure 1. ***Ferocactus viridescens*****, Longitudinal Section.**

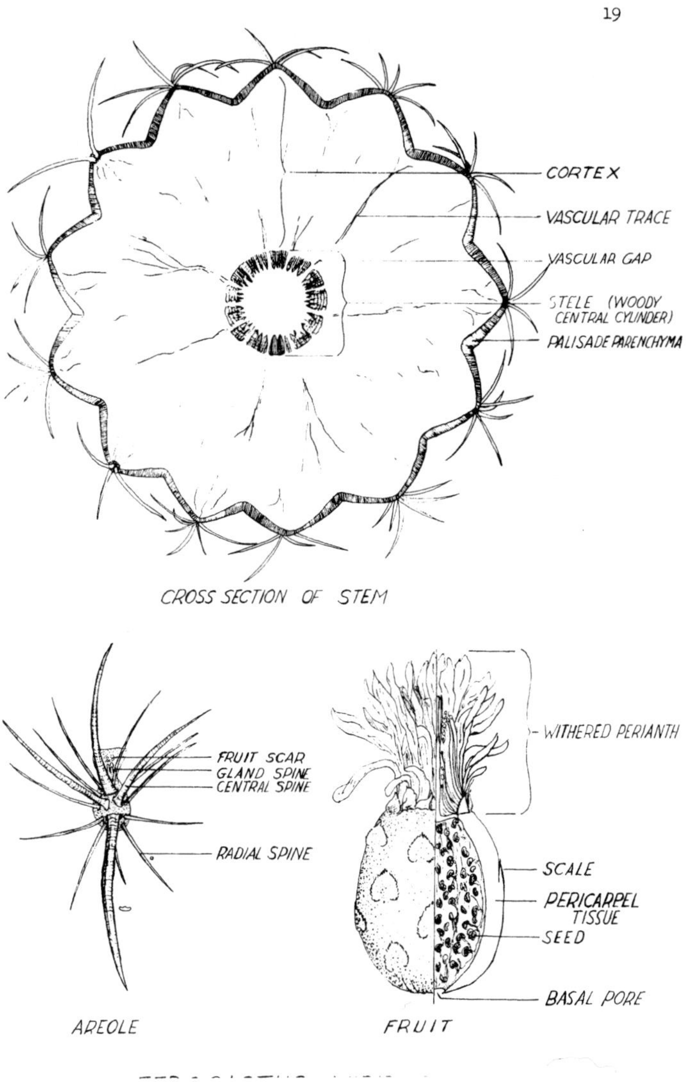

Figure 2. ***Ferocactus viridescens*, Cross section, Fruit, and Areole.**

in the Crassulaceae, and oxalic acid in the Mesembryanthemaceae - are produced instead. This is an incomplete form of respiration with reduced energy production, but it also means the retention of carbon compounds in the plant. During the day these plants carry on assimilation partly at the expense of their stored acids, and with only partial utilization of the atmospheric carbon dioxide, thus decreasing necessity of transpiration during the hours when the environmental factors are most disadvantageous. During the day the amount of acid in the sap may be reduced to one tenth of its night value. The necessity of gas exchange with the atmosphere is reduced. The ratio of carbon dioxide absorbed by cacti to oxygen given off is far less than for non-succulent plants.

The efficiency of the devices which have been developed by desert plants to prevent the loss of body moisture was investigated by Dr. Daniel T. MacDougal and his associates at the Desert Botanical Laboratory at Tucson. A number of succulent plants were removed from soil and stored under different conditions of exposure to the environment. The weight loss and morphological changes the species underwent were observed and recorded. A large specimen of *Ferocactus wislizenii* lost 1/500 of its original weight in one day after the excision of its root system, but the same plant, after six years of storage in a shaded laboratory, and no change in conditions except that transpiration had reduced its weight by one third, lost only 1/17,000 of its weight per day. In fact the plant had a decrease in sap density which could only be explained on the basis of the disintegration of the carbohydrates, which in one case amounted to 13 per cent of the dry weight of the cortex, where the catabolic destruction of cell material was extended to include the walls of whole masses of cells. The plant was apparently utilizing metabolic water, 0.6 gram of which is theoretically produced for each gram of carbohydrate reduced. After six years the proportion of water in the tissue remained about the same. At the end of the experiment it was found the plant had digested portions of its cortical system, leaving lacunae 8 cc in volume. Even during this breakdown of tissue the apex of the plant grew and produced flowers each year.

Other basic differences in the physiology of succulent and non-succulent xerophytes are indicated by their osmotic pressures. Cacti have osmotic pressures of six to ten atmospheres, or about the same as those of mesophytes, but woody xerophytes have osmotic pressures which vary with the moisture content of the soil, sometimes as high as 100 atmospheres. It is sometimes assumed that high osmotic pressures in woody xerophytes make it possible for them to absorb water from soil which is less moist, but this has been questioned. High osmotic pressures may retard water loss from leaves. The low osmotic pressures of cacti may indicate they do not absorb water from the soil except when it is abundant, and there is other evidence that this is true. Woody desert plants have enormous root systems which often penetrate to great depths. The mesquite has roots which sometimes go down 100 feet in order to tap underground water supplies. The creosote bush has widely spreading roots and others which also go deep. The wide spacing of creosote bushes is a result of the killing of seedling plants by the low water content of the soil, which has been sucked dry by the roots of established individuals. Shreve has suggested that if the desert were turned "inside out" it would present an aspect of abundant vegetation, because the root development of xerophytes is so much greater than the aerial portions of the plants. We have already seen that the roots of Ferocacti are very shallow, in order to take advantage of the short lasting moisture in the surface layers of soil which has been dampened by light desert showers. The extensive system of absorptive roots is confined to the top few centimeters of the soil, where they can collect the moisture from light showers and transfer it to the succulent stem for storage.

One considering the autoecological relations of Ferocacti cannot fail to be impressed with the adaptations which make it possible for them to survive in their harsh environment. They are not in direct competition with neighboring desert plants, because their shallow roots take up soil moisture when it is abundant. That moisture is stored in an expansible succulent stem. Structural and physiological modifications for the retention of the moisture are so effective as to enable specimens used in experiments to survive without other water for six years.

Most Ferocacti grow in rocky, well drained soil, usually on slopes. However, *Ferocactus latispinus* in central Mexico is abundant on the silt flats of broad valleys, and *F. wislizenii* sometimes occurs in similar habitats in Arizona and Sonora. Those barrel cacti found in central Mexico are calciphytes, and all species are at least tolerant of basic soils. Not all Ferocacti are desert plants. *Ferocactus viridescens* from San Diego County, California, and coastal northern Lower California grows in a chaparral association, while *F. herrerae* is found in the thorn forest area of Sinaloa, often growing in silty flats in very dense arid tropical vegetation, in an area of 20 to 30 inches of summer rainfall.

The principal limiting factor for the southern distribution of *Ferocactus* is too much moisture. Most species grow where the annual rainfall is between three and 20 inches. Where there is over 20 inches of rainfall the specialized succulent storage system is unnecessary for water retention and becomes a liability because of susceptibility to decay in a moist environment. Low temperatures prevent the northward migration of the genus. Barrel cacti can withstand 14 degrees to 20 degrees Farenheit temperatures for short periods, but prolonged exposure to temperatures under 28 degrees Farenheit will cause their destruction. Plants turgid with water damage more easily than flaccid, desiccated ones. Cactus seeds require warm moist conditions for germination, so must have rainy periods when the minimum temperature is at least 70 degrees Farenheit if seedlings are to become established.

Biotic factors disturbed the barrel cacti very little before the increase in the human population of the desert areas. Insects sometimes damage the plants but are also the significant agents of pollination. Flowers of *Ferocactus* apparently are self-sterile, because the anthers and stigmatic surfaces mature at different times. Ants, bees, and other honey and pollen feeding insects are attracted to the nectaries in the flowers and also to the sugar-secreting gland spines produced by the flowering areoles. Some insects do damage a few species of *Ferocactus*. The scale insect *Diaspis echinocacti* (Bauche) has a number of host plants among various cactus genera but seems to attack only *Ferocactus latispinus* among the barrel cacti. This scale does not seriously damage plants in the desert, but in the protection of greenhouse collections becomes a serious pest. Cochineal scales are parasites of *Opuntia* and related genera, but do not attack *Ferocactus*. The larvae of a lepidopterous insect, probably *Eremberga creabates* (Dyar), bore into the stem of *Ferocactus fordii* var. *fordii* but do not kill the plant, and apparently feed on only the one species. Mortensen (1930, p. 172) reported the larvae of another moth, *Cactobrosis fernaldianis*, attack *F. wislizenii* in Arizona. I found large black beetles in cavities in the underground base of *Ferocactus macrodiscus* but saw no evidence that they were eating the plant. Adults of the coleopterous flat-headed borers, *Acmaeodera quadrivattata* and *A. lucana*, eat the pollen of Ferocacti, but may also aid in pollination.

The dense spine armament of desert barrel cacti serves to protect the succulent stem from herbiverous animals, but offers little protection for the flowers. The antelope ground squirrel, *Citellus leucurus*, can often be observed eating the flowers of *Ferocactus acanthodes*. Later in the season it neatly cuts off the top of the fruit and collects the seeds. Gophers, *Thomomys* sp., eat the roots of barrel cacti, chewing them off at the base of the plant. In times of drouth distress their spiny armament is inadequate to protect the plants from thirsty mammals. Rabbits somehow work through the spines at the base of the stem and eat the succulent interior. *Ferocactus acanthodes* var. *lecontei* is sometimes kicked apart by desert mountain sheep, *Ovis canadensis nelsoni*, which then eat the damp pulp. Mr. Fritz Schwarz has seen deer, horses and burros kick away a patch of spines on *Ferocactus histrix*, and then carefully nuzzle into the interior of the plant.

In spite of these isolated instances it can be said that biotic factors presented no grave danger to barrel cacti before the recent settlement of arid areas by man. The situation has changed. Many species have been so heavily collected they are becoming rare in some areas, and conservation laws for their protection have been passed in every region in which they occur. Barrel cacti are utilized for stock food in many sections of Mexico. Cattle and goats are raised in deserts where the plant life simply cannot support them on a sustained basis. As the vegetation becomes scarce the ranchers uproot and cut the spines from the barrel cacti and feed the plant body to the stock. A mature *Ferocactus* is at least fifty years old, and offers little in food value, so this use of an irreplaceable resource will soon lead to the extinction of the species. *Ferocactus diguetii* was once common on Coronados Island, near Loreto, Lower California, but has been exterminated on that island through use for stock food. In 1937 I saw a large number of tall barrel cacti on the southern Magdalena plain, in Lower California, but in 1951 I was unable to find a single specimen. The same is true of giant specimens of *F. covillei* near Guaymas, Sonora.

Ferocacti are used for making "cactus candy" both in the United States and Mexico. Sections of the pulpy cortex of the stem are boiled in a sugar syrup, and simply act as a vehicle for the flavoring which is added. This use too should be discouraged. The fruit of at least two species, *Ferocactus pilosus* and *F. histrix*, are used locally for food by the Mexicans.

TAXONOMY

Taxonomic History. Cacti were among the natural curiosities which intrigued the first European explorers of this continent, and the first written account of them seems to have been that of Gonzalo Fernandez de Oviedo y Valdez, which appeared in 1526. Oviedo had accompanied an early colonization attempt in New Spain, as Chronicler of the expedition for Charles V. His reports to his sovereign were published under the title *Sumario de la Historia Natural de las Indias*, and included rather detailed descriptions of the large columnar Cerei and Opuntias.

I know of no record of the first introduction of cacti into European horticulture, but the herbals of the period offer some clues. Mathias Lobelius and Petrus Pena, in their *Stirpium adversaria nova*, published in London in 1570, described a *Melocactus* which was growing there. In his *Iconis stirpium seus plantarum tan exoticarum quam indigenarum*, which was published in Antwerp in 1576, Lobelius illustrated the *Melocactus* and also described plants of *Cereus* and *Opuntia*, which he called *Iniorum tunae ficifera*. The *Opuntia* had been introduced into Spain, and from there to France and Italy, where it became established and produced fruit. These descriptions were picked up by later herbalists, who perhaps were acquainted with the plants, but in any case were adept at plagiarizing from their predecessors. Rembertus Dodonaeus (1583, p. 801) illustrated an *Opuntia* which he called *Ficus indica*, and John Gerarde in the 1597 edition of *The Generall Historie of Plants* illustrated several kinds of cacti.

In the early seventeenth century the herbalists continued to use copies of the early wood cuts, and books concerned with the botanical aspect of plants, rather than medicinal, began to appear. In 1613 Basil Besler published a tremendous folio volume, *Hortus Eystettensis*, which contained excellent engravings of Opuntias and Melocacti.

The increasing number of plant introductions during the following period resulted from the expansion of colonization and commerce with the New World. When Tournefort, the "father of the genus concept," published

Institutiones Rei Herbariae in 1700 he proposed the genus *Opuntia*, in which he recognized 11 forms or "species," and shortened *Echinomelocactusul* to *Melocactus.* Under *Melocactus* he listed 13 forms, which included such presently recognized taxa as *Cereus peruvianus, C. triangularis, Cactus* intortus, etc. Linnaeus further reduced the name *Melocactus* to *Cactus* in the first edition of *Species Plantarum.* It was the only genus he recognized, but the 22 species he included in it were segregated into the subdivisions of Echino-Melocacti, Cerei, and Opuntia.

The eighth edition of Miller's *Gardeners Dictionary*, published in 1768, adopted the binomial system of nomenclature and used Linnaeus' genus *Cactus*, but in addition reinstated the pre-Linnaean genera *Cereus, Opuntia*, and *Pereskia.* The first valid description of a modern *Ferocactus* appeared in this work, under the name *Cactus recurvus.* There was strong interest in cacti throughout the nineteenth century. Many large private collections were built up by wealthy European plant fanciers. Collectors penetrated new regions and the number of new species swelled. Baron Wilhelm von Karwinsky made three trips to Mexico between 1827 and 1832, from whence he sent large collections of plants and seeds to Munich and St. Petersberg. Prince Joseph Salm-Reifferscheid-Dyck amassed a huge collection of cacti and other succulent plants, and between 1817 and 1853 published a long series of articles and books about it. A French industrialist named Monville assembled a fine collection in Normandy, most of which was later destroyed in a disastrous storm. The French cactologist Charles Lemaire was associated with these gardens, and published three books with descriptions of many new species which had been first imported for Monville.

The volume of literature which appeared in the 1800s reflects the growth of knowledge of the Cactaceae through that century. Haworth, in 1812, mentioned about 45 species of cactus in his *Synopsis Plantarum Succulentarum.* In 1827 Linke and Otto erected the genera *Echinocactus* and *Melocactus*, separating them from the Linnean genus *Cactus.* The great systematist, A.P. de Candolle included 183 species in the cactus section of his *Prodromus- Systematis Naturalis Regni Vegetabilis* published in 1828. The first large book about cacti is accredited to Ludwig Pfeiffer, who included 570 species in his *Beschreibung und Synonymik der Cacteen* in 1837. In 1853 J. Labouret, a French collector, published his *Monographie des Cactees*, with descriptions of 670 species.

Dr. George Englemann, a St. Louis physician with a strong avocational interest in botany, became the authority on the cacti of the United States and northern Mexico. He described the many cacti which were collected by members of various government surveys in the west, and published fourteen important papers on the Cactaceae between 1845 and 1876.

Englemann worked closely with Karl Schumann, a life long student of the Cactaceae, and curator of the Royal Botanical Museum in Berlin.

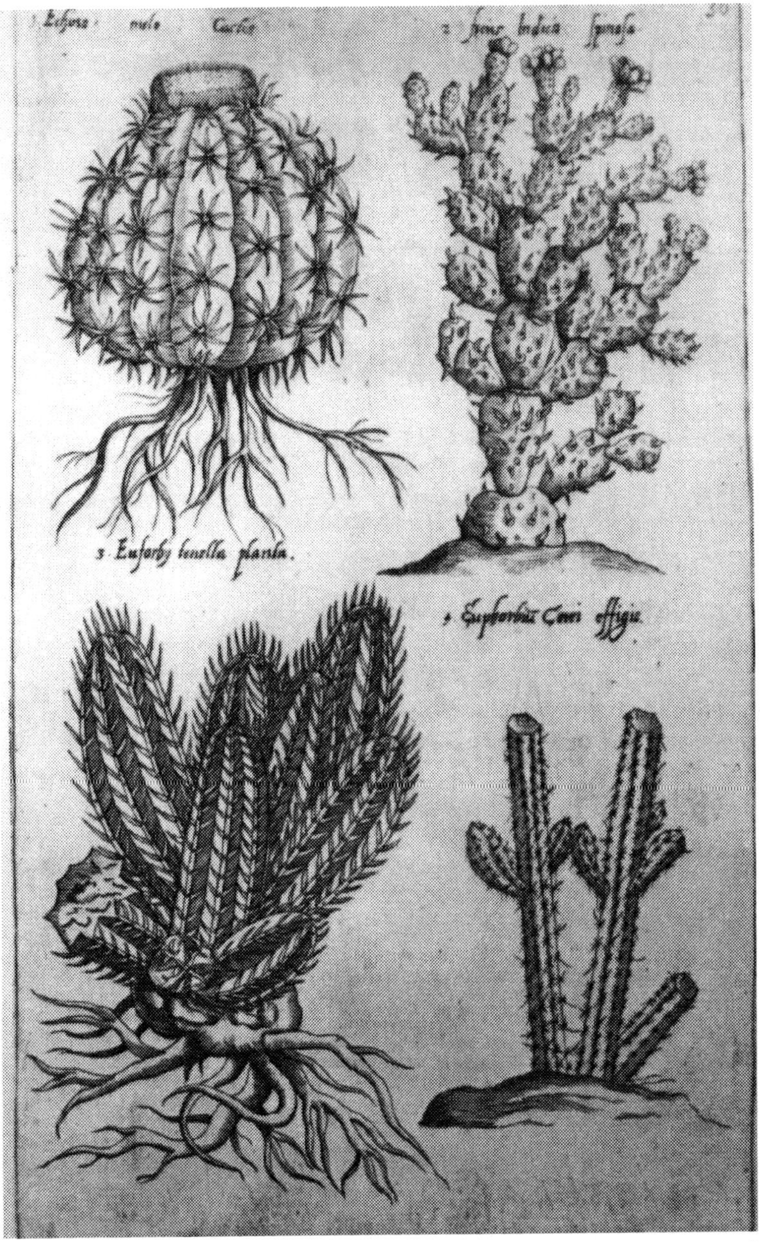

Figure 3. Illustrations of three cacti and one *Euphorbia*, from Emanuel Sweert's *Florilegium*, published at Frankfurt-am-Main in 1612. The figures in this metal engraving had appeared as woodcuts in Gerard's *Generall Histoire of Plantes*, published in 1597.

Schumann published an 832 page monograph of the Cactaceae in 1898, followed by a 170 page supplement in 1903. This work, *Gesamtbeschreibung der Kakteen*, is still standard. It divides the Cactaceae into three subfamilies, Peireskiodeae, Opuntiodeae, and Cereiodeae, which are split into 21 genera. Schumann had considered the phylogeny within the Cactaceae and realized that his relatively few genera did not indicate the phylogenetic lines. He was dubious about splitting the family into a number of small genera, however, and felt that those he used indicated the broad relationships. Schumann's classification has become known as the "German," or "Conservative", system as contrasted with the later "Liberal" or "American" system of Britton and Rose.

In 1904 N. L. Britton and J. N. Rose began a critical study of the Cactaceae, expecting to produce a general description of the North American species. In 1911, however, the Carnegie Institution agreed to finance a study of the whole family, which resulted in a very comprehensive investigation. Field work was undertaken in the accessible cactus regions and a large collection of herbarium and living material was assembled in New York and Washington. The various important world herbaria and botanic gardens were visited in order to study their collections and arrange exchanges. The resulting four volume monograph, the *The Cactaceae*, was published between 1919 and 1923.

No other botanists had the opportunity to study the wealth of cactus material which was enjoyed by Britton and Rose, or had been assisted by as many co-workers. In *The Cactaceae* Schumann's three major subdivisions *Pereskia*, *Opuntia*, and Cereeae were used essentially as he had defined them. These, however, were divided into 124 genera, as opposed to Schumann's 21, and 1235 species were recognized. The new classification resulted from a fuller knowledge of the taxa and a more "liberal" philosophy of taxonomy than that of most previous workers. Britton and Rose apparently were not concerned with phylogenetic relationships as such, but their final treatment, based on the gross morphology of the plants, naturally is largely in accordance with our present conception of the phylogeny.

The nomenclatural system proposed in *The Cactaceae* was generally accepted by American and Mexican, as well as some European, botanists, but it was regarded with reservation by most of the latter. Recently that situation has reversed. Werdermann, Knuth, Borg and Backeberg have used the "American" system in their latest treatments. Backeberg has further subdivided a number of genera. On the other hand, Marshall uses the system of Britton and Rose in his *Cactaceae* and *Arizona's Cactuses*, but is more conservative in his species concept. Peebles, in Kearney and Peebles, *Flowering Plants of Arizona* (1942) used the collective genera of Schumann, but in their *Flora of Arizona* (1951) adopted the genera of Britton and Rose except for combining *Coryphantha* and *Mammillaria*. Benson, in his *Cacti of Arizona*, published in 1940 and 1950, uses a very conservative system at both the genus and species levels, reducing the 16 cactus genera which Britton and Rose listed as occurring in Arizona to five.

Let us give additional consideration to the taxonomic history of the globular cacti. I mentioned that in 1827 H. F. Link and F. Otto proposed two genera, *Echinocactus* and *Melocactus*, to include those globular species which previously had been called *Echinomelocactus*, *Melocactus*, and later, by Linnaeus, shortened to *Cactus*. *Echinocactus* was erected to include the globular plants which had cereus-like flowers born at the apex rather than the side of the plant, and lacked the cephalium which distinguished *Melocactus*. Fourteen species were listed under *Echinocactus*, these including plants now referred to at least five different genera, *Echinocactus*, *Ferocactus*, *Malacocarpus*, *Cactus*, and *Echinofossulocactus*. Only one of the original 14 species of *Echinocactus* is retained in that genus as interpreted by Britton and Rose.

The new genus *Echinocactus* was adopted by A. P. de Candolle the following year, and by Pfeiffer, Lemaire, Labouret, Salm-Dyck, and all subsequent workers. It was used as an all-inclusive genus, and plants were often placed in it for negative reasons - that is, they were not Cerei because they were too short, not Melocacti because they lacked a cephalium, not *Echinopsis* because they did not have long tubular flowers, and not Mammillarias because they did not have the small tubercles characteristic of that genus.

With the great increase in the number of species it became evident that *Echinocactus* was a polyphyletic complex, and a number of authors segregated genera from it. Among these were *Astrophytum* by Lemaire in 1839, *Gymnocalycium* by Pfeiffer in 1845, *Malococarpus* by Salm-Dyck in 1850, Coulter's *Lophophora* in 1894 and Schumann's *Rebutia* in 1895. However, when Schumann monographed the Cactaceae in 1898 he included all of those in his collective genus *Echinocactus*, in which he recognized 138 species. Schumann did divide the genus into 11 subgenera, but these were not always along precise lines. Of the species now considered to belong to *Ferocactus*, for example, five were placed in his subgenus *Euechinocactus* and eight in his subgenus *Ancistrocactus*.

Britton and Rose split the collective genus *Echinocactus* into 28 genera, under their subtribe Echinocactanae. It was necessary to establish the type of *Echinocactus* before making the segregates and Britton and Rose selected *Echinocactus platyacanthus* as the lectotype. *Echinocactus* Link and Otto retained, but only nine species remained in it.

The genus *Ferocactus* was one of the segregates proposed by Britton and Rose, with *Echinocactus wislizenii* as its type. Croizat (1943b) suggested that *Ferocactus* is invalid, arguing that *Echinocactus platyacanthus* which was designated lectotype for *Echinocactus* by Britton and Rose was "a binomial of uncertain application, that is, a classic nomen dubium."

Croizat further treated *E. platyacanthus* as a synonym of *Cactus latispinus* Haworth, on the basis that de Candolle (1828) had listed both as synonyms of *Echinocactus cornigerus* DC. Since Britton and Rose made *E. platyacanthus* the lectotype of *Echinocactus* and placed *Cactus latispinus* in their new genus *Ferocactus*, Croizat indicated that *Ferocactus* would automatically be reduced to a synonym of *Echinocactus*.

Moran (1953) recently revised the Cactaceae for *Hortus Third*, and considered the question which Croizat had raised. Moran indicated that *Echinocactus platyacanthus* can in fact with little reservation be referred to a central Mexican plant, as has been done by Bravo and also by Rost. In any case *E. platyacanthus* could only belong with the other large Mexican plants Britton and Rose retained in *Echinocactus*. *Echinocactus platyacanthus* and *Cactus latispinus* are decidedly distinct and different species, according to their original descriptions, and the names are associated with distinct taxa today. Even if *Cactus latispinus* were found to be synonymous with the lectotype of *Echinocactus*, as Croizat contends, it would not necessarily follow that *Ferocactus* would be automatically reduced to synonomy, since *Cactus latispinus* is not the type of that genus.

In 1926 Charles R. Orcutt proposed the genus *Bisnaga* as a segregate of *Ferocactus*. Orcutt (1926, p. 1) gave the following as his total discussion:

> *BISNAGA* Orcutt.
>
> Distinguished from *Ferocactus* by the edible fleshy fruits, not dehiscent by a basal pore, and the brown seeds. Type: *Echinocactus cornigerus* DC.
>
> *Echinocactus echidne*, *rafaelensis*, *crassihamatus*, *glaucescens*, and *recurvus* probably belong here, but the fruits seem to be yet unknown.

I see no reason to retain *Bisnaga* Orcutt.

Taxonomic Treatment. Britton and Rose (1922, p. 123) included 31 species in their new genus *Ferocactus*. Of these 25 were transferred from *Echinocactus*, and six were new species which they described in *The Cactaceae*. In this treatment I have accepted 18 of the original species of Britton and Rose, excluded four because they belong to other genera, found four to be full synonyms, reduced two to varietial rank under other species, and adopted earlier names for three species on the basis of priority.

When I started this study I found that five new species and one new variety had been proposed for *Ferocactus* since its original publication. In addition nine species and three varieties had been combined in the genus, bringing in taxa which Britton and Rose considered to be synonyms. I have retained two of the new species and treated the other three as varieties. Of the recent combinations two are retained as legitimate prior names of established taxa, and one is included in the section of inadequately known taxa.

As a result of the present study I have described two new species and three new varieties of *Ferocactus*, and have reduced six established species to varieties of other species. The genus *Ferocactus* as here treated includes 25 species and 10 varieties.

Britton and Rose did not use infraspecific categories in their taxonomic system. I feel that many species of *Ferocactus* are actually actively evolving complexes of distinct populations which are quite different from each other. I believe the use of units of classification below the level of species is often essential for the recognition of these divergent and morphologically distinct units which are possibly incipient species which have not yet evolved genetic isolation. In my treatment I have recognized several of these formerly undescribed units as varieties of established species. Also, I have reduced some of the taxa which other authors have considered to be distinct species to varieties of earlier species. In some instances these differences in treatment result from a different taxonomic philosophy, and others from a possibly fuller knowledge of the plants resulting from field work and other advantages which I have enjoyed.

Some explanation of the criteria which I used in determining the following taxonomic treatment may be of value. When one works with a particular group of plants he naturally evaluates the characters which he feels are most dependable in analyzing the taxa. There is variation in the stability and value of any character, and overemphasis of a particular one and disregard or ignorance of the rest is to be avoided. In *Ferocactus* the habit of the plant; the number, shape, and type of ribs; the arrangement and character of spines; the shape, size, color, type of tube scales, and time of appearance of the flower; size, shape, color, fleshiness, type of scales, and time of maturation of the fruit; as well as the shape, size, color, and morphology and surface sculpturing of the seeds, all are important. Any one character may be diagnostic in one taxon and too variable to be of value in another, so it must be evaluated according to the group with which it is used. For example, spine characters are important because they are usually fairly stable and are always present. The contrasting qualities of hooked versus straight spines always appear in keys, and were used by de Candolle, Schumann, and others to separate subtribes and sections. However, one can find straight spined and hooked spined individuals within a single species, and sometimes both spine forms occur on a single plant. *Ferocactus covillei* has very strongly hooked central spines in Arizona, but adult plants near Guaymas, Sonora, always have straight spines, which has resulted in repeated misidentification of the plants in that area. Another example is flower color, which is a dependable key character for separating *Ferocactus gracilis* and *F. acanthodes* var. *tortulospinus* which are sympatric in Lower California. *Ferocactus gracilis* always has red flowers, and those of *F. acanthodes* var.

tortulospinus are always yellow. In other species, such as *F. latispinus*, the flowers may be purple, red, yellow, or white. The type specimen of *F. wislizenii* had yellow flowers, but the great majority of the plants in this taxon have red flowers. Plants near Benson, Arizona, have red or yellow flowers.

Most species of Ferocacti are poorly represented in herbaria, and in many cases only one or two preserved specimens were found. The species from southwestern United States were well represented. In citing specimens I have included all of the specimens examined of the poorly represented species, and only a sample of the others. I have used the standard abbreviations for herbaria cited, as given by Lanjouw and Stafleu (1954) in *Index herbariorum.*

The few samples of *Ferocactus* in herbaria are not sufficient to indicate the distributions of the species. For that reason I have not indicated individual specimens on the distribution maps, but rather have tried to show the approximate ranges of each taxon, based on field observations, preserved specimens, personal communications, and reports in the literature. The distributions as shown are only approximate, and plants may be located only in isolated areas within the overall area of distribution as it is indicated.

Key To The Species of Ferocactus

Editors' Note: *Changes have occurred in the* Ferocactus *taxa since the publication of George Lindsay's 1955 thesis, such as the discoveries of the species* F. lindsayi *and* F. reppenhagenii. *There also have been field and laboratory studies which have attempted to group Ferocacti according to their evolutionary development from the appearances of their plant parts and seeds, most notably the work of Nigel Taylor [Bradleya 2/1984 & 5/1987]. Taylor has made several changes in taxonomy, including the changing of some species to varieties. Whether these changes will endure will probably be determined not from more studies of appearances, but from molecular genetic studies, such as those being performed by Hugo Cota, described elsewhere in this book. This book has as one of its goals the review of progress in* Ferocactus *taxonomy. Its major goal is to present Lindsay's work with updating additions, making the original work complete in its descriptions. Lindsay occasionally differs from others in naming and grouping. We have placed editorial notes to highlight synonyms. These differences are minor and probably unimportant as Cota's work will probably result in substantial rearrangements.*

We have expanded the original key. We also have changed its form, which originally used eight levels of indents, to a simpler numerical form modeled after that of Nigel Taylor. The key includes Lindsay's descriptions, added to by descriptions drawn from Nigel Taylor (NT) and Backeberg's Cactus Lexicon *(Bb).*

The editors have taken liberties with this key by deviating from being dichotomous (having only two possibilities) in a few items. This deviation from usual practice was done in order to include species identified since Lindsay and some of the useful insights of Nigel Taylor while keeping to Lindsay's chapter arrangement. For example, Key item 24 has four species possibilities. Two of these, Ferocactus herrerae *and* Ferocactus townsendianus, *appear as Lindsay species and chapter headings. Taylor considers them as varieties, hence are not included in his key. The genus* Ferocactus *is small, and we believe that such deviations from orthodoxy won't confuse the reader.*

Following the Key are two additions: *Ferocactus* Distributions, a listing of *Ferocactus* species, varieties, and their distributions; *Ferocactus* Synonyms, a list of historical and current names.

1. Plants strongly cespitose, forming broad low mounds of many (more than 10) heads. 2

1. Plants simple, or if cespitose normally with less than 10 stems, not forming low mounds. 3

2. Fruit red, densely covered with linear apiculate, ciliate scales; stem not crowded; ribs about 13; (Tehuacan to Oaxaca) . . . . 1. *F. flavovirens*

2. Fruit yellow, with widely spaced lunate scales; stems crowded; ribs about 8; (Tehuacan to Zapotitlan, Puebla). . . . . 2. *F. robustus*

3. Spines 1-10/areole, straight and needlelike, none strongly flattened above or recurved to hooked at apex. 4

3. Spines 10/areole, or at least one strongly flattened and/or recurved to hooked at apex, or stem ribs 13-16 and spiraled. 15

4. Seeds smooth or with reticulate markings, but not pitted. 5

4. Seeds pitted. 8

5. Spines 1-6, more or less equal (+/-), to 2.5 cm. long, stems 15-50 cm diameter Spines usually 7, central longer, 3-10 cm; stems to about 25 cm diameter 7

6. Stem distinctly glaucous, blue green; fruit nearly white; seeds very smooth; (Hidalgo Mexico). . . . . 3. *F. glaucescens*

6. Stem dark green, largest specimens over 30 cm tall and broad, seldom cespitose; seeds with a reticulate pattern of raised testa-cell margins; spines 1-3, sometimes 5 in juvenile specimens; (from mtns. of Sinaloa in west Mexico). . . . . 5. *F. schwarzii*

7. Areoles well separated on the ribs, 2-4 cm apart; stems often clustered; stigmas 10-14; stems under 30 cm tall, often cespitose; (eastern Sierra Madre, SL Potosi and Hidalgo, Mexico). . . . . 4. *F. echidne*

7. Areoles about 1 cm apart or +/- confluent on the ribs; stem solitary; stigmas (about 7); (Michoacan, south-west Mexico). . . . . 26. *F. reppenhagenii*
Editors' Note: F. reppenhagenii *was not in the original text.*

8. Fruit red to purple, indehiscent, and/or very juicy and deliquescent; ribs acute; stem not exceeding 1.2 m high. 9

8. Fruit yellow (red in 21b) or dihiscing by a basil pore; ribs obtuse or acute; stem 30 cm-4 m high. 12

9. Flowers yellow; seed about 1 mm. 10

9. Flowers red to purplish pink; seed about 1.8-2 mm. 11

10. Stem ribs, 13-18; spines 6-7/areole; seed elongate, curved; (Michoacan Mexico) . . . . 27. *F. lindsayi*
Editors' Note: F. lindsayi *was not in the original text.*

10. Stem ribs 20-40; spines golden yellow, usually 7/areole, typically 9, 1 central and 8 radials; seed +/- isodiametric; (Durango to Jalisco and Puebla, north-central Mexico).. . . . . 6. *F. histrix*

11. Stem globular to cylindric, 30-120 cm high; flower 6-7 cm long; (Puebla-Vera Cruz border).. . . . . 28. *F. haematacanthus*
Editors' Note: F. haematacanthus *was not in the original text.*

11. Stem disc shaped, depressed globose, more than twice as wide as tall, deep seated in ground, to 10 cm tall; (central and southern Mexico).
. . . . 8. *F. macrodiscus*

12. Central spine, 1 per areole, conspicuous; seeds 2-3 mm. 13

12. Central spines 4 or not distinct from radials; seeds 1.5-2 mm. . . 14

13. Flower to 4.5 cm long; stem to 1 m high (SW Chihuahua, SE Sonora, and N Sinaloa). . . . . 7. *F. pottsii*

(listed as F. alamosanus*, a synonym, in Lindsay)*

13. Flower 6-7.5 cm long; stem to 2.5 m high; (S Arizona to N Sinaloa, BC Sur).. . . . . 14. *F. emoryi*
(F. covillei *synonym in Lindsay)*

13. Central spine 1, always straight, 9-15 or even 25 cm long; r. sp. 8-12, upper ones stouter; flower yellow, 6 cm long; (San Ignacio to Commondu, central BC). . . . . 15. *F. rectispinus*
(F. emoryi *variety per NT)*

14. Areoles with 13-20 hairlike whitish marginal bristles or setaceous spines, usually red, some +/- flattened or angled ; central spines all similar; stems often in clumps; (Central N Mexico).
. . . . 11. *F. pilosus*

14. Spines 22-25, similar in shape and size; stem short cylindric; ribs 24-31, wavy; flower yellow, reddish outer, 5 cm long(Angel de la Guardia Island, BC). . . . . 24. *F. johnstonianus*
(Species/Bb ,F. acanthodes *variety/NT).*

14. Stem ribs 25-35; spines clear yellow, rarely reddish brown, terete, all of one type; stem solitary; (BC Islands). . . . . . . 25. *F. diguetii*

15. Scales on receptacle tube and fruit with long narrowly attenuated apices; stem biscuit shaped (or depressed globular); ribs about 21; (central Mexico). . . . . 10. *F. latispinus*

15. Stem globular to short cylindric to 25 cm high; ribs spiralled, 13-15, 3 cm high; radial spines subulate, 8, 2 of these +/- compressed, banded, to 2.5 cm long; central spine 1, very stout, to 7

cm long; flower red, bordered white or pink; (Puebla and Oaxaca, Mexico). . . . . 9. *F. recurvus* (F. latispinus *var. per NT, sp. per Bb)*

15. Scales not as for the preceding. 16

16. Fruit pinkish red and indehiscent, and/or very juicy, deliquescent, releasing the seeds in fluid. 17

16. Fruit yellow or dehisciing by a basal pore when ripe. 19

17. Spines straight or curved, but not hooked at apex; flower 3-4 cm short tubed. 18

17. Spines, at least one per areole hooked at apex; flower 6-10 cm with a long tube; (El Paso, Cameron City TX to SL Potosi Mexico). . . . . 29. *F. hamatacanthus*

18. Flowers purplish pink to red, tepals with paler margins; seed to 2 mm. (Cumbre (10,000 ft., El Renosco). . . . . 8. *F. macrodiscus*

18. Flowers yellow; seeds c. 1mm. . . . . 6. *F. histrix*

19. Radial spines, 7 per areole, terete, only slightly thinner than the solitary terete or radially compressed central; (S AZ, Sonora). . . . . 14. *F. emoryi*

19. Radial spines 9 or at least some thinner than the one or more centrals.

. . . . 20

20. Perianth segments remaining +/- erect at anthesis; flowers to 2.5 cm diameter; stems often clustering, to 3 m high; principal spines 6-12, none curved or hooked at apex, often with marginal hairlike radials; central spines all similar; (northern to central Mexico). . . . . 11. *F. pilosus*

20. Perianth-segments spreading; flowers 3.5-6 cm diameter., stems rarely clustering; spines not as above or centrals and radials intergrading. .. 21

21. Flowers reddish to wine purple; principal central spine hooked or strongly curved at tip; (W coast BC). . . . . 21. *F. fordii*

21. Flowers green, yellow, orange, or red. 22

22. Spines clearly differentiated into stout dark colored centrals plus upper and lower radials, and finer whitish laterally directed radials, or the latter absent and seeds with tabular testa-cells. 23

22. Spines in each areole intergrading in size and color; seeds with concave testa-cells. 25

23. Central spines red, 4, the principal one distinctly flattened instead of diamond-shaped, only the principal one twisted; flowers red; fruits to 7.5 cm long; (from Rosario to Millers Landing BC). .... 18. *F. gracilis*

23. Central spines 4, twisted and tortuous (except rarely *F. gracilis* var. *coloratus*); radial spines about 16, radiating, terete; flower 6 cm diameter and long, red; (Smith Island group, Bahia Los Angeles, BC) .... 19. *F. gatesii*
(Sp./ Bb; var. F. gracilis*/NT)*

23. Largest central spine more flattened than the others or otherwise dissimilar, often strongly recurved or hooked; flowers red to yellow; fruits to 6 cm long. 24

24. Ribs 20-30; stem wide and heavy; seeds with finely verrucose, +/- isodiametric testa-cells, the raised anticlinal walls at the cell margin not prominent; (from Sonora, Chihuahua, N Sinaloa, W Durango andAZ) .... 12. *F. wislizenii*

24. Central spines dissimilar in character, one or two more developed than others; radial spines 8, 2 of these white, the others flecked red; central spine 1, hooked initially, becoming straight; ribs, 12-20; stem thinner than *F. wislizenii*; flower funnelform, reddish, bordered yellow; (S Sonora, Sinaloa, and Durango) .... 13. *F. herrerae*
(species per Bb, F. wislizenii *variety per NT)*

24. Central spines 4, cruciform, hooked; radial spines variable, usually about 11; seeds with tabular to concave, coarsely verrucose testa-cells, the verrucae few and separate, the raised cell margins prominent or the cells oblong; (central BC to Cape). .... 16. *F. penninsulae*

24. Central spines 4, lateral two not distinctly flattened; radial spines bristle-like; flowers about 6 cm long, middle pink, greenish-yellow border; (BC gulf and Isla San Jose). ..... 17. *F. townsendianus*
(species per Bb, F. penninsulae *variety per NT)*

25. Flowers greenish-yellow; spines not hooked or strongly curved at tip; spines to 5 cm long; seed about 1.5 mm; stem not conical, as broad as tall; radial spines not bristle-like; (San Diego USA and nearby BC)........................... 22. *F. viridescens*

25. Flowers yellow, orange or reddish, or green but with other colors in the same population; spines to 5-17 cm long; seeds about 2-3 mm. 26

26. Central spines golden yellow or rarely bright red, usually +/-diamond-shaped in cross section and twisted flattened and fairly uniform, central and radial spines about equal in number (10); flowers orange to red with 4-5 mm wide inner perianth-segments; (Isla Cedros and W Baja). . . . . 20. *F. chrysacanthus*

26. Central spines fewer than radials and 4 of the centrals are much larger than the others, to 7-17 cm long; inner perianth-segments 7-11 mm wide, flowers yellow; (SW USA, NW Sonora, NE BC). . . . . 23. *F. acanthodes*

A Review of *Ferocactus* Britton and Rose

J. Hugo Cota

Department of Botany, Iowa State University, Ames, IA 50036

and

Centro de Educación Ambiental e Investigación Sierra de Huautla (CEAMISH),

Universidad Autónoma del Estado de Morelos,

Av. Universidad # 1001, Cuernavaca, Morelos, Mexico.

Prelude

The following text, my contribution to this book, combines the field observations made by many people with the revolutionary molecular approach under way in taxonomy. This involves the analysis of DNA, such as sequencing and restriction site data. Field taxonomy often deals with the interspecific comparisons of morphological and physiological traits, both subject to convergence. The study of DNA provides new evidence which supplements conventional taxonomic studies, and lessens the amount of homoplasy (where two or more organisms independently acquire the same character state due to convergent evolution). DNA sequencing is the source of many new characters (the order and position of bases in the strings of DNA). Many of these characters are stable and highly conserved during evolution; some are evolving rapidly. From a comparison of similarities and differences between species, genealogical trees (cladograms) are built, with a distant relative (outgroup) serving to anchor (root) the tree. There are several methods to build and analyze trees. The method using "parsimony" (principle of maximum parsimony) constructs cladograms with a minimum number of evolutionary steps (changes). The construction of these trees from the sequencing and restriction site data was done objectively, by the software within the computer. My work involves the study of *Ferocactus* chloroplast DNA. Differences between cladograms, such as branching patterns, occur for several reasons, e.g., different number of species sampled, unequal rates of evolution between the regions of the genome being investigated, hybridization, gene duplication, and lineage sorting. As with all statistical methods, confidence increases with an increase of sampling. At the end of this section I have included a glossary of terms which may be unfamiliar to the reader.

Introduction

More than four decades have elapsed since Lindsay (1955a) wrote his doctoral dissertation, a study of the taxonomy and ecology of *Ferocactus* Britton and Rose. Lindsay's studies represent a valuable source of field documented material in which he includes both morphological and ecological data, and his own concepts about the classification of *Ferocactus*. His extensive field work at that time was challenging especially in remote regions of the Baja California Peninsula and surrounding islands as well as in mainland Mexico in the 1950's. The extent of his field work proves that there was no obstacle which could stop George from accomplishing his goals and conducting his field studies. His passion for cactus taxonomy and adventurous spirit have inspired other people to follow his example. George has been one of my mentors and his support and advice during my graduate studies and career in cactus taxonomy have been meaningful. Many fruitful discussions with him have given me a broader perspective of the genus and encouragement to seek the answers of the taxonomic relationships and evolutionary history of *Ferocactus*. I feel honored to contribute with this chapter of the book, in particular because of my personal interest in *Ferocactus* and because Lindsay's pioneer field studies of the genus represent an excellent example of his love and devotion for plants and his understanding of their taxonomic relationships.

Subsequent to the conclusion of Lindsay's dissertation, several authors have conducted separate studies dealing with diverse biological aspects of the genus. Such studies have considered a single species or major taxonomic groups within the genus and have referred to nomenclatural, biological, ecological, or physiological matters (e.g., Blom and Clark, 1980; Bravo-Hollis, 1966; Cota and Wallace, 1996; Nobel, 1977; Ruffner and Clark, 1986; Taylor, 1979a, 1979b, 1980, 1984, 1987; Taylor and Clark, 1983; Unger, 1992). Lindsay contributed descriptions of new taxa, nomenclatural changes, and ecology of *Ferocactus* (e.g., 1942, 1955b, 1955c, 1955d, 1964, 1965, 1968).

In the following sections, I briefly describe the main topics that have been investigated in *Ferocactus* from 1955 to the present. My objectives in this chapter are to summarize the knowledge of the genus in different areas of study and to discuss the importance of understanding its phylogenetic relationships at the interspecific, generic and tribal levels. It is my intent to review Lindsay's taxonomic treatment and associate it with the results from modern techniques (molecular studies) used in phylogenetic analyses of *Ferocactus*. I hope that the up-to-date view of *Ferocactus* presented here is useful to anyone interested in cacti.

Because of the diverse array of topics investigated since 1955, several studies have been omitted not because they are irrelevant, but because their goals are considered distant from the main issues addressed in this chapter. In additon, to mention every paper dealing with the genus would imply the discussion of several areas of research that are not my specialty. Therefore, and with my apologies to those authors who have contributed to the knowledge of the genus in the topics excluded herein, I restrict myself mainly to those studies that in one way or another are more closely related to the understanding of the biosystematics of *Ferocactus*. At the end of this chapter there is a list of additional bibliographic references dealing with various aspects of the genus.

Ferocactus is distributed in arid and semiarid regions of central and northern Mexico and southwestern United States (Fig. 4), and it has been hypothesized to occupy a critical phylogenetic position in the classifications of the Cacteae (Fig.5) (Buxbaum, 1951, 1958; Barthlott, 1988; Barthlott and Hunt, 1993). Within the Cacteae, *Ferocactus* is the third largest genus in number of species after *Mammillaria* Haw. and *Coryphantha* (Engelm.) Lem. (Gibson and Nobel, 1986; Barthlott and Hunt, 1993).

The understanding of the phylogeny of *Ferocactus* and its phylogenetic position within the Cacteae (the largest tribe within subfamily Cactoideae in North America), along with its patterns of speciation, is significant to understand the relationships at the interspecific and tribal level (in particular between the tribes Pachycereeae and Cacteae). The development of a robust phylogenetic hypothesis for the genus will provide a basis for the subsequent determination of its evolutionary patterns with other genera of the Cacteae as well to potentially clarify the relationships between the tribes Pachycereeae and Cacteae. Likewise, a methodical study of *Ferocactus* will help to explain the interspecific phylogenetic relationships and most likely provide a scenario of the evolutionary patterns of radiation.

Taxonomic Background

The taxonomic history of *Ferocactus* is addressed by Lindsay earlier in this book, and no further discussion is needed. At present, the taxonomy of the genus remains in a somewhat confused state. Different taxonomic philosophies, disagreement as to species boundaries, and under-representation of some taxa in herbarium collections have contributed to the complexity of its taxonomic circumscriptions. Another factor involved is the relatively high level of morphological homoplasy, which obscures the degree of relatedness due to convergence. Additionally, cactus taxonomy in general is complex because morphological variability is associated with gradients in habitats and geographic ranges (Cody et al., 1983). In *Ferocactus*, the use of primarily vegetative morphological characters (which are likely to display different degrees of plasticity in response to local environmental conditions) has also contributed to its taxonomic difficulty. As a result, natural subpopulations subject to varied selective pressures may diverge both morphologically and genetically, occasionally providing discontinuities that are useful to distinguish taxonomic complexes in the process of speciation. As a consequence of natural variation and taxonomic delineations, the number of species circumscribed in the genus has been a matter of disagreement and is reflected in several taxonomic treatments (Table 1).

Prior to Lindsay, Britton and Rose (1922) proposed a taxonomy in which they included 30 species [Lindsay (1955a: 40) indicates 31]. Lindsay's classification (1955a) considered a total of 25 species and ten varieties. More recently, in a taxonomic treatment of *Ferocactus sensu stricto* Taylor and Clark (1983) included 29 species; Taylor (1984) recognized 23 species and 20 infraspecific taxa, while Bravo and Sanchez-Mejorada (1991) accepted 29 species and 25 varieties. Finally, Unger (1992) provided a review of the genus in which descriptions and distributional data are discussed. Although his taxonomic delimitations were based on previous treatments, he presented a classification scheme which included four sections (Table 1) and a list of naturally occurring hybrids. In the broad sense of the genus, Taylor (1980) transferred some species of *Stenocactus* (Schum.) Berger to *Ferocactus*, based on morphological affinities such as similarities in rib pattern and presence of glandular areoles, and created the subgenera *Ferocactus* (in which are placed all of Lindsay's species) and *Stenocactus*.

Despite the substantial amount of taxonomic work conducted during the past seven decades, the controversy in species boundaries within the genus is evident: no classifications are similar yet the number of species are similar (e.g., 30, 29, 28, 25, 23). Neither Britton and Rose (1922) nor Lindsay (1955a) used infrageneric categories, whereas Bravo and Sanchez-Mejorada (1991), Taylor (1984), Taylor and Clark (1983), and Unger (1992) classified the genus using other taxonomic hierarchies, such as sections, groups and subgenera (Table 1). A common feature of these classifications is that the delimitation of species has been based primarily on gross morphological features of the stem, flower and fruit.

Of these taxonomic treatments, those by Taylor and Clark (1983) and Taylor (1984) are of special importance because they have correlated gross morphology with micromorphological seed coat characters. These studies have led to the establishment of sectional boundaries and the consideration of new ideas about the evolution of *Ferocactus*. In spite of Taylor's (1984) comprehensive treatment combining all the data available at that time, a robust phylogeny of the genus has not been presented to date, and key issues regarding its origin and radiation remain unresolved.

The extensive use of varietal rank in the different classifications is further indication of the taxonomic confusion of this genus. To some extent, the use of varietal rank may be helpful in distinguishing infraspecific groups in *Ferocactus*, and might accurately reflect the relatively recent origin of some species groups, especially for some Baja Californian species. Indeed, Lindsay (1955a, 1965) and Taylor (1984) indicated that those species occurring in mainland Mexico are taxonomically well-defined, while several taxa from northwestern Mexico and the Baja California peninsula remain problematic, probably due to incipient processes of speciation.

In the following sections, I review new data from cytological and molecular sources that reveal preliminary information about the relationships at the interspecific level as well as the inferred relationships of *Ferocactus* with the columnar cacti of Tribe Pachycereeae. Both sources of information are used to discuss the issues of phylogeny and hybridization. To avoid confusion and to facilitate the taxonomic circumscriptions of *Ferocactus*, the specific epithets and authorities used in this chapter are those included in Lindsay's classification for two reasons. First, to honor him for contributing to the understanding of the infra- and interspecific categories of the genus and second, because the other taxonomies (Taylor and Clark, 1983; Taylor, 1984; Bravo and Sanchez-Mejorada, 1991; Unger, 1992), also recognize the majority of species proposed by Lindsay. This is not meant to discredit the valuable taxonomic contribution of these authors. Also, it is worth mentioning the outstanding contributions of Taylor (1979a, 1979b, 1984, 1987) in the nomenclature of the genus clarifying the application of several specific epithets and authorities that should be discontinued. I must repeat, however, that while I am aware of these nomenclatural changes, here I follow those names used by Lindsay (1955a) for the reasons indicated above.

To date, the most modern taxonomic treatments of *Ferocactus* are those of Taylor (1984) and Taylor and Clark (1983), in which phylogenetic ideas about the evolution and radiation of the genus based on vegetative and reproductive characters, geography, and macro- and micromorphology of the seed coat have been proposed. This information is essential to understanding the modern concept of classification of the genus, and these recent evolutionary hypotheses will be used to discuss phylogenetic aspects of *Ferocactus*, especially in the section which includes molecular studies.

Reproductive Biology in *Ferocactus*

Reproductive strategies in plants are numerous and they are reflected in an array of floral morphology and breeding systems, which have evolved in response to genetic, environmental, and selective forces. In sexually reproducing plants, as is the case in *Ferocactus*, breeding systems determine, in part, patterns and levels of genetic variation. Although little is known regarding the pollination biology and breeding systems of the genus, in the following paragraphs I summarize our current knowledge of the topic.

Floral Biology and Pollination

The flowers of *Ferocactus* are perfect and bowl-shaped (Fig. 6); they open during the day, and have a slight fragence (Bravo and Sanchez-Mejorada, 1991). The color spectrum varies from yellow, orange, red, pink, lavender, to purple (Fig. 6); the stamens are numerous (Fig. 6A), usually with yellow anthers that mature before the style becomes receptive, thus they are protandrous (Richards, 1986). The plants bloom from early spring to late summer, and the flowers remain open for several days (Bravo and Sanchez-Mejorada, 1991).

In *Ferocactus* there is an apparent coadaptation of pollinating agents and its flowers. The floral attributes such as the funnelform to bell-shaped, diurnal, bright yellow, medium-to large-sized flowers, with nectar and little or no fragance at all, are characteristic of bee pollinated flowers (Rowley, 1980a). The flowers of *Ferocactus* are pollinated by several species of bees. Bee pollinated flowers have been documented in *F. wislizeni* (Engelm.) Britton and Rose (Grant and Grant, 1979a) which is usually pollinated by medium sized bees of the family Megachilidae (*Megachile sidalcea* Cockerell and *Lithurge echinocacti* Cockerell) and Apiidae (*Diadasia australis* Cresson) (Grant and Grant, 1979b). Cockerell (1900) also indicated that *Auglochlora neglectula* Cockerell visits the flowers of *F. wislizeni*. Unidentified bees have been observed crawling around the stamens and stigmas of the flowers of *F. histrix* (DC) Lindsay and *F. robustus* (Otto) Britton and Rose in areas of Central Mexico (pers. obs.). Although the flowers of *Ferocactus* are also visited by other species of insects, the pollination syndrome has evolved to promote bees as the principal vector. In additon to bees, beetles are common visitors of *Ferocactus* flowers and feed on pollen and may accidentally pollinate the flower (Grant and Grant, 1979b) acting as secondary pollinators.

Mechanisms such as herkogamy (the spatial isolation of stamens and stigma lobes) and protandry in the flowers of *Ferocactus*, coupled with the active behavior of bees, are important factors that discourage self-fertilization and promote gene exchange. In addition, there are several stigma lobes that expand when they are receptive and provide a landing platform for pollinators (Fig. 6), facilitating cross-pollination. Therefore, open floral morphology and full exposure of anthers and stigmatic surface probably allows pollination by more than one bee species. Similar floral attributes have been reported for *Echinocereus* Engelm. (Cota, 1993) and the cactus flora of the southwestern United States (Grant and Grant, 1979b).

Other floral characteristics in *Ferocactus* are nectar and pollen rewards. Nectar production seems to be relatively low and despite the lack of experimental tests, measurable amounts of this fluid are difficult to detect (at least to the human eye!). Similarly, low nectar production has been reported in the flowers of *Echinocactus grusonii* Hildm. and other genera of the Cactoideae (Scogin, 1985). Low nectar amount has also been observed in *Echinocereus engelmannii* (Parry) Lem. (Cota, 1993) species which shares similar floral attributes to *Ferocactus*. It is likely that low nectar production in the flowers of *Ferocactus* is compensated for by the correspondingly abundant pollen (as evidenced by the numerous stamens) which probably is the major floral reward. The same pattern (i.e., little nectar and abundant pollen) has been reported in *Opuntia lindheimeri* Engelm. (Grant and Hurd, 1979). Moreover, pollen amount is also associated with pollinator efficiency: high amounts of pollen produced per flower correlate with higher pollinator efficiency (Richards, 1986). In the wild, the anthers of the numerous stamens in the flower of *Ferocactus* produce massive amounts of pollen which satisfy demands by pollinators and assure its transfer to another flower. Correspondingly, seed production usually occurs in large numbers, which seems to be sufficient for the perpetuation of the species in nature.

Ants and Extrafloral Nectaries

Extrafloral nectaries are glands that secrete nectar from different parts of the plant. These glands are characteristic in *Ferocactus* and they occur apically in the areole, in particular in actively growing areoles where new floral structures are in the process of development. The number of extrafloral nectaries per areole varies from one to five in *F. gracilis* Gates (Blom and Clark, 1980). These glandular structures produce an ant-attracting nectar of varied sugar composition (glucose, sucrose, and fructose) of which only glucose has been detected in higher concentrations early in fruit production in *F. acanthodes* (Lem.) Britton and Rose (Ruffner and Clark, 1986).

It is generally accepted that extrafloral nectaries play a role in a mutualistic relationship between plants and protective ants (Formicidae) (Bentley, 1977a, 1977b; Pickett and Clark, 1979). In this protectionist scenario, ants are attracted by nectar produced in these glands, and while foraging for nectar they protect the plants from potential herbivores. Ruffner and Clark (1986) indicated that ant visitation and activity is correlated with nectar production and phenology of the plant. For instance, in *F. acanthodes* var. *lecontei* (Engelm.) Lindsay, the composition and amount of extrafloral nectar changes according to plant phenology, and ant visitation is more common during the blooming and fruiting periods. Also, ants depending on liquid food in desert environments may respond to fluctuations in the water content of their food (Ruffner and Clark, 1986).

Though several species of ants visit the plant, some species are more frequent visitors than others. Among the species of ants visiting extrafloral nectaries in *Ferocactus*, the honey ants (*Crematogaster depilis* Wheeler) have been reported to be the most frequent in *F. gracilis* (Blom and Clark, 1980) and *F. acanthodes* var. *lecontei* (Ruffner and Clark, 1986). In addition, del Castillo (1982, 1988) documented the presence of *Irydomyrmex* and *Dorymyrmex* in *F. histrix* in mainland Mexico. Other species associated with the extrafloral nectaries of *F. gracilis* are *Iridomyrmex pruinosum, Camponotus ocreatus,* and *Pheidole grallipes* (Blom and Clark, 1980). Unidentified ants have been observed visiting flowers and extrafloral nectaries in wild plants of *F. histrix, F. latispinus* (Haw.) Britton and Rose, *F. recurvus* (Miller) Y. Ito, and *F. robustus* (pers. obs.).

Seed Morphology

Both seeds and pollen grains are important sources of morphological characters useful for elucidating evolutionary trends and phylogenetic lineages. The importance of the architectural design of these structures is evident when they are applied to the classification of taxa in which characters based on gross morphology are not the best source of data to assess the degree of relationship.

In the Cactaceae, several studies of seed macro- and micromorphology have been successfully applied at different taxonomic levels (e.g., Barthlott and Voit, 1979; Friedrich and Glaetzle, 1983; and Glaetzle and Prestlé, 1986). The shape, variation in the testa cells and wall sculpture of seeds provide information of taxonomic importance. In *Ferocactus,* studies on seed coat attributes are limited; the most relevant is that of Taylor and Clark (1983), in which the importance of seed characters was demonstrated in the classification of the genus. In their study, the authors correlated characteristics of the fruit and the hilum-micropilar rim (HMR) which allowed them to define the two sections of *Ferocactus*, namely section *Ferocactus* (seeds with massive HMR, fruit dry, dehiscent by a basal pore, and glossy seed coat) and section *Bisnaga* (Orcutt) N. P. Taylor (seeds with narrow HMR, juicy fruit and shiny seed coat). To date, the most complete description of the distribution of seed coat attributes in 31 species of the genus is found in Taylor and Clark (1983), which also provide hypotheses about the evolutionary trends of *Ferocactus* based on micromorphology of seeds, plant habit, and stem morphology.

In terms of the current knowledge of macro- and micromorphoplogical seed characters, the following are some of the defining seed attributes of *Ferocactus* (variations to this pattern should be expected due in part to convergent evolution, malformation, and genetic factors among others). According to Taylor and Clark (1983), the seeds of *Ferocactus* subgenus *Ferocactus* are in general mussel-shaped, and range in size from 1 to 3 mm; the seed coat may be smooth to rugose (with testa-cells tabular to tabular-concave). Some species (*F. robustus* and *F. wislizeni*) have a reticulate pattern with verrucose periclinal walls. In the case of *F. rectispinus* (Engelm.) Britton and Rose and *F. acanthodes* var. *lecontei* the seeds have tabular testa cells (Fig. 7A, C, D). The seed coats of the species analyzed exhibited cracks (Fig. 7B) probably due to the exposure of seed to the beam of the Scanning Electron Microscope; the same situation was reported by Taylor and Clark (1983).

Pollen Morphology

Palynology, the study of pollen grains and spores, is another source of comparative data for taxonomic purposes practically at all levels of hierarchy. Reliable palynological data is related to the pollen grain itself, e.g., aperture number, shape and position of apertures, and exine sculptural patterns. In the Cactaceae, it has been shown that the distribution of some morphological features of the pollen grain are useful in defining major lineages. For instance, the three subfamilies (Pereskioideae, Opuntioideae and Cactoideae) can be distinguished based on pollen types and exine structural design (Kurtz, 1948; Tsukada, 1964). Moreover, pollen grain morphology is relatively uniform at the tribal level (Leuenberger, 1976).

At the specific level, pollen analyses are limited in *Ferocactus*. According to Kurtz (1948) and Tsukada (1964) the pollen grains of *F. acanthodes*, *F. covillei,* and *F. wislizeni* are tricolpate with a punctibaculate ektexine (finely pitted exine), and equatorial diameter ranging from 48-68 (85) μm. Whether these morphological patterns in pollen are common throughout the genus remains unclear, until further studies are conducted in a broader range of species.

Cytological Studies

In general, the classification of the Cactaceae has used traditional methods and has been based on shared morphological characters. In the last 40 years, several tools to address questions in plant systematics and reconstruct phylogeny at different taxonomic levels have blossomed. Cytotaxonomy and modern molecular techniques based on DNA analyses are clear examples of the revolution that plant systematics has experienced to produce genetic based phylogenies.

The study of chromosomes (structures that contain the genetic material) is a good source of comparative data in plant classification. Cytological data of various types (chromosome number, behavior at meiosis, size and shape of chromosomes, and DNA amount) are widely used in plant taxonomy. In the Cactaceae, cytological studies have provided insight into polyploid complexes, hybrid lines, chromosome morphology, and chromosomal rearrangements. Additionally, studies of mitotic and meiotic chromosomes have shown that species of *Ferocactus* have a base number (lowest haploid humber) of $x = 11$ (Fig. 8) (which is also the base number for the family; Pinkava et al., 1977). Thus far, all chromosome counts for *Ferocactus* reported in the literature (17 species) are consistent with the basic number for the family (Table 2). The number of taxa analyzed to date represent 68% of the total of species recognized in Lindsay's taxonomy.

Overall, the morphology of mitotic chromosomes among the species of *Ferocactus* is homogeneous: primarily metacentric with a few pairs of submetacentric chromosomes, and size ranging from 3 to 7 μm (Figs. 8B-C).

The chromosomes of *Ferocactus* happen to be the largest among those taxa surveyed in the Cactaceae (Cota et al., submitted); however, the significace of large chromosomes is unclear. Some taxa, *Ferocactus acanthodes* var. *lecontei, F. chrysacanthus* (Orcutt) Britton and Rose (Fig. 8B), and *F. wislizeni*, exhibit satellites or secondary constrictions (small extensions at the end of the arms of the chromosomes) (Cota et al., submitted). Similar patterns in chromosome morphology have been observed in unrelated genera of the Cactaceae such as *Echinocereus* Engelm. (Cota, 1991; Cota and Wallace, 1995), *Mammillaria prolifera* (Miller) Britton and Rose (Johnson, 1980), and *Nyctocereus* (Berger) Britton and Rose (Palomino et al., 1988).

The uniformity in shape and number of chromosomes and lack of satellites does not necessarily reflect evidence of close phylogenetic relationship. Chromosomal rearrangements at the molecular level may account for the distinctiveness of some species. Alternatively, the presence of satellites in some northern species, such as *F. acanthodes* var. *lecontei* , *F. chrysacanthus*, and *F. wislizeni* indicates that satellites might be used as taxonomic markers (Cota et al., submitted), and that further analyses of chromosome morphology might be advantageous to understand interspecific relationships in *Ferocactus.*

As mentioned previously, some of the taxonomic confusion that characterizes *Ferocactus* has been attributed to hybridization and introgression events. Lindsay (1955a) and more recently Taylor (1984) have both indicated that Baja Californian species are taxonomically problematic due to probable introgressive processes, which brings new genetic attributes to actively evolving species. This hypothesis is based upon observations of individuals with intermediate morphologies in areas where two species are sympatric. Indeed, cases of intermediacy have been suggested in two related species groups: *F. gracilis* and the *F. peninsulae* (Engelm.) Britton and Rose group (Taylor, 1984). Polymorphism in spine shape and color in addition to intermediacy of stem and flower characters are common in individuals of the same population. At present, it is unclear to what degree this variation is genetically and/or environmentally induced. Analyses of meiotic configurations in different individuals of *F. gracilis* (Fig. 8A) and *F. peninsulae* failed to provide evidence for hybridity (Cota et al., submitted) at least for the populations examined. Contrary to those hypothesized introgressive events that have contributed to the taxonomic confusion in some Baja Californian species, chromosomal analyses of these taxa at different stages of meiosis show normal pairing and formation of bivalents at diakinesis, which may suggest the lack of hybridization in sympatric species (Cota et al., submitted) or simply a lack of genetic barriers. In addition, previous meiotic counts of some Baja Californian and Mexican mainland species (Beard, 1937; Pinkava et al., 1973, 1977, 1985) have not reported abnormalities during meiosis. To date, in spite of cases of morphological intermediacy, there is no cytological evidence such as univalents, trivalents, chromosome bridges, fragments, lagging chromosomes, or any other abnormalities during cell division to support the possibility of hybridization. Also, hybrids may not show meiotic abnormalities because there is little chromosomal differentiation between species. It should be mentioned, however, that even though there is no evidence of hybridization based on chromosome behavior and morphology, this event can not be ruled out until further analyses are conducted on the remaining species, especially in those problematic populations indicated by Taylor (1984).

In addition to hybridization, polyploidy has been indicated as an important factor in the evolution of certain cacti, e.g., some species of *Opuntia* (Tournef.) Miller (Pinkava et al., 1985) and *Echinocereus* (Cota and Philbrick, 1994; Cota and Wallace, 1996). Both processes are yet to be documented in *Ferocactus* and is likely that they have not contributed substantially to speciation events in this genus (Cota et al., submitted). The frequency of polyploidy in the subfamily Cactoideae in which *Ferocactus* is circumscribed is low: approximately 12.5% (Pinkava et al., 1985). Unlike some other genera of the subfamily in which polyploidy is relatively common, e.g., *Echinocereus* (Cota and Philbrick, 1994; Pinkava et al., 1992; Weedin and Powell, 1978), to date all the species of *Ferocactus* which have been cytologically investigated are diploid (Table 2). Moreover, *F. robustus*, one of the putatively least derived species (Taylor and Clark, 1983), has not experienced changes in chromosome number. The same apparently stable diploid number has been observed in putative sister genera of *Ferocactus* such as *Echinocactus grusonii* and *Stenocactus* (*Echinofossulocactus*) *crispatus* (DC) Berger (Katagiri, 1952); *Echinocactus polycephalus* (Engelm.) Bigel. (Pinkava et al., 1977); *E. horizonthalonius* Lem. and *E. texensis* Hoppfer (Weedin and Powell, 1978); and *S. pentacanthus* (Lem.) Berger (Pinkava and Parfitt, 1982). The homogeneity of chromosome numbers in *Ferocactus* and allied taxa does not provide useful information for understanding interspecific and intergeneric relationships by correlating it with patterns of chromosomal evolution. Cota et al. (submitted) suggest that the relatively recent origin of the genus may account for the lack of polyploid individuals in *Ferocactus* and its suspected sister taxa (*Echinocactus* Link. and Otto and *Stenocactus*), and that changes in chromosome number have not played a major role in the evolution of *Ferocactus*. They have hypothesized that chromosome evolution in the genus is likely taking place at the molecular level, and consequently, chromosome rearrangements remain cryptic. Indeed, the non-coding region (intron) loss of the chloroplast gene *rpo*C1 has been reported in representative members of the Cactoideae, including *F. flavovirens* (Wallace and Cota, 1996). Further cytological investigations with a wider taxonomic sampling within *Ferocactus* may be useful in determining the extent of the diploid condition and the occurrence of chromosomal rearrangements. In addition, studies of crossability to examine the genetic basis of taxonomic characters and isozyme analyses to estimate the genetic distance between taxa would certainly be effective detecting cases of natural hybridization and/or introgression in populations where individuals with intermediate morphology are common.

On the other hand, and in spite of the lack of evidence to document natural hybrids based on the study of meiotic figures, artificial hybridization is an approach from which cactophiles obtain bizarre specimens. Intergeneric hybrids involving *Ferocactus* are precious novelties, and documented cases are those crosses between *F. acanthodes* and *Leuchtenbergia principis* Hook. to produce the hybrid X *Ferobergia* (Glass, 1966), and the cross between *Stenocactus* (*Echinossofulocactus* sp.) X *Ferocactus* sp. that produced X*Ferossofulocactus* (Rowley, 1980b). Disregarding fertility issues in these intergeneric hybrids, the ability to recover viable offspring from intergeneric crosses probably indicates a relatively low degree of genetic divergence; therefore, the apparent lack of reproductive isolation allows chromosomes to pair at meiosis to create artificial hybrids. If artificial and even naturally occurring intergeneric hybrids are created within certain groups of cacti, then it is quite likely that interspecific hybrids of *Ferocactus* do occur in the wild as suggested by Lindsay (1955a) and Taylor (1984). Nonetheless, sources of evidence (other than intermediacy) are still missing.

Current Molecular Phylogenetic Knowledge

Several molecular biological techniques involving macromolecules (in particular chloroplast and nuclear DNA), are being applied to the study of phylogenetic relationships and evolution of certain plant groups. Because the advantages of molecular tools in plant systematics and evolution are discussed at length in several papers (e.g., Avise, 1994; Palmer, 1987; Palmer et al., 1988; Olmstead and Palmer, 1994; Whitkus et al., 1994) I will only mention two of their strengths: 1) they provide virtually unlimited number of characters to analyse and compare in relatively short periods of time, and 2) they are less subject to convergent evolution, so that homoplasy is minimized and phylogenetic reconstruction is less problematic. Previous papers (Wallace, 1986, 1995a, 1995b; Wallace and Cota, 1996; Cota and Wallace, 1996) have explained the importance and application of macromolecular techniques to the study of cactus evolution in more detail.

Pioneering studies using molecular techniques in the systematics of the Cactaceae at different taxonomic levels were initiated in the early 1990s at Iowa State University under the direction of Robert S. Wallace, and are providing new insights into the systematics, evolution, and phylogeny of the cactus family. In this facility, various molecular methods [in particular gene sequencing and restriction site variation studies of chloroplast DNA (cpDNA)] are being applied to both North and South American groups of cacti in order to generate a phylogeny of this family. Among the numerous promising projects in progress in this lab are:

1. Within the subfamily Cactoideae, a major study using different regions of the chloroplast genome to elucidate the interspecific relationships in *Ferocactus* and its relationships with North American columnar cacti of Tribe Pachycereeae. The preliminary results of this project are discussed in the following sections.

2. The assessment of the phylogenetic relationships and major lineages between North and South American columnar cacti.

3. In the subfamily Opuntioideae, a study of the interspecific phylogenetic relationships in *Opuntia* and related taxa (*Pereskiopsis* Britton and Rose, *Pterocactus* MacDouglas and Mir., *Quiabentia* Britton and Rose, and *Tacinga* Britton and Rose), using several regions of the chloroplast genome represents a major effort which is providing new insight to clarify the taxonomy of this complex group.

4. The phylogenetic study of the Tribe Rhipsalidae (including *Hatiora* Britton and Rose, *Lepismium* Pfeiffer, *Rhipsalis* Gartn., *Rhipsalidopsis* Britton and Rose, and *Schlumbergera* Lem.) to determine the putative terrestrial lineage from which this epiphytic tribe evolved and the pattern for divergence within the tribe.

5. Analyses of the major lineages within the tribe Hylocereeae to clarify their phylogenetic relationships and intergeneric boundaries.

6. An intergeneric study in members of the South American tribes Trichocereeae, Cereeae, and Browningieae to investigate their phylogenetic relationships has been initiated recently. Additionaly, several other projects that will complement those outlined here are being planned for the near future.

Relevant descriptions and preliminary results of the main projects in progress in Wallace's lab in diverse lineages of the Cactaceae, and a review of the major techiques in the molecular systematics of this family using cpDNA are provided in Wallace (1995a, 1995b), Wallace and Cota (1996), and Cota and Wallace (1996). The reader is advised to consult these references for a more comprehensive understanding of terminology and methods used in the following section.

Molecular Studies in *Ferocactus*

The putatively basal phylogenetic position in which *Ferocactus* has been placed in the Tribe Cacteae of the Subfamily Cactoideae (Fig. 5) (Buxbaum, 1958; Barthlott, 1988; Barthlott and Hunt, 1993) suggests the possibility that several lineages evolved from it. However, the pattern of intergeneric relationships within the members of the Cacteae tribe and possibly taxa of other tribes remains unclear despite a few shared morphological characters that suggest some degree of relationship. The phylogenetic reconstruction of *Ferocactus* confronts a series of issues, some of which are related to the following questions: Is this genus monophyletic and a basal lineage within the Cacteae? Did other genera arise from *Ferocactus* or evolve in parallel? If so, What are those? And finally, Does the presence of chartaceous scales in the flowers of *F. flavovirens* (Scheidw.) Britton and Rose suggest any phylogenetic relationship with North American columnar cacti of the Pachycereeae which also display this character? The answers to these enigmas are certainly significant in elucidating the origin, evolution and phylogeny of this controversial genus. In this section, it is my aim to address some of these issues, namely the monophyly of *Ferocactus* and its relationships with columnar cacti of North America, based on preliminary molecular data obtained from cpDNA restriction site analysis and DNA sequences of coding (exon) and non-coding (intron) regions of the chloroplast genome. Because these studies are still in progress, it is necessary to note that the relationships presented in the following discussions are subject to future changes as new data becomes available from within the genus and within the tribe. Also, the arguments approached are only briefly discussed because they are at present based on preliminary data; detailed discussions are in preparation for publication elsewhere.

Molecular Phylogenetics of *Ferocactus* and its Relationships with North American Columnar Cacti of North America (Tribe Pachycereeae) Based on Restriction Site Variation of cpDNA and Gene Sequence Analyses of the Chloroplast Gene *ndhF*

The enormous diversity encompassed by *Ferocactus* and the presence of similar morphological structures in other genera (*Echinocactus* and *Stenocactus*) raise the possibility that this diverse assemblage may not be monophyletic. Initially, no specific hypotheses were suggested about the origin of *Ferocactus*. Lindsay (1955a) considered the genus to be a "non-natural group," interpreted today to mean perhaps polyphyletic; later, Taylor (1980), based on morphological similarities in rib pattern and presence of areolar glands in *Ferocactus* and *Stenocactus coptonogonus* (Lem.) Berger, considered that these two lineages should be united because the affinities suggested a common origin and close evolutionary relationship. Consequently, four species previously placed in *Stenocactus* were transferred to his newly established subgenus *Stenocactus* of *Ferocactus* (Taylor, 1980) in the broad sense of the genus. It is remarkable that these authors' ideas converged in the same assumption of a paraphyletic, possibly polyphyletic *Ferocactus*. Moreover, the presence of morphologically similar flower scales has suggested some degree of relationship between *Ferocactus* and columnar cacti of North America (Gibson, 1992). Sclerification in the bract tips or scales of the pericarpel and floral tube occurs in both Mexican columnar cacti of the Tribe Pachycereeae, subtribe Pachycereinae [*Pachycereus* (Berger) Britton and Rose], and subtribe Stenocereinae [*Escontria chiotilla* (F. A. C. Weber) Rose, *Myrtillocactus cochal* (Orcutt)

Britton and Rose, *Stenocereus stellatus* (Pfeiff.) Riccob., and Tribe Cacteae (*F. flavovirens* (Scheidw.) Britton and Rose. Some authors (Buxbaum, 1951; Gibson and Nobel, 1986) have suggested that homoplasious character transformation in the Cactaceae may be common. Molecular data in the next section demonstrate that the presence of sclerified scales in distantly related taxa is due to parallelism.

The molecular part of a biosystematic study of *Ferocactus* based on cpDNA restriction site variation and sequence of the gene *ndh*F, to investigate the monophyly of the genus, its interspecific relationships, and major lineages (as proposed by Taylor, 1984) has provided new insight into its taxonomy and phylogeny. The gene *ndhF* is located at one end of the small single copy region of the chloroplast (Figure 9), and encodes a subunit of the NADH dehydrogenase (Scotland et al., 1995). In the next paragraphs I combine the preliminary results obtained from these projects because both studies focus on the same objectives. In both the restriction site variation and gene sequence studies, selected taxa from throughout the genus have been examined along with representative columnar cacti of North America (Tribe Pachycereeae) and other cylindric cacti of Tribe Cacteae to clarify the relationships within the genus and the allied taxa of these tribes.

The 250 mutations (representing changes in restriction sites) detected in the restriction site study and the sequences obtained from the *ndh*F gene were analyzed independently using the principle of maximum parsimony with the program PAUP [Phylogenetic Analysis Using Parsimony (Swofford, 1993)] to construct trees. Since taxonomic sampling in the sequencing study is still limited, the sequencing results must be considered preliminary.

Because the restriction site study includes a larger number of taxa from the different lineages, the relationships determined from this study will be used to discuss aspects related to the phylogeny of *Ferocactus*. Although different in topology and species investigated, both phylogenies will be used in concert to discuss the relationships of *Ferocactus* with North American columnar cacti. For the restriction site study, a modified molecular phylogeny [*F. hamathacanthus* (Muehlenpf.) Britton and Rose was excluded as in Lindsay's treatment)] of that published by Cota and Wallace (1996; submitted) obtained from this analysis is shown in Figure 10. In turn, Figure 11 shows the most parsimonious tree with the preliminary phylogeny obtained from sequences of the *ndh*F gene. Both phylogenies suggest the following:

1. *Ferocactus* is a paraphyletic assemblage as presently circumscribed in the different classifications, i.e., *Echinocactus grusonii* is included within the *Ferocactus* clade and is basal to *F. glaucescens* (DC) Britton and Rose and *F. histrix*, making *Ferocactus* paraphyletic (this result is not evident in the *ndh*F phylogeny, and *E. grusonii* has not yet been sequenced for the *ndh*F phylogeny).

2. There is no direct phylogenetic relationship of *Ferocactus*, in particular *F. flavovirens*, with columnar cacti of the Pachycereeae. This evidence eliminates the possibility of relationships between *Ferocactus* and North American columnar cacti, particularly with *Escontria chiotilla* based on similarities of chartaceous flowers scales as indicated by Gibson (1992).

3. This evidence confirms the monophyletic origin of Subfamily Cactoideae as proposed by Wallace and Cota (1996).

4. The North American columnar cacti of Tribe Pachycereeae and its two subtribes (Pachycereinae and Stenocereinae) are all monophyletic lineages.

The most remarkable result in this study is the possibility of paraphyly of *Ferocactus* as presently circumscribed, which confirms Lindsay's and Taylor's earlier suspicions on the origin of the genus. If *Ferocactus* were a monophyletic group it should include all of the descendants (which is not the case as *E. grusonii* has traditionally been treated as a separate taxonomic unit). It is evident that this preliminary phylogeny will likely raise more controversy. If we favor monophyletic groups, making *Ferocactus* monophyletic (including *E. grusonii*) we would require a new taxonomic treatment and consequently, nomenclatural changes. That is, the International Code of Botanical Nomenclature (Greuter, et al., 1994) calls for the principle of priority of the earliest name formally published. In fact, the oldest valid generic name is *Echinocactus* because Engelmann in 1884 originally described the type species for the genus as *Echinocactus wislizeni*, and it was later proposed as *Ferocactus wislizeni* by Britton and Rose in 1922, when they segregated it from *Echinocactus*. Since this phylogeny is preliminary, and the remaining species need to be investigated, no further discussion is provided here to avoid more taxonomic confusion and misinterpretation. Some species of *Ferocactus* are still missing from this study as well as of species from *Echinocactus* and allied taxa from within the Cacteae; therefore, it is premature to ascertain the paraphyly of *Ferocactus*, until the study is completed.

The lack of molecular evidence to support the association between *Ferocactus* and the columnar cacti based on the presence of floriferous chartaceous scales led to a new hypothesis about the origin of *Ferocactus*. As suggested by Cota and Wallace (submitted), it is feasible that *Ferocactus* probably evolved early in the divergence of the present Cacteae, and most likely shared a common ancestor with *Echinocactus* and *Stenocactus* as evidenced by some shared morphological characters (e.g., *Ferocactus* and *Stenocactus* have flattened central spines and naked scales of the pericarpel), features that might also indicate their close phylogenetic relationship. In addition, the similarity in rib pattern and glandular spines in *S. coptonogonus* and *Ferocactus* reflect close relationship (Taylor, 1980).

Based on the molecular data, to date, the phylogenetic relationships of *Ferocactus, Stenocactus* and *Echinocactus* appear to be clarified and resolved in part. The molecular evidence based on restriction site analysis of the cpDNA genome indicates that within the Subtribe Echinocactinae, *Stenocactus* is in a basal position relative to *Ferocactus* and *Echinocactus* (Fig. 10) (Cota and Wallace, submitted). Conversely, on morphological grounds it is difficult to demonstrate the basal position of any one of these three genera. Nonetheless, in early classifications of the Cacteae, *Echinocactus* has been placed in a putatively basal position (Buxbaum, 1958; Barthlott and Hunt, 1993).

Although gene sequencing is one of the most effective methods to estimate the amount of DNA variation by comparing the order of nucleotides in different taxa, analysis of preliminary data failed to confirm the phylogenetic relationships at the interspecific level in *Ferocactus.* Two factors may account for this. First, a limited number of taxa were sampled, and second, the *ndh*F gene is evolving rapidly so that the phylogenetic signal is not the most appropriate for estimating the degree of relationship. It has been reported that this gene is evolving 2-3 times faster that the *rbc*L (large subunit of ribulose biphosphate carboxylase/oxygenase) gene (Olmstead and Sweere, 1994). Similar results were obtained in the comparative analysis based on sequences of the non-coding region of the *trn*L-*trn*F (intergenic region of the transfer RNA genes) with 17 species of *Ferocactus* (Cota and Wallace, unpub. data): the degree of relatedness was partially resolved (cladogram not included). However, the phylogenetic relationships of *Ferocactus* with columnar cacti corroborated those obtained from the restriction site and *ndh*F phylogenies, confirming that the presence of sclerified scales in distantly related lineages represents one more example of convergence in the Cactaceae.

The Biogeography of *Ferocactus*

The geological history of Baja California explains in part the origin as well as the composition and affinities of the flora of the Sonoran Desert. Axelrod (1979) provides an excellent interpretation of the geological scenario that was involved in the origin and evolution of the flora of this area. Because the geographic distribution of *Ferocactus* includes northwestern mainland Mexico, the Baja California Peninsula, and southwestern U.S., it is also possible to explain, in part, its geographic range based on the series of geological events that took place during the Pliocene and Pleistocene as described below. For a complete review of the geological history of this area, the reader should consult Axelrod (1979), Gastil et al. (1983), and Wiggins (1960) plus references included therein.

Before Peninsular California separated, it was connected to mainland Mexico in western Sonora, Sinaloa, and Nayarit. During the middle Miocene the peninsula first separated from continental Mexico (Axelrod, 1979) beginning the formation of the Gulf of California. The tip of the Peninsula (La Paz and Los Cabos regions) was presumably attached to Jalisco during the Miocene and joined the peninsula in the Pleistocene (Gastil et al., 1983). As the incipient gulf expanded, the islands formed through several natural processes such as submergence, uplift, erosion, and volcanism. Throughout this time, the islands probably acted as land bridges contributing to the expansion and colonization of new areas for plants. In others cases, they may act as centers in which divergence and thus speciation events were favored due to geographic isolation. It is quite likely that the islands in the Sea of Cortez played a major role in the diversification of *Ferocactus* as they provided new ecological conditions and suitable habitats for establishment of immigrant individuals. In addition, time may have been a major ally in the divergence and differentiation of these populations that became isolated from their mainland relatives. Examples of these are those endemic species [e.g., *F. chrysacanthus, F. diguetii* (Weber) Britton and Rose, *F. gatesii* Lindsay, and *F. johnstonianus* (Britton and Rose) Fosb.] that probably arose from a common stock but diverged as they became geographically isolated. It is remarkable that these taxa appear to have mainland relatives and that morphological differences are subtle or incipient. Indeed, some of these island endemics have been described as varieties by some authors, which may reflect the actively evolving status of the genus.

The occurrence of 11 of the 25 species (44%) recognized by Lindsay (1955a) in the Baja California Peninsula and surrounding islands is evidence that this area has been important in the diversification of the genus. To date, it is unknown whether these species originated after the separation of the peninsula from the Mexican coast. As a manner of speculation, a possible scenario of the distribution of the species of *Ferocactus* in Baja California can be explained by a bidirectional, possibly tridirectional pattern. That is, if the species originated after the formation of the Sea of Cortéz, it is possible that some taxa (e.g., *F. acanthodes*) entered Baja California from the north, whereas the Baja California relatives of *F. covillei* and *F. wislizeni* reached the peninsula via a migratory route through the islands in the young Gulf of California. As these species moved into new habitats, most likely they diverged and evolved into new entities. Conversely, if some species evolved in the peninsula itself, then the ancestors of the extant floristic elements drifted along with the peninsula and then became isolated by subsequent geological events.

Although the ideas I present here lack evidence such as fossil records to document migratory pathways, they are supported in part by plate tectonics events related to the origin of the Baja California Peninsula itself, and to the affinities of its flora to mainland Mexico [e.g., *F. robustus* (from central Mexico) has similar architectural design of the seed coat with that of *F. wislizeni* (from northwestern Mexico) and the Baja Californian species *F. townsendianus* (Taylor and Clark, 1983), and other genera of the Cactaceae (*Cochemiea* (Brandegee) Walton and *Stenocereus* Riccob.) are allied with mainland genera of cacti (Wiggins, 1960) among other flowering plants]. Also, some floristic elements in southern Baja (La Paz and Cabo San Lucas) are similar to plant species distributed in mainland Mexico in the areas of the Pacific Coast (Axelrod, 1979; Rzedowski, 1973). These affinities imply that some elements of the flora probably originated in mainland Mexico and migrated west towards the Baja California peninsula and southwestern U.S. (Axelrod, 1979). Moreover, the similarity in ecological conditions between the desert areas of Baja California, Sonora and Sinaloa, with those of Central Mexico, in particular the Tehuacan Valley, suggested the same predominant conditions for the semideserts of the Tertiary (Axelrod, 1979).

It is interesting to note the parallelism in ecological conditions in these two desert areas because this information adds more insight into the patterns of radiation of *Ferocactus*. Taylor and Clark (1983) hypothesized that two major evolutionary lines (section *Ferocactus* and section *Bisnaga*) arose independently. The former originated from *F. robustus* and the latter from *F. flavovirens*, two species that have retained plesiomorphic characters in gross morphology of stem and growth habit. Interestingly, the authors suggested the Tehuacan Valley as the center from which *Ferocactus* evolved. In section *Bisnaga*, most of the species are restricted to east-central Mexico and appear to be well defined. However, according to Taylor and Clark (1983) and Taylor (1984) those taxa in section *Ferocactus* radiated and evolved into northwestern Mexico and Baja California, and have little morphological resemblance with their putative ancestor (*F. robustus*) from which they became isolated. It is likely that the "linking species" is missing. Could it then have been possible that the connection between the taxa of this phylad was lost during evolution? Likewise, it could have become extinct during the geological events that took place during the origin of the peninsula of Baja California, enhancing the morphological divergence between the descendants and the putative ancestor. It is clear that the evolution of the genus was in the direction of similar desert environments from those predominant in the Valley of Tehuacan. Although no addditional evidence is available, this explanation seems reasonable and based on the geological history provides a stronger basis for the interpretation of the origin and radiation of the genus as suggested by Taylor and Clark (1983). Clearly, more data are needed to fully understand the patterns of radiation of *Ferocactus*.

Conclusions

Ferocactus is indeed a complex taxonomic unit. In spite of the effectiveness of molecular tools in systematic studies of the Cactaceae at different hierarchical levels, the interspecific relationships in the genus will remain unclear until taxonomic sampling is completed. However, the application of these techniques in the systematics of *Ferocactus* has proven to be of importance in understanding the intergeneric relationships and the evolution of certain morphological traits, such as the presence of chartaceous scales in the flowers. It is possible that some change in taxonomic circumscription will be made as future studies are conducted. Those molecular systematic studies in progress will certainly clarify the relationships at the infra- and interspecific levels and will lead to a phylogeny which provides more insight into character evolution. Also, it is important to keep in mind that after more than 70 years of taxonomic work, the pieces are gradually coming together, and that the phylogenetic reconstruction of *Ferocactus* in particular, and of the Cactaceae in general, is possible thanks to these revolutionary studies in molecular systematics. Although additional taxonomic sampling is needed, it is satisfying to see that the modern phylogeny based on cpDNA restriction site data correlates well with Lindsay's classification. Overall, most of the species considered in his taxonomy and other authors' taxonomies (with the exception of *F. histrix* and *F. glaucescens*) are included in the cpDNA phylogeny as a monophyletic group. In addition, the inclusion of these two species within the *Ferocactus* clade confirms previous ideas about the paraphyletic origin of the genus. The next step for clarifying the patterns of evolution should allow determination of the major lineages within *Ferocactus* and how they have diverged in time into such a morphologically plastic taxonomic unit.

Finally, I would like to mention that molecular studies for phylogenetic reconstruction are not being done to prove whether a certain taxonomic treatment is correct; they are done to test proposed taxonomies in terms of phylogeny, and more importantly, to understanding the patterns of radiation in the different lineages, as well as the evolution of floral and other morphological characters. It is noteworthy that the existence of previous treatments based on classical taxonomy allows us to directly apply molecular techniques in concert with morphological traits to generate what we think will be a more sound phylogenetic foundation for the Cactaceae. Molecular systematics in combination with morphology are rich sources of data which can explain evolutionary patterns and phylogenetic relationships in the cactus family.

REFERENCES

Avise, J. C. 1994. *Molecular Markers, Natural History and Evolution.* Chapman & Hall, Inc., N. Y.

Axelrod, D. I. 1979. Age and Origin of Sonoran Desert Vegetation. Calif. Acad. Sci. *Occ. Pap.* 132: 1-74.

Barthlott, W. 1988. Uber die systematischen Gleiderungen der Cactaceae. Beitr. Biol. Pflanzen 63: 17-40.

Barthlott, W., and D. R. Hunt. 1993. Cactaceae. In: *The Families and Genera of Vascular Plants.* Vol. II. Flowering Plants, Dicotyledons. Kubitzki, K., J. G., Rohwer, and V. Bittrich (eds.), Springer-Verlag, Berlin.

Barthlott, W., and G. Voit. 1979. Mikromorphologie der Samenschalen und Taxonomie der Cactaceae: ein rastrer-elektronenmikroskopischer Uberlich. Pl. Syst. Evol. 32: 205-229.

Beard, E. C. 1937. Some chromosome complements in the Cactaceae and a study of meiosis in *Echinocereus papillosus.* Bot. Gaz. 99: 1-21.

Bentley, B. L. 1977a. Extrafloral nectaries and protection by pugnacious bodyguards. Annu. Rev. Ecol. Syst. 8: 407-427.

Bentley, B. L. 1977b. The protective function of ants visiting the extrafloral nectaries of *Bixa orellana* (Bixaceae). J. Ecol. 65: 27-38.

Blom, P. E., and W. H. Clark. 1980. Observations of ants (Hymenoptera: Formicidae) visiting extrafloral nectaries of the barrel cactus, *Ferocactus gracilis* Gates (Cactaceae), in Baja California, Mexico. Southwestern Nat. 25: 181-196.

Bravo-Hollis, H. 1966. *Ferocactus lindsayi*, una especie nueva. Cact. Suc. Mex. 11: 9-12.

Bravo-Hollis, H., and H. Sánchez-Mejorada. 1991. *Ferocactus* Britton and Rose. In: *Las Cactáceas de México.* Vol. III. Universidad Nacional Autónoma de México. Mexico, D. F.

Britton, N. L., and J. N. Rose. 1922. *Ferocactus.* In: *The Cactaceae.* Vol. II. Dover Pub. Inc., New York.

Buxbaum, F. 1951. Stages and lines of evolution of the Tribe Euechinocactinae. Cact. Succ. J. (U.S.) 23: 193-197.

Buxbaum, F. 1958. The phylogenetic division of the subfamily Cereoideae, Cactaceae. Madroño 14: 177-206.

Cockerell, E. D. 1900. The cactus bees: genus *Lithurge.* Amer. Nat. 34: 487-488.

Cody, M. L., R. Moran, and H. Thompson. 1983. The Plants. Pages 49-97. *In*: T. J. Case and M. L. Cody (eds.), *Island Biogeography of the Sea of Cortéz*. Univ. California Press, Los Angeles.

Cota, J. H. 1991. Karyotype evolution in the genus *Echinocereus* (Cactaceae). Master's Thesis. The Claremont Graduate School/Rancho Santa Ana Botanic Garden. Claremont, CA.

Cota, J. H. 1993. Pollination syndromes in the genus *Echinocereus*: A review. Cact. Succ. J. (U.S.) 65: 19-26.

Cota, J. H., and C. T. Philbrick. 1994. Chromosome number variation and polyploidy in the genus *Echinocereus* (Cactaceae). Amer. J. Bot. 81: 1054-1062.

Cota, J. H., and R. S. Wallace. 1995. Karyotypic studies in the genus *Echinocereus* (Cactaceae) and their taxonomic significance. Caryologia 48: 105-122.

Cota, J. H., and R. S. Wallace. 1996. La citología y la sistemática molecular en la familia Cactaceae. Cact. Suc. Mex. 41: 27-46.

Cota, J. H., and R. S. Wallace. Submitted. A phylogeny of *Ferocactus* and its relationships with North American columnar Cacti of Tribe Pachycereeae. Systematic Botany.

Cota, J. H., J. P. Rebman, and R. S. Wallace. Submitted. Chromosome numbers in *Ferocactus* (Cactoideae: Cactaceae). Cytologia.

del Castillo, R. F. 1982. Estudio ecológico de *Ferocactus histrix* (DC) Lindsay. Bachelor Thesis. Universidad Nacional Autónoma de México. Mexico.

del Castillo, R. F. 1988. Nota sobre los nectarios extraflorales en cactàceas. Cact. Suc. Mex. 33: 99-100.

Friedrich, H., and W. Glaetzle. 1983. Seed-morphology as an aid to classifying the genus *Echinopsis* Zucc. Bradleya 1: 91-104.

Gastil, G., J. Minch, and R. P.Phillips. 1983. The geology and ages of islands. Pages 13-25. *In*: T. J. Case and M. L. Cody (eds.), *Island Biogeography in the Sea of Cortéz*. Univ. Cal. Press., Los Angeles.

Gibson, A. C. 1992. The Peruvian Browningias of *Gymnathocereus*. Cact. Succ. J. (U.S.) 64: 62-68.

Gibson, A. C., and P. S. Nobel. 1986. *The Cactus Primer*. Harvard Univ. Press. Cambridge, MA.

Glaetzle, W., and H. Prestlé. 1986. Seed-morphology of the genus *Notocactus*. Bradleya 4: 79-96.

Glass, C. 1966. An incredible new bigeneric cultivar. Cact. Succ. J. (U.S.) 38: 177-178.

Grant, V., and K. A. Grant. 1979a. Pollination of *Echinocereus fasciculatus* and *Ferocactus wislizeni*. Pl. Syst. Evol. 132: 85-90.

Grant, V., and K. A. Grant. 1979b. The pollination spectrum in the southwestern American cactus flora. Pl. Syst. Evol. 133: 29-37.

Grant, V., and P. D. Hurd. 1979. Pollination in *Opuntia liendheimeri* and related species. Pl. Syst. Evol. 133: 15-28.

Greuter, W., F. R. Barrie, H. M. Burdet, W. G. Chaloner, V. Demoulin, D. L. Hawksworth, P. M. Jorgensen, D. H. Nicolson, P. C. Silva, P. Trehane, and J. McNeil. 1994. *International Code of Botanical Nomenclature* (Tokyo Code) adopted by the Fifteenth International Botanical Congress, Yokohama, August-Sept. 1993. *Regnum Veg.* 131.

Johnson. M. A. 1980. Further cytological investigations in *Mammillaria prolifera* and other *Mammillaria* species. Cact. Succ. J. (Great Britain) 42: 43-47.

Katagiri, S. 1952. Chromosome numbers and polyploidy in certain Cactaceae. Cact. Succ. J. (U.S.) 25: 141-143.

Kurtz, E. B. Jr. 1948. Pollen grain characters of certain Cactaceae. Bull. Torr. Bot. Club 75: 516-522.

Leuenberger, B. E. 1976. Pollen morphology of the Cactaceae. Cact. Succ. J. (Great Britain) 38: 79-94.

Lindsay, G. E. 1942. A new variety of *Ferocactus alamosanus*. Cact. Succ. J. (U. S.) 14: 139-143.

Lindsay, G. E. 1955a. The Taxonomy and Ecology of the Genus *Ferocactus*. Ph. D. Diss. Stanford University. Stanford, CA.

Lindsay, G. E. 1955b. *Ferocactus schwarzii* - A new species. Cact. Succ. J. (U.S.) 27: 70-72.

Lindsay, G. E. 1955c. *Ferocactus gatesii* - A new species. Cact. Succ. J. (U.S.) 27: 150-151.

Lindsay, G. E. 1955d. Some new varieties and nomenclatural changes in *Ferocactus*. Cact. Succ. J. (U.S.) 27: 163-175.

Lindsay, G. E. 1964. A new variety of *Ferocactus*. Cact. Succ. J. (U.S.) 36: 8-10.

Lindsay, G. E. 1965. Los Ferocacti de Baja California. Cact. Suc. Mex. 10: 73-91.

Lindsay, G. E. 1968. The rediscovery of *Ferocactus haematacanthus*. Cact. Succ. J. (U.S.) 40: 3-6.

Nobel, P. S. 1977. Water relations and photosynthesis of a barrel cactus, *Ferocactus acanthodes*, in the Colorado Desert. Oecologia 27: 117-133.

Olmstead, R. G., and J. D. Palmer. 1994. Chloroplast DNA systematics: A review of methods and data analysis. Amer. J. Bot. 81: 1205-1224.

Olmstead, R. G., and J. A. Sweere. 1994. Combining data in phylogenetic systematics: an empirical approach using three molecular data sets in the Solanaceae. Syst. Biol. 43: 467-481.

Palmer, J. D. 1987. Chloroplast DNA evolution and biosystematic uses of DNA variation. Amer. Nat. 130S: 6-29.

Palmer, J. D., R. K. Jansen, H. J. Michaels, M. W. Chase, and J. R. Manhart. 1988. Chloroplast DNA variation and plant phylogeny. Ann. Miss. Bot. Gard. 75: 1180-1206.

Palomino, H. G., S. Zuleta, and L. Scheinvar. 1988. Estudios citogeneticos de dos especies y una variedad de *Nyctocereus* (Cactaceae). Bol Soc. Bot. Mex. 48: 75-80.

Pickett, C. H., and W. D. Clark. 1979. The function of extrafloral nectaries in *Opuntia acanthocarpa* (Cactaceae). Amer. J. Bot. 66: 618-625.

Pinkava, J. D., and M. G. McLeod. 1971. Chromosome numbers in certain cacti of western North America. Brittonia 23: 171-176.

Pinkava, J. D., and B. D. Parfitt. 1982. Chromosome numbers in certain cacti of western North America-IV. Bull. Torr. Bot. Club 109: 121-128.

Pinkava, D. J., M. A. Baker, B. D. Parfitt, M. W. Mohlenbrock, and R. D. Worthington. 1985. Chromosome numbers in some cacti of western North America-V. Syst. Bot. 10: 471-483.

Pinkava, D. J., L. A. McGill, T. Reeves, and M. G. McLeod. 1977. Chromosome numbers in some cacti of western North America-III. Bull. Torr. Bot. Club 104: 105-110.

Pinkava, J. D., M. G. McLeod, L. A. McGill, and R. C. Brown. 1973. Chromosome numbers in some cacti of western North America-II. Brittonia 25: 2-9.

Pinkava, J. D., B. D. Parfitt, M. A. Baker, and R. D. Worthtington. 1992. Chromosome numbers in some cacti of western North America-VI, with nomenclatural changes. Madroo 39: 98-113.

Richards, A. J. 1986. *Plant Breeding Systems*. G. Allen and Unwin (Pub.) Ltd., London.

Rowley, G. 1980a. Pollination syndromes and cactus taxonomy. Cact. Succ. J. (Great Britain) 42: 95-98.

Rowley, G. 1980b. *Name that Succulent*. Stanley Thornes Ltd., Cheltenham.

Ruffner, G. A., and W. D. Clark. 1986. Extrafloral nectar of *Ferocactus acanthodes* (Cactaceae): composition and its importance to ants. Amer. J. Bot. 73: 185-189.

Rzedowski, J. 1973. Geographical relationships of the flora of the Mexican dry regions. Pages 61-72. *In*: A. Graham, ed., *Vegetation and Vegetational History of Northern Latin America.* Elsevier Sci. Publ. Co. Amsterdan, London & New York.

Scogin, R. 1985. Nectar constituents of the Cactaceae. Southwestern Nat. 30: 77-82.

Scotland, R. W., J. A. Sweere, P. A. Reeves, and R. G. Olmstead. 1995. High level systematics of Acanthaceae determined by chloroplast DNA sequences. Amer. J. Bot. 82: 266-275.

Shinozaki, K., M. Ohme, M. Tanaka, T. Wakasugi, N. Hayashida, T Matsubayashi, N. Zaita, J. Chungwongse, J. Obokata, K. Yamaguchi-Sinozaki, C. Ohto, K. Torazawa, B. Y. Meng, M. Sugita, H. Deno, T. Kamogashira, K. Yamada, J. Kusuda, F. Takaiwa, A. Kato, N. Tohdoh, H. Shimada, M. Sugiura. 1986. The complete nucleotide sequence of the tobacco chloroplast genome. Plant Mol. Biol. Rep. 4: 110-147.

Stockwell, P. 1935. Chromosome counts in some Cactaceae. Bot. Gaz. 96: 565-570.

Swofford, D. L. 1993. PAUP: Phylogenetic Analysis Using Parsimony, version 3.1. Illinois Natural History Survey, Champaign.

Taylor, N. P. 1979a. New combinations in *Ferocactus.* Cact. Succ. J. (Great Britain) 41: 30-31.

Taylor, N. P. 1979b. Notes on *Ferocactus* B. & R. Cact. Succ. J. (Great Britain) 41: 88-94.

Taylor, N. P. 1980. *Ferocactus* and *Stenocactus* united. Cact. Succ. J. (Great Britain) 42: 108.

Taylor, N. P. 1984. A review of *Ferocactus* Britton and Rose. Bradleya 2: 19-38.

Taylor, N. P. 1987. Additional notes on some *Ferocactus* species. Bradleya 5: 95-96.

Taylor, N. P., and J. Y. Clark. 1983. Seed-morphology and classification in *Ferocactus* subg. *Ferocactus*. Bradleya 1: 3-16.

Tsukada, M. 1964. Pollen morphology and identification. II. Cactaceae. Pollen et Spores 6: 45-84.

Unger, G. 1992. *Die Grossen Kugelkakteen Nordamerikas.* Art-Buchbindrei. Graz, Austria.

Wallacc, R. S. 1986. Biochemical taxonomy and the Cactaceae: An introduction and review. Cact. Succ. J. (U.S.) 58: 35-38.

Wallace, R. S. 1995a. Molecular evidence for the systematic placement of *Echinocereus pensilis* (K. Brandegee) J. Purpus (Cactaceae). Haseltonia 3: 71-76.

Wallace, R. S. 1995b. Molecular systematic study of the Cactaceae: Using chloroplast DNA variation to elucidate cactus phylogeny. Bradleya 13: 1-12.

Wallace, R. S., and J. H. Cota. 1996. An intron loss supports the monophyletic origin of the subfamily Cactoideae. Curr. Gen. 29: 275-281.

Weedin, J. F., and M. A. Powell. 1978. Chromosome numbers in Chihuahuan Desert Cactaceae. Amer. J. Bot. 65: 531-537.

Whitkus, R., J. Doebley, and J. F. Wendel. 1994. Nuclear DNA Markers in Systematics and Evolution. Pages 116-141 *In*: R. L. Phillips and I. K. Vasil (eds.). *DNA-Based Markers in Plants,* Kluwer Academic Publ., The Netherlands.

Wiggins, I. L. 1960. The origin and relationships of the land flora. Pages 148-165. In: *The biogeography of Baja California and adjacent seas.* Syst. Zool. 9: 148-165.

Authority	Subgenus	Section	Group	Species
Britton and Rose, 1922	—	—	—	**30**
Lindsay, 1955a	—	—	—	**25**
Taylor, 1980	*Stenocactus*	—	—	4
Taylor and Clark, 1983	*Ferocactus*	*Ferocactus*	*F. robustus*	13
			F. pottsii	4
	—	*Bisnaga* (Orcutt) Taylor and Clark	*F. glaucescens*	5
	—	—	*F. recurvus*	7
				29
Taylor, 1984	*Ferocactus*	*Ferocactus*	*F. robustus*	9
	—	—	*F. pottsii*	3
	—	*Bisnaga*	*F. glaucescens*	5
	—	—	*F. latispinus*	6
				23
Bravo and S<nchez, M., 1991	*Ferocactus* Britton and Rose	—	—	27
	Hamatacanthus Bravo	—	—	1
	Pennisquama Buxb.	—	—	1
				29
Unger, 1992	*Ferocactus*	*Ferocactus*	—	13*
	—	*Pottsia* Unger	—	5
	Bisnaga (Orcutt) Unger	*Bisnaga* (Orcutt) Unger	—	5
	—	*Glaucescenti* Unger	—	5
				28

Table 1. Comparison of the taxonomic hierarchies used in the different classifications of the genus *Ferocactus*. Bold numbers indicate number of species in each treatment. * Includes five natural hybrids.

Taxon	Reported as	Chromosome number	Reference(s)
F. chrysacanthus (Orcutt) Britton & Rose	*F. chrysacanthus*	2n = 22	Cota et al. (submitted).
F. acanthodes (Lem.) B&R	*F. acanthodes*		
var. *acanthodes*	var. *acanthodes*	n = 11	Pinkava et al. (1977).
	F. rostii	n = 11	Stockwell (1935).
var. *lecontei* (Engelm.) Lindsay	var. *lecontei*	n = 11	Pinkava and McLeod (1971); Pinkava et al. (1977, 1992).
		2n = 22	Cota el al. (submitted).
F. echidne (DC) B&R	*F. echidne*	2n = 22	Katagiri (1952).
F. covillei B&R	*F. covillei*	2n = 22	Katagiri (1952).
F. fordii (Orcutt) B&R	*F. fordii*		
var. *fordii*	var. *fordii*	n = 11	Pinkava et al. (1973); Cota et al. (submitted).
F. gracilis H. E. Gates	*F. gracilis*		
var. *gracilis*	var. *gracilis*	n = 11	Pinkava et al. (1973, 1977, 1985); Cota et al (submitted).
*F. hamatacanthus** (Muehlpf.) B&R	*F. hamatacanthus*	n = 11	Beard (1937).
var. *hamatacanthus**	var. *hamatacanthus*	n = 11	Weedin and Powell (1978).
F. histrix (D. C.) G. E. Lindsay	*F. histrix*	n = 11	Cota et al. (submitted).
F. latispinus (Haw.) B&R	*F. latispinus*	2n = 22	Katagiri (1952); Cota et al. (submitted).
F. macrodiscus (Mart.) B&R	*F. macrodiscus*	n = 11	Cota et al. (submitted).
F. peninsulae (Engelm. ex Weber) B&R			
var. *peninsulae*	var. *peninsulae*	n = 11	Cota et al. (submitted).
F. pilosus (Galeotti) Werderm.	*F. pringlei*	n = 11	Pinkava et al. (1977).
	F. pilosus	n = 11	Pinkava and Parffit (1982).
	F. stainesii	n = 11	Katagiri (1952).
F rectispinus (Engelm.) B&R	*F. rectispinus*	2n = 22	Cota et al. (submitted).
F. recurvus (Miller) Y. Ito	*F. recurvus*	2n = 22	Cota et al. (submitted).
F. robustus (Otto) B&R	*F. robustus*	2n = 22	Cota et al. (submitted).
F. townsendianus B&R	*F. peninsulae*		
	var. *townsendianus*	2n = 22	Cota et al. (submitted).
F. viridescens (Nuttal) B&R	*F. viridescens*	n = 11	Pinkava et al. (1973; 1977).
	var. *viridescens*	n = 11	Cota et al. (submitted).
F. wislizeni (Engelm.) B&R	*F. wislizeni*	n = 11	Pinkava et al. (1973).
		2n = 22	Katagiri (1952); Cota et al. (submitted).

Table 2. Chromosome counts reported for *Ferocactus*.Taxonomy and authority names in the taxon column follow that of Lindsay (1955a). Asterisk indicates species excluded from Lindsay's classification.

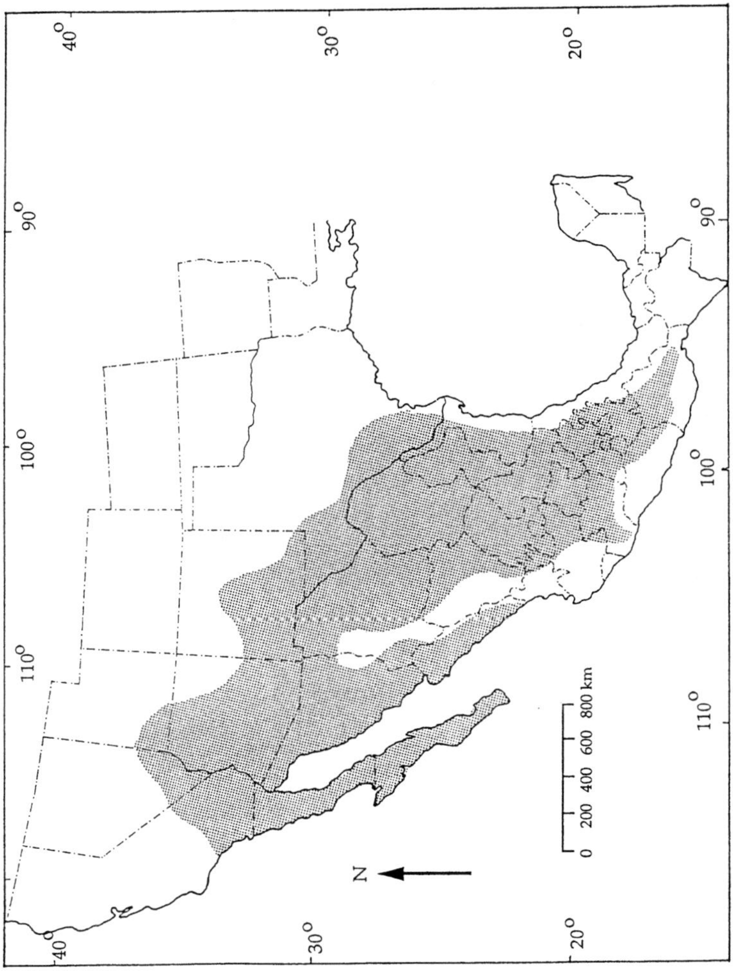

Figure 4. Overall geographic distribution of *Ferocactus* based on data from Lindsay (1955a) and Taylor (1984). The Baja California Islands have been omitted from the map.

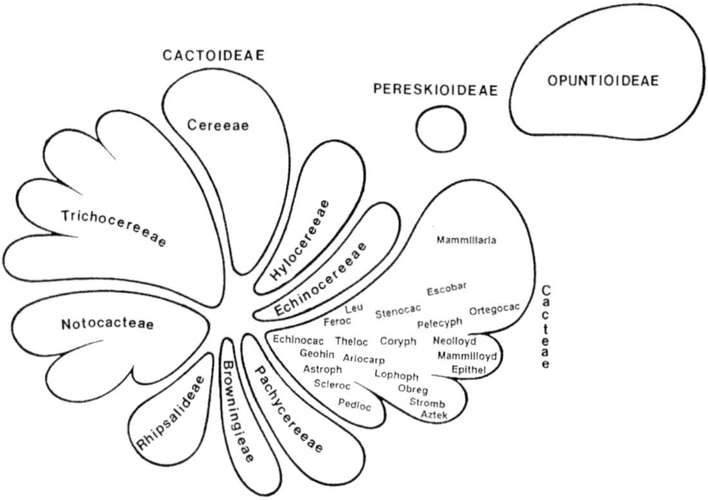

Figure 5. Diagram showing the presumably evolutionary position of *Ferocactus* within the Tribe Cacteae of the Subfamily Cactoideae. Note the position of *Ferocactus* relative to *Echinocactus* and *Stenocactus*. Figure modified from Barthlott and Hunt (1993).

Figure 6. Floral morphology of *Ferocactus*, A). *F. macrodiscus*, G. Lindsay 2607. B). *F. echidne* var. *echidne* from Barranca of Mazitlan, G. Lindsay, 2069. C). *F. flavovirens* from Zapotitlan Salinas, G. Lindsay 205.

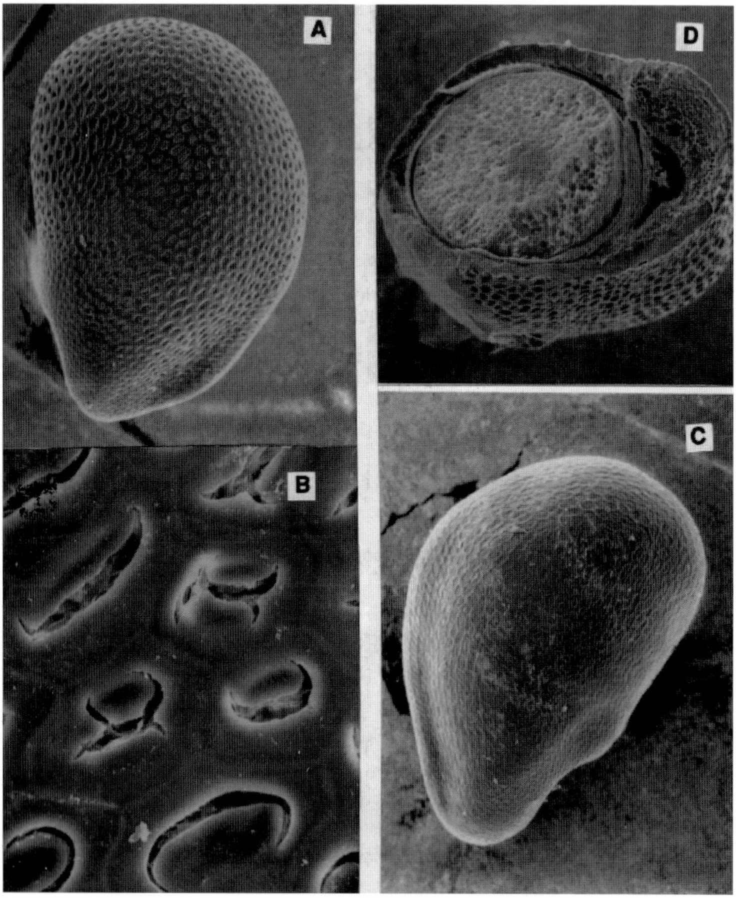

Figure 67. Seeds of Ferocactus. A. Seed of F. rectispinus (H. Cota, 8027) with tabular-concave testa-cells. B. Detail of seed-coat of F. rectispinus showing portions of testa-cells with cracks in seed-coat. C. Seed of F. acanthodes var. lecontei (W. Wisura, s.n., RSA). D. Cross Section of seed of F. acanthodes var. lecontei.

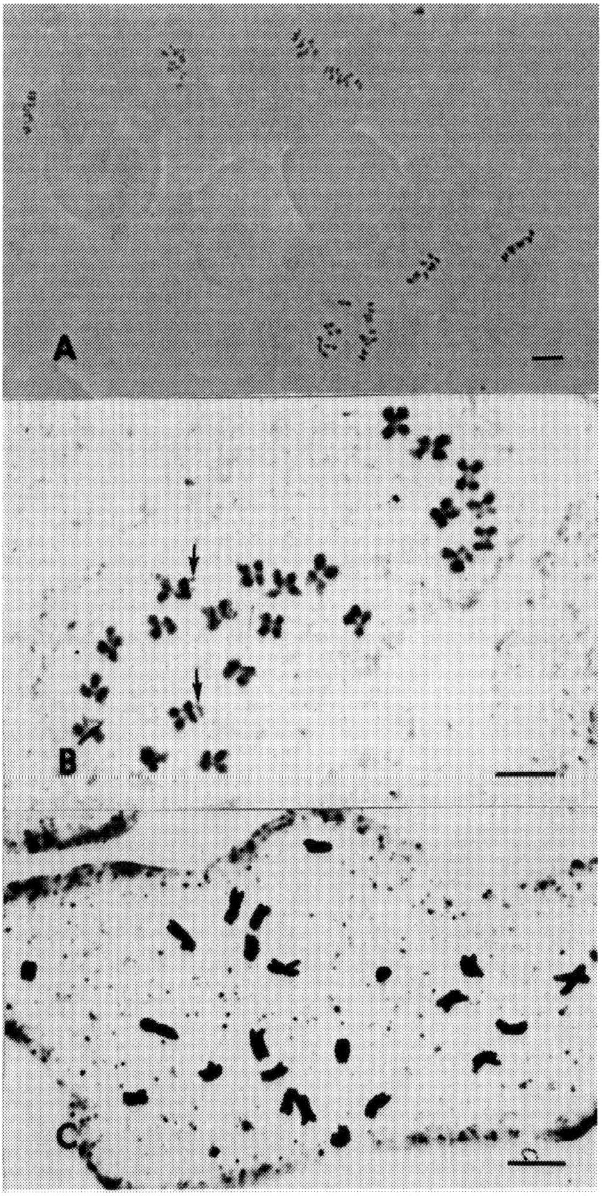

Figure 8. Representative species of *Ferocactus* showing meiotic and mitotic chromosomes. A.) *F. gracilis* var. *gracilis*, J. Rebman 2728, Metaphase II. Scale bar = 20 m. B.) *F. chrysacanthus*, H. Cota 7441. Arrows indicate satellites. Scale bar = 10 m. C.) *F. latispinus*, H. Cota, 8039. Scale bar = 10 m.

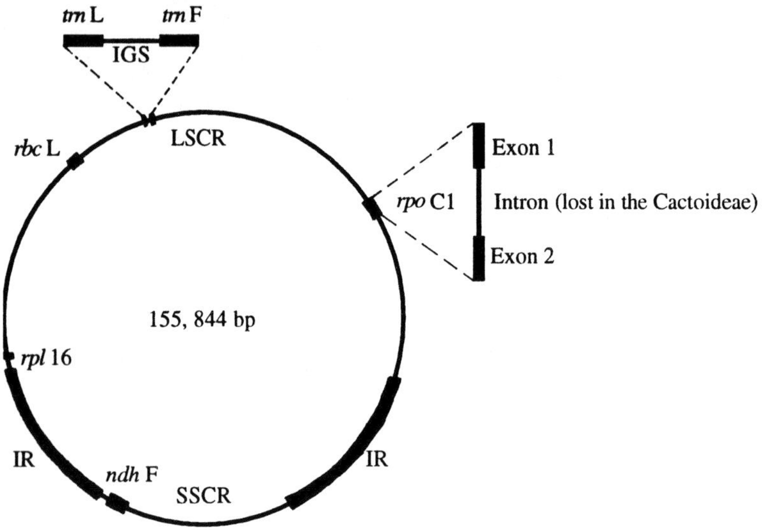

Figure 9. Diagram showing the circular molecule of the cpDNA in *Nicotiana tabacum* (modified from Shinozaki et al., 1986) and the approximate positions of the genes and regions used in the phylogenetic analyses of the Cactaceae, including *Ferocactus*. LSCR = Large Single Copy Region, SSCR = Small Single Copy Region, IR = Inverted Repeat, IGS = Intergenic Spacer between the *trnL* (UAA) 3' exon and the trnF (GAA)genes. The abbreviations for the genes are: *ndhF* = NADH dehydrogenase, *rbcL* = Large subunit of rubisco, rp116 = ribosomal protein, *rpoC* = RNA polymerase, *trnL* and *trnF* = transfer RNA genes. For details about the structure and gene order of the cpDNA molecule the reader is referred to Shinozaki et al., 1986 and Wallace, 1995b.

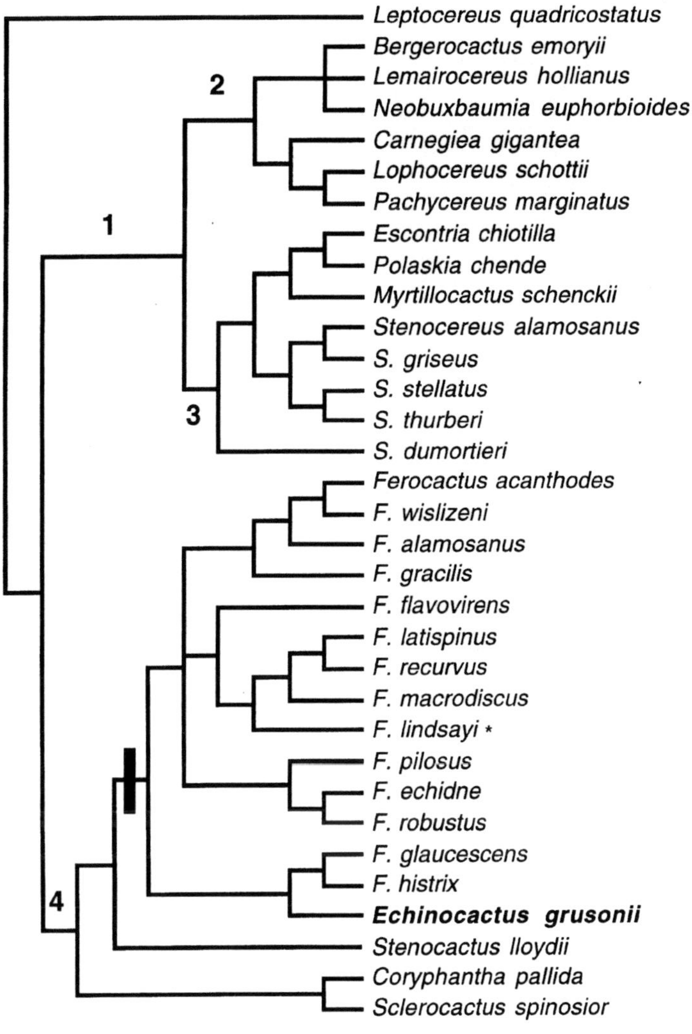

Figure 10. 50% Majority rule consensus tree of 42 equally parsimonious trees (length = 320 and consistency index = 0.772) depicting the preliminary phylogeny for the genus *Ferocactus* obtained from cladistic analysis of cpDNA restriction site data (data from Cota and Wallace, submitted). The thick bar indicates the inclusion of *E. grusonii* within *Ferocactus* making it paraphyletic. Also, there is no relationship of any of the columnar cacti with *Ferocactus*. 1 = represents evidence for monophyly in the Pachycereeae; 2 = monophyly for the Pachycereinae; 3 = monophyly for the Stenocereinae, and 4 = monophyly for the Cacteae. Asterisk represents species described by Bravo-Hollis (1966).

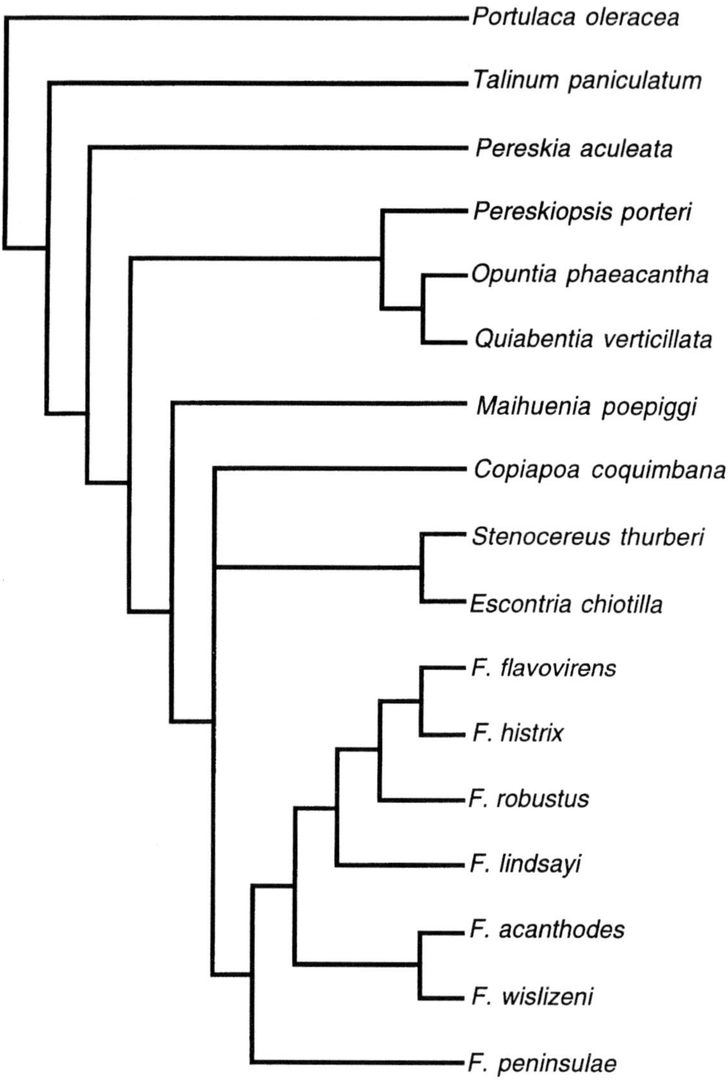

Figure 11. Strict consensus tree of three equally parsimonious trees (length =1434 and consistency index= 0.79) showing preliminary phylogenetic relationships of *Ferocactus* based on sequences of the chloroplast gene *ndhF* (data from Cota and Wallace, unpub). See text for a detailed explanation about the phylogenetic relationships of the cladogram.

SUPPLEMENTARY REFERENCES ON *FEROCACTUS*

Ault, J. R., and W. J. Blackmon. 1987. In vitro propagation of *Ferocactus acanthodes* (Cactaceae). HortScience 22: 122-127.

Barcikowski, W., and P. S. Nobel. 1984. Water relations of cacti during desiccation: distribution of water in tissues. Bot. Gaz. 145: 110-115.

Barthlott, W. 1981. Epidermal and seed surface characters of plants: systematic applicability and some evolutionary aspects. Nord. J. Bot.1: 345-355.

Bates, A. 1975. Flowering Ferocacti. Nat. Cact. Succ. J. (U.S.) 30: 25.

Benson, L. 1969. *The Native Cacti of California.* Stanford Univ. Press. Stanford, CA.

Benson, L. 1982. *The Cacti of the United States and Canada.* Stanford University Press, Stanford, CA.

Blakely, E. R. 1960. The San Diego Barrel Cactus. Saguaroland Bull. 14: 6.

Bravo-Hollis, H. 1937. *Las Cactàceas de México.* Universidad Nacional Autónoma de Mexico. Mexico.

Bregman, R., and F. Bouman. 1983. Seed germination in Cactaceae. Bot. J. Linn. Soc. 86: 357-374.

Buxbaum, F. 1950. *The Morphology of Cacti.* Abbey Garden Press. Pasadena CA.

Buxbaum, F. 1965. Die Systematische Stellung des *Echinocactus flavovirens* Scheidweiler. Beiträge zur Biologie der Pflanzen 41: 143-156.

Cota, J. H. 1984. Influencia de la luz, temperatura y substancias quìmicas en la germinación de semillas de *Ferocactus latispinus* (Haw.) Britton y Rose. Bachelor Thesis. Escuela Nacional de Ciencias Biológicas, IPN. Mexico.

Cota, J. H. 1985. Pruebas de viabilidad con sales de tetrazolio en semillas de *Ferocactus latispinus*. Cact. Suc. Mex. 30: 51-56.

Cota, J. H. 1990. The Cacti of Cedros Island, Baja California. Mexico. Cact. Succ. J. (U.S.) 62: 294-301.

Cutak, L. 1944. Spine Chats - Dr. Wislizenus. Cact. Succ. J. (U.S.) 16: 27.

Cutak, L. 1947. Spine Chats - *Echinocactus grussonii.* Cact. Succ. J. (U.S.) 19: 79.

del Castillo, R. F. 1983. *Ferocactus histrix* - Distribución geográfica y hábitat. Cact. Suc. Mex. 28: 3-12.

del Castillo, R. F. 1986. Semillas, germinación y establecimiento de *Ferocactus histrix*. Cact. Suc. Mex. 31: 5-11.

del Castillo, R. F. 1987. Efectos de disturbio y la orientación de ladera en *Ferocactus histrix*. Cact. Suc. Mex. 32: 8-16.

del Castillo, R. F. 1988. Fenolog'a y remoción de semillas en *Ferocactus histrix*. Cact. Suc. Mex. 33: 5-14.

del Castillo, R. F., and S. Trujillo A. 1991. Ethnobotany of *Ferocactus histrix* and *Echinocactus platyacanthus* (Cactaceae) in semiarid Central Mexico: past, present and future. Economic Botany 45: 495-502.

Diguet, L. 1928. *Les Cactacées Utiles du Mexique*. Archives d'Histoire Naturelle. Paris.

Eggli, U. 1984. Stomatal types of Cactaceae. Pl. Syst. Evol. 146: 197-214.

Ehleringer, J., and D. House. 1984. Orientation and slope preference in barrel cactus (*Ferocactus acanthodes*) and its northern distribution limit. Great Basin Naturalist 44: 133-139.

Felger, R. S., and M. B. Moser. 1985. *People of the Deserts and Sea*. University of Arizona Press. Tucson.

Gason, P. 1981. Epidermal anatomy of some North American globular cacti. Cact. Succ. J. (G. Britain) 43: 101-108.

Gates, H. E. 1931. *Ferocactus rectispinus*. Cact. Succ. J. (U.S.) 2: 390-391.

Gates, H. E. 1933. Four new species of *Ferocactus* from Lower California, Mexico. Cact. Succ. J. (U.S.) 4: 323-325.

Gates, H. E. 1949. Barrel cactus of Lower California. Cact. Succ. J. (Great Britain) 11: 78-80.

Geller, G. N., and P. S. Nobel. 1987. Comparative cactus architecture and PAR interception. Amer. J. Bot. 74: 998-1005.

Glass, C. 1968. *Ferocactus recurvus* var. *greenwoodii*, a new variety from Oaxaca. Cact. Succ. J. (U.S.) 40: 158-161.

González-Quintero, L. 1972. Las cactáceas subfósiles de Tehuacán. Cact. Suc. Mex. 17: 3-15.

Habermann, V. 1971a. *Ferocactus acanthodes*. Kaktusy 7: 34.

Habermann, V. 1971b. *Ferocactus viridescens*. Kaktusy 7: 98.

Hajek, F. 1980. *Ferocactus robustus*. Kaktusy 16: 95-96.

Harralson, J. T., and S. M. 1966. Diameter of the Barrel Cactus *Echinocactus wislizeni*. Cact. Succ. J. (U.S.) 38: 178.

Haugg, E. 1985. *Ferocactus fordii*. Kakt. and Sukk. 36: 6.

Haugg, E. 1991. *Ferocactus glaucescens*. Kakt. and Sukk. 42: 15.

Hawkes, M. W. 1982. Hybridization in the Cactaceae. Cact. Succ. J. (U.S.) 54: 223-225, 243-246.

Hawkes, M. W. 1983. Hybridization in the Cactaceae-Conclusions. Cact. Succ. J. (U.S.) 55: 31-36.

Henshaw, J. L. 1978. The fascinating *Ferobergia*. Nat. Cact. Succ. J. 33: 77.

Humphrey, R. R. 1936. Growth habits of barrel cacti. Madroño 3: 281-290.

Hunt, D. R., and N. P. Taylor. 1990. The Genera of Cactaceae: towards a new consensus. Bradleya 8: 85-107.

Hunter, W. D., F. C. Pratt, and J. D. Mitchell. 1921. The principal cactus insects of the United States. U. S. Department of Agriculture. Enthomologym Bull. No. 113. Washington, D.C.

Jordan, P. W., and P. S. Nobel. 1981. Seedling establishment of *Ferocactus acanthodes* in relation to drought. Ecology 62: 901-906.

Jordan, P. W., and P. S. Nobel. 1982. Height distributions of two species of cacti in relation to rainfall, seedling establishment, and growth. Bot. Gaz. 143: 511-517.

Jordan, P. W., and P. S. Nobel. 1984. Thermal and water relations of roots of desert succulents. Annals of Botany 54: 705-717.

Katagiri, S. 1953. Chromosome numbers and polyploidy in the Cactaceae. Cact. Succ. J. (U.S.) 25: 141-143.

Kishi, M. 1978. *Ferocactus*. A quarterly Cact. Succ. J. (Japan) 1: 44-49.

Kleiner, E. 1977. *Ferocactus latispinus*. Kakt. Sukk. 18: 249.

Kråhenbühl, F. 1980. *Ferocactus haematacanthus*. Kakt. Sukk. 31: 14-17.

Kråhenbühl, F. 1982. *Ferocactus robustus*. Kakt. Sukk. 33: 170-171.

Kråhenbühl, F. 1983. *Ferocactus flavovirens*. Kakt. Sukk. 34: 40-41.

Kråhenbühl, F. 1983a. *Ferocactus latispinus*. Kakt. Sukk. 34: 162-163.

Krainz, H. 1963. *Ferocactus glaucescens*. Kakt. Sukk. 14: 101.

Lau, A. B. 1981. The habitat of *Ferocactus johnstonianus*. Cact. Succ. J. (U.S.) 53: 221-223.

Lewis, D. A., and P. S. Nobel. 1977. Thermal energy exchange model and water loss of a barrel cactus, *Ferocactus acanthodes*. Plant Physiology 60: 609-616.

Lindsay, G. E. 1942. A new variety of *Ferocactus alamosanus*. Cact. Succ. J. (U.S.) 14: 139-143.

Lindsay, G. E. 1948. *Ferocactus diguetii* - The giant visnaga. Desert Pl. Life 20: 20-23.

Lindsay, G. E. 1952. The use of cactus as stock food. Desert Pl. Life 24: 4-6.

Lindsay, G. E. 1968. The rediscovery of *Ferocactus haematacanthus*. Cact. Succ. J. (U.S.) 40: 3-6.

Lloyd, F. E. 1908. Extrafloral nectars in the cacti. Plant World 11: 138-140.

Lyons, G. W. 1968. A note on *Ferocactus alamosanus*. Cact. Succ. J. (U.S.) 40: 1-2.

Mann, J. 1969. Cactus-feeding insects and mites. Smithsonian Institute Bull. No. 256. Washington, D.C.

MacDougal, D. T., and E. S. Spalding. 1910. *The Water-Balance of Succulent Plants*. Pub. 141, Carnegie Inst. Washington, Washington, DC.

Maddams, W. F. 1975. Ferocacti for flowers. Cact. Succ. J. (Great Britain) 37: 76-77.

Marshall, W. T. 1956. The barrel cactus as a source of water. Saguaroland Bull. 10: 64-71.

Mauseth, J. D., Y. Uozomi, B. J. Plemons, and J. V. Landrum. 1995. Structure and systematic study of unusual tracheid type in cacti. J. Plant Res. 108: 517-526.

Mays, H. 1979. Ferocacti from seed. Nat. Cact. Succ. J. 34: 20-21.

McCarten, N. F. 1973. Fossil cacti and other succulents from the late Pleistocene. Cact. Succ. J. (U.S.) 53: 122-123.

McIntosh, C. T. 1981. Flowering Ferocacti. Nat. Cact. Succ. J. 29: 126.

Meyrán-García, J. 1987. *Ferocactus macrodiscus* var. *septentrionalis*. Cact. Suc. Mex. 25: 33-37.

Moran, R. 1954. On Buxbaum's phylogeny of the "Euechinocactineae". Cact. Succ. J. (U. S.) 26: 45-48.

Moulis, B. 1982. A *Ferobergia* flower. Cact. Succ. J. (U.S.) 54: 217.

Mozingo, H. N., and P. L. Comanor. 1975. Implications of the thermal response of *Ferocactus acanthodes*. Cact. Succ. J. (U.S.) 47: 22-28 (supplemental volume-yearbook).

Nobel, P. S. 1980a. Morphology, surface temperatures, and northern limits of columnar cacti in the Sonoran Desert. Ecology 61: 1-7.

Nobel, P. S. 1980b. Influences of minimun stem temperatures on ranges of cacti of southwestern United States and Chile. Oecologia 47: 10-15.

Nobel, P. S. 1981. Influences of photosyntetically active radiation in cladode orientation, stem tilting, and height of cacti. Ecology 62: 982-990,

Nobel, P. S. 1986. Relation between monthly growth of *Ferocactus acanthodes* and environmental productivity index. Amer. J. Bot. 73: 541-547.

Nobel, P. S. 1988. *Environmental Biology of Agaves and Cacti*. Cambridge Univ. Press.

Nobel, P. S. 1989. Temperature, water availability, and nutrient levels at various soil depths - consequences for shallow-rooted desert succulents, including nurse plant effects. Amer. J. Bot. 76: 1486-1492. Oku, R. 1968. Various spines of *Ferocactus acanthodes*. Succ. Japon 66: 10-11.

Patten, D. T., and B. E. Dinger. 1969. Carbon dioxide exchange patterns of cacti from different environments. Ecology 50: 686-688.

Ready, K. F., and J. B. Bancroft. 1985. The assembly of barrel cactus virus protein. Virology 141: 302-305.

Riha, J., and R. Subik. 1980. *Ferocactus schwarzii*. Kaktusy 16: 29-30.

Riha, J., and R. Subik. 1982. *Ferocactus stainesii*. Kaktusy 18: 1-3.

Robberecht, R., and P. S. Nobel. 1983. A Fibonacci sequence in rib number for a barrel cactus. Annals of Botany 51: 153-155.

Roque-Puente, J. P. 1988. Envasado de cabuches encurtidos en vidrio y hojalata. Cact. Suc. Mex. 33: 48-52.

Rose, M. J., and W. Barthlott. 1994. Coloured Pollen in Cactaceae: A Mimetic Adaptation to Hummingbird-Pollination. Bot. Acta 107: 402-406.

Sánchez-Mejorada, H. 1965. Los *Ferocactus* de la Barranca de Meztitlan, Hgo. Cact. Suc. Mex. 10: 61-72, 101.

Sánchez-Mejorada, H. 1966. Breve contribución al conocimiento de *Ferocactus haematacanthus*. Cact. Suc. Mex. 11: 29-40.

Sánchez-Mejorada, H. 1980. Nota sobre las semillas de *Ferocactus lindsayi* y *F. reppenhagenii*. Cact. Suc. Mex. 25: 66-68.

Sánchez-Mejorada, H. 1982. *Some Prehispanic Uses of Cacti among the Indians of Mexico*. Secretaria de Desarrollo Agropecuario, Toluca, Mexico.

Schütz, B. 1974. *Ferocactus gracilis*. Kaktusy 10: 49-50.

Schütz, B. 1975. *Ferocactus viridescens*. Kaktusy 11: 73-74.

Schütz, B. 1979. *Ferocactus pilosus*. Kaktusy 15: 118-120.

Sedlar, J. 1984. *Ferocactus fordii*. Kaktusy 20: 59-60.

Smith, S. D., B. Didden-Zopfy, and P. S. Nobel. 1984. High-temperature responses on North American cacti. Ecology 65: 643-651.

Unger, G. 1971. *Ferocactus pottsii*. Kakt. and. Sukk. 22: 184-187.

Unger, G. 1974. *Ferocactus reppenhagenii*. Kakt. and. Sukk. 25: 50-54.

Unger, G. 1976. *Ferocactus wislizeni*. Kakt. and. Sukk. 27: 272-273.

Unger, G. 1977. *Ferocactus fordii*. Kakt. and. Sukk. 28: 171-172.

Unger, G. 1978a. *Ferocactus macrodiscus*. Kakt. and. Sukk. 29: 65-67.

Unger, G. 1978b. *Ferocactus glaucescens*. Kakt. and. Sukk. 29: 186-187.

Unger, G. 1980. Nochmals *Ferocactus haematacanthus*. Kakt. and. Sukk. 31: 148.

Unger, G. 1981. Bemerkungen zu *Ferocactus emoryi* und *Ferocactus acanthodes*. Kakt. and. Sukk. 32: 25-27.

Zimmer, K. 1980. Einfluss der Temperatur auf die Keimung von Kakteensaatgut X. Keimung einiger *Ferocactus*-Arten. Gartenbauwissenschaft 45: 121-125.

GLOSSARY

Allozymes (Alloenzymes). Different forms of the same enzyme formed by differrent alleles at the same locus. Often used to study the amount of genetic variation within and between populations at or below the species level.

Apomorphy. Cladistic term used to define a derived character state (opposite to plesiomorphy.

Chartaceous Scales. Paper-like scales (chartaceous = paper-like).

Character. Any attribute of an organism that can be consistently measured, counted, or otherwise defined.

Chemotaxonomy. The use of comparative biochemistry in systematic studies.

Chloroplast. Organelle containing the membranes, pigments and enzymes necessary for photosynthesis in an eukaryote organism.

Chromosomes. Structures located in the nucleus of a plant or animal cell that carry the gentic information encoded in the molecular structure of the DNA.

Cladistics. A type of analysis of phylogenetic relationships in which monophyletic taxa are grouped on the basis of shared derived characters.

Cladogram. A branching diagram of taxonomic entities in which the branching sequence is based on inferred historical connections between entities as evidenced by shreded, unquely derived features (synapomorphies).

Coding Regions (Exon). The part of the transcribed nuclear RNA of eukaryotes which forms the messanger RNA after the excision of the introns.

Convergence (Convergent Evolution). The development of similar structures in plants with distantly related ancestors.

Cryptic. Non-visible, occult.

Cytology. The study of cell, as used in taxonomy the study of chromosomes.

Diploid. A tissue or plant with two sets of chromosomes in each cell.

DNA. Deoxyribose Nucleic Acid. Double stranded genetic material of most organism and organelles.

Ektexine. Outer region of the exine (see exine).

Enzyme. Proteins which mediate chemical reactions in living organisms.

Eukaryote. A higher organism which possesses a nucleus bounded by a membranous nuclear envelope and has many cytoplasmic organelles. Its DNA is associated with histones to form chromosomes.

Exine. The outer part of the wall of pollen grain.

Exon (Coding Region). The part which is expressed in the protein product.

Gene. A particular sequence of nucleotides along a molecule of DNA.

Genome. The totality of the DNA sequences of an organism or organelle.

Haploid. A tissue or plant in which each cell has one set of chromosomes.

Heterozygosity. The proportion of individuals in a population that are heterozygous at a specified locus or at a number of loci.

Homoplasy. The result of parallel or convergent evolution in which two or more kinds of organisms independently acquire the same character state. Homoplasy sometimes also results from reversals when in a particular lineage a character reverts from an apomorphic to plesiomorphic state. In phylogenetic analysis homoplasy can cause character conflicts or misinterpretation of relationships.

Hybrid, Hybridization. The offspring of a cross between two different strains that are genetically more or less dissimilar from each other.

Ingroup. In cladistic analysis a monophyletic group under investigation for character polarity by comparizon with an outgroup.

Interspecific. An event such as between individuals from separate (different) species.

Introgression. ***Introgressive hybridization.*** Incorporation of genes of one species into the gene pool of anothe *via* an interspecific hybrid.

Intron (Non-coding Region). Genes in eukaryotes are organized in such a way that while the whole sequence is transcribed, only part of it forms the messanger RNA. Introns or intervening sequences are excised during the maturation of the RNA.

Isozyme (Isoenzymes). Different forms of the same enzyme formed at different loci on the chromosome of a plant.

Least Derived. The putatively most "primitive" taxon within a group.

Locus. The position on a chromosome occupied by a specified gene and its alleles. pl. *loci.*

Metacentriic. Chromosomes in which both arms are of equal or approximately the same length.

Meiosis. The process in which chromosomes are duplicated, exchange segments through crossing-over and divide in two successive nuclear divisions with each of the resulting cells having half as many chromosomes as the one cell had before division began.

Mitosis. The process in which the chromosomes of a nucleus are duplicated and then divided equally between two daughter cells.

Monophyletic. A natural taxonomic group composed of and ancestral species and all of its descendants.

Mutation. Any detectable and heritable change in the genetic material. Any change in a gene sequence, chromosomal structure, or number.

Nectary. Gladular structure that secretes nectar (fluid containing sugars and amino acids).

Nucleotide. The individual components of a nucleic acid. A nucleoside to which a phosphate group is attached at the 5' position on the sugar.

Outgroup. A monophyletic taxon that is used in phylogenetic analysis to determine which of two or more states of a character in the group being investigated (ingroup) is apomorphic.

Paraphyletic. A taxonomic group that includes an ancestral species and some, but not all, of its descendants. In claditic analysis such a group is rejected in favor of a monophyletic group.

Phenology. The study of plant development in relation to seasons.

Phyllad. A lineage, an evolutionary line.

Phylogeny. The evolutionary history of a group of organisms.

Plesiomorphic. Cladistic terms which refers to the primitive state of character.

Pollen. The structures produced in the anthers or microsporangia that result from the maturation of a microspore.

Polyphyletic. A non-natural taxonomic group hypothesized to have a multiple origin (from two or more different evolutionary lines).

Polyploid. Having more than twice the normal haploid number of chromosomes.

Protandry (Protandrous). A condition in which the anthers mature and shed pollen before the stigma becomes receptive.

Puntibaculate. Pollen grain with finely pitted exine.

Sclerified. Similar to chartaceous.

Seed. A ripened ovule containing an embryo within a seed-coat, often with additional storage tissues (e.g., endosperm).

Seed Coat. Testa, the covering of the seed.

Sensu Lato (s.l.). In the broad sense; as broadly defined.

Sensu Stricto (s.s.). In the restricted sense; as narrowly defined.

Speciation. The formation of a new biological species including formation of polyploids by various evolutionary processes.

Specific Epithet. The second part of a species name; a Latin word, usually either an adjective or a possesive noun.

Sympatric. Together in the same geographic area; term used to describe populations, races, species, etc. living in the same place.

Symplesiomorphy (symplesiomorphic character). A plesiomorphic character shared by two or more taxa.

Synapomorphy (synapomorphic character). An apomorphic (derived) character state shared by two or more taxa. In cladistic studies it is evidence of relationship.

Systematics. The study of relationships among organisms and the classificaction and naming of those organisms.

Taxonomy. The description, identification, naming and classifying of objects or organisms.

Tetraploid. A plant or tissue whose cells have four sets of chromosomes.

Topology. The shape of a cladogram with the relative position of the branches.

Translocation. An exchange between non-homologous chromosomes whereby a part of one becomes attached to the other, or a re-arrangement within a chromosome.

Ferocactus Distributions

Editors' *Note:* *The following alphabetically lists all of the known species and varieties of* Ferocactus *in an arrangement that we consider reasonable. We have used the most currently accepted names, which occasionally are not those used in the text. They are those used in the key, and synonyms are given in both text and Key. The numbering follows that used in the Key. Some listed plants may someday be transferred from* Ferocactus *to some other genus. For example, we have placed* F. setispinus *on this list for completeness. It is considered by Lindsay and other authorities to belong in Genus* Echinocactus. *Benson, however, retains it in* Ferocactus. *Another problem species is* F. hamatacanthus, *also from the Rio Grande area. Benson considers it to be a* Ferocactus, *as does Taylor. Benson splits it into two varieties, var.* hamatacanthus *and var.* sinuatus; *Taylor recognizes only the species. To blend both viewpoints, it could be an evolving species where interbreeding is possible except for separation by flowering cycles or geography. We have included mention of* F. setispinus *within* F. hamatacanthus.

# Species	Variety	Area	Location
23 *acanthodes*	*acanthodes*	US BC	SB and Rvrsd Ctys, CA; AZ; Sonora MX; NE. BC;
	lecontei	US	S. CA; AZ; NV(Clark Co);Utah
	tortulispinus		BC Laguna Chapala Seca
	eastwoodiae	US MX?	E.CA, S.AZ (high cliffs), Pima, Pinal, and Gila Cty
20 *chrysacanthus*		IL	Isla Cedros and Isla W. San Benito
14 *covillei (emoryi)*		US MX	S. AZ, Sonora
25 *diguetii*	*diguetii*	IL	Isla Santa Catalina; Cerralbo
	carmenensis	IL	Isla Carmen
4 *echidne*	*echidne*	MX	S L Potosi and Hidalgo, E. Sierra Madre
	victoriensis	MX	Cuidad Victoria, Tamalupas
1 *flavovirens*		MX	Tehuacan to Oaxaca
21 *fordii*	*fordii*	BC IL	Isla San Martin and El Socorro Garden
	grandiflorus		Punta Eugenio to Punta Abreojos, Isla Natividad
19 *gatesii*		IL	Smith Isla group, N of Bahia de los Angeles
3 *glaucescens*		MX	Hidalgo
18 *gracilis*	*gracilis*	BC	El Rosario, Central BC
	coloratus		Punta Prieta to Millers Landing
28 *haematacanthus*		MX	Puebla-Veracruz border
29 *hamatacanthus*	*hamatacanthus*	US MX	El Paso,Cameron Cty TX to SL Potosi MX
	sinuatus	US	Big Bend TX
13 *herrerae*		MX	Sonora, Sinaloa, Durango
6 *histrix*		MX	Durango to Jalisco and Puebla

24 *johnstonianus*		IL	Isla Angel de la Gardia
10 *latispinus*		MX	Central MX
27 *lindsayi*		MX	Michoacan (Rio Balsas)
8 *macrodiscus*		MX	Cumbre (10,000'), El Renosco
16 *peninsulae*	*peninsulae*	BC	B de LA, Sierra S Borja to Cape
	viscainensis	BC	Near Mesquital
11 *pilosus*		MX	northern to central Mexico.
7 *pottsii*	*pottsii*	MX	Alamos, Sonora (high in canyons)
	alamosanus	MX	Mtns E of Alamos, S Chihuahua
15 *rectispinus*		BC	San Ignacio to Commondu.
26 *reppenhagenii*		MX	Michoacan
9 *recurvus*	*recurvus*	MX	Puebla and Oaxaca
	greenwoodii	MX	Nejapa Valley, Oaxaca.
2 *robustus*		MX	Tehuacan to Zapotitlan, Puebla
5 *schwarzii*	*schwarzii*	MX	N Sinaloa (steep cliffs and mountains)
30 *setispinus*		US	*Echinocactus*? Colorado River area, TX
17 *townsendianus*	*townsendianus*	BC IL	Isla Magdalena, S Jose, and Mararita; Loreto to Cape
	santa-maria	IL	Isla Santa Maria
22 *viridescens*	*viridecens*	US BC	W. SD Cty, Sierra Juarez BC foothills
	littoralis	BC	Coast zone, N of Ensenada to Mn. Sta. Dmgo,
12 *wizlizenii*	*wizlizenii*	US MX	S. AZ, NM, TX and Sonora MX (summer rain areas)
	tiburonensis	IL	Isla Tiburon

Ferocactus Synonyms

Compiled by Madelyn Lee

Editors' Note: *Genus* Ferocactus *names have been fairly stable over the past 40 years, with some species becoming varieties and some names being identified as redundant and eliminated. This list covers currently and previously accepted names. There is an occasional iconoclast who prefers an older name (*cylindraceus *instead of* acanthodes*), and there are occasional differences between authorities such as Backeberg (BB), Benson, Bravo, and Lindsay. Rediscoveries may bring back old names. New work may eliminate or create names. If, in this compilation, there is no comment beneath a species name, then it is the one selected as current.*

acanthodes variety *acanthodes*
acanthodes variety *eastwoodiae*
acanthodes variety *lecontei*
acanthodes variety *tortulospinus*
alamosanus variety *alamosanus* is *pottsii* variety *alamosanus* Benson
alamosanus variety *platygonus* is *pottsii* variety *pottsii* Benson
arizonicus is *wislizenii*
californicus (unknown)
chrysacanthus
coloratus is *gracilis* variety *coloratus*
cornigerous is *latispinus*
covillei is *emoryi* BB (see *emoryi*)
crassihamatus is *Thelocactus crassihamatus*
cylindraceus is *acanthodes*
diguetii variety *diguetii*
diguetii variety *carmenensis*
echidne variety *echidne*
echidne variety *victoriensis*
electracanthus is *histrix*
emoryi is *wislizenii* (near Coolidge Dam) is *covillei* (near Gila River)
emoryi variety *rectispinus* is *rectispinus*
falconeri is *wislizenii*
flavovirens
fordii variety *fordii*
fordii variety *grandiflorus*
gatesii
glaucescens
gracilis variety *gracilis*
gracilis variety *coloratus* was *gracilis* Lindsay
haematacanthus is *stainesii* variety *haematacanthus* per BB

hamatacanthus variety *hamatacanthus*
hamatacanthus variety *sinuatus*
herrerae
hertrichii questionable species per BB
histrix
horridus possibly a hybrid
johnsonii is *Echinomastus johnsonii*
johnstonianus
latispinus
latispinus variety *flavispinus* is *latispinus*
lecontei is *acanthodes* variety *lecontei*
lindsayi
macrodiscus
macrodiscus variety *multiflorus* is *macrodiscus*
melocactiformis is *histrix*
nobilis is *recurvus*
orcuttii is *viridescens* Lindsay
peninsulae variety *peninsulae*
peninsulae variety *viscainensis*
pfeifferi is probably *glaucescens*?
pilosus
pilosus Lindsay and Benson
phoenicus is *wislizenii*
pottsii variety *pottsii*
pottsii variety *alamosanus*
pringlei is *pilosus* Lindsay
rafaelensis is *echidne* variety *victoriensis*
rectispinus
recurvus variety *recurvus*
recurvus variety *greenwoodii*
reppenhagenii
robustus
rostii is *acanthodes*
santa-maria is *townsendianus* variety *santa-maria*
schwartzii
setispinus
stainesii variety *stainesii* BB is *pilosus* per Lindsay
stainesii variety *pringlei* is *pilosus*
stainesii variety *pilosus* is *pilosus*
tiburonensis is *wislizenii* variety *tiburonensis*
tortulispinus is *acanthodes* variety *tortulospinus*
townsendianus variety *townsendianus*
townsendianus variety *santa-maria*
uncinatus is *Thelocactus uncinatus*

victoriensis is *echidn*e variety *victoriens i*s Lindsay
viridescens variety *viridescens*
viridescens variety *littoralis*
viscainensis is *peninsula*e variety *viscainensis*
wislizenii variety *wislizenii*
wislizenii variety *albispinus* is *wislizenii*
wislizenii variety *tiburonensis*

1. FEROCACTUS FLAVOVIRENS (Scheidweiler) Britton and Rose, Cactaceae 3: 138. 1922.

Echinocactus flavovirens Scheidweiler, Allg. Gartenz. 9: 50. 1841.

PLANT cespitose, forming large mounds sometimes over 2 meters in diameter and nearly 1 meter tall; individual stems to 3 or 4 dm tall and 2 dm wide, light green, globular to elliptical. RIBS 13, acute, 3.5 cm deep, vertical, not tuberculate. AREOLES oval, 1.5 cm long and 8 mm wide, bearing slight gray tomentum which ultimately disappears, distantly spaced on ribs, from 2 to 4 cm apart. SPINES tan or gray, acicular, terete; central spines 4 to 6, radiating, the lower central directed downward, longer than the others, to 8 cm long; radial spines 12 to 20, radiating, the lower ones like the centrals but the upper ones sometimes lighter colored, bristle-like and occasionally twisted. FLOWERS yellow, produced on the youngest areole on the rib and thus in the center of the stem; scales of the ovary linear-lanceolate, 15 mm long and 3 mm wide, very ciliate with an attenuate-aristate tip, the cilia on lower portion dichotomously branched, those near apex simple, the tips of cilia and of scale hyaline, sharp; scales intergrading into the outer perianth segments, these 18 mm long, margin entire at base with upper portion like the scales; inner perianth segments linear-lanceolate, 20 mm long and 2 to 3 mm wide, margin at base entire but the acute tip serrate to ragged; filaments 4 to 10 mm long, very fine, anthers minute; style 15 mm long and 1.2 mm thick, yellow, striated longitudinally and divided into 13 unequal stigma lobes 1 to 4 mm long. FRUIT elliptical, 28 mm long and 18 mm wide, completely covered with long brown ciliate aristate scales, these arranged linearly giving the appearance of rows; wall of ovary fleshy, red, 2 mm thick, the locule filled with soft, red, acid pulp containing scattered black seeds; perianth persisting, also covered with scales, the withered perianth about 2 cm long. SEED small, black, 1 mm long, with fine polygonal sculpturing.

Neotype: Hills 9 km from Tehuacan, Puebla, Mexico, on road to Zapotitlan de Salinas, *Lindsay 2596* (DS). The original description was of plants from "Mexico, Tehuacan, 6,000 ft. elevation."

Distribution: Vicinity of Tehuacan and Zapotitlan de Salinas, Puebla. Mr. Schwarz states this species extends from the Tehuacan region toward the Mistecas Altas of Oaxaca. Map number one. Representative specimens: MEXICO: PUEBLA: 5.6 miles from Tehuacan on road to Zapotitlan de Salinas, 6,000 ft. elevation, *Lindsay 2596* (DS,SD); Zapotitlan de Salinas, *Lindsay 2059* (DS,SD). Living material of *Lindsay 2596* is at the Desert Botanical Garden of Arizona.

Scheidweiler described *Echinocactus flavovirens* in 1841, from living plants which had been sent from Tehuacan, Mexico, some years before. The collection, probably by Karwinsky, had been thought to represent *E. robustus*. Dr. Rose reintroduced *Echinocactus flavovirens* into cultivation in 1906, and in 1922 included it in *Ferocactus*. Two other names have been associated with this species, *Echinocactus polyocentrus* Lemaire (Salm-Dyck, Cact. Hort. Dyck. 1844. 22. 1845), which appeared in a list but was never published with description, and *E. orthacanthus* Link and Otto, the type of which came from Montevideo and the description of which is not of *Ferocactus flavovirens*.

Bravo (1937, p. 429) states the flowers are yellow. Britton and Rose did not know the flowers and fruit. I have not seen fresh flowers material, and have drawn the description from treated withered perianths on the fruit. The uniquely scaled, fleshy fruit, which is filled with red pulp resembling that of a *Lemaireocereus*, the scale-like spine-tipped perianth segments of the flower, and the very small seeds are unlike those of any of the other Ferocacti; in fact they do not fit well in any known genus. It is possible that a new genus should be established for this species, but I hesitate to do this without a better understanding of the flower.

Ferocactus flavovirens grows in the same area as *F. robustus*, and has the same associate species, but usually is found on higher limestone hillsides. *Ferocactus robustus* is much more common in the valley flats near Tehuacan, but in the mountains at Zapotitlan *F. flavovirens* is the most abundant, and *F. robustus* is scattered.

Figure 12. ***Ferocactus flavovirens*** **at Zapotitlan de Salinas, Puebla.**

Figure 13. Fruit of *Ferocactus flavovirens*. Note the acute, ciliate scales and fleshy character of the fruit.

2. FEROCACTUS ROBUSTUS (Otto) Britton and Rose, Cacteae 3: 135. 1922.

Echinocactus robustus Otto, in Otto and Dietrich, Allg. Gartenz. 1:364. 1833.

Echinocactus robustus var. *prolifer* Pfeiffer, Enum. Cact. 61. 1837.

Echinocactus robustus var. *monstrosus* Pfeiffer, loc. cit.

Echinofossulocactus robustus Lawrence, in London, Gard. Mag. 17: 318. 1841.

STEMS very cespitose, forming huge clusters of hundreds of branches, the clumps to 5 meters in diameter and over 1 meter tall; individual stems globuse to clavate, 8 to 16 cm wide, deep green. RIBS 8, prominent, acute, thickened under areoles, tuberculate. AREOLES widely separated on the ribs, round, 8 mm wide, with a superior floriferous portion, this becoming inconspicuous in age. SPINES purple, reddish, or horn-colored; central spines 4 or sometimes 6, erect, radiating, straight, annulate, square or angled in cross section, sometimes flattened laterally, the lower one longer, to 6 cm long; radial spines 10 to 14, radiating, the lower ones much like the centrals and the upper ones acicular or bristle-like and lighter in color. FLOWERS 3 to 4 cm long and about as wide, yellowish; ovary covered with broad, rounded imbricated scales, these intergrading into the outer perianth segments; outer perianth segments yellow with red midstripe, mucronate; inner perianth segments yellow, oblong, acute; stigma lobes 10, red. FRUIT yellow, fleshy, 2 to 3 cm long and 2 cm wide, with broad, widely separated, fleshy scales. SEED black, 1.5 mm long and 1 mm wide, finely sculptured with polygonal ridges.

Neotype: Zapotitlan de Salinas, near Tehuacan, Puebla, Mexico, *Lindsay 2058*, Sept. 4, 1951, (DS).

Distribution: Arid area in the vicinity of Tehuacan, Puebla. I have observed this species from Tepeaca to Zapotitlan de Salinas, Puebla. Map number one.

Representative specimens: MEXICO: PUEBLA: Zapotitlan de Salinas, *Lindsay 2058* (DS). Living specimens are to be found at Huntington Botanical Garden, Desert Botanical Garden, and the University of California Botanical Garden at Berkeley.

Karwinsky apparently discovered this species in the vicinity of Tehuacan in 1828. He sent fruit and probably plants to Cells in France that year. The name first appeared without description in a list of cactus plants authored by Friedrich Otto in the *Allgemeine Gartenzeitung* in 1833, and this reference has generally been cited as the valid publication. Britton and

Rose (1922 3: 135) cite Link and Otto as the authors, but the article was written by Otto, although both Link and Otto were editors of the periodical in which it appeared.

In 1837 Ludwig Pfeiffer treated *Echinocactus robustus*, crediting the species to "H. Berol.", and describing two varieties, *prolifer* and *monstrosus*. The first seems to fit the typical species, while var. *monstrosus* was an irregularly ribbed form which appeared among seedlings. This treatment appeared in *Enumeratio diagnostica Cactearum*, by Ludwig Pfeiffer, and also in *Beschreibung und Synonymik der Cacteen*, by Louis Pfeiffer, the same year. One of these works is apparently a translation of the other, and the treatment of *E. robustus* is the same in both. I do not know which was published first.

Labouret and Schumann listed *Echinocactus galeottii* as a possible synonym of *E. robustus*, but both questioned it. *Echinocactus galeottii* is obviously one of the large Echinocacti, probably *E. grusonii*.

The remarkable polycephalic habit of *Ferocactus robustus* is quite unlike that of any other species in the genus. The compact clumps grow to enormous size, sometimes fifteen feet across. These clusters are probably not from the same original root system, but are a complex which has developed from seedling plants which have grown up around the parent. The blossoming period is long. I have collected flowers and mature fruit in March, when they were scarce, and in September, when both were more abundant. The stems are firmly attached to the clusters and clonal reproduction is not important as it is in some clumping cacti with easily detached joints.

Ferocactus flavovirens, another cespitose species, grows in the same area and has been confused with *F. robustus*. The plants are quite unlike and belong to different subgenera. *Ferocactus flavovirens* has larger and fewer stems and very different fruit. In the flats near Tehuacan, *F.* robustus is the more common species, but at Zapotitlan de Salinas *F. flavovirens* is the most abundant.

Ferocactus robustus grows in calcareus soil, with *Lemaireocereus stellatus*, *L. hollianus*, *L. weberi*, *Pachycereus marginatus*, *Cephalocereus tetetzo*, *C. macrocephalus*, *C. hoppendstedtii*, *Ferocactus recurvus*, *F. flavovirens*, *Echinocactus grandis*, etc.

Figure 14. *Ferocactus robustus*, near Tehuacan, Puebla, Mexico.

Figure 15. *Ferocactus robustus*, flowers and fruit.

3. FEROCACTUS GLAUCESCENS (De Candolle) Britton and Rose, Cactaceae 3: 137. 1922.

Echinocactus glaucescens de Candolle, Mem. Mus. Hist. Nat. Paris 17: 115. 1828.

Echinocactus pfeifferi Zuccarini, in Pfeiffer, Enum. Cact. 58. 1837

Echinocactus theionacanthusul Lemaire, Cact. Aliq. Nov. 22. 1838.

Echinofossulocactus pfeifferi Lawrence, in London, Gard. Mag. 17: 18. 1841.

Bisnaga glaucescens (De Candolle) Orcutt, Cactography 1: 1. 1926.

STEM simple or cespitose from base, globular, to 30 cm tall and broad, top flat or slightly depressed, distinctly glaucous. RIBS 12-17, acute, about 2.5 cm high and 3.5 cm wide, vertical, not tuberculate. AREOLES elongate, 1.5 to 2 cm long, 5 mm wide, the top and botton attenuate, constricted between spiniferous and floriferous sections, bearing tan tomentum which extends both above and below body of areole to nearly or completely connect with those adjacent. SPINES yellow, erect spreading, nearly equal, subulate, barely annulate, to 3.5 cm long and 1.5 mm wide near base, usually 1 central and 6-7 radials, but in some cases a total of 4, in all cases little differentiation between central and radial series. FLOWERS yellow, campanulate, 4.5 cm long and 3.5 cm wide; scales on ovary yellowish, about 2 mm long, intergrading with outer perianth segments which are 2 cm long, brownish with yellow, ciliate margins; inner perianth segments about 21, lanceolate, 3.5 cm long and 5 mm wide, clear yellow with serrulate margins and acute to apiculate tip; filaments yellow, 1 cm long, anthers yellow, minute; style 2 cm long, narrow, divided into 8 stigma lobes which tend to recurve. FRUIT globular, fleshy, 1.5 to 2 cm long and nearly as broad, with the withered perianth totaling about 3 cm long, whitish or yellowish with red blush, covered with yellowish, ciliate scales, the locule filled with sweet white pulp composed of funicular tissue which surrounds the seeds. SEED small, shiny, mahogany to almost black, 1.5 mm long, 1 mm wide, and 0.6 mm thick, testa with only traces of sculpturing, hilum very small, round, deep, white.

Neotype: Limestone boulders and outcrops, 5,000 ft. elevation, 5 mi. south of Jacala, Hidalgo, Mexico, *Lindsay 2611* (DS). The type specimen was sent to de Candolle by Thomas Coulter, from "Mexico."

Distribution: Hidalgo, Mexico. Known from Toliman, Zimapan, Meztitlan, and Jacala, Hidalgo. Probably to be expected in similar habitats in adjacent states. Map number one.

Representative specimens: MEXICO: HIDALGO; 5 mi. S. Jacala, *Lindsay 2611* (DS,SD), *Schwarz* s.n. (DS); Canon de Venado, 20 km E. Meztitlan, *Lindsay 2063* (DS).

Echinocactus glaucescens was described by A.P. de Candolle in 1828, from a small plant which he had received from Thomas Coulter the year before. In 1837 Zuccarini described *Echinocactus pfeifferi*, which he recognized was close to *E. glaucescens*, based on material collected by Karwinsky at Toliman. This species is referable to *F. glaucescens*. In 1838 Lemaire published *E. theionacanthus*, a glaucous blue-green plant with sulphur-colored spines, which would seem to belong here, although the older spines were reddish towards the base. The next year, however, Lemaire published *E. theiacanthus*, based on *E. mammillifer* Miquel. The similarity of the two names may indicate they were based on the same material, and *E. mammillifer* was apparently described from a seedling plant, which Britton and Rose (1922, p. 122) think might belong to the present genus *Echinofossulocactus*. In that case *E. theionacanthus* Lemaire, *E. theiacanthus* Lemaire, *E. mammillifer* Miquel, and *E. mammillarioides* Hooker should all be excluded from this species. Schumann (1898, p. 329) states that *E. dietrichianus* Forster appears to belong here.

Ferocactus glaucescens is a trim species, desirable for horticultural purposes because it grows well in cultivation, and is attractive with its golden spines and tailored appearance. The waxy, glaucous blue-green color is unique.

The distribution of this species is rather restricted, and apparently it occurs only in the state of Hidalgo. I photographed specimens near Jacala, Hidalgo, on April 5, 1955. There the plants, about one foot tall and the same diameter, had two four inch branches from its base. That plant had 17 ribs, each of which bore 3 or 4 round, white fruit at its upper areoles. I counted a total of 43 fruit on the one plant, and four unopened buds. The small side branches also bore fruit. The Jacala plants were growing on limestone outcrops and boulders, in very small pockets of leaf mold which had accumulated in shallow depressions in the rock. The roots solidly filled the pockets. The Ferocacti were usually most common on north-facing mountain slopes in a juniper-oak forest, at an elevation of about 5,000 feet.

On September 4, 1951, Dr. Helia Bravo and I collected herbarium material from a clustered *Ferocactus* at Canon de Venado, near Meztitlan, Hidalgo (*Lindsay 2063*). The plant was a cluster of about nine globular heads, which appeared naked because each areole bore only 3 or 4 spines. Dr. Bravo revisited the area in April, 1955, and collected fruit of our "Ferocactus dudoso" which she sent to me. Both fruit and seed are identical with those of *F. glaucescens* from Jacala, and the plant is that species.

Figure 16. ***Ferocactus glaucescens*** **photographed 5 miles south of Jacala, Hidalgo, Mexico, at an elevation of 5,000 feet. The specimen was about one foot high, and was growing in a very shallow pocket of soil on top of a limestone boulder.**

Figure 17. ***Ferocactus glaucescens*** **in flower at Stanford University on April 17, 1955.**

Figure 18. *Ferocactus glaucescens*. Above, cespitose plant (*Lindsay 2063*) at Canon de Venado, near Meztitlan, Hidalgo. Below, fruiting specimen (*Lindsay 2611*) from near Jacala, Hidalgo.

4. FEROCACTUS ECHIDNE (De Candolle) Britton and Rose, Cactaceae 3: 136. 1922.

Key to the varieties

a. Central spine usually less than 4.5 cm long, plant stem usually flattened-globose, scales on fruit with rounded tip, margin not strongly ciliate . . . . *F. e.* var. *echidne*

b. Central spine usually longer than 4.5 cm, plant stem usually globose to globose-cylindric, scales on fruit ciliate with acute tip . . . .*F. e.* var. *victoriensis*

4a. FEROCACTUS ECHIDNE (De Candolle) Britton and Rose var. ECHIDNE

Echinocactus echidne A. P. de Candolle, Mem. Cact. 19. 1834.

Echinocactus vanderaeyi Lemaire, Cact. Aliq. Nov. 20. 1838.

Echinocactus dolichacanthus Lemaire, op. cit. 25.

Echinofossulocactus vanderaeyi Lawrence, in London, Gard. Mag. 17: 318. 1841.

Echinofossulocactus vanderaeyi var. *ignota longispina* Lawrence, in London, loc. cit.

Echinofossulocactus echidne Lawrence, in London, loc. cit.

Echinocactus gilvus Dietrich, Allg. Gartenz. 13: 170. 1845.

Echinocactus echidne gilvus Salm-Dyck, Cact. Hort. Dyck. 1849, 27. 1850.

Ferocactus echidne (De Candolle) Britton and Rose, Cactaceae 3: 136. 1922.

Bisnaga echidne (De Candolle) Orcutt, Cactography 1: 1. 1926.

STEM simple or cespitose, flattened-globose or sometimes globular, to 30 cm tall and broad, rich green in color. RIBS about 13, vertical, rather acute but not distinctly tuberculate, about 2.5 cm high. AREOLES oval with a superior, floriferous, truncated extension, tomentose in youth. SPINES amber, acicular, smooth, thin; central spine 1 to 5 cm long, porrect; radial spines about 7, shorter than the central, radiating, sometimes with traces of annulations; small gland-spines in flowering areoles persistent. FLOWERS from center of plant, clear yellow, 4.5 cm long and 3 cm wide, funnelform; small yellow imbricated ciliate scales of ovary and tube intergrading with outer perianth segments; outer perianth segments yellow, spatulate, entire, to 2 cm long and 5 mm wide, tip obtuse; inner perianth segments yellow, lanceolate or oblanceolate, entire or serrulate, 3 cm long and 4 mm wide; filaments pale yellow, very fine, to 1 cm long, anthers minute; style to 25 mm long, the upper 1 cm divided into 10-14 stigma lobes. FRUIT globular, fleshy, 2 cm long and 1.25 cm wide, to 4 cm long including withered perianth; ovary covered with yellowish obtuse scales, 4 mm long and 3 mm wide, the fruit apparently not opening by basal pore. SEED smooth, dark red, plump, rounded and not angled, to 1.5 mm long and about 1 mm wide, 0.8 mm thick, the testa without pits or sculpturing.

Neotype: Venados, Hidalgo, Mexico, *Bravo 34/22* (DS).

The holotype specimen was collected in "Mexico" by Thomas Coulter. Dr. Baehni, Director of the Botanical Gardens and Herbarium at Geneva, wrote that they were unable to find any material regarding *Echinocactus echidne* in the De Candolle collections.

Distribution: Hidalgo, San Luis Potosi, Guanajuato and Queretaro, Mexico. Mr. Fritz Schwarz says this species ranges through the Eastern Sierra Madre from Tamaulipas to Guanajuato. Map number one.

Representative specimens: MEXICO: TAMAULIPAS: Ing. *Hernandez s. n.* (MEXU); Hidalgo: Puente Tasquilla on Laredo Highway, *Dawson 3052* (AHFH); Barranca de Mezquitlan, *Lindsay 2069* (DS). Living material is growing at the Huntington Botanical Garden, the Desert Botanical Garden, and the Instituto de Biologia in Mexico. The neotype specimen consists of photographs and dried flowers, fruit and seed from a living plant at the Instituto de Biologia. I photographed the plant *Bravo 34/22* in flower there April 4, 1955. Dr. Bravo later sent me the mature fruit, and the flower, fruit, and seed descriptions are based on that material.

A. P. de Candolle described *Echinocactus echidne* in 1834 from plants obtained from Thomas Coulter. The original description is complete except for fruit and seed, and is accompanied by an excellent illustration. This is fortunate, because the species is variable and has often been confused with other similar taxa. De Candolle had first considered *E. echidne* to be a variety of his *E. histrix*, but after the plants flowered in Geneva he decided it was a distinct species.

Lemaire published *E. vanderaeyi* in 1838, from a sterile specimen in Monville's collection. The description indicates that it is the same as *E. echidne*. Lemaire also described *E. dolichacanthus* in the same paper. Labouret, Schumann, and Britton and Rose included both *E. vanderaeyi* and *E. dolichacanthus* as synonyms of *E. echidne*, and I have followed them in this treatment. It seems doubtful, however, that *E. dolichacanthus* belongs there. The original description of that species indicates a globular plant with sinuous, tuberculate ribs, very strong spines, and other characters atypical of *E. echidne*. Also, Lemaire apparently had the specimens on which he based his new species before him, and did not indicate that they were closely related — rather he thought that *E. dolichacanthus* was "related to yet sufficiently distinct" from *E. histrix.*

Lawrence, in 1838, published a catalogue of the cacti in the collection of the Rev. Theodore Williams, in which he established the genus *Echinofossulocactus.* Lawrence included no descriptions other than gross size, but listed *vanderaeyi, vanderaeyi* var. *ignota longispina*, and *echidne* under *Echinofossulocactus.* He did indicate the specimen of *E. vanderaeyi* was "1-1/4 ft. high, and 1 ft. 10 in. in diameter", which is larger than *Ferocactus echidne* is thought to grow.

Echinocactus gilvus was described by Albert Dietrich in 1845, when he pointed out it was very close to *E. echidne* and would be considered a form of that species except that it had amber colored flowers. The outer perianth segments were described as brown with purple midstripe and the inner ones cream with a small purple midstripe. Also, the stem of *E. gilvus* was a blue-green. Salm-Dyck reduced *E. gilvus* to a variety of *E. echidne*, while Schumann and Britton and Rose consider it to be only a synonym. I have no modern information about *E. gilvus*, and have followed Schumann in placing it in the synonomy of *E. echidne*. Mr. Fritz Schwarz has told me there is a red-flowered form of *Ferocactus echidne* in the mountains near Ciudad Maise, San Luis Potosi. This form has not appeared in the literature.

A living specimen of *Ferocactus echidne, Bravo 34/22*, in Dr. Bravo's study collection at the Instituto de Biologia in Mexico City, agrees with the original description and illustration of this species in all details, and I have selected it for the neotype. The plant is from Venados, Hidalgo. I collected a small *Ferocactus, Lindsay 2069*, in the same region in 1951, and it flowered at Stanford on May 1, 1955. The flowers are typical of *F. echidne*, but the plant body is more globular, the ribs are sinuate-tuberculate, the spines are heavier, and the areoles bear more radials. Bravo illustrates a very similar plant in Las Cactaceas de Mexico (p. 431) as *F. echidne*, and the plant should probably be considered as a wide variant of that species.

Ferocactus echidne grows well under cultivation and flowers freely, but is rather rare in collections. Plants which have been growing outside at the Huntington Botanical Garden for over thirty years have formed large clumps of many stems, but the spines are much reduced, possibly because of environmental conditions.

4b. FEROCACTUS ECHIDNE (De Candolle) Britton and Rose var. VICTORIENSIS (Rose) Lindsay, Cact. and Succ. Journ. 27: 168. 1955

Echinocactus victoriensis Rose, Contr. U. S. Nat. Herb. 12: 291.1909.

STEM simple to quite cespitose, globular to globose-cylindric, bright green, apex slightly depressed and bearing brown tomentum. RIBS 11-14, acute, slightly undulating and tuberculate, 2-3 cm deep. AREOLES elliptical, not truncated above, bearing gray-white tomentum, spaced 3 or 4 cm apart on the ribs. SPINES acicular, yellowish to brown or gray, brittle; central spine 1, 5-8 cm long, erect; radial spines about 7, to 6 cm long, spreading. FLOWERS apparently yellow (described from treated withered specimens), about 4 cm long and 3 cm wide, funnelform; scales on ovary small, 2 mm long and 3 mm wide, ciliate, tip acute; outer perianth segments obovate, to 2 cm long and 8 mm wide; inner perianth segments lanceolate, to 3 cm long and 4-5 mm wide, entire with acute tip; filaments 5-15 mm long; style 2 cm long, 2.5 mm wide, the terminal 10 mm divided into 14 linear stigma lobes. FRUIT globular, white with pink blush to red, 2 cm long and broad, with withered perianth included about 3.5 cm. long; scales of ovary widely separated, light yellow or purplish, acute, broader than long; locule filled with white pulp composed of thickened, gelatinous funiculi. SEEDS shiny black or very deep red, 1.75 mm long, 1.35 mm wide, 0.75 mm thick, testa smooth.

Holotype: Vicinity of Victoria, Tamaulipas, Mexico, altitude about 320 meters, *Edward Palmer 267* (US), the type of *Echinocactus victoriensis* Rose.

Distribution: Mountains between Ciudad Victoria and Jaumauve, Tamaulipas, Mexico. Map number one.

Representative specimens: MEXICO: TAMAULIPAS: Vicinity of Victoria, *Palmer 276* (US, type); 11 km. southwest Ciudad Victoria, on road to Jaumauve, *Lindsay 2612* (DS,SD).

Dr. Edward Palmer collected this *Ferocactus* near Ciudad Victoria, on the east side of Mexico, in 1907. Living material was sent to Dr. Rose in Washington, and he described the species, as *Echinocactus victoriensis*, in 1909. When Britton and Rose established the genus *Ferocactus* in 1922 they thought *E. victoriensis* was the same as *Ferocactus echidne*, and for that reason did not combine it in the new genus.

Dr. Helia Bravo studied the cacti of southeastern Tamaulipas in 1952 and reported (Bravo 1953, p. 538) a species of *Ferocactus* in Cuchilla Verde Canyon, near Ciudad Victoria, which appeared to partially fit the incomplete description of *Echinocactus rafaelensis* Purpus. Dr. Ira L. Wiggins and I collected the same species on April 6, 1955, and I also assigned it to *Ferocactus rafaelensis*. However, a comparison of our material with the type specimen of *Ferocactus victoriensis* has convinced me they are in the same taxon.

The original description of *Echinocactus victoriensis* states "Plants never cespitose .... spines all bright yellow" (Rose 1909, p. 291), which does not agree with the plants which we collected, but possibly can be attributed to the small sample available to Rose in Washington. Our specimens and the type specimen of *E. victoriensis* do match. However, our specimens did have a different appearance than *Ferocactus echidne*, to which *Echinocactus victoriensis* had been assigned. I have carefully compared the material of *E. victoriensis* with what I feel is typical material of *Ferocactus echidne* and am convinced that they belong to the same complex, but that there are sufficient differences for the separation of *E. victoriensis* as a variety.

Ferocactus echidne var. *victoriensis* differs from var. *echidne* in having the stems more columnar and are usually more cespitose; longer, more brittle spines; slightly larger seeds; floriferous areoles which are oblong but not truncate; acute, ciliate scales on the fruit rather than nearly entire scales with rounded apices; and the intangible character of a different appearance.

Echinocactus rafaelensis Purpus is discussed in another section of this paper. If it is the same as the plants from the Victoria-Jaumave area it will fall into the synonomy of *Echinocactus victoriensis*, which was described three years earlier. According to the present treatment it would be a synonym of *Ferocactus echidne* var. *victoriensis.* The description and photograph in the original publication of *Echinocactus rafaelensis* appear to represent a different species.

My collections of *Ferocactus echidne* var. *victoriensis* were made at 1,650 feet elevation in the hills 11 km southwest of Ciudad Victoria, on the road to Jaumave. There it grew on limestone cliffs and boulders, usually in partial shade of *Ptelea trifoliata*, in association with *Jatropha spatulata*, *Dioon edule*, *Mascagnia* sp., *Buddleia* sp., *Opuntia* sp., etc. The Ferocacti were occasionally simple but usually were branched from the base to form many-stemmed clusters, the larger heads 6 to 8 inches in diameter and to 14 inches tall. Spines were yellow to brown or gray, very brittle, acicular, and to 4 inches long. The fruit was green or yellowish green, turning red, to 2 cm long and 1.5 cm broad, with reddish or purplish scales. The fruit was pulpy, with the small seeds enclosed in white, sweet pulp composed of enlarged, gelatinous funiculi. The seeds were very small, smooth, and shiny black or under magnification very deep red. The testa is shiny and smooth, but magnification sometimes shows traces of sculpturing near the hilum, which is small and oval.

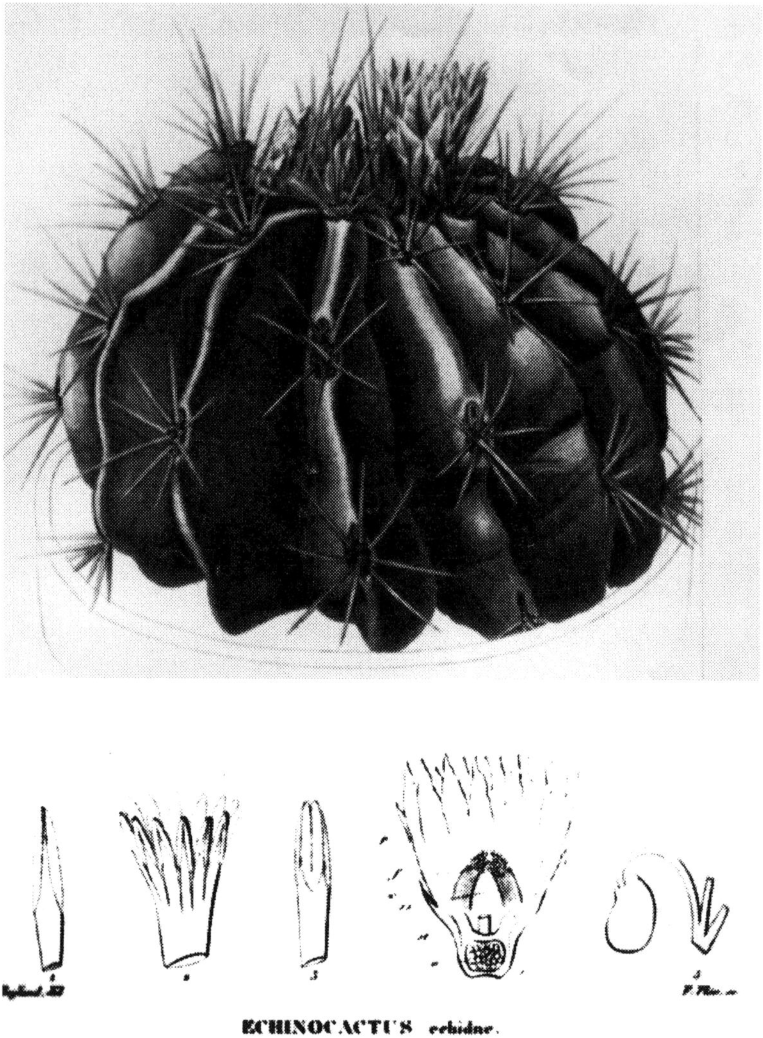

Figure 19. ***Ferocactus echidne*** **var.** ***echidne*****. Copy of the illustration by Heyland which accompanied the original publication of** ***Echinocactus echidne*** **De Candolle in Mem. Cact., plate 11. 1834.**

Figure 20. *Ferocactus echidne* var. *echidne*. Above, *Bravo 34/22* from Venados, Hidalgo, the specimen from which the neotype was taken. Below, specimen from the Barranca de Mezauitlan, Hidalgo, (*Lindsay 2069*).

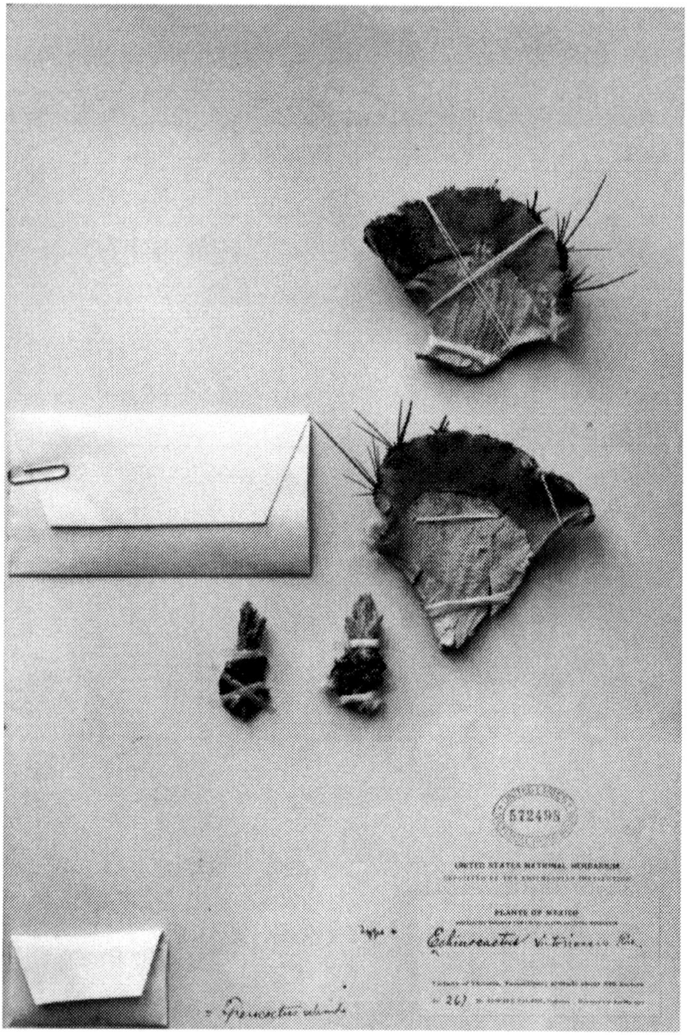

Figure 21. *Ferocactus echidne* var. *victoriensis*. Holotype specimen of *Echinocactus victoriensis* Rose and *Ferocactus echidne* var. *victoriensis*.

Figure 22. *Ferocactus echidne* var. *victoriensis* (*Lindsay 2612*) growing in limestone hills 11 km. southwest of Ciudad Victoria, on the road to Jaumauve, Tamaulipas, Mexico.

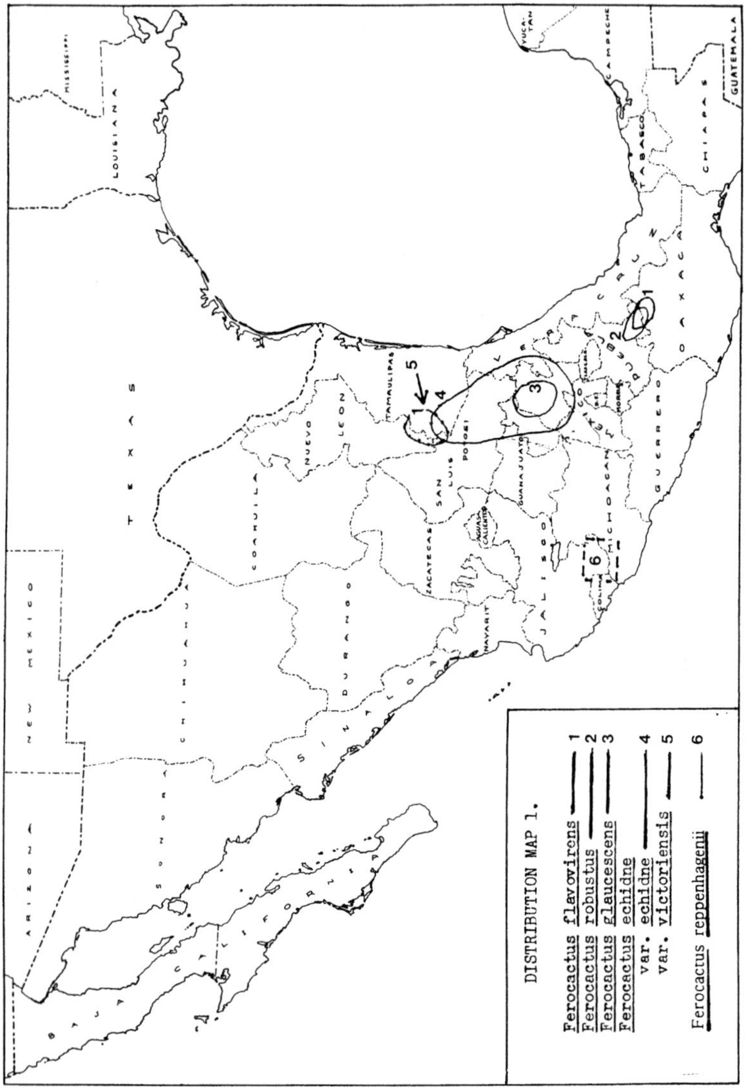

Distribution Map 1

5. FEROCACTUS SCHWARZII Lindsay, Cact. and Succ. Journ. 27: 70. 1955.

STEM always simple, from globose to broadly elliptical, tending toward broadly obovoid in maturity, to 8 dm tall and 5 dm in diameter, apex very slightly depressed, velvety, 2 to 5 cm wide. RIBS 13 to 19, acute, perpendicular, 3 to 5.5 cm deep, pale green, not tuberculate. AREOLES elliptic to obovate, 5 to 12 mm wide and 11 to 22 mm long, lanate in youth, the deciduous wool light tan at first, ageing to light or dark gray, the areoles confluent or nearly so. SPINES at first yellow ageing through gray to light horn, very slightly recurved, almost porrect, faintly annulate, plano-convex to terete in cross section, 1.5 to 5.5 cm long and 1 to 2 mm broad at base, not differentiated into a central and lateral series, usually 4 in immature plants but sometimes 3 or 5 or more, mature plants bearing 1 to 3 spines per areole, when 2 the lower is slightly recurved and the upper slightly curved upward, with both on the same plane as the rib; nectareous gland-spines appearing in flowering areoles, above regular spines and below flower, usually 2 at an areole, usually unevenly placed, later up to 5 may appear, pale orange, slightly flattened with rounded tip, 1.8 to 2.2 mm wide, becoming slightly mammillate on drying in age. FLOWERS produced in circle around the apex of the plant, appearing on second aerole from the top; buds scaled, the scales ciliate-fimbriate, red with yellow margin; flowers yellow, to 5 cm long and 4 cm across when fully opened, scales of ovary grading into outer perianth segments, these yellow with red midstripe, margins slightly ciliate; inner perianth segments clear yellow, about 2 to 2.5 cm long and 8 mm wide, tip acuminate, margin slightly ciliate; anthers and stamens yellow; style yellow, 2 cm long, stigma-lobes about 12 to 20, spreading, light yellow. FRUIT when dry 1.5 cm long and 12 mm broad, not dehiscing, covered with recurved shield-shaped scales, the withered perianth persisting making total length of dried fruit 3 cm, the walls of the ovary reddish and the dried scales yellow. SEEDS black, reticulate, 1.5 mm long, 1 mm wide, 0.6 mm thick, hilum oval, sunken, white; the seeds in the fruit surrounded by a mass of dried white sugary pulp.

Holotype: Barrancas between El Rancho del Padre and Rio Sinaloa, in northern Sinaloa, Mexico, *Schwarz s.n. Dudley Herbarium No. 371145* (DS).

Distribution: Steep cliffs and mountains of the barrancas between El Rancho del Padre, near Bacubirito, Sinaloa, and the Sinaloa river, Sinaloa, Mexico. Also at Cerro Colorado, near Cofradia, about thirty miles east of Culican, Sinaloa. Map number two.

Representative specimens: MEXICO; SINALOA: Mountains between El Rancho Padre and the Sinaloa river, *Schwarz s.n.*, Dudley Herbarium No. 371145, tylpe (DS); Cerro Colorado, near Cofradia, about 30 miles east of Culiacan, *Brandegee s.n.* Nov. 6, 1904 (UC).

Mr. Herman Marcks and Mr. Fritz Schwarz discovered the specimens from which this species was described in 1940, and have had it in cultivation since then. Mr. Schwarz listed the name in his catalogues and distributed the plant to principal collections in the United States and Europe. I had a specimen in my study collection since 1951, but the original description and type material is from a plant in Mr. Schwarz' garden in San Luis Potosi.

At the time I described this species I was not aware of a herbarium specimen collected by T. S. Brandegee at Cerro Colorado, Sinaloa, Nov. 6, 1904, and deposited in the herbarium of the University of California. The specimen was unidentified, and consists of short fragments of ribs with eight areoles, each of which bears four straight acicular spines. Brandegee's notes on the sheet say "Sinaloa, *Echinocactus*, Cerro Colorado. T. S. Brandegee Nov. 6, 1904. Spines not hooked - growing on cliffs." The specimen is *Ferocactus schwarzii*.

Brandegee made a large collection of plants in the vicinity of Culiacan between August and November, 1904. In 1905 he published a paper which included many new species which he collected on that trip, but he did not mention the unidentified *Echinocactus*. His article gave the following locality data. "In November the plants growing about Cofradia and in the Cerro Colorado were collected. Cofradia and Cerro Colorado are east from Culiacan thirty or more miles, and near the boundary line of the State of Durango. Cerro Colorado is a small mountain with peaks of red rock that are perhaps 2,000 feet above sea level."

Ferocactus schwarzii has the aspect of the larger Echinocacti when it is mature, but the flowers and fruit are typical of *Ferocactus*. Juvenile plants have four or five equal spines per areole, but the mature plants have but one or two.

Mr. Fritz Schwarz has been a leading cactus collector and exporter for many years, during which time he discovered a number of new Mexican cacti and introduced them into horticulture. This *Ferocactus* is named for him.

Figure 23. *Ferocactus schwarzii,* a mature specimen from the type locality, growing in the collection of Mr. Fritz Schwarz in San Luis Potosi.

Figure 24. *Ferocactus schwarzii,* a juvenile specinen in the author's collection.

6. FEROCACTUS HISTRIX (De Candolle) Lindsay, Cact. and Succ. Journ. 27: 171. 1955.

Echinocactus histrix De Candolle, Mem. Mus. Hist. Nat. Paris 17: 115. 1828.

Echinocactus coulteri G. don, Gen. Gard. 3: 162. 1834.

Echinocactus oxypterus Zuccarini, in Pfeiffer, Enum. Cact. 57. 1837.

Echinocactus electracanthus Lemaire, Cact. Aliq. Nov. 24. 1838.

Echinofossulocactus oxypterus Lawrence, in London, Gard. Mag. 17: 318. 1841.

Echinocactus electracanthus (Lem.) var. *capuliger* Monville, in

Labouret, Monogr. Cact. 184. 1853.

Ferocactus melocactiformis sensu Britton and Rose, Cactaceae 3: 138, 1922, not *Echinocactus melocactiformis* De Candolle.

STEM simple, broadly subovate to globular, usually less than 5 dm tall and 5 dm in diameter, but in some areas specimens may be to 1 m tall; top of stem rounded with a massive, somewhat depressed, tomentose apex. RIBS 20 to 38, straight, acute, 2 to 3 cm high, with small tubercles between the areoles. AREOLES oval, to 2 cm long, with yellow tomentum in youth, this turning gray. SPINES strong, yellow or yellow tinged with red toward the base, sometimes aging to brown; central spine 1 to 9 cm long, erect, straight or slightly curved, annulate, sometimes flattened laterally and sometimes dorsiventrally, in which case they are saber-shaped, or often they are triangular or polygonal in cross section; radial spines shorter, radiating, terete, about 8 but sometimes more, almost equal in length, slightly curved; actively nectareous gland-spines, to 3 mm long, produced in flowering areoles and persisting. FLOWERS yellow, 3.5 cm long and 2.5 cm wide, campanulate; imbricate ovarian scales yellow with ciliate margins, intergrading with scales of the tube, these longer, red with yellow margins, ciliate, spirally imbricate and blending into the outer perianth segments; outer perianth segments yellow with red midstripe, to 1.5 cm long and 4 mm wide, margins serrulate; inner perianth segments yellow, linear-oblong, acute, serrate, spreading; filaments many, pale greenish yellow, to 1 cm long; anthers minute, yellow; style 15 mm long, the upper 8 mm divided into 16 stigma lobes. FRUIT squamous, 2 to 3 cm long, fleshy and edible. SEED small, dark brown.

Neotype: A water-color plate by Heyland on which A.P. de Candolle wrote the determination of *Echinocactus histrix*, in the general collection of the Herbier Delessert, Conservatoire et Jardin Botaniques, Geneva. The holotype seems not to have been preserved.

Distribution: Hills of the tablelands of central Mexico, in the states of Zacatecas, Durango, Jalisco, Guanajuato, Hidalgo, and Puebla. Map number two.

Representative specimens: MEXICO: ZACATECAS: hills 7 mi. N.E. of Troncoso, *Lindsay 2576* (DS,SD); JALISCO: rocky hills 23 mi. W. of Ojuelos, on road to Aguas Calientes, *Lindsay 2031* (DS,SD); SAN LUIS POTOSI: Bocas, *Orcutt 19241581* (DS); PUEBLA: Esperanza, *Purpus 5358, 5497* (UC).

Two Echinocacti were among the many new species described by de Candolle in 1828. The first of the two to be published was *E. melocactiformis*, which was based on a drawing, and this was followed by *E. histrix*, which was based on a plant received with a shipment of cacti from Thomas Coulter, in Mexico, in 1827. Most taxonomic treatments have considered the two names to be synonyms, and have used *E. melocactiformis* on the basis of priority. I do not feel that the taxon which *E. melocactiformis* was intended to describe can be identified with any certainty, and for that reason have combined *E. histrix* De Candolle in *Ferocactus*, and have referred to it the synonyms of *F. melocactiformis* sensu Britton and Rose. This move was made with reluctance, because of the changes in the literature which would be involved. I would like to review the history and circumstances of the description of *Echinocactus melocactiformis* which made it necessary.

Echinocactus melocactiformis was discovered by members of the Royal Botanical Expedition to New Spain which surveyed the botanical resources of Mexico between 1788 and 1801, under the direction of Dr. Martin Sesse y Lacasta. Sesse, and a Mexican physician who had joined him in the undertaking, Dr. Jose Mariano Mocino, returned to Spain in 1804. They took with them their herbarium specimens, 1,400 colored drawings of plants by Cerda and Echeverria, and manuscripts of proposed publications, including Flora Mexicana and Plantae Novae Hispaniae.

Plans to publish the works failed and Sesse died in 1809. Mocino did scientific work and taught in Madrid, but became involved in political difficulties during the French occupation, and when the French withdrew he fled to France, taking his plants, manuscripts and drawings with him. Mocino settled in Montpellier and there became acquainted with de Candolle, who helped him work up some of his material, and to whom he turned over his drawings and manuscripts. In 1817 Mocino obtained permission to return to Spain, and requested the return of his papers from de Candolle, who hastily had the manuscripts and 1,100 of the colored drawings copied. The original drawings were lost after Mocino's death, but his manuscripts and part of his herbarium were preserved at the Botanical Garden of Madrid.

De Candolle published 274 new species based on his copies of the Mocino drawings, *Echinocactus melocactiformis* appearing in 1828. In the manuscript of *Icones Florae Mexicanae* Mocino had tentatively named the species *Cactus multangularis*, but de Candolle did not use that name because of its previous use by Willdenow in 1813.

The drawing from which the description of *Echinocactus melocactiformis* was made was poor and the description was necessarily vague and inconclusive. No dimensions are given, the number of spines is lacking, and the reported position of the flowers is rather improbable. The flower and spine color do not fit any known species, and possibly were inexactly copied from the original drawing. The plate shows a plant with the rib structure typical of an *Echinofossulocactus.*

On the other hand, *Echinocactus histrix,* which de Candolle described the same year as *E. melocactiformis* from a plant he had received from Coulter, is clearly described as to shape, ribs, and spines. The type specimen was small, and in dying condition when received by de Candolle, so the description lacks information about flowers and fruit. In any case, it is complete enough to be readily identifiable as belonging to the taxon which we are considering.

I think it is impossible to apply the name *Echinocactus melocactiformis.* The original description and illustration from which it was made are vague. The position of flowers and color of flowers and spines are unlike the taxon to which it has been assigned. The rib structure is like that of an *Echinofossulocactus.* Also, the fact that de Candolle described both *E. melocactiformis* and *E. histrix* the same year, and that the latter is applicable to the plants we are considering, would indicate that *E. melocactiformis* is not the applicable name.

G. Don described *E. coulterii* in 1834, also from a small plant obtained from Thomas Coulter, and included *E. histrix* of de Candolle as a synonym. This was followed by the description of *Echinocactus oxypterus* Zuccarini in Pfeiffer, in 1837. Pfeiffer thought it might be referred to *E. histrix*, but lacked material for comparison.

Echinocactus electracanthus was described by Lemaire in 1838, from a small dead plant 4 inches high and 6 inches in diameter, which had been brought from Mexico by a "Dom. Desch." I question placing this name in the synonomy of *E. histrix*, because of the 30 ribs on a plant 4 inches tall, red tomentum, and the red color and form of the spines. However, Britton and Rose did, and Schumann used *E. electracanthus* as the name of the taxon, noting that some one of the earlier names had priority, but retaining the well established name because of the confusion surrounding the earlier ones.

Labouret, Schumann, and Britton and Rose indicate that *Echinocactus lancifer* Reichenbach in Terscheck, Cact. Suppl., without date, belongs in this complex. I have been unable to locate this reference.

Echinocactus electracanthus Lem. var. *capuliger* Monville in Labouret, *Monographie des Cactees*, 184., is a type described as possessing radial bristles. I do not know this plant.

Ferocactus histrix is a beautiful golden-spined species which is often confused with *Echinocactus grusonii.* In San Luis Potosi large specimens nearly one meter tall are sometimes found. The plants usually grow on rocky hills and cliffs, stopping abruptly at the base of the slope, but in some areas occasional specimens may occur on flat plains. Usually *Ferocactus histrix* grows as scattered individuals, but on the hills near Troncoso, Zacatecas, they were in very dense stands, the golden plants about 18 inches tall and as broad. There they were in flower on March 20, and ants were actively feeding on the gland-spines which are produced between the spine cluster and flowers in flowering areoles. The ants were licking the bud scales, as well, indicating that the scales may also secrete nectar.

Echinocactus histrix is one of the visnagas used in Mexico for making candy, the pulp serving as a vehicle for sugar and flavoring. The fruit is edible, and is sold in the markets under the name of "tuna de visnaga." Mr. Fritz Schwarz told me that the plants are often eaten by deer, horses, and burros, who kick away part of the spine armament and devour the pulp.

The specific epithet *histrix* has often been spelled *hystrix* in the literature.

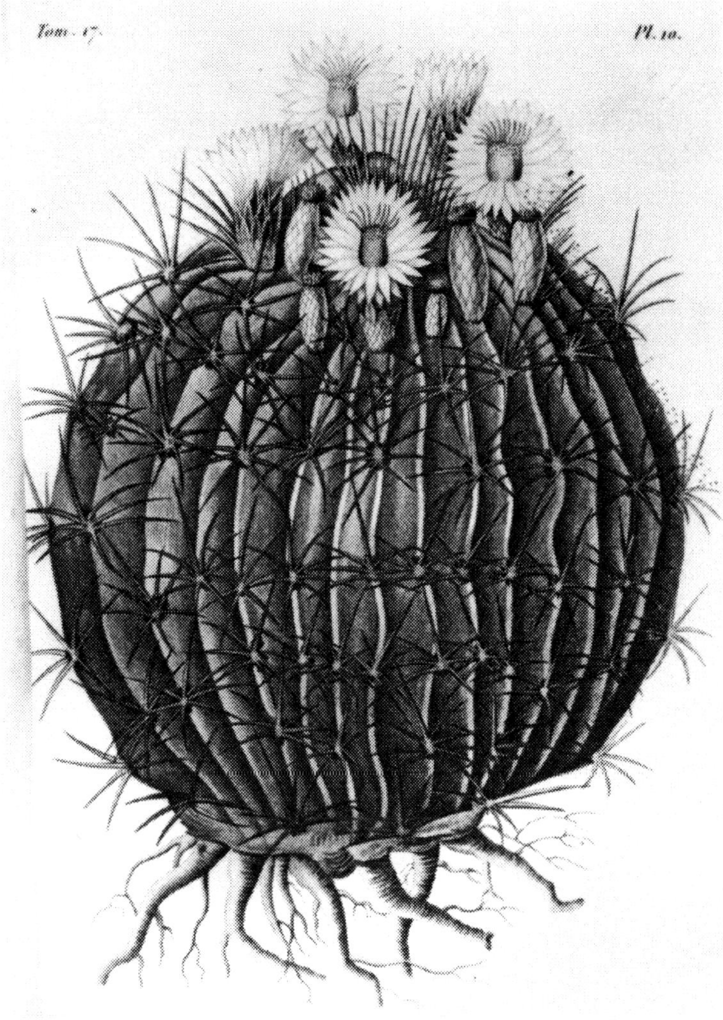

Figure 25. ***Echinocactus melocactiformis*. This illustration appeared with the original description of the species, and had been copied from a plate in Mocino's *Icones Florae Mexicanae*.**

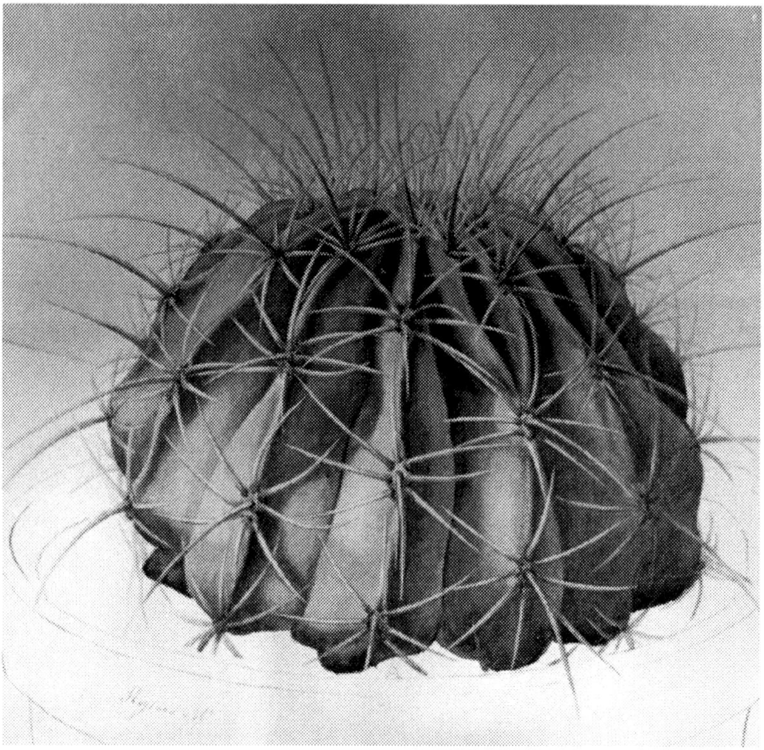

Figure 26. *Ferocactus histrix*. This is a photograph of a water color drawing by Heyland, on which A. P. De Candolle wrote the determination *Echinocactus histrix*. The plate has not been published, and is preserved in the Herbier Delessert, Geneva. It is now designated the neotype of *Ferocactus histrix*.

Figure 27. *Ferocactus histrix* (*Lindsay 2576*) in the hills near Troncoso, Zacatecas.

Figure 28. *Ferocactus histrix* in flower, photographed near Troncoso, Zacatecas, March 20, 1955.

7. FEROCACTUS ALAMOSANUS Britton and Rose, Cactaceae 3: 137. 1922

Editors' Note: Ferocactus *plain Dalamosanus var.* alamosanus *and* F. a. var. platygonus *are named by Nigel Taylor and others as* F. pottsii *var.* alamosanus *and* Ferocactus pottsii *var.* pottsii*, respectively, which are the current names.*

Key to the varieties

a. Ribs about 20, acute, stem densely covered with spines, plants to 3 dm. tall . . . . *F. a.* var. *alamosanus*

b. Ribs about 13, obtuse, spines not intermeshed, plants to 10 dm tall . . . . *F. a.* var. *platygonus*

7a. FEROCACTUS ALAMOSANUS Britton and Rose var. ALAMOSANUS

Echinocactus alamosanus Britton and Rose, Contr. U. S. Nat. Herb. 16: 239. 1913.

Ferocactus alamosanus Britton and Rose, Cactaceae 3: 137. 1922.

STEM simple or sometimes cespitose, somewhat flattened from above, 30 cm or more in diameter. RIBS about 20, narrow, acute, vertical. AREOLES oval, tomentose, about 15 mm long. SPINES yellow, acicular; central spine 1, porrect, flattened laterally, angled, 6 cm long; radial spines usually 8, 3-4 cm long, spreading slightly; the spines intermeshed forming a dense covering over stem. FLOWERS and FRUIT unknown.

Holotype: High up in the canyons of Alamos Mountain, Sonora, Mexico, *Rose*, *Standley* & *Russell 12850*, March 18, 1910 (US).

Distribution: Known only from type locality and from Cienegita and Black Canyon at Guirocoba Ranch, 50 km east of Alamos, Sonora. Map number two.

Representative specimens: MEXICO: SONORA: High up in canyons of Alamos Mountain, *Rose*, *Standley* & *Russell 12850* (US) type; Guirocoba Ranch, 50 km E Alamos, *Lindsay s. n.*, March 22, 1941 (DS). Living material of the Rose, Standley and Russell collection is growing at the Huntington Botanical Garden, Garden No. 43-194.

Ferocactus alamosanus var. *alamosanus* is known only from the type locality on Alamos Mountain, Sonora, and from canyons at Guirocoba

Ranch, near Alamos, Sonora. This variety is small and very heavily armed with long acicular spines which tend to be slightly angular in cross section. The ribs are acute and rather tuberculate.

7b. FEROCACTUS ALAMOSANUS Britton and Rose var. PLATYGONUS , Lindsay, Cact. and Succ. Journ. 14: 139. 1942.

STEM simple, to 1 m tall and 5 dm wide, globular to short cylindric. RIBS to 20, usually about 13 in small specimens, 3-4 cm broad and deep, obtuse. AREOLES oval, about 12 mm long and 10 mm wide, bearing tan tomentum; in addition there is a superior elliptical floriferous portion connected with the spiniferous portion by a narrow isthmus, this bearing short gland spines. SPINES amber yellow with reddish base, gray in age; central spine 1, to 7.5 cm long, porrect; radial spines about 8, 2.5 to 4.5 cm long, terete or slightly flattened laterally. FLOWERS funnelform, to 4.5 cm long and 3.5 cm broad; outer perianth segments about 20, 10 mm long and 6 mm broad, spatulate, light greenish yellow, margins white; inner perianth segments spatulate, light greenish yellow, margins serrate; stamens to 15 mm long, filaments yellow, anthers about 1 mm long, yellow; style yellow, stigma lobes 12, 12 mm long. FRUIT ovoid, to 4 cm long and 3 cm broad, yellow, bearing broad scales, perianth persistent, fruit opening by basal pore. SEEDS deep brown or black, to 3 mm long and 2 mm broad, hilum at base of tiny terminal tubercle.

Holotype: Guirocoba Ranch, 50 km E Alamos, Sonora, Mexico, *Bool & Lindsay s.n.* April 20, 1940 (DS).

Distribution: Mountains east of Alamos, Sonora, the western slopes of the Sierra Tarahumara, southern Chihuahua, and northeastern corner of Sinaloa, Mexico.

Representative specimens: MEXICO: SONORA: Guirocoba Ranch, *Lindsay s. n.* 1939, (DES); *Bool & Lindsay s. n.*, April 20, 1940 (DS), type. Living specimens from Guirocoba Ranch are growing at the Huntington Botanical Gardens, Desert Botanical Garden of Arizona, and the University of California Botanical Garden at Berkeley.

Ferocactus alamosanus var. *platygonus* grows much larger than var. *alamosanus*, and has a naked appearance because its distantly separated areoles bear short spines. It occupies a wide altitudinal range, from an arid tropical thorn forest habitat at Guirocoba Ranch, Sonora, to pine forests in the Sierra Tarahumara, above Cerro Colorado and Metate, Chihuahua. There it grows with *Echinocereus scheeri* in scant soil on tops of large boulders, possibly because of heavy winter snows. I photographed a flowering plant at Guiropaco, Chihuahua, on March 29, 1939.

I established both varieties of *Ferocactus alamosanus* at the Desert Botanical Garden of Arizona in 1940, and in two years the plants of var. *platygonus* had more than doubled in size. This variety was a favorite food of desert rodents and had to be protected with wire netting.

Recent catalogues of Mr. Fritz Schwarz list *Ferocactus guirocobensis*, which has not been described and is the same as *F. alamosanus* var. *platygonus*. Mr. Schwarz and Mr. Robert Flores report a third form of this complex form near San Bernardo, Sonora, which is north of Alamos. The barrel cacti in that region resemble *F. alamosanus* var. *platygonus* but are very large. Seedlings in Mr. Flores' collection have annulate, hooked central spines, but spines of mature specimens are like those of var. *platygonus*.

Johnston (1924, p. 1110) reported *Ferocactus alamosanus* from the head of San Carlos Bay, near Guaymas, Sonora, but the plants in that area are a straight-spined form of *Ferocactus covillei*.

Figure 29. ***Ferocactus alamosanus*** **var.** ***alamosanus*****. holotype specimen.**

Figure 30. ***Ferocactus alamosanus*** **var.** ***platygonus*** **at the type locality, Guirocoba Ranch, 50 Km. east of Alamos, Sonora, Mexico.**

Figure 31. *Ferocactus alamosanus* var. *platygonus*, a large specimen at Guirocoba Ranch, Sonora.

Figure 32. *Ferocactus alamosanus* var. *platygonus* in flower at Guiropaco, Chihuahua, in the Sierra Madre, March 29, 1939.

8. FEROCACTUS MACRODISCUS (Martius) Britton and Rose, Cactaceae 3: 139. 1922.

Echinocactus macrodiscus Martius, Nov. Act. Acad. Nat. Cur. 16: 341. 1832.

Echinocactus macrodiscus laevior Monville, in Labouret, Monogr. Cact. 197. 1853.

Echinocactus macrodiscus decolor Monville, in Labouret, loc. cit.

Echinocactus macrodiscus multiflorus R. Meyer, Monatsschr. Kakteenk. 25: 150. 1914.

STEM simple, disc-shaped, to 3-4 dm wide and 1 dm tall, usually very flat and deep seated in the soil. RIBS 13-35, acute, usually tuberculate, flattened and thickened under areoles. AREOLES oval, truncate at top where pressed against tubercle above, about 8 mm long and 6 mm wide, bearing light tan tomentum in youth, the areoles widely separated, in low depressions on the ribs. SPINES red, yellow or horn-colored, recurved against plant body, annulate; central spines 4, somewhat flattened, cruciform with the lateral two inclined upward, the lower sometimes longer and larger, but in some plants all four central spines about equal; radial spines 6-8, recurved, often lighter colored than the centrals, the uppermost sometimes acicular. FLOWERS campanulate, lavender or dark red, 3-4 cm long and as broad; tube short and thick-walled, covered with reddish-brown scales; outer perianth segments oblong, purple with white margins; inner perianth segments oblong-linear, fimbriate with mucronate tip, dull red with purple midstripe; stamens dull yellow green, anthers yellow; style bearing about 12 dark red stigma lobes. FRUIT magenta, irregularly globular, born in a cluster in the center of the stem, to 4 cm long and 3 cm wide, covered with fleshy scales with white hyaline margins; the scales ovate-deltoid, 3-5 mm long, auriculate at base; perianth persisting; walls of ovary fleshy and colored; locule filled with sweet parenchymatous tissue. SEED dark brown or black, 2 mm long, 1.5 mm wide and 0.8 mm thick, covered with small, somewhat angular pits; hilum small, lateral-terminal.

Neotype: Hill just above San Juan de Teposcolula, Oaxaca, Mexico, about 37 miles south of Huahuapan de Leon, altitude 2550 m, *Lindsay 2607*, April 1, 1955 (DS). Holotype presumed lost, but probably from high mountains at El Renoso, San Luis Potosi, Mexico, and collected by Baron von Karwinsky. Galeotti collected this species in San Luis Potosi about the same time.

Distribution: Central Mexican highlands, in the states of San Luis Potosi, Queretaro, Guanajuato, Puebla and Oaxaca. Map number two.

Representative specimens: MEXICO: OAXACA: San Juan de Teposcula, *Lindsay 2607* (DS, neotype); Low elevations between Mitla and Oaxaca, *Schwarz s. n.* (DS); GUANAJUATO: Hills of Alejon, San Miguel de Allende, *Schwarz s. n.* (DS).

Ferocactus macrodiscus was probably discovered by Karwinsky during his botanical expeditions to Mexico between 1827 and 1832. Galeotti collected the species in San Luis Potosi about the same time. In any case *Echinocactus macrodiscus* was well represented in European collections by 1853, when Labouret published two varieties, which he attributed to Monville, from plants raised from seed. These were *Echinocactus macrodiscus* var. *laevior*, which was separated because it had more spines, and var. decolor, separated because the spines were lighter colored.

In 1840 Scheidweiler published *Echinocactus campulacanthus* in the Allgemeine Gartenzeitung (8: 337), which Salm-Dyck referred to *E. macrodiscus* with a question mark in 1845. In 1850, however, Salm-Dyck included *E. campulacanthus* in the synonomy of *E. macrodiscus* without question, as have Labouret and Schumann since. Britton and Rose felt that *E. campulacanthus* belonged elsewhere. The original description by Scheidweiler indicated his species had 1 strongly recurved, transversely striated, reddish central spine and 7 unequal, recurved, radial spines, which differs from those of *E. macrodiscus*. The original description was entitled Beschreibung einiger neuen Cacteen aus Mexiko, aus der Regend von Potosi, which would indicate *E. campulacanthus* was a Mexican plant. On the other hand, Scheidweiler indicated it was very close to *E. arcuatus*, which is a *Malococarpus* from South America, and Britton and Rose in refecting it from the synonomy of *E. macrodiscus*.

Echinocactus macrodiscus var. *multiflorus* Meyer was proposed to designate a plant with darker and more abundant flowers and pale yellow spines.

Ferocactus macrodiscus is an imperfectly known species, and more than one taxon may be represented in the complex which I have included under that name. I feel that the three varietal forms already described for the species represent only normal variation. Specimens sent by Mr. Fritz Schwarz, from near San Miguel de Allende, Guanajuato, have a somewhat different habit and heavier armament, with very heavy straight spines which are not recurved toward the plant. I do not know the flower of this form, but fruit supplied by Mr. Herman Marks from specimens of this type in his garden were similar to those of *F. macrodiscus* from Oaxaca.

I have felt some doubts about retaining *F. macrodiscus* in the genus *Ferocactus*. It is very closely related to *Homalocephala texensis* (Hopffer) Britton and Rose, which it strongly resembles in appearance, armament, depressed habit, and the position and character of the fruit. The flower of the monotypic genus *Homalocephala* has dense wool in the axils of the scales of the ovary, and the seeds are large and smooth, while the scales of the ovary of *Ferocactus macrodiscus* of course have naked axils and the seeds are smaller and pitted. In spite of these and other differences, *F. macrodiscus* appears to be nearly as closely related to *Homalocephala texensis* and *Ferocactus macrodiscus* may represent transitional forms between *Ferocactus* and *Echinocactus*, although *Homalocephala* is generally considered to be a side development from *Echinocactus* (Bauxbaum 1951, p. 193; Berger 1926, p. 67).

Ferocactus macrodiscus is found on the Mexican central plateau from San Luis Potosi to the highlands of central Oaxaca. It is a flat, low plant, and is unusual in having two distinct series of roots. One to several thick tap roots extend deep into the ground, and a second, lateral system of slender roots radiate out from the plant just under the surface. The plants may be several centimeters tall during periods when they are turgid with water, but tend to become depressed below the surface of the ground during periods of drouth, and at that time are exceedingly difficult to find.

Ordinarily *Ferocactus macrodiscus* grows in rich soil between rocks, often in half shade. I have collected the species only once, at 7910 feet elevation on a hill just above San Juan de Teposcolula, about 60 km south of Huahuapan, Oaxaca. Dr. Helia Bravo had found them there in 1953 (Bravo 1954, p. 520) and had given precise directions for locating the spot, but even with this help Dr. F. Miranda, Dr. Ira L. Wiggins, and I had some difficulty in finding the elusive heads which often were below the surface of the ground and blended with the grass. The plants there grew in pockets of heavy silt between limestone outcrops. Associated plants were species of *Juniperous*, *Cupressus*, *Quercus*, *Arctostaphylos*, *Nothalena*, *Selaginella*, *Sedum*, *Coryphantha*, etc. Dr. Bravo also collected *Ferocactus macrodiscus* in the oak association between Tejupan and Suchixtlahuaca, Oaxaca. A similar type occurs at much lower elevations between Oaxaca City and Milta, Oaxaca. There, at elevations of 5,500 to 6,000 feet, it grows on low hills in the floor of the wide valley, growing with more xerophytic associates, *Opuntia*, Nopalea, *Ferocactus nobilis*, *Mammillaria karwinskiana*, and other trees and shrubs. I was unable to locate the plant there, where most of the land has been disturbed by cultivation.

Mr. Fritz Schwarz gave me directions for finding *F. macrodiscus* near San Miguel de Allende, Guanajuato, but several hours search failed to reveal a single specimen. As has already been noted, plants from this district appear to be a distinct form.

Ripe fruit of *Ferocactus macrodiscus* is sweet and juicy, and is used for food by local inhabitants.

Figure 33. ***Ferocactus macrodiscus*** **from San Juan de Teposcula, Oaxaca, Mexico, the neotype specimen (*Lindsay 2607 DS*).**

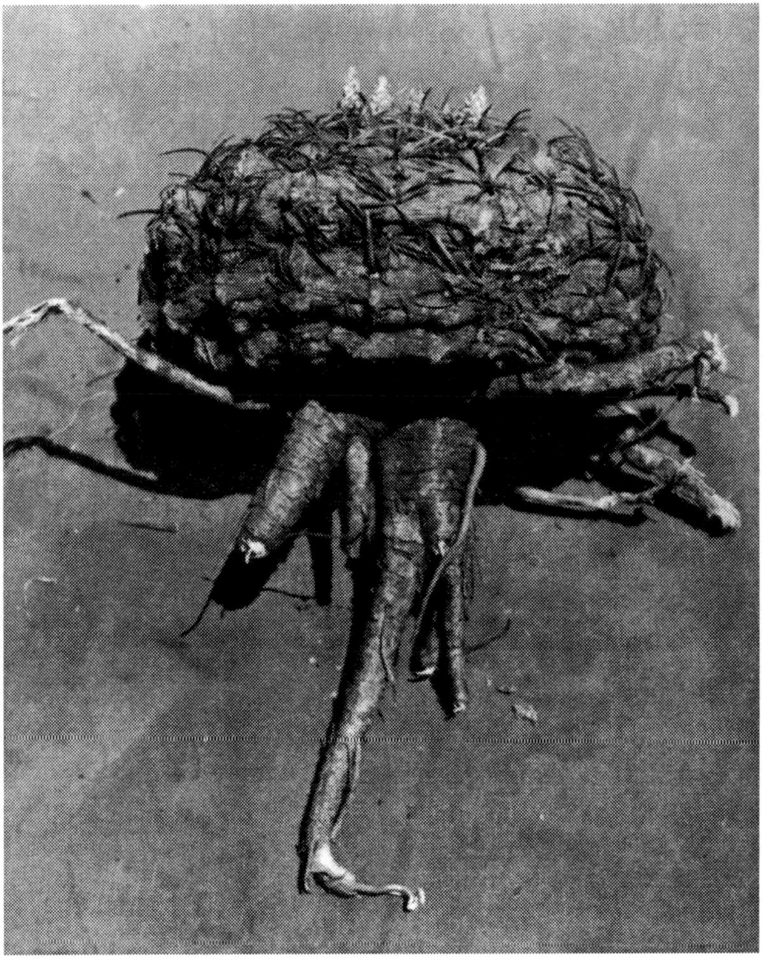

Figure 34. *Ferocactus macrodiscus*, showing the depressed stem and contractile tap roots.

Figure 35. ***Ferocactus macrodiscus*****, above,** ***Schwarz s.n.*****, from near Mitla, Oaxaca, and below from hills of Alejan, San Miguel Allende, Guanajuato.**

Figure 36. Depressed habit of *Ferocactus macrodiscus* at San Juan de Teposcula, Oaxaca. The photographs, made from kodachrome transparencies, show Dr. Ira L. Wiggins examining plants the tops of which are below the level of the surface of the ground.

Figure 37. Habitat photograph of *Ferocactus macrodiscus* at San Juan de Teposcula, Oaxaca. Many plants are growing in the grass among the limestone rocks. Photographs by Dr. Ira L Wiggins.

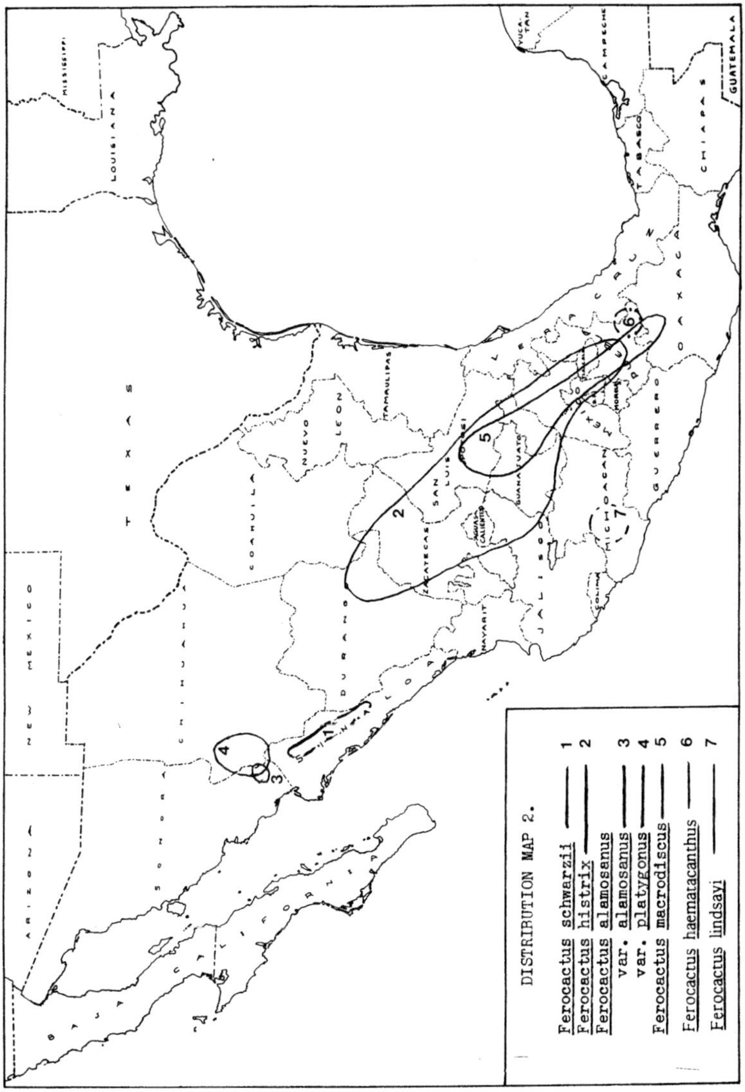

Distribution Map 2

9. FEROCACTUS RECURVUS (Miller) Y. Ito, Cacti 1952 105. 1952.

Cactus recurvus Miller, Dict. Gard. ed. 8. 1768.

Cactus nobilis Linnaeus, Mantissa Plantarum 243. 1771.

Echinocactus recurvus sensu Link and Otto, Verh. Ver. Beford.

Gartenb. 3: 426. 1828, as to citation, not as to description or figure (incorrectly labeled *Melocactus recurvus*).

Echinocactus spiralis Karwinsky, in Pfeiffer, Enum. Cact. 60. 1837.

Echinocactus solenacanthus Scheidweiler, Allg. Gartenz. 9: 50. 1841.

Echinocactus recurvus spiralis Schumann, Gesamtb. Kakteen 348. 1898.

Ferocactus nobilis (Linnaeus) Britton and Rose, Cactaceae 3: 141.1922.

Bisnaga recurvus (Miller) Orcutt, Cactography 1: 1. 1926.

STEM simple, globose to short-cylindric, usually less than 4 dm tall but sometimes to 1 m tall and 3.5 dm thick, large specimens often decumbent. RIBS usually 13-16, often spiraled, tuberculate, deep green, acute and sometimes undulate. AREOLES circular in spiniferous portion, to 1.5 cm long and broad, with a truncated floriferous portion above, this concealed on older ribs by the next tubercle; young areoles bearing tan tomentum which ages gray. SPINES ashy-red to horn-colored; central spines 4, the 3 superior straight, ascending, annulate, flattened laterally, to 4 cm long and 2.5 mm wide; the lower central spine curved or hooked at the end, porrect or sometimes descending, much longer and wider, to 5 or 6 cm long and 7 mm wide, strongly annulate and sometimes concave in cross section; radial spines 5-7, radiating, straight or slightly recurved, flattened or terete, annulate, shorter than the centrals. FLOWERS wine or purple color, narrowly campanulate, 5 cm long and 2.5 cm wide, appearing in December or January; scales of ovary triangular, 2-3 mm long and broad, purple with white sclerous ciliate margin, imbricated in spirals and intergrading with outer perianth segments, these purple with white fimbriate margins and acute tips; inner perianth segments narrow lanceolate, 3 cm long and 4 mm wide at widest point, lighter colored, white or silvery with purple midstripe or base, margin undulate, tip acuminate; inside of the tube greatly thickened, forming a solid disk or shoulder around the lower portion of the style, with a deep nectary between; stamens very numerous, the filaments attached to the horizontal surface of the swollen hypanthium shoulder, and from 3 to 17 mm long, brown or purple; style 3 cm long and 1.25 mm thick, wine color, the top 5 mm divided into 16 yellow stigma lobes. FRUIT red or yellow, columnar, elongating during maturation to 5-8 cm long and 2 cm wide, covered with spirally arranged, ciliate, sclerous, triangular scales. SEED very small, reddish-brown, to 1.25 mm long, 0.6 mm wide, and 0.4-0.5 mm thick; the shiny brown testa pitted with small, deep, elongate perforations which may completely penetrate it; hilum small, oval, brown.

Neotype: Hills at Zapotitlan de Salinas, near Tehuacan, Puebla, Mexico, *Lindsay 2060* (DS). The holotype was procured from Mexico by Dr. William Houston, sometime before 1733, and probably was not saved.

Distribution: Puebla and Oaxaca, Mexico, occupying diverse habitats from near Tehuantepec, Oaxaca, northward to the arid region about Mitla and the city of Oaxaca, the Mixtecas Altas of southern Puebla, where they grow in oak groves at 8,000 feet elevation, to the arid region around Tehuacan, Puebla. A specimen cultivated at the Instituto de Biologia in Mexico City is said to have been collected in Zacatecas. Map number three.

Representative specimens: MEXICO: PUEBLA: Zapotitlan de Salinas, near Tehuacan, *Lindsay 2060* (DS), *Lindsay 2597* (DS); OAXACA: 14 mi. N. Huahuapan, *Lindsay 2609* (DS); 12 mi. S. Huahuapan, *Lindsay 2608* (DS,SD); Mixtecas Altas, 53 mi. N. Oaxaca, alt. 7,610 ft., *Lindsay 2606* (DS); 1.9 mi. S. Tlacalula, at 5,400 ft. el., *Lindsay 2600* (DS).

Ferocactus recurvus was the first species to be described in the genus. It was collected in Mexico sometime before 1733 and was mentioned in Miller's *Dictionary of Gardening*, 7th edition, in 1759. This description became the basis for the name *Cactus recurvus* Miller in the 8th edition of the *Dictionary of Gardening* in 1768, which was the valid publication of the species. Linnaeus based his *Cactus nobilis*, published on page 243 of *Mantissa Plantarum*, on Miller's *C. recurvus*. Britton and Rose (1922 3:123) accepted 1767 as the publication date for *Mantissa Plantarum*, and for that reason gave *Cactus nobilis* priority over Miller's *C. recurvus*. However, *Mantissa Plantarum* was published in two sections, pages 1-142 in 1767, and pages 143-588 in 1771. *Cactus nobilis* appeared on page 243, which was published in 1771, and for that reason belongs in the synonomy under *Cactus recurvus*.

Miller, following the description of *Cactus recurvus*, made these interesting comments about that species.

> The third sort was brought into England by the late Dr. William Houston, who procured the plants from Mexico; but as they were long in their passage, and had received wet, they were decayed before they arrived in England; but from the remains of them which were left, they appeared to be the most singular of all the species yet known. This had two orders of thorns; one of which was straight, and set on at the joints in clusters, spreading out from the center each way like a star; and in the middle of each cluster is produced one broad flat thorn near two inches in length, which stands erect, and is recurved at the point, and is brownish red

colour. These thorns are, by the inhabitants of Mexico, set in gold and silver, and made use of for picking their teeth, and the plant is by them called Visnaga, i.e. toothpick.

In 1827 Link and Otto (p. 426) combined *Cactus recurvus* in their new genus *Echinocactus*. Their description was of a juvenile plant, no mature specimens having been at hand. They illustrated *Echinocactus recurvus* with a plate captioned *Melocactus recurvus*, possibly because the plates had been engraved before they decided to erect the genus *Echinocactus*. The plant illustrated is not this species, and *Melocactus recurvus*, based on that plate, should not be included in the synonomy, as it has been in the past.

Karwinsky collected *Ferocactus recurvus* in Mexico in 1828. In 1837 *E. spiralis* was named by Pfeiffer, but attributed to Karwinsky. The species was separated because of spiraled ribs found on seedling plants raised from seed Karwinsky had sent from Mexico. Spiraled ribs are characteristic of *E. recurvus*. *Echinocactus curvicornis* Miquel was placed under this species by Schumann and Britton and Rose, but the biscuit-shaped habit and the 11 or 12 radial spines indicate it belongs with *F. latispinus*. Probably *Echinocactus stellatus* Scheidweiler should also be referred by *F. latispinus*, because the description calls for 21 ribs, and the plant came from San Luis Potosi. In 1841 Scheidweiler described *Echinocactus solenacanthus* which unquestionably is *Ferocactus recurvus*. *Ferocactus recurvus* and *F. latispinus* are closely related and often confused. The two species are unquestionably distinct, although there is evidence of interspecific hybridization in some populations of Puebla. *Ferocactus recurvus* is taller in habit, globular to short-cylindric, with about 13 ribs, while *F. latispinus* is depressed globular, usually biscuit-shaped, with about 21 ribs. The flowers of *F. recurvus* appear in mid-winter, are about 5 cm long, and the fruits elongate to be columnar when mature. *Ferocactus latispinus* plain is summer flowering, the flowers are usually only 2.5 or 3 cm long, and the fruit is also much shorter. Radial spines of *F. recurvus* are fewer, 5 to 7, and the seeds are comparatively straight, while radial spines of *F. latispinus* average about 12-15, and the seeds are reinform.

Not all of the differences hold in every case. Specimens of *F. recurvus* from the higher elevations in the Mixtecas Altas of Puebla were depressed and sometimes had as many as 21 ribs. Plants from near Matamoros, Puebla, seemed to be intermediate between the two species. An excellent collection of intermediate variations was seen at Matamoros. A wide central traffic island in a new avenue had been landscaped with native cacti, and was literally "paved" with many thousands of plants of *Ferocactus*. All intergrades from typical *F. recurvus* to *F. latispinus* were to be seen, and apparently represented an interspecific hybrid swarm.

Ferocactus recurvus has the southernmost range of the genus.

Some years ago Indians brought Mr. Thomas MacDougall, who was living in Tehuantepec, specimens of a "visnaga" which they had found growing nearby. Mr. MacDougall told Dr. Wiggins and me about the *Ferocactus* when we visited him in Tehuantepec in 1955, but we were unable to find the locality they came from. Mr. MacDougall returned to New York and sent me negatives of excellent photographs he had taken of the original Tehuantan *Ferocactus* specimens, reproduced in plate 33, which showed them to be *F. recurvus.* Mr. MacDougall said that natives found additional specimens near San Jose Lachiguiri, Oaxaca, after our visit, and these are to be shipped to me.

Rather small specimens of *F. recurvus* which I collected near Mitla, Oaxaca, in 1937 have been growing at the Desert Botanical Garden of Arizona since 1939. The plants have become enormous procumbent things, four feet long, and produce a great mass of flowers every Christmas time, continuing to flower into April. One which I collected in 1951 at Zapotitlan, Puebla, blossomed on December 17, 1954, at Stanford University. The flowers are unusual in having a very much thickened inner wall of the hypanthium, which forms a fleshy shoulder or disk around the base of the style. The stamens are attached to the flat upper face of this shoulder. The flowers remain open several days, partially closing during the dark hours. During the first four or five days the stigma lobes remain appressed together, but the anthers apparently are ripe. The stigma lobes then expand and appear to be receptive, by which time the anthers are dry and withered. The different time of maturation of the male and female elements probably prevents self-fertilization within the flower itself. Single flowers on Ferocacti in cultivation rarely if every produce fruit with seed.

Figure 38. *Ferocactus recurvus,* a specimen growing near Tehuacan, Puebla, Mexico. The neotype specimen, *Lindsay 2060 DS*, was made from this plant.

Figure 39. ***Ferocactus recurvus*** **from Zapotitlan de Salinas, Puebla, in flower at Stanford University December 17, 1954.**

Figure 40. *Ferocactus recurvus*. Above, plant in fruit (*Lindsay 2600*) from south of Tlacalula, Oaxaca, at 5,400 ft. elevation. Below, *Lindsay 2606* from highlands 53 miles north of Oaxaca, Oaxaca, at 7,610 feet.

Figure 41. ***Ferocactus recurvus*** **from near Tehuantepec, Oaxaca, photographed by Mr. Thomas MacDougall.**

10. FEROCACTUS LATISPINUS (Haworth) Britton and Rose, Cactaceae 3: 143. 1922.

Cactus latispinus Haworth, Philos. Mag. 63: 41. 1824.

Echinocactus cornigerus A. P. de Candolle, Mem. Mus. Hist. Nat. Paris 17: 36. 1828.

Echinocactus curvicornis Miquel, Linnaea 12: 5. 1838.

Mammillaria latispina Tate, in Loudon, Gard. Mag. 16: 26. 1840.

Echinocactus stellatus Scheidweiler, Allg. Gartenz. 8: 338. 1840. @BODY ITEM = *Echinofossulocactus cornigerus* Lawrence, in London, Gard. Mag. 17: 318. 1841.

Echinofossulocactus cornigerus elaitor Lawrence, in London, loc. cit.

Echinofossulocactus cornigerus rubro-spina Lawrence, in London, loc. cit.

Echinofossulocactus cornigerus angustispinus Lawrence, in London, loc. cit.

Echinocactus cornigerus flavispinus Hagge, ex Forster, Handb. Cact. 318. 1846.

Echinocactus cornigerus latispinus Forster, Handb. Cact. 318. 1846.

Echinocactus latispinus Hemsley, Biol. Centr. Amer. Bot. 1: 533. 1880.

Echinocactus latispinus flavispinus Weber, Dict. Hort. Bois. 467. 1896.

Echinocactus cornigerus var. *rubrispinosus* Vaupel, Monatssch. Kakteenk. 12: 59. 1902.

Echinocactus cornigerus var. *flavispinosus* Vaupel, Monatsschr. Kakteenk. 12: 59. 1902.

Bisnaga cornigerus (DeCandolle) Orcutt, Cactography 1: 1. 1926.

Ferocactus latispinus var. *flavispinus* (Weber) Y. Ito, Cacti 1952 105. 1952

.

STEM simple, depressed globose or flattened, to 3 dm tall and 4 dm wide, light green. RIBS about 21, vertical, acute, tuberculate, with a large protuberance above each areole. AREOLES large, oval truncated floriferous section above, this concealed in older areoles by the overlapping tubercle. SPINES reddish to yellowish; central spines 4, the upper 3 straight, annulate, flattened, ascending, to 4 cm long and 4 mm wide; the lower central spine longer, curved or hooked at the tip, flattened, annulate, to 5 cm long and 9 mm wide, usually descending; radial spines 12-15, radiating, straight or very slightly recurved, some flattened and some terete, most annulate, the lowest directly below the central spine and shortest, the next two flattened more than the rest; gland-spines produced in flowering areoles, above the spine bundle, persistent but soon covered by the tubercle above. FLOWERS produced in the summer months, funnelform, purple or yellow, to 4 cm long and as broad; scales of ovary very densely imbricate, 3 mm long and 2 mm wide, sclerous, ciliate, with acute tip, intergrading with scales of tube and outer perianth segments; scales of tube with fleshy, ciliated basal portion about 5 mm long and wide, with an attenuate ciliate sclerous tip extending about 5 mm above; outer perianth segments lanceolate, 18 mm long and 4 mm wide, with a thickened basal portion and a ciliate-fimbriate sclerous aristate tip; inner perianth segments lanceolate, 16 mm long and 3 mm wide, margins entire but tip mucronate; inner walls of hypanthium very fleshy, to 6 mm thick; filaments numerous, 3-10 mm long, anthers minute; style 25 mm long, the upper 5 mm divided into about 16 unequal stigma lobes; color of flowers varies from orchid to yellow, the most common being mahogany outer perianth segments, orchid inner perianth segments, red stamens, red style, and yellow stigma lobes, but on many plants, particularly those with yellow spines, the flower parts may be shades of yellow. FRUIT oval, to 2.5 cm long and 1.75 cm wide, with the withered perianth 4 cm long; covered with densely imbricate acute sclerous scales. SEED small, elongate-reniform, shiny dark brown, deeply pitted, to 1.5 mm long, 1 mm wide and 0.6 mm thick.

Neotype: 8.5 miles east of the city of San Luis Potosi, San Luis Potosi, Mexico, *Lindsay 2583* (DS). The holotype from which Haworth described the species was brought from "Mexico" by a Mr. Bullock, and is presumed lost.

Distribution: Central Mexico, the plateau states of Hidalgo, Mexico, Queretaro, Guanajuato, Puebla, Jalisco, San Luis Potosi, Aguas Calientes, Zacatecas, etc. Map number three.

Representative specimens: MEXICO: SAN LUIS POTOSI: flats 4 mi E San Luis Potosi, S.L.P., *Lindsay 2034*, *2035*, (DS); 8 mi. E San Luis Potosi, S.L.P., *Lindsay 2583* (DS,SD); dry gravelly mesas near San Luis Potosi, *Pringle 3270* (UC, MEXU); ZACATECAS: 7 mi. NE Troncoso, *Lindsay 2581* (DS,SD); GUANAJUATO: 2 mi. from Dolores Hidalgo on road to San Miguel de Allende, *Lindsay 2594* (DS,SD); rocky rolling hills, 2 mi. from Dolores Hidalgo on road to Guanajuato, el. 6,700 ft., *Lindsay 2593* (DS,SD); QUERETARO: Del Ciervo a San Juan, *Altimirano 1730* (MEXU); San Juan del Oro, *Orcutt 2660* (DS); HIDALGO: 3 mi. N Ixmiquilpan, *Dawson 3084* (AHFH); dry sunny ridge, Tula, *Matuda 19436* (UC).

Ferocactus latispinus was brought from Mexico to England by a Mr. Bullock, and was described in the genus Cactus by A. H. Haworth in 1824. In 1828 A. P. de Candolle published and illustrated *Echinocactus cornigerus* from one of Mocino's drawings of Mexican plants, using Mocino's manuscript name, but suggested that the plant might be Haworth's species. Six years later de Candolle supplemented his original description of *E. cornigerus* with information obtained from a living plant sent to him from Mexico by Thomas Coulter. This was accompanied by an excellent plate of Coulter's plant.

Fr. A. Guil. Miquel named a seedling plant *Echinocactus curvicornis* in 1838, indicating it was related to the species now known as *Ferocactus recurvus*, in which synonomy it has usually been placed. The habit of the plant and the illustrations of the spines which accompanied the original description indicate that it belongs with *F. latispinus*. In 1840 Tate used the name *Mammillaria latispina* in referring to Haworth's plant, without intent to describe it. *Echinocactus stellatus* was a name proposed by Scheidweiler in 1840 for a plant with 21 ribs, from San Luis Potosi. It probably belongs in the synonomy of *F. latispinus* rather than with *F. recurvus*, where it has usually been placed. Lawrence's infamous list of cacti, published in 1841, listed *Echinofossulocactus cornigerus* with varieties *elatior*, *rubro-spina*, and *angustispina*, all without descriptions except gross size. There is no way to evaluate these names, but Britton and Rose included them all under *F. latispinus*.

Hemsley combined *Cactus latispinus* with *Echinocactus* in 1880, and in 1896 Weber proposed the name *Echinocactus latispinus flavispinus* for the form with yellow spines and flowers. The red-spined and yellow-spined specimens of *Ferocactus latispinus* look distinct, but in the field they are found mixed in most populations, with series of intergrades. The flower color is usually indicated by the color of the spines, but yellow-spined plants sometimes bear purple-colored flowers, and Mr. Fritz Schwarz told me that occasionally red-spined plants have yellow flowers. I feel that the name *flavispinus* cannot be maintained at the varietal level, and that it should only be considered a form.

Ferocactus latispinus is common in the grasslands of central Mexico, where it usually is found growing on silty flats and plains. It may also occur on rocky hillsides. The range of this species is north of that of closely related *F. recurvus*, but they may meet in Puebla. The differences between the two species have been discussed under *F. recurvus*.

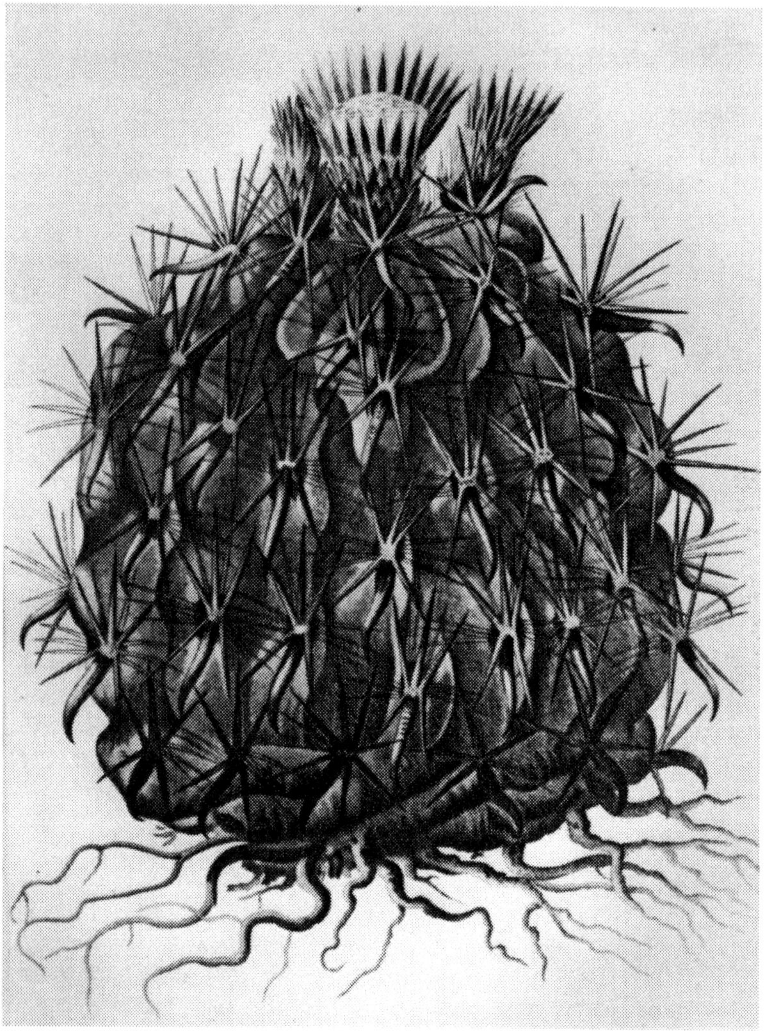

Figure 42. Photograph of the illustration which accompanied the original description of *Echinocactus cornigerus* de Candolle. The description, as well as the illustration, was made from one of Mocino's plates of Mexican plants.

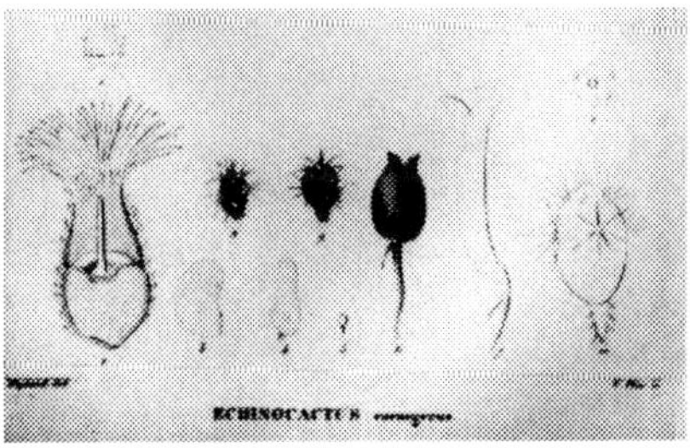

Figure 43. Illustration of *Echinocactus cornigerus* made from a colored plate which Heyland drew of plants sent to de Candolle by Thomas Coulter. From *Mem. Cact.*, plate 10. Paris, 1834.

Figure 44. *Ferocactus latispinus* in flower, San Luis Potosi, S.L.P., Mexico, August 28, 1951.

Figure 45. Habitat photograph of *Ferocactus latispinus* growing in silt flats four miles east of San Luis Potosi, S.L.P. Mr. Fritz Schwarz is examining two plants, one with red and the other with yellow spines.

11. FEROCACTUS PILOSUS (Galeotti) Werdermann, In Fedde, Rep. Spec. Nov. Sonder-Beiheft C. Lief 18: pl. 72. 1933.

Echinocactus pilosus Galeotti in Salm-Dyck, Cactac. Hort. Dyck. 1849. 148. 1850.

Echinocactus pilosus (Galeotti) var. *speinesii* Salm-Dyck, op. cit. p. 149.

Echinocactus pilosus (Galeotti) var. *pringlei* Coulter, Contr. U. S. Nat. Herb. 3: 365. 1896.

Echinocactus pringlei Rose, Contr. U. S. Nat. Herb. 10: 127. 1906.

Ferocactus stainesii Britton and Rose, Cactaceae 3: 124. 1922.

Echinocactus stainesii incorrectly attributed to Hooker by Britton and Rose)

Ferocactus pringlei (Coulter) Britton and Rose, Cactaceae 3: 125. 1922.

STEM simple or cespitose, globular to columnar, to 3 m tall and 5 dm wide, often forming massive clumps from the base. RIBS 13 to 20, not tuberculate in adults, rather acute. AREOLES ovid, to 20 mm long and 8 mm broad, with dense tan tomentum in youth but contiguous on ribs of mature plants. SPINES red or yellow or blotched with both, slightly curved and spreading, subulate, annulate, not strongly differentiated into a central and radial series, the four more central ones cruciform with the upper and lower often flattened laterally, these to 5 cm long; often a series of 2 to 5 somewhat shorter, smaller spines occur above and below the central four; conspicuous brown or white twisted bristles 2 to 4 cm long radiating from the edge of the aerole are characteristic but may be lacking in some individuals; several persistent nectareous gland-spines are produced in the upper portion of the flowering areoles. FLOWERS numerous, yellow to red, small, produced in a circle around apex of plant, to 4 cm long and 2.5 cm wide, enclosed by spines of adjacent areoles and not opening broadly, the tips of perianth segments incurved and the mouth of the corolla only a few millimeters broad; ovary short ovoid, covered with short circular scales which intergrade with the scales of tube and outer perianth segments; outer perianth segments lanceolate, pointed, red or orange; inner perianth segments more spatulate, serrate above, usually lighter yellow or orange than the outer; stamens yellow, filaments to 1 cm long, anthers yellow; style yellow, stigma lobes about 15, yellow. FRUIT ovoid, yellow, 3 to 4 cm long, walls of ovary fleshy and succulent, covered with rounded scales; perianth persistent.

The amount of red pigmentation in spines and flowers varies considerably from plant to plant in the same colony. A tendency for yellow flowers to be smaller in size than more deeply colored ones was noted in a colony near Saltillo, Coahuila, where the yellow flowers were about 2.5 cm long and 2 cm wide and the red flowers were 4 cm long and 2.5 cm wide.

Neotype: San Luis Potosi, Mexico, 69 mi. east of the city of San Luis Potosi on the road to Antiguo Morelas, hillsides at 4,700 ft. elevation, *Lindsay 2588* (DS). The original type specimen was probably from San Luis Potosi. Sir Edward Salisbury, Director of the Royal Botanic Gardens at Kew, has written to me that there is no material of this species preserved there.

Distribution: Northern Mexico, States of San Luis Potosi, Zacatecas, Durango, Coahuila, and Nuevo Leon, common throughout the whole sierra. Map number three.

Representative specimens: MEXICO: SAN LUIS POTOSI: 120 km NE city of San Luis Potosi, *Lindsay 2043* (DS,SD); 69 mi. NE San Luis Potosi, *Lindsay 2588* (DS,SD); COAHUILA: limestone ledges, Carneros, *Pringle s.n.*, Sept. 27, 1890 (UC); 15 mi. from Saltillo on road to Carneros, *Lindsay 2614* (DS,SD); Sierra de Parras,

C.A. Purpus, *s.n.* (UC); limestone ledges, mountains, Jimulco, *Pringle 154* (US). Mr. Fredrick Stains, an official of a mining company in San Luis Potosi, sent a large specimen of this plant to Kew Gardens. It was mentioned as *Echinocactus stainesii* in an unsigned article, concerning activites at Kew, which appeared in Audot's *Revue Horticole* (6:248) in 1845. The article implied that the species had been named by Hooker. Britton and Rose (1922, 3:124) accepted this reference as the original description for the species, and placed subsequent names in synonomy. However, no adequate description of the plant was published in *Revue Horticole* and apparently there was no intent to describe the new species in that article.

In the same year, 1845, the name *Echinocactus pilosus* Galeotti was mentioned by Salm-Dyck (1845, p. 21), but here again there was no description, the name simply occurring in a list. Later, however, Salm-Dyck (1850, p. 148) gave a full description of *E. pilosus* Galeotti which in the absence of earlier descriptions should be accepted as the valid publication of the species. The plant on which the description was based was juvenile, only 7 inches in diameter, possibly furnished by Galeotti, who had collected in Mexico. Salm-Dyck (1850, p. 149) also described a variety *steinesii* under *E. pilosus*, which differed in the distribution of its spines and bristles. Schumann (1898, p. 308) believed the variety *steinesii* of Salm-Dyck belonged to another complex and did not include it with his synonyms of *E. pilosus*. He did include *E. stainesii* of horticulture. Mr. Fredrick Stains, for whom the species was named, often had his name spelled Staine or Steins in the German literature, and the specific name *steinesii* used by Salm-Dyck is incorrect.

In April, 1885, C. G. Pringle collected plants in the mountains near Jimulco, Coahuila, and distributed them under the name *Echinocactus pilosus* Galeotti. John M. Coulter (1896, p. 365) proposed the variety *pringlei* based on this material, which he said "differs in that the radial spines are represented by 3 or 4 flexuous spines at the upper edge of pulvinus and 4 or 5 at the lower edge; centrals 6 or 7; flowers 3.5 to 4 cm long, brownish-red." J. N. Rose (1906, p. 127) elevated the variety to specific rank, listing the new combination "*Echinocactus pringlei*" with the cryptic statement "This species is very distinct from the true *E. pilosus*. Both are under cultivation in Washington."

Britton and Rose (1922, p. 124) placed *stainesii* in their new genus *Ferocactus*, and listed *pilosus* as a synonym, based on their interpretation of the rules of priority. In their discussion of *Ferocactus stainesii* they noted "This species differs from the following one (*Ferocactus pringlei* (Coulter) Britton and Rose) in having more distinct ribs, the areoles more widely separated, the spines duller colored, more numerous, somewhat curved, two of them decidedly flattened and hairs white. We know the plant only from description and illustration." The last sentence seems strange in view of Rose's earlier statement that both species were in cultivation in Washington.

The characters on which Coulter based his variety *pringlei* and on which Britton and Rose maintained *pringlei* and *stainesii (pilosus)* as distinct species are all within the limits of variation found in many species of *Ferocactus*. In general the northern plants which have been called *pringlei* exhibit more white areolar bristles, but this is not constant, and as Werdermann (1933, pl. 72) points out, is possibly correlated with altitudinal factors. I have observed variation in number, shape, and color of spines, as well as the size and color of flowers in *Ferocactus pilosus* in San Luis Potosi and Coahoula, but these variations were conspicuous even in local populations and within the acceptable limits of any modern species concept. I am unable to find adequate constant characters upon which to maintain *pringlei*, even as a variety.

Ferocactus pilosus is a beautiful species which inhabits the high desert plateau of central northern Mexico. Usually it is found on rocky limestone hillsides, but it also occurs on alluvial slopes and even silty flats, between 4,500 and 6,500 feet elevation. The plants are always colorful and often enormous, sometimes eight feet tall with a number of branches rising from the base. The bright red spines, backed with white bristles, give the plant a striking appearance.

Ferocactus pilosus is common in San Luis Potosi on highway Mexico 80 between El Huizache and Soledad. Here it grows with other cacti on hillsides covered with desert shrubs. Some of the associated plants are *Echinocactus palmeri, Mammillaria candida, Astrophytum myriostigma, Leuchtenbergia principis, Lophophora williamsii, Myrtillocactus geometrizans*, and species of *Opuntia, Agave, Yucca, Prosopis, Larrea, Fouquieria,*

Lysiloma, Chrysothamnus, etc. In Coahuila, between Saltillo and Carneros, smaller specimens of the type which has been called *Ferocactus pringlei* grow in broad deep silt plains, particularly in clumps of *Agave scabra*. Here the plants are small, usually about 18 inches tall and 14 inches in diameter. Near Carneros, Conception del Oro, and Agua Nueva the plants are found on hillsides, and attain large size.

The fruit of *Ferocactus pilosus* is rather fleshy and acid, and is used much like lemons. The fruit is marketed, and the common name for the species is "visnaga de limon."

Figure 46. *Ferocactus pilosus* (Galeotti) Werdermann, photographed 120 km. northeast of San Luis Potosi, S.L.P.

Figure 47. ***Ferocactus pilosus*****, showing the typical polycephalic habit of this species in San Luis Potosi. The specimen is about five feet tall.**

Figure 48. *Ferocactus pilosus*, detail of the stem of the plant shown in figure 47.

Figure 49. *Ferocactus pilosus* in flower, *Lindsay 2588*, from 69 miles east of San Luis Potosi, elevation 4,700 feet. Photographed March 22, 1955.

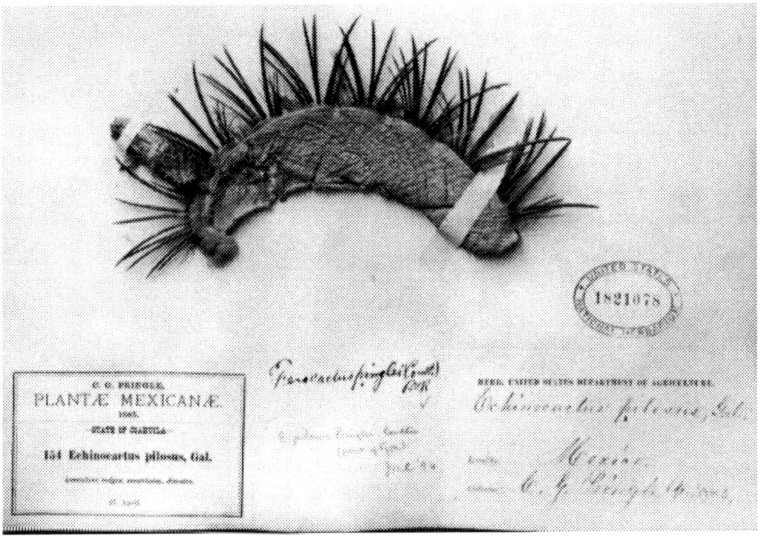

Figure 50. Holotype specimen of *Ferocactus pringlei*.

Figure 51. *Ferocactus pilosus*, *Lindsay 2614*, photographed 15 miles from Saltillo, Coahuila, on the road to Carneros. Associated plants are *Agave scabra*.

Figure 52. *Ferocactus pilosus*, detail of the flowers of the plant shown in figure 51, photographed April 7, 1955.

12. FEROCACTUS WISLIZENII (Engelmann) Britton and Rose, Cactaceae 3: 127. 1922.

Editors' Note: *There is a small controversy as to whether this* Ferocactus *should be written as* wislizenii, *as per Lindsay, or as wislizeni, as per Nigel Taylor. We have opted for the Lindsay version for two reasons. It is largely his book; the use of single "i"s after vowels and doubles after consonants is standard practice.*

Key to the varieties

a. Red or sometimes yellow flowers, blossoming in mid-summer, fruit maturing the following winter, areoles usually with setaceous radial spines . . . . *F. w.* var. *wislizenii.*

b. Yellow flowers in the spring, fruit maturing by early summer, no setaceous radial spines . . . . *F. w.* var *tiburonensis.*

12a. FEROCACTUS WISLIZENII (Engelmann) Britton and Rose var. WISLIZENII

Echinocactus wislizeni Engelmann, in Wislizenus, Mem. Tour. North. Mex. 96. 1848.

Echinocactus emoryi Engelmann, in Emory, Mil. Reconn. 157. 1848.

Echinocactus wislizeni var. *decipiens* Engelmann, in Rothrock, Rep. U. S. Geogr. Surv. 6: 128. 1878.

Echinocereus emoryi Rumpler, in Forester, Handb. Cact. ed. 2. 804. 1885.

Echinocactus wislizeni var. *albispina* Toumey, Gard. and For. 8: 154. 1895.

Echinocactus falconeri Orcutt, West Amer. Sci. 12: 162. 1902.

Echinocactus arizonicus Kunze, Monatsschr. Kakteenk. 19: 149. 1909.

Echinocactus wislizeni var. *phoeniceus* Kunze, Torreya 13: 75. 1913.

Ferocactus wislizeni (Engelmann) Britton and Rose, Cactaceae 3: 149. 1919.

Ferocactus arizonicus (Kunze) Orcutt, Cactography 6. 1926.

Ferocactus falconeri Orcutt, loc. cit.

Ferocactus phoeniceus (Kunze) Orcutt, loc. cit.

Echinocactus hertrichii Weinberg, Desert 1: 40. 1929. (as *hertichii*)

Ferocactus emoryi (Engelmann) Y. Ito. Cacti 1952 104. 1952.

Ferocactus wislizeni var. *phoeniceus* (Kunze) Y. Ito. Cacti 1952 105. 1952.

Ferocactus wislizeniplain var. albispinus (Toumey) Y. Ito, Cacti 1952 105. 1952.

STEM simple or occasionally sparsely branched from base, globular to columnar, to 3 m tall and 6 dm wide. RIBS 20-30, not strongly tuberculate, about 3 cm tall. AREOLES large, oval to elliptic, to 2.5 cm long, brown tomentose in youth, spaced 2-3 cm apart in flowering portion, later becoming approximate. SPINES variable in size, number, and color; 4 central spines cruciform, ashy gray to white or red, annulate, the upper 3 usually similar, terete, straight and about 5 cm long, the lower strongest, flattened laterally and often hooked at the tip, often 8-10 cm long and 5 mm wide, usually somewhat deflexed; radial spines variable from setaceous to acicular, usually about 12, to 5 cm long; short gland-spines are produced between the spine fascicle and flower in flowering areoles. FLOWERS red to yellow, funnelform, 4-5 cm long and broad; scales on ovary deltoid with ciliate margins, imbricate, about 5 mm wide and 4 mm long, intergrading with larger scales of tube and outer perianth segments; outer perianth segments rather fleshy, to about 16 mm long and 10 mm wide, with serrulate margins and mucronate tip; inner perianth segments ovate to lanceolate, about 2 cm long and 5-10 mm wide, red with yellow margins or sometimes pure yellow, serrulate with mucronate tip; walls of tube thickened with a shallow nectary pit between the tube and base of style; stamens numerous, the filaments 5-10 mm long, red; style yellow, 3 mm wide and 20 mm long, the terminal 13 mm divided into about 20 yellow stigma lobes. FRUIT yellow, narrow ovoid, to 5 cm long and 3 cm wide, including the persistent perianth to 8 cm long; scales of ovary fleshy with ciliate margin. SEED reddish brown to almost black, 2.25-2.5 mm long, 1.75 mm wide, rounded or sometimes angled, the testa covered with shallow intricate sculpturing, the depressions wrinkled.

Holotype: Southern end of Jornada del Muerto, near Dona Ana, New Mexico, *Wislizenus "cactus No. 6*", August 5, 1846, in the George Engelmann Herbarium (MBG). The specimen consists of a dried flower bud and two dried flowers, and an accompanying specimen consists of a sketch of an areole and outline of a flower, with a short note of description.

Distribution: Southern Arizona, southern New Mexico, the southwestern tip of Texas, northwestern Chihuahua, northern and western Sonora, and northwestern Sinaloa. Maps three and four.

Representative specimens: ARIZONA: YUMA CO: Sandy flat 5 mi. SW Stoval, about 3 mi. E Mohawk Mts., plants to 1.2 m tall, *Wiggins 8642* (DS). PIMA CO. Tucson, (flowers 8 cm long on some sheets) *Palmer 72* and *73*, Aug. 10, 1867 (MBG); 11 mi. S. Tucson, *Cutler 1072ul* (MBG); Florida Canyon, Santa Rita Mts., el. 4,000 ft., *Benson 9745* (POM,ARIZ); N. of Fresnal, Baboquivari Mts., el. 2,700 ft., *Benson 9988* (POM); Redington Pass, Santa Catalina Mts., el. 3,800 ft., *Benson 9848* (POM); N. base Coyote Mts., rocky soils, el. 2,500 ft., *Benson 9976* (POM). MARICOPA

CO. Gravelly flats 7 mi. S. Gila Bend, *Wiggins 8725* (DS). COCHISE CO. Camp Bowie (then New Mexico) *Rothrock 492*, 1874, (MBG, Holotype of *E. wislizeni* var. *decipiens* Engelmann); Benson, *Trelease s.n.* April 1892 (MBG). PINAL CO. Dudleyville, *Toumey s.n.* Sept. 25, 1896 (US,UC); 5 mi. S. Florence, el. 1,600 ft., *Graham 7-26-1* (UC); near Sacaton, *Leding S.F.8*, 1920 (ARIZ). GRAHAM CO. 10 mi. E. Coolidge Dam on road to Safford, ribs 28, variation in spines of adjacent plants, *Lindsay 2025* (DS,SD). NEW MEXICO. DONA ANA CO. Southern end of Jornada del Muerto, near Dona Ana, Wislizenus "*cactus no. 6*", 1846, Holotype, contains fruit 6 cm. long including perianth, the ovary 3.5 cm. long, a dried flower 3 cm long, and dried bud 18 mm long. A second packet on the same sheet is labeled "*Dr. Bigelow No. 12, Echinocactus wislizeni*, Paso del Norte, N. Mex., Nov. 12, 1857," (MBG); mesa W. Organ Mts., *Wooton & Standley 3204* (ARIZ, Topotype); near type locality, Mesilla Park, *Standley 565* (MBG); Rincon, *Jones s*.n. Sept. 9, 1884 (POM). LUNA CO. Floridas, *Mulford 1038* (MBG). TEXAS. El Paso, *Jones s.n.* Sept. 12, 1884 (CAS,UC,POM,ARIZ); "above El Paso," *Lt. Kribber s.n.* Dec. 1849 (MBG). MEXICO. CHIHUAHUA. Dry limestone hills near Lake Guzman, (central spines not flattened or hooked, 3.5 cm long) *Pringle 6875* (US,MBG,POM,MEXU). SONORA. 20 m. S. Hermosillo, ribs 22, *Lindsay 2554* (DS,SD); Tetas de Cabra, San Carlos Bay, *Dawson s.n.* Feb., 1940 (AHFH); Near Potam, in Yaqui Valley, 13 deep ribs, *Lindsay 2556, 2557* (DS,SD); 23 km W. Alamos, on road to Navajoa, growing in semi-shade, 13 deep ribs, *Lindsay 2219* (DS,SD); 51 mi. S. Navajoa, el. 460 ft., few or no setaceous spines, *Lindsay* 2562 (DS,SD). SINALOA. 6.5 mi. S. Los Mochis junction on highway Mexico 15, 5 ft. tall, 20 in. wide, 18 ribs 3 in. deep, no setaceous spines, *Lindsay 2563* (DS,SD).

In 1846 Dr. A. Wislizenus, a professional partner of Dr. George Engelmann, undertook a self-sponsored exploratory tour of northern Mexico and Upper California. Wislizenus collected natural history and geological specimens, and was one of the scientific pioneers through much of the region he crossed. Outfitting himself with a light covered wagon, he joined a caravan of Missouri traders for the journey to Santa Fe, New Mexico, which was then Mexican territory. In Santa Fe the party learned that the United States and Mexico were at war, but in spite of this Governor Armijo granted Wislizenus a passport to proceed southward into the interior. On August 5, enroute to El Paso, Wislizenus discovered the large *Ferocactus* which Engelmann was to name for him. His journal (1848, p. 39) describes the incident as follows:

> Before reaching Donana, I met on the road with the largest cactus of the kind that I have ever seen. It was an oval Echinocactus, with enormous fishhook-like prickles, measuring in height four feet, and in the largest circumference six feet eight inches. It had

> yellow flowers, and at the same time seed, both of which I took along with some of the ribs: but I really felt sorry that its size and weight prevented me from carrying the whole of this exquisite specimen with me. Dr. Engelmann, preceiving that it was a new, undescribed species, has done me the honor to call it after my name.

Wislizenus proceeded to El Paso and Chihuahua City, where he was detained for six months as an enemy alien, until that city was taken by the American forces under Col. Doniphan. Joining the Americans as a civilian surgeon, Wislizenus returned to the United States via Saltillo and Monterrey. The botanical collections which he had made were worked up by Engelmann, and were published, the new *Echinocactus wislizeni* included, as an appendix to Wislizenus's report in 1848."

Dr. Engelmann had become interested in the Cactaceae some years before, and in 1845 (pp. 246-247) described seven species from Texas sent to him by Lindheimer. Engelmann became the American authority on cactus, and received a great amount of botanical material from private expeditions, such as that of Wislizenus, as well as the government military and civil expeditions which were surveying the new western territories.

In 1846 Lt. W. H. Emory collected and also sketched a few cacti while he was with the American Expeditionary force under Col. Kearny, during the conquest of New Mexico and California, and Engelmann treated these in an appendix to Emory's report in 1848.

Between 1849 and 1856 Emory, then Major, directed the United States and Mexican Boundary Survey. The personnel of this expedition were under instructions to make comprehensive studies of the natural history of the region traversed. A number of naturalists made large botanical collections. Among the botanists were Dr. Charles C. Parry, Prof. George Thurber, and Charles Wright. Important plant collections were also made by Dr. John L. LeConte and Arthur Schott, who were civilian geologists connected with the survey. Major Emory himself was an enthusiastic collector. All of the cactus specimens were sent to Dr. Engelmann.

During this period Dr. J. M. Bigelow and other naturalists with various Pacific Railroad Surveys were also sending cacti to Dr. Engelmann, who thus accumulated a tremendous herbarium collection from the rich, virgin cactus territory of southwestern United States. Engelmann published fourteen major papers on the Cactaceae between 1845 and 1878, in which he described well over 100 new species and about 50 new subspecies and varieties. Probably the two most important of Engelmann's publications were his *Synopsis of the Cactaceae of the United States*, in 1856, and the *Cactaceae of the Boundary*, in 1859, with 75 superb steel engraved plates.

Engelmann described *Echinocactus emoryi* in 1848, from drawings made by Lt. W. H. Emory of plants which he found on the Gila River between the mouths of "Rio Prieta" and the San Carlos River. Emory was with the reconnaissance party of Col. Kearny's United States Army force which was engaged in the conquest of the Mexican territories of New Mexico and California. Emory (1848, p. 65) gives the following account of the cactus:

> Following the course of this fire, as it bared the ground of shrubbery, and exposed the soil, etc., to view, I found what was to us a very great vegetable curiosity, a cactus, 18 inches high, and 18 inches in its greatest diameter, containing 20 vertical volutes, armed with strong spines. When the traveler is parched with thirst, one of these split open, will give sufficient liquid to afford relief. Several of these cacti were found torn from the earth, and lying in the dry bed of a stream.

Emory's drawings of cacti were submitted to Dr. Engelmann, who prepared tentative descriptions of them which were published in Emory's report. The drawings were inadequate for thorough botanical diagnosis, and Engelmann said (Emory 1848, p. 157) "my descriptions, however, and the names given by me, must remain doubtful till we are able to obtain some more data to characterize the species." The sketch of the *Echinocactus* was small and lacked detail, which prevented Engelmann's recognizing it as his own *E. wislizenii*. As a result of the necessarily inadequate original description of *E. emoryi*, another taxon became associated with that name. This is discussed under *Ferocactus covillei*.

Echinocactus wislizenii became well known from collections made by the Boundary Commission party and other government surveys. Engelmann's *Cactaceae of the Boundary* has two excellent plates illustrating the species 1859, plates 25 and 26).

Ferocactus wislizenii is a variable taxon with a broad distribution which includes ecological habitats with wide altitudinal and climatic range. The species probably also has gene exchange with *F. acanthodes* var. *lecontei* and *F. herrerae*. The large number of more or less distinct appearing forms has resulted in the description of several species and varieties. In 1878 Dr. Engelmann treated *Echinocactus lecontei*, which he had earlier described as a species, as a variety of *E. wislizenii*. In the same paper he described another variety, *E. wislizenii* var. *decipiens*, from plants collected by Rothrock at Camp Bowie, Arizona. The holotype specimen apparently represents the typical form of *E. wislizeni*, although the spines are only 4 cm long and the lower central spine is only slightly flattened. Specimens collected in Chihuahua by Dr. C. G. Pringle, his number 6875, are very much the same except that all of the central spines are straight.

In 1895 J. W. Toumey described *Echinocactus wislizeni* var. *albispina* as a form with yellow spines and flowers which was found in the foothills near Tucson. This variety has since been attributed to both *Ferocactus wislizenii* and *F. acanthodes*. Toumey (1895, p. 154) also mentioned a mountain form of the *F. wislizenii* relationship, which he said occurred north and east of Phoenix, and called the plant *Echinocactus thurberi*, but gave no description.

Mr. Charles Russel Orcutt published *Echinocactus falconeri* in 1902, based on a barrel cactus in the *wislizenii* complex from Batamoral, Sonora. In 1909 R. E. Kunze described *Echinocactus arizonicus* to name a red-flowered form of *wislizenii* from Pinal County, Arizona, and in 1913 published the name *Echinocactus wislizeni* var. *phoeniceus* for the purple-flowered plants which occur near Phoenix. Flower color apparently is not significant in *Ferocactus wislizenii*. The plants from near the type locality in New Mexico have yellow flowers, and Mr. Wm. Taylor Marshall showed me a colored photograph of two specimens growing side by side near Benson, Arizona, which were morphologically alike, but one had red flowers and the other clear yellow.

I have recognized but one varietal form in this treatment of *Ferocactus wislizenii*. It is possible that some of the other rather distinct forms deserve varietal recognition, but the material I have studied is not conclusive.

Plants in the *Ferocactus wislizenii* complex from the coastal region of Sonora and Sinaloa are perplexing. *Ferocactus herrerae* is a closely related species with 13 ribs, short gray central spines and twisted setaceous radial spines, which occurs in Sinaloa. A barrel cactus from western Sonora and northern Sinaloa appears to be intermediate between *F. herrerae* and *F. wislizenii* which occurs in its typical form in northern Sonora. The intermediate form has been referred to in the literature as *F. horridus* (Lowry 1936, p. 189), because it has 13 ribs, and has also appeared in the trade under that name. *Ferocactus horridus* was a name proposed for a little known plant in Lower California, which is actually *F. peninsulae*. In the spring of 1955 Dr. Ira L. Wiggins and I drove down the west coast of Mexico, from Nogales to Mazatlan. We paid particular attention to *F. wislizenii* as well as the 13 ribbed intermediate form to the south, and made collections at intervals of from 25 to 75 miles along the entire route. North of Ciudad Obregon the plants were referable to *F. wislizenii* although they had a reduced number of ribs. From Ciudad Obregon southward the plants came to resemble *F. herrerae*, with 13 deep ribs, short straight central spines, and radiating twisted white bristles. The change from *F. wislizenii* to *F. herrerae* was not constant, however. For example, a specimen taken 27.5 miles south of Ciudad Obregon, Sonora, (*Lindsay 2560*), was quite typical of *F. herrerae*, while other specimens from near Los Mochis, Sinaloa, (*Lindsay 2563*), were closer to *F. wislizenii*.

Another problem is the degree of relationship between *Ferocactus wislizenii* and *F. peninsulae*, which is a variable species common in central Lower California. There appear to be some constant characters which separate the two. *Ferocactus peninsulae* usually has fewer ribs than *F.*

wislizenii, but not fewer than the southern Sonoran "intermediate" population of that species. Also, *F. peninsulae* is usually a clavate plant with a smaller diameter, and its seeds lack the intricate secondary sculpturing in the depressions of the reticulations which appears to be characteristic of *F. wislizenii* and *F. herrerae*. It is difficult to justify separating the Sonoran population of *F. wislizenii* from *F. peninsulae*, and the two could probably be combined within a very broad species. On the other hand it would be even more difficult to consider the type specimens of *F. peninsulae* and *F. wislizenii* as representing the same taxon. I feel that *Ferocactus wislizenii* does not occur in Lower California or the islands on the western side of the Gulf of California.

Ferocactus wislizenii grows in an area where summer rains supply most of the moisture. They have great altitudinal range, from sea level in Sonora to 5,000 feet in Arizona, and may be found on grassy mesas, rocky ridges or hillsides, alluvial flats, and in the southern extension of their range in silt flats in thorn forests. The plants tend to incline toward the south and the directional orientation has resulted in the common name of "compass cactus." The root system is shallow and as the plants grow they may become off center and topple over, but they continue to grow and blossom in this prostrate position. Benson (1950, p. 97) states that the fruit are a favorite food of deer and rodents, and that the abundance of mammals in a region can be determined by the number of cactus fruit left in the spring.

Monstrous specimens of *Ferocactus wislizenii* are common and in these the rib structure is intermittent and the stem is covered with irregular tubercles and knobs. The apical meristem may divide and form a monstrous mass of heads. *Echinocactus hertrichii* Weinberg is probably one of these monstrous forms, although it has sometimes been attributed to a similar monstrous type of *Ferocactus acanthodes* var. *lecontei*.

12b. FEROCACTUS WISLIZENII (Engelmann) Britton and Rose var. TIBURONENSIS Lindsay, Cact. and Succ. Journ. 27: 166. 1955.

STEM simple, globose to short columnar, to 1 m tall and 3.5 dm wide. RIBS about 21, 3 cm tall, slightly tuberculate. AREOLES large, oval, to 3 cm long and 1.5 cm wide, becoming approximate in age; brown tomentose in youth. SPINES usually heavily annulated, not clearly differentiated into a radial and central series; the 4 most central spines terete, cruciform in arrangement, straight or somewhat tortuously twisted, the lower sometimes flattened and to 9 cm long; radial spines subulate, annulate, strongly resembling the centrals but not as heavy, though never setaceous; nectiferous gland-spines produced between flower and spine bundle of flowering areoles. FLOWERS yellow, funnelform, 6 cm long and 5 cm wide; scales on ovary broad, obtuse, with auriculate base and slightly ciliate margins, the ovary scales intergrading with those on the tube; lower outer perianth segments very broad, 20 mm long and 17 mm wide, sub-deltoid, yellow or reddish; inner perianth segments yellow, broad lanceolate, to 40 mm long and 11 mm wide, margins serrulate; walls of tube 7 mm thick; stamens very numerous, yellow to red, 5-15 mm long, attached to thickened tube between the base of perianth segments and the nectary pit located between the base of the tube and style; style 30 mm long, 4 mm thick, yellow, furrowed, the top 5 mm divided into about 20 yellow stigma lobes. FRUIT fleshy, yellow, when dried 2-3 cm long and to 2.5 cm wide, with the persistent withered perianth included about 6 cm long. SEED black, 2.5 mm long and 1.75 mm wide, rounded, with double reticulate sculpturing but only a trace of figuring inside the central depressions; hilum small, round, and white.

Holotype: Southeast corner of Tiburon Island, Gulf of California, Mexico, *Lindsay 2229* (DS).

Distribution: Known only from Tiburon Island, Gulf of California, Mexico. Map number four.

Representative specimens: MEXICO: TIBURON ISLAND: Ensenada Perro, SE corner of island, *Lindsay 2229* (DS, holotype); SE corner of island, *Johnston 4270* (CAS); 3 mi. N Willard's Point, frequent on rocky hillsides, 20 ribs, 22 in. high and 11 in. in diameter, *Johnston 4251* (CAS).

The barrel cactus on Tiburon Island is doubtlessly of the *Ferocactus wislizenii* complex, but a number of differences separate it from the typical form. I first saw the plants of Tiburon on April 3, 1947, when they were in sterile condition, and assumed that they were the normal form of *F. wislizenii* which occurs on the Sonoran mainland. Dr. Reid Moran and I again visited Tiburon on May 5, 1952, while we were with the Sefton Foundation—Stanford University expedition to the Gulf of California. This time the barrel cacti were in full bloom, with a compact cluster of clear yellow flowers in the center of each plant. Apparently the blossoming period was well advanced because there were few buds, but many spent flowers with almost fully developed fruit. The typical variety does not blossom before mid-summer, and the fruit mature the following winter, remaining on the plants through spring. Also, the flowers of the typical form in Sonora are red, and appear in a crown away from the apex of the plant, rather than in a compact central cluster. The spines of the Tiburon plant were variable, but lacked the characteristic setaceous radials and distinctly flattened, hooked lower central of the typical variety. The seed of the Tiburon plant had reticulations similar to those of typical *F. wislizenii* but the secondary figuring in the depressions was not as conspicuous. The above combination of factors indicated that the Tiburon barrel cactus required varietal recognition so I described it as *Ferocactus wislizenii* var. *tiburonensis.*

Johnston had collected two specimens of var. *tiburonensis* in 1921, his number 4270 from the southeast corner of the island, and number 4251 from near Willard's Point. Johnston *no.* 4270 from the type locality furnished the material from the description of the fruit and seeds, and was a particularly heavily armed plant, with coarse, tortuous heavily annulated spines to 9 cm long.

Figure 53. ***Ferocactus wislizenii*** **var.** ***wislizenii*** **photographed ten miles east of Coolidge Dam, Arizona, August 23, 1951. The first blossoms of the season had just opened.**

Figure 54. *Ferocactus wislizenii*, detail of the flowers of the plant shown in figure 53. The six flowers shown were the first to appear, and the blossoming period would extend through September.

Figure 55. ***Ferocactus wisllzenii*** **var.** ***wislizenii*****, monstrose specimen photographed 20 miles north of Tucson, Arizona. This is probably the form on which Weinberg based his** ***Echinocactus hertrichii*****.**

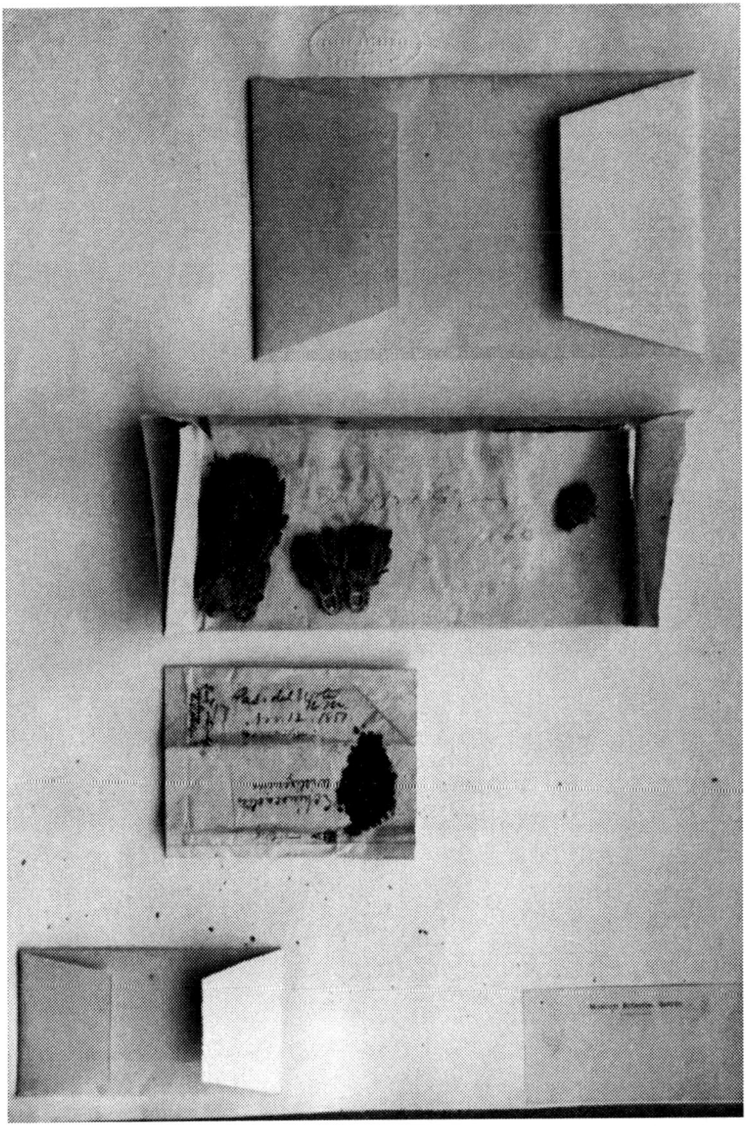

Figure 56. Holotype specimen of *Echinocactus wislizenii*, the upper specimen the original collection by Dr. Wislizenus in 1846. From the Geoege Engelmann herbarium, now preserved at the Missouri Botanical Garden.

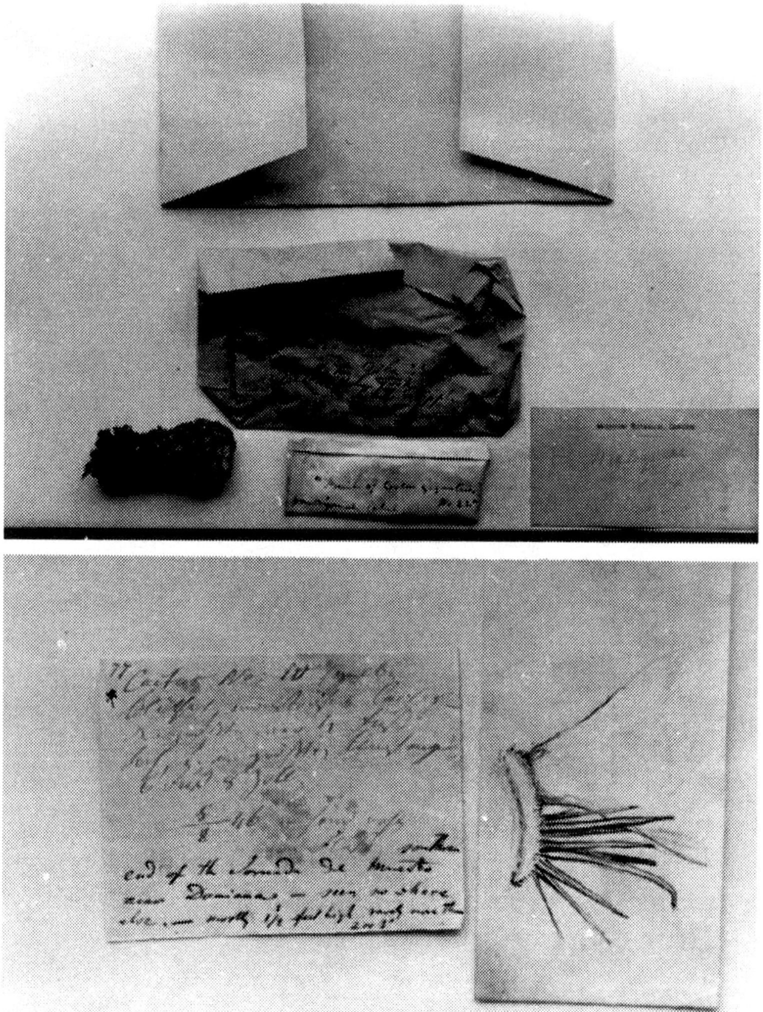

Figure 57. Early specimens of *Echinocactus wislizenii* from the George Engelmann herbarium. Above, specimen collected by Lt. Whipple. Below, the original sketch by Dr. Wislizenus, which formed part of Engelmann's type material.

Figure 58. *Ferocactus wislizenii* var. *wislizenii*, *Lindsay 2563*, from near Los Mochis, Sinaloa.

Figure 59. ***Ferocactus wislizenii*** **var.** ***wislizenii*****, fruit of the Sinaloa specimen shown in figure 58.**

Figure 60. *Ferocactus wislizenii* var. *tiburonensis*, the plant from which the holotype specimen was taken, photographed at the southeast corner of Tiburon Island, Gulf of California, Mexico.

Figure 61. ***Ferocactus wislizenii*** **var.** ***tiburonensis*****, detail of flowers. Note that the blossoming period is well advanced and some of the fruit are nearing maturity, on May 5, 1952.**

13. FEROCACTUS HERRERAE Ortega, Mexico Forestal 5: 52. 1927.

STEM simple, globose to columnar, to 2 m tall and 4.5 dm wide. RIBS 13, acute, deep, often spiraled, strongly tuberculate in juvenile plants but not in mature specimens. AREOLES elliptic, 2 dm long, with white to gray tomentum, widely spaced on the ribs. SPINES vary with the maturity of the plant; seedlings 6 cm wide have one reddish hooked central spine and 8 straight radial spines, with no bristles; plants 25 cm tall and broad have 6 gray, annulate central spines, the principal one to 10 cm long and 5 mm wide with an angled or hooked tip, and a series of white, twisted, radiating bristles; in plants over 5 dm tall the principal central spine is straight and diamond-shaped instead of flattened, and the radial bristles are few or absent. FLOWERS funnelform, 6 cm long and wide, the ovary 15 mm long and wide; scales of ovary cordate, 3 mm long and 4 mm wide, red at the base and with yellow margins; outer perianth segments narrow at base, widening above, red with yellow margins; inner perianth segments lanceolate with acute tip, 5 cm long and 9 mm wide, with a red midstripe and clear yellow margins; stamens numerous, 15-20 mm long, filaments yellow to red; pistil 25 mm long, with about 24 stigma lobes. FRUIT oblong, 4-6 cm long and 25-30 mm wide, greenish yellow, fleshy, dehiscing through a large basal pore. SEED black or dark brown, 2.25 mm long, 1.5 mm wide, rather angular, sometimes somewhat crested, with shallow polygonal sculpturing.

Holotype: A band along the coast 10 km wide, from Mazatlan to Ahome, Sinaloa, Mexico, and in Sianori, Durango, Mexico, to 1,200 meters above sea level, *Ortega s. n.* (MEXU). The specimen in the Biological Institute of the University of Mexico, which is assumed to be the holotype, has no definite locality data. It includes flowers, fruit, the original publication and a number of photographs.

Distribution: Coastal plains of Sinaloa, and southwestern Sonora, and mountains of western Durango, Mexico. Map number three.

Representative specimens: MEXICO: SINALOA: A band along the coast 10 km wide, from Mazatlan to Ahome, *Ortega s. n.* (MEXU, holotype); Rocky hills and flats, not far from highway, Pericos, *Schwarz 229* (DS); Altata, Brandegee s. n. Sept. 2, 1902 (UC); San Blas, *Jones 22967* (POM); Sonora, 27.5 mi. S Ciudad Obregon, *Lindsay 2560* (DS,SD).

The spines of *Ferocactus herrerae* vary with the age of the plant. Young seedlings have one hooked central spine with eight radiating radials, all of which are comparatively heavy, and there are no bristles. Specimens between 25 and 50 cm tall have six central spines, the principal one flattened and usually curved or hooked at the tip, and a series of twisted white bristles. In specimens over 5 dm tall the main central spine is straight and the radial bristles are often lacking. Dr. Ortega reported that he first thought two species were represented. The natives in the region agreed, and called the smaller plants, which they used for making cactus candy, "visnaga hembra," and the larger plants were called "visnaga macho." Dr. Ortega came to suspect that the two types were simply different stages of maturity of a single species when he was unable to find small plants of the straight-spined form or large plants with curved central spines and twisted bristles. He also observed that large plants, which hunters cut off to attract deer during periods of drouth, produced small offshoot branches with the juvenile type spines. Additional observations showed that only one species was represented.

The character of a hooked or straight central spine is not particularly significant. The population of *Ferocactus covillei* near Guaymas has strongly hooked central spines in young plants and all straight spines in the adults. Straight-spined forms of *F. wislizenii* appear in Chihuahua, and straight-spined specimens of *F. townsendianus* are not unusual in Lower California.

Ferocactus herrerae is closely related to *F. wislizenii*, but has only 13 ribs, as contrasted with about 25 for *wislizenii*, and differs also in the character of the spines and the reticulation of the seed coat. The habitat of the two species is quite different. *Ferocactus herrerae* grows on the floor of arid tropical forests, often in flats covered with dense vegetation which becomes impenetrable during the summer rainy season, and the habitat of the species is not particularly xerophytic. Associated species include such tropical types as *Haematoxylum brasiletto, Ceiba acuminata, Ipomoea arborescens, Tabebuia palmeri, Pachycereus pecten-aboriginum*, etc.

A large population of southern Sonoran barrel cacti which appear to be intermediate between *Ferocactus herraeae* and *F. wislizenii* is discussed under the latter species.

Figure 62. *Ferocactus herrerae*, a Plant collected by Mr. Frltz Schwarz between Culiacan and Perlcos, Sinaloa, Mexico.

Figure 63. ***Ferocactus herrerae*** **(*Lindsay*) photographed 27.5 miles south of Ciudad Obregon, Sonora.**

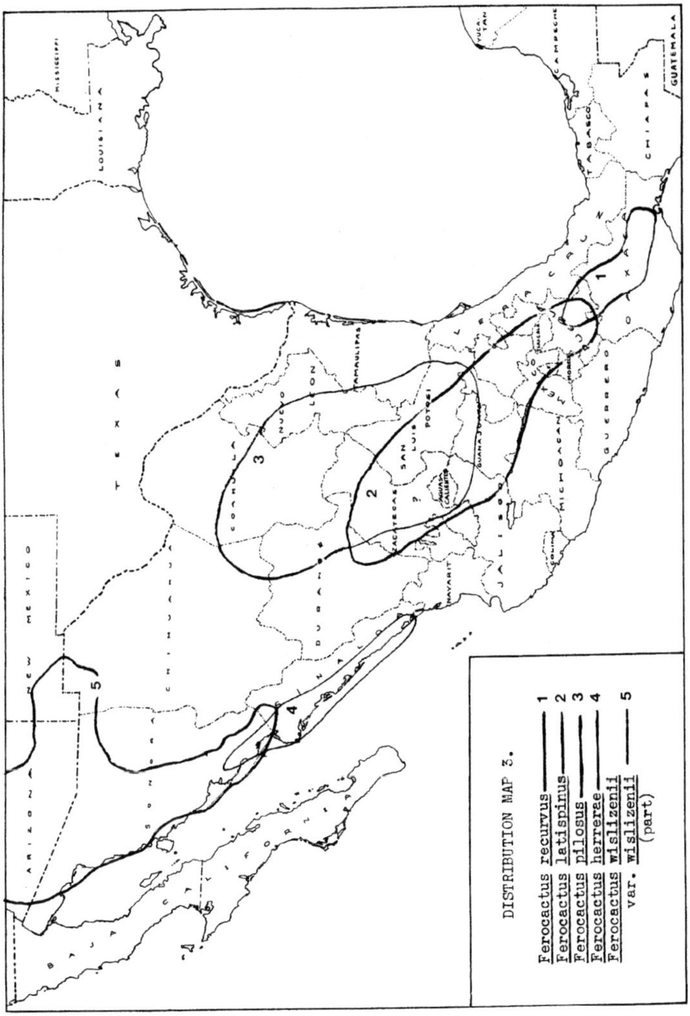

Distribution Map 3

14. FEROCACTUS COVILLEI Britton and Rose, Cactaceae 3: 132. 1922.

Editors' Note: *The species name* covillei *has been changed back to* emoryi (Engelmann).

Echinocactus covillei (Britton and Rose) Berger, Kakteen 238. 1929.

Ferocactus emoryi (Engelmann) Y. Ito, Cacti 1952 104. 1952.

STEM simple, globular to cylindric, to 2.5 m tall and 6 dm in diameter. RIBS 15-32, to 5 cm deep and as broad, often very distinctly tuberculate in youth, but not in mature specimens. AREOLES large, flowering areoles sometimes 4 cm long and 17 mm wide, the spine-bearing portion nearly 3 cm long, young areoles bearing dense yellow tomentum, this eroding away and turning gray; SPINES variable as to number, size, shape, and color; usually pinkish gray or horn color, very robust, annulate, bristles never present; central spine 1, porrect, terete or sometimes flattened dorsi-ventrally, straight or hooked, 4-10 cm long, in some specimens 4 mm in diameter towards the base; radial spines 6-8, erect spreading, straight or slightly curved, terete or angled or flattened dorsi-ventrally, usually about two thirds as long as the central, nectareous gland-spines conspicuous, in a central position between spine-bearing and flower-bearing portion of the areole, a single central one appearing first, but older areoles showing up to 12, some of which may be 5 mm long and 2 mm broad, becoming spinescent. FLOWERS mahogany, red, red tinged with yellow, or clear yellow, to 7 cm long and 5 cm broad, broad scales on the ovary and tube blending into outer perianth segments; inner perianth segments linear oblong, acuminate, often serrate, mahogany red to lemon yellow. FRUIT obovoid to oblong, to 5 cm long and 3 cm broad, with broad cordate scales, ovary walls thick and fleshy, persisting on plant and drying to very hard capsule, often not opening by basal pore. SEED dark brown or black, rounded, 2 mm long, 1.5 mm wide, and 1 mm thick, pitted with fine circular or oval depressions, sometimes somewhat crested on side opposite the hilum.

Holotype: Hills and Mesas near Altar, Sonora, Mexico, *C. G. Pringle 342*, August 11, 1884 (US).

Distribution: South Central Arizona to south to Guaymas, Sonora. In Arizona usually found between 1,500 ft. and 3,000 ft. elevation, mostly in the Organ Pipe National Monument and the Papago Indian Reservation in Pima County, with isolated colonies in Maricopa and Pinal counties. Common in the area about Magdalena, Sonora, at about 2,000 ft. elevation, and at sea level at Guaymas, San Carlos Bay, and San Pedro Bay. Map number four.

Representative specimens: ARIZONA: PIMA CO.: Fedington Canyon, Baboquivari Mts., *Benson s.n.*, Oct. 18, 1939 (ARIZ); Growler Mts. near Bates Well, alt. 1,300 ft., *Benson 9895* (POM); Wash 10 mi. south Bates Well, *Benson 9917* (POM); 1 mi. east Bates Well, *Benson 9896* (POM); Quijotoa Mts., *Blakley & Speck 262* (DES); 7 mi. east Papago Wells, *Harbison s.n.*, Mar. 14, 1937 (SD); Fresnal Canyon, Papago Indian Reservation, *Loomis SF112* (ARIZ); Fresnal Canyon, *Loomis SF84* (ARIZ); near Bates Well, Growler Mts., *Peebles 14546*, and *14546A* (ARIZ); Hills near Sells, *Peebles SF160* (ARIZ); Bates Well to Quitovaquito, *Peebles 14551* (ARIZ); rocky hillside at NW end Coyote Mts., 48 mi. W. Tucson on road to Ajo, *Wiggins 8696* (DS); SONORA: Road between Caborca and Quitovac, 3 mi. N. San Pedro, *Keck 4115* (DS); Plains between Veruga Pass and Pozo Cerna, *Wiggins 6028* (DS); hills and mesas near Altar, *Pringle 342*, holotype (US); 4.8 mi. N. Magalena, *Lindsay 2550*, *2551*, and *2552* (DS,SD); dry hillsides, El Alamo, near Magdalena, *Kennedy 7115* (CAS); 66 mi. S. Magdalena, *Lindsay 2553* (DS,SD); San Pedro Bay, *Johnston 4292* (CAS), *Lindsay 2222* (DS,SD); San Carlos Bay, *Johnston 4348* (CAS), *Dawson 1009*, and *1009A* (AHFH); Guaymas, *M.E. Jones s.n.*, Nov. 2, 1926 (POM).

Britton and Rose proposed the name *Ferocactus covillei* for the taxon which had theretofore been called *Echinocactus emoryii* when they found that the latter was actually based on material of another taxon, *E. wislizeni*.

In 1846 and 1847, the then First Lieutenant W. H. Emory made a reconnaissance for an overland route from Ft. Leavenworth to San Diego, in connection with the western expeditionary army of Col. Kearney. Lt. Emory collected botanical specimens on the trip, which were later reported by John Torrey, and made drawings of the cacti which he encountered. The drawings were submitted to Dr. Engelmann, who used them as the basis of a number of new species which were published as an appendix to Emory's report in 1848.

Among the drawings was a rather small sketch of a plant which Emory had found on October 25, 1846, on the Gila River between Prieto and San Carlos creeks. Engelmann described *Echinocactus emoryii* from this sketch and from seed from the plant. Emory's journal for Oct. 25 notes "I found what was to us a very great vegetable curiosity, a cactus, 18 inches high, and 18 inches in its greatest diameter, containing 20 vertical volutes, armed with strong spines. When the traveler is parched with thirst, one of these split open, will give sufficient liquid to afford relief."

The original sketch was small and inaccurate, and the description based on it was vague and generalized. As a result the name was applied to new species being discovered during the western exploration. Bigelow, in Engelmann and Bigelow's report of the Cactaceae in the Pacific Railway

Report, said that *Echinocactus emoryii* had been collected west of the Colorado, in the Valley of the Mojave, mixed with *E. polycephalus*. This must have been *Ferocactus acanthodes* var. *lecontei*. Bigelow also reported purchasing, in San Francisco, a plant which had been brought from Guaymas, Sonora, and this specimen was sent to Washington under the name of *Echinocactus emoryii*. The figure of two areoles of *E. emoryii* in Plate Three of the *Cactaceae of the Pacific Railway Report* was probably drawn from the Guaymas specimen. The original drawing from which the plate was made is number 1519 in Engelmann's notes preserved at the Missouri Botanical Garden, and is marked "Bigelow's" at the bottom.

Engelmann's treatment of *Echinocactus emoryii* in the *Cactaceae of the Boundary Survey* was based on plants collected by Schott south of the Gila River, where *Ferocactus covillei* occurs. By this time the association of *Ferocactus covillei* with the name *Echinocactus emoryii* was firmly established, until Britton and Rose found that the type locality of *E. emoryii* indicated that the original specimen could only have been *E. wislizeni*, and proposed the new name *Ferocactus covillei* for the orphaned taxon.

Britton and Rose (1922, p. 132) state that the type locality of *E. emoryii* was in southwestern New Mexico. Actually it is in southeastern Arizona, near Coolidge Dam. I have collected the *Ferocactus* there and it is typical *F. wislizeni* (*Lindsay 2025* (DS)).

Ferocactus covillei is a neat and distinct species. Young plants have a clean appearance because their long spines, which encase them in a cage, are widely separated and the plant body is plainly visible. In southern Arizona this species grows on rocky slopes and alluvial plains between 1,500 and 3,000 feet elevation. There the plants are usually under three feet tall, and form a characteristic element of the foothill vegetation. Associated plants include *Carnegiea gigantea, Opuntia fulgida, Lemaireocereus thurberi, Echinocereus engelmanni, Fouquieria splendens, Olneya tesota, Krameria gravi, K. parvifolia, Cercidium floridum, C. microphyllum, Prosopis juliflora* var. *velutina, Acacia greggii*, etc.

Ferocactus covillei becomes very large in the southern section of its range. I have seen specimens eight feet tall and two feet in diameter growing in silty plains near Guaymas, and plants over five feet tall are to be found on the rocky headlands at San Pedro and San Carlos Bays, Sonora. The spines of mature plants in the southern area are all straight, but young plants less than ten inches in diameter have the strongly hooked central spines characteristic of the species in Arizona. In the Guaymas area *Ferocactus covillei* grows at sea level, often on broad silt plains, and is associated with *Lophocereus schottii, Pachycereus pecten-aboriginum, Opuntia fulgida, Acacia willardiana, Larrea tridentata, Olneya tesota, Simmondsia chinensis, Cercidium microphyllum, C. sonorae, Forchammeria watsonii*, etc.

The spines of *Ferocactus covillei* are quite variable, but are always strong, annulate, and few in number. Lateral bristles which are found in many barrel cacti are never present. The central spine is always hooked in juvenile specimens, but may be straight in adults. In some specimens the central spines are five inches long, in others only one and a half inches. Often the spines are flattened dorsi-ventrally in contrast to the laterally flattened spines more characteristic of the genus.

Ferocactus covillei is used to make cactus candy, and the pulp has been crushed and the liquid it contains extracted to use for an emergency water supply. During times of drouth the spines are removed from the large plants, and the pulp is chopped up and used for stock food. This use is common with many of the larger species of *Ferocactus,* but is particularly obvious with this one, because the large specimens which formed a conspicuous feature of the landscape near Guaymas only a few years ago have nearly all been utilized. *Ferocactus covillei* was named for Dr. F. V. Coville, who was curator of the U. S. National Herbarium.

Figure 64. *Ferocactus covillei*, holotype specimen.

Figure 65. ***Ferocactus covillei*, a large specimen growing on the plains north of Guaymas, Sonora.**

Figure 66. *Ferocactus covillei*, a juvenile specimen from Guaymas, Sonora. Note the tuberculate ribs and strongly hooked central spines which are characteristic of young plants of this species.

Figure 67. *Ferocactus covillei*, (*Lindsay 2251*), from 4.8 miles north of Magdalena, Sonora. The rather straight central spines are typical of adult plants in the southern part of the range of this species. Plants from Arizona usually have strongly hooked central spines.

Figure 68. *Ferocactus covillei*, (*Lindsay 2251*), showing details of fruit and the dorsi-ventrally flattened spines.

15. FEROCACTUS RECTISPINUS (Engelmann, in Coulter) Britton and Rose, Cactaceae 3:134. 1922.

Echinocactus emoryi rectispinus Engelmann, in Coulter, Contr. U.S. Nat. Herb. 3: 362. 1896.

Echinocactus rectospinus (Engelmann, in Coulter) Britton and Rose, Journ. N.Y. Bot. Gard. 12: 269. 1911. (Spelled *rectospinus* in this reference.)

STEM simple, globose to cylindric, to 1.5 m tall and 4.5 dm wide. RIBS about 21, tuberculate, deep, sometimes twisted or spiraled. AREOLES large, 3 cm long and 1 cm wide, the spiniferous portion oval, above which is a protuberance with several persistent nectareous gland-spines, and at the top a large oval scar where the fruit abscissed; young areoles bear short light gray tomentum; areoles at first about 1 cm apart, becoming approximate in age, the top becoming truncate by being curled under the tubercle above. SPINES all straight, terete, annulate, reddish or blotched red and yellow; central spine 1, porrect, 9-25 cm long and 2.5 mm wide; radial spines 7-9, like the central but only 1.5-6 cm long, the three upper radials sometimes longer than the lowers. FLOWERS 6 cm long, clear light yellow, the scales on the ovary rounded, thin margined, sometimes ciliate; inner perianth segments lemon yellow, lanceolate, 5 cm long, acuminate. FRUIT yellow, fleshy, 3.5 cm long and 2.5 cm wide, 7 cm long including the persistent withered perianth; ovary covered with wide, brown, ciliate scales, the basal pore not opening. SEEDS black, about 2 mm long and 1.5 mm wide, pitted with small round or oval depressions, not reticulate; hilum small, round, terminal.

Holotype: Near Muleje, Lower California, Mexico, *Gabb 12* (MBG).

Distribution: San Ignacio to Commondu, Lower California, Mexico. Map number four.

Representative specimens: MEXICO: LOWER CALIFORNIA: Near Muleje, *Gabb 12* (MBG, holotype); 5 mi. W. Canipole, growing on rocky ridges, *Lindsay 1989* (DS,SD); foot of Coyote Grade (Cuesta del Coyote) 20 mi. S.Muleje, *Wiggins 11,414* (DS,SD); Head of Conception Bay, *Rose 16671* (CAS).

William M. Gabb collected two areoles and spine clusters of this species in 1867, and the specimens, with sketches of the plant, were turned over to Dr. Engelmann. Engelmann prepared a description from the material, which he thought represented a variety of *Ferocactus covillei*, then known as *Echinocactus emoryii*, because of the absence of secondary radial spines. Engelmann did not publish the species during his lifetime, but John Coulter formally described it from the Engelmann manuscripts, as *Echinocactus emoryii rectispinus.* In error the length of the central spine was given as 30-32 cm, instead of 12- 13 as indicated in Engelmann's manuscript and the type specimen. Mr. Howard E. Gates, however, collected a specimen with spines over 26 cm long, in the Sierra Giganta, near Carrizal Ranch in the mountains near Comondu (Gates 1931, p. 390). This must be a record spine-length for the Echinocactanae.

Britton and Rose raised the variety to specific rank in 1911, after Rose had collected it at Conception Bay. They misspelled the name as *Echinocactus rectospinus.*

I know the flowers of this species only from illustrations and the description. A colored illustration in *The Cactaceae* 3, plate 5, is from a plant collected by Dr. Rose at the head of Conception Bay and sent to the New York Botanical Garden. It indicates the scales and perianth segments are very broad. Mr. John P. Figg-Hoblyn photographed a plant in flower six miles southwest of Canipole, Lower California, on August 30, 1955. The photographs are in color, and show an exceptionally brilliant clear yelow flower. Mr. Figg-Hoblyn has kindly allowed me to make and include monochrome copies of his photographs, which are reproduced in Plates 62 and 63. It is interesting to note the late date of appearance of the flowers, the first one of which had opened the last of August.

On April 28, 1952, Dr. Howard Scott Gentry photographed *Ferocactus rectispinus* at La Champagna, Sierra de las Palmas, Lower California, where the plants were globose, 6-10 dm tall. This was between 4,000 and 5,000 feet elevation, which seems rather high for the species, which occurs also at sea level, along Conception Bay.

Figure 69. ***Ferocactus rectispinus*****, (*****Lindsay 1989*****), from 5 miles west of Canipole, Lower California, Mexico.**

Figure 70. *Ferocactus rectispinus* from six miles southwest of Canipole, Lower California, in flower August 30, 1955. From a kodachrome transparency by Mr. John P. Figg-Hoblyn.

Figure 71. *Ferocactus rectispinus*, flower detail of the plant in figure 70. From a kodachrome transparency by Mr. John P. Figg-Hoblyn.

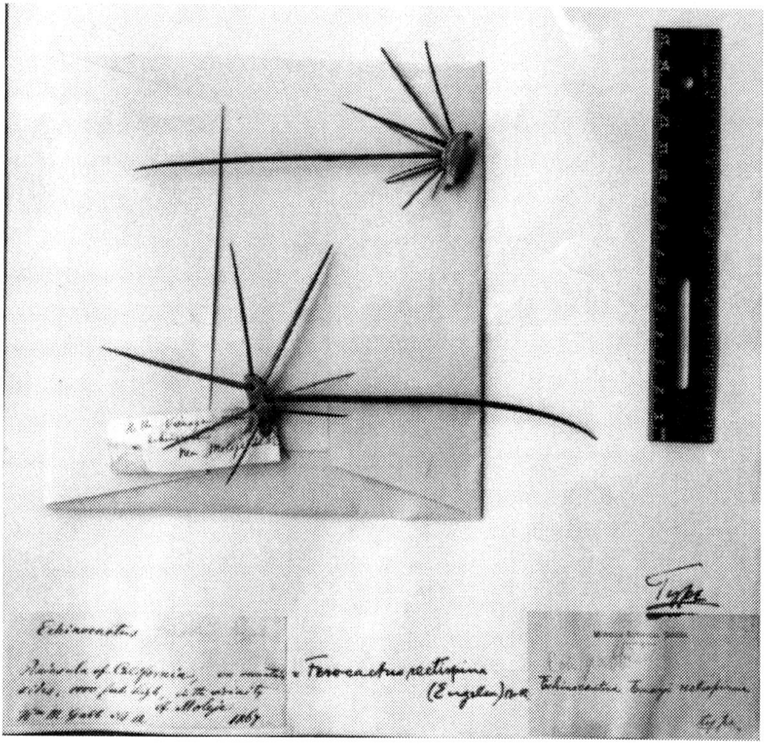

Figure 72. Holotype specimen, *Echinocactus emoryii rectispinus*.

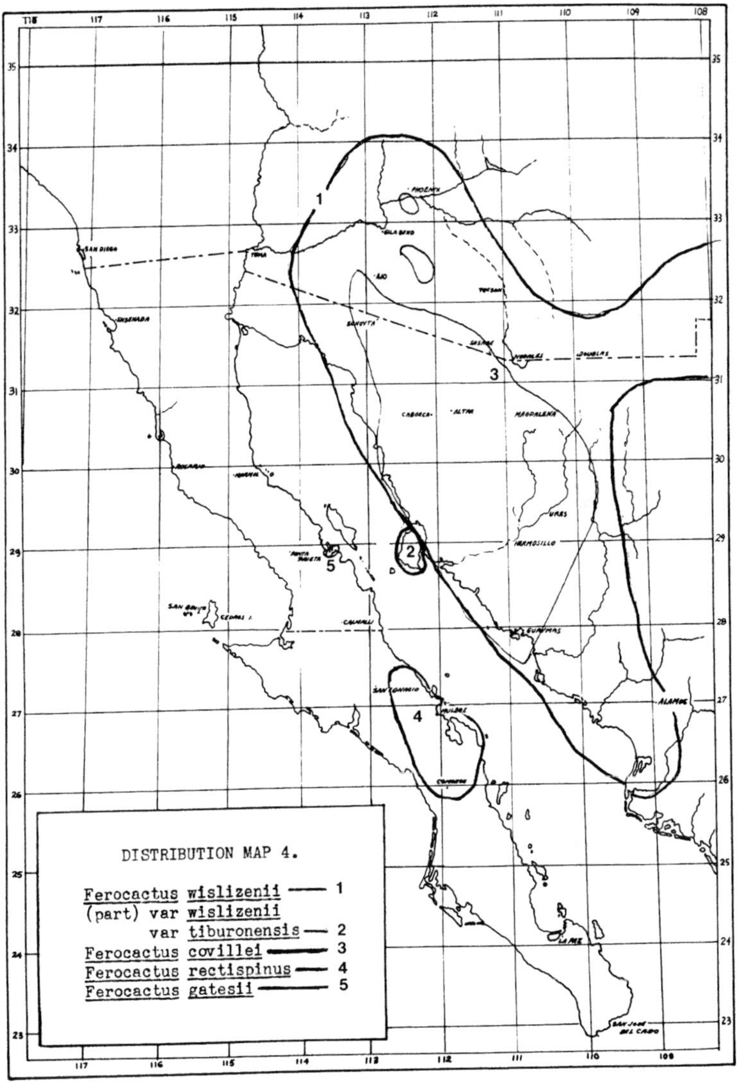

Distribution Map 4

16. FEROCACTUS PENINSULAE (Engelmann, ex Weber) Britton and Rose, Cactaceae 3: 133. 1922.

Key to the varieties

a. Spines usually gray, the principal central spine only slightly flattened but strongly hooked, flowers over 5 cm long, outer perianth segments broad, spatulate . . . . *F. p.* var. *peninsulae*.

b. Spines usually red, the principal central spine usually much flattened and not strongly hooked, flowers under 5 cm long, outer per ianth segments narrow, lanceolate, acuminate . . . . *F. p.* var. *viscainensis*.

16a. FEROCACTUS PENINSULAE (Engelmann, ex Weber) Britton and Rose var. PENINSULAE

Echinocactus peninsulae Engelmann, ex Weber, Bull. Mus. Hist. Nat. Paris 1: 320. 1895.

Ferocactus horridus Britton and Rose, Cactaceae 3: 128. 1922.

Ferocactus peninsulae (Engelmann, ex Weber) Britton and Rose, Cactaceae 3: 133. 1922.

STEM simple, ovoid becoming clavate, to 2.5 m tall and 4 dm wide. RIBS 12-20, prominent, rather deep. AREOLES 20 mm long and 8 mm wide, with gray tomentum in youth, and constricted between the flower and spine bearing portions. SPINES grayish red with yellow tips; central spines 4, cruciform, annulate, all straight and not particularly flattened except the lower one, which is flattened, hooked at the end, 4-15 cm long and 6 mm wide; radial spines variable, usually about 11, usually annulate, subulate, and straight, but sometimes twisted setaceous; the 3 lower radial spines are well developed and much like the centrals in character, but occupy a radial position; about 6 small persistent nectariferous gland-spines are produced above the spine fascicle in flowering areoles. FLOWERS funnelform, 5-6 cm long, with smooth imbricate scales on ovary and tube; perianth segments golden yellow with red midstripe; stamens orange, appressed against the style; from the outside the flower appears orange, from the inside, yellow. FRUIT globular, yellow, to 3 cm long, 2-2.5 cm wide, with yellow fleshy scales; dried persistent perianth about 4 cm long. SEED reddish brown or black, about 2 mm long and 1.5 mm wide, sculptured with oval or elongate reticulations.

Holotype: "Cape San Lucas to near San Diego along the coast of the Peninsula of California in gravelly soil, rarer in the mountains, *William M. Gabb No. 11*, 1867," from the George Engelmann herbarium (MBG). The specimen consists of a section of rib with two spine clusters. It was probably collected near Muleje, because Engelmann's notes for *Echinocactus emoryi* var. *rectispinus*, based on *Gabb's number 12*, say: "Resembles No. 11 (*Echinocactus peninsulae*) in form, habit, etc. except in the character of the spines, therefore undoubtedly a distinct species; found only in the vicinity of Moleje, on the mountain sides, 1,000 feet high . . .Found in the same locality where No. 11 (*Echinocactus peninsulae*) was found but much more restricted."

Distribution: Central Lower California, Mexico, from Los Angeles Bay and the Sierra San Borjas to the Cape region, where it is replaced by *Ferocactus townsendianus*. Map number five.

Representative specimens. MEXICO; LOWER CALIFORNIA: Lower California, probably near Muleje, *Gabb 11* (MBG); Los Angeles Bay, *Johnston 3453* and *3454* (CAS); San Francisquito Bay, *Rose 16746* (US, holotype of *F. horridus*); *Johnston 4190* (CAS); *Lindsay 515, 2242* (DS,SD); *Moran 4118* (DS,SD); 20 mi. inland from Santa Rosalia, *Lindsay 1996* (DS,SD); Muleje, *Wiggins 5718* (DS); Guadalupe Point, Conception Bay, *Johnston 4162* and *4163ul* (CAS); Coyote Point, Conception Bay, *Moran 3942* (DS,SD); 4 mi. W. San Luis Gonzaga, *Lindsay 1979* (DS,SD).

Mr. William M. Gabb, of the California State Geological Survey, made a mule-back mineral prospecting trip through Lower California from Cape San Lucas to San Diego in 1867. Gabb collected a number of fragments of cacti on the journey, and sent them to Dr. Engelmann in St. Louis. Engelmann prepared manuscript descriptions and proposed tentative names for the new species, which he did not publish. Among these was one based on Gabb's number 11, from near Muleje, which he proposed to call *Echinocactus peninsulae*. Before Engelmann died in 1884 he apparently wrote to Dr. Weber about the proposed species, which he felt was in the *Echinocactus wislizeni* complex.

Between 1891 and 1894 Dr. John Coulter wrote a preliminary revision of the North American Cactaceae, and in the course of its preparation studied Engelmann's specimens, notes, and "the diagnoses of many unpublished species which had come into his hands, notably those collected by Mr. William Gabb in 1867 in Lower Californis," (Coulter 1894, p. 92). Coulter published *Echinocactus pennsulae* in 1896, attributing both the name and description to Engelmann.

In 1894 Leon Diguet, a scientific explorer and collector for the Paris Museum, sent Dr. Weber a photograph and possibly some herbarium material of a large barrel cactus from near the 27th parallel in Lower California. Weber described the plant as *Echinocactus peninsulae* in a paper, *Les Cactees de la Basse Californie*, in 1895. Weber did not attribute the name to Engelmann, but indicated that Engelmann had agreed that it was a new species, saying "D'accord avec feu Engelmann (*in litteris*), je le considere comme une espece distincte, que je propose d'appeler *Echinocactus Peninsulae*." Weber did not credit the species to Engelmann, who had tentatively proposed the name more than ten years before Diguet made the photograph used by Weber in his description. The name at least is Engelmann's, and Weber's original description includes no data not in Engelmann's manuscript. Schumann, in 1898 (page 355), attributed the species to Engelmann, citing it "*Echinocactus peninsulae* Eng. ms. bei Web. in Bull. mus. Paris I. 5 (sonderabd.) (1894)." No material of *Echinocactus peninsulae* is preserved at the Paris Museum, and it seems safe to assume that Weber's description was at least partially based on the Gabb specimen, which I have cited as the holotype. The name of the species, and probably also at least part of the original description, was doubtlessly furnished by Engelmann, in spite of the fact that Weber did not so indicate. Engelmann had proposed the name, in manuscript, more than ten years before Diguet took the photograph cited by Weber.

Ferocactus peninsulae is the common barrel cactus through much of Lower California, as Weber pointed out in his articles. Dr. Rose did not recognize the species when he collected it at San Francisquito Bay in 1911, and with Britton later published it as *Ferocactus horridus*. Dr. Ivan M. Johnston collected *F. peninsulae* at Los Angeles Bay, San Francisquito Bay, and Conception Bay in 1921, but thought those specimens belonged with *F. wislizeni* (Johnston 1924, p. 1111). *Ferocactus peninsulae* is very close to *F. wislizeni*, or at least to the variant of *F. wislizeni* which occurs in central Sonora, but is separated from that taxon by having a clavate stem, fewer ribs, fewer spines, slightly different flowers, simply sculptured seeds, and possibly other characters. It is also closely related to *F. townsendianus*, which replaces it in the Cape region of the peninsula.

Ferocactus peninsulae apparently intergrades with *F. rectispinus*, a yellow-flowered species with very long straight spines and no fine radial spines. The two species share the same habitat from San Ignacio to Comondu, and intergrades which appear to be hybrids are fairly common, particularly between Santa Rosalia and San Ignacio. Johnston's number 4163, from Guadalupe Point, Conception Bay, is a good example of the suspected hybrid form. Some of the areoles lack fine radial spines and others have them, and the principal central spines are to 11 cm long and only slightly curved at the tips.

16b. FEROCACTUS PENINSULAE (Engelmann, ex Weber) Britton and Rose var. VISCAINENSIS (GATES) Lindsay, Cact. and Succ. Journ. 27: 169. 1955.

Ferocactus viscainensis Gates, Cat. and Succ. Journ. 4: 324. 1933.

STEM simple, globose to subcylindric, clavate, to 1.5 m tall and 3 dm wide. RIBS 13-21, distinctly tuberculate, thin, deep, undulate, dull olive green. AREOLES elliptic, 1.5-2 cm long, 1-4 cm apart. SPINES variable; central spines 4, annulate, cruciform, the 3 upper nearly straight, ascending, to 6.5 cm long and 2.5 mm wide, the lower central spine flattened, curved or hooked at the tip, to 10 cm long and 5 mm wide; radial spines about 11 but often less, the lower 3 heavy, terete, annulate, and resembling the centrals, the others radiating, sometimes setaceous, and sometimes lacking. FLOWERS about 4.5 cm long, perianth segments lanceolate, with red or purple midstripe and straw-yellow margins. FRUIT yellow, oblong, 4 cm long, with a few broad scales. SEEDS dark reddish brown or black, irregularly rounded, approx. 1.75 mm long and 1-1.25 mm wide, reticulate, the reticulations without secondary sculpturing in the depressions.

Holotype: Mesquital, Lower California, Mexico, *Gates 43* (D.S., holotype of *F. viscainensis* Gates).

Distribution: From near San Andreas to Calmalli, Lower California, Mexico. Map number five.

Representative specimens: MEXICO: LOWER CALIFORNIA: Mesquital, *Gates 43* (DS, holotype); Low granite hills 5 mi. N. Mesquital, *Lindsay 2012* (DS); Los Angeles Corral, about 35 mi. NW. San Ignacio, *Lindsay 2003* (DS,SD) 18 mi. S. Mesquital, *Lindsay 2008* (DS,SD).

Ferocactus peninsulae var. *viscainensis* was described as *F. viscainensis* by Mr. Howard E. Gates, from plants he found at Mesquital, Lower California, in 1932. The population from which the type specimen was taken apparently represents a taxon rather intermediate between *Ferocactus peninsulae* var. *peninsulae* and *F. gracilis* var. *coloratus*. It is not confined to a small, localized colony, but is found for at least 30 miles on either side of the type locality. The holotype specimen of *Ferocactus viscainensis* consists of three sections of ribs, with a number of areoles, and two dried fruit. The spines on each rib are variable, but the two best preserved areoles with spine bundles are indistinguishable from those of the Gabb holotype specimen of *Ferocactus peninsulae*. If one were to consider only the holotype specimen of *F. viscainensis* he would be inclined to treat it as a synonym of *F. peninsulae*. I do not think the holotype specimen of *F. viscainensis* accurately represents the taxon ascribed to it, but that is a rather wide variant. Photographs with the type sheet show three specimens from near Mesquital which appear to better represent the population there. I feel that the "viscainensis" population is distinct from *F. peninsulae*, although the two are obviously in the same complex, and that its relationship can best be indicated by treating it as a variety of *F. peninsulae*. *Ferocactus peninsulae* var. *viscainensis* differs from the typical form in having shorter, stiffer, more tubular flowers, shorter, less differentiated spines, which somewhat resemble those of *Ferocactus gracilis* var. *coloratus*, and other rather inconstant and intangible differences.

Figure 73. *Ferocactus peninsulae* var. *peninsulae*, from a photograph taken in Lower California by Leon Diguet and used by Dr. Weber to illustrate *Echinocactus peninsulae*. From Bull. Mus. Hist. Nat. 4: 101. 1898.

Figure 74. *Ferocactus peninsulae* var. *peninsulae*, (*Lindsay 515*), from San Francisquito Bay, Lower California. This is a topotype of *Ferocactus horridus* Britton and Rose.

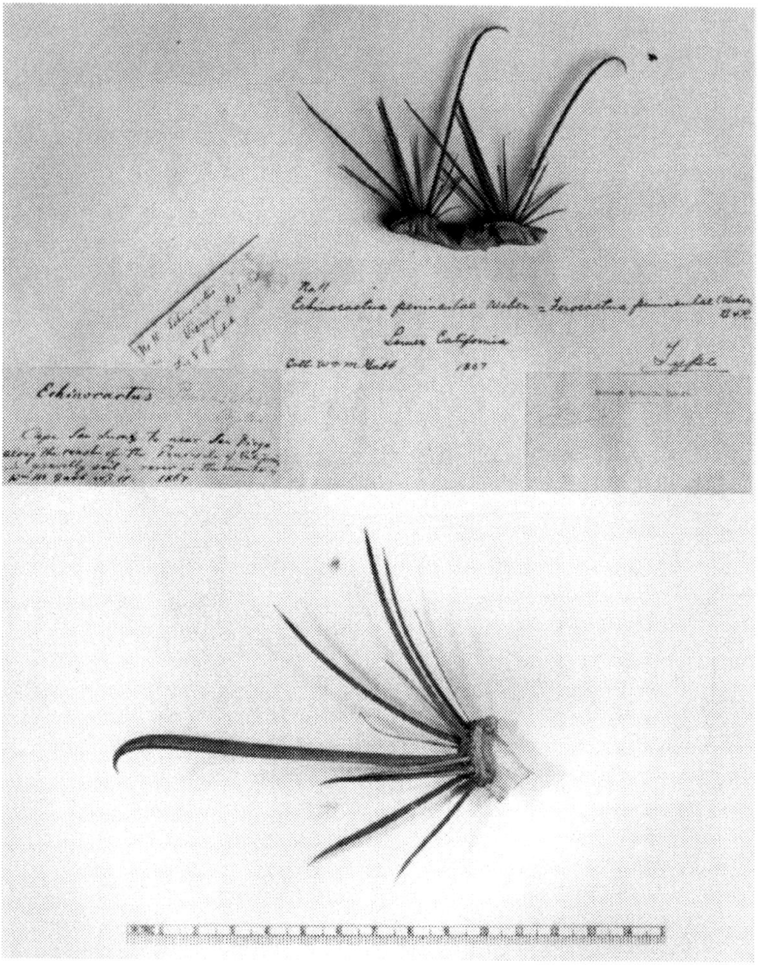

Figure 75. Holotype specimen of *Echinocactus peninsulae*, collected by William Gabb near Muleje, Lower California, in 1867. Below, spine cluster from the holotype specimen of *Ferocactus viscainensis* Gates, for comparison.

Figure 76. Holotype specimen of *Ferocactus viscainensis* Gates and *Ferocactus peninsulae* var. *viscainensis* (Gates) Lindsay.

Figure 77. ***Ferocactus peninsulae*** **var.** ***viscainensis*** **(*Lindsay 2012*) photographed five miles north of Mesquital, Lower California.**

Figure 78. ***Ferocactus peninsulae* var. *viscainensis* (*Lindsay 2008*), 18 miles south of Mesquital, Lower California. This specimen lacks**

Figure 79. ***Ferocactus peninsulae*** **var.** ***viscainensis*****, details of flowers. Above,** ***Lindsay 2012*****, from five miles north of MesquitaI, and below,** ***Lindsay 2008*** **from 18 miles south of Mesquital, Lower California.**

17. FEROCACTUS TOWNSENDIANUS Britton and Rose, Cactaceae 3: 127.1922.

Key to the varieties

a. Stem subconical, flowers orange or red, principal central spine usually strongly curved at tip . . . . *F. t.* var. *townsendianus*

b. Stem globular, flowers yellow, principal central spine straight or only slightly curved at tip . . . . *F. t.* var. *santa-maria*

17a. FEROCACTUS TOWNSENDIANUS Britton and Rose var. TOWNSENDIANUS

Ferocactus townsendianus Britton and Rose, Cactaceae 3:127 1922.

STEM simple, short cylindric, more or less conical or constricted toward the apex, to 5 dm tall and three dm wide. RIBS about 16, slightly tubercled, rather deep, usually spiralled. AREOLES oval, the spiniferous portion about 1 cm long and 8 mm wide, with a superior floriferous section extending above, this becoming truncate when pressed against the adjacent tubercle; young areoles bear short tan tomentum. SPINES gray or brown; central spines usually 4, sometimes 3, annulate, cruciform, the upper 3 ascending, straight or slightly recurved, the lower longer, flattened, with curved or hooked tip, to 10 cm long and 3.5 mm wide; radial spines 14-16, radiating, setaceous to subulate, sometimes curled, the 3 lower ones heavier and somewhat resembling the centrals; nectariferous gland-spines produced between flower and spine fascicle of flowering areoles. FLOWERS large, funnelform, 5-6 cm long and nearly as broad; scales on ovary imbricate, fleshy with ciliate margins, intergrading with larger ovate scales of the tube which have ciliate margins and an apiculate tip; outer perianth segments broad, ovate, red with yellow ciliate margin; inner perianth segments yellow with red midstripe and base, oblong-lanceolate, with serrulate-undulate margins and acute tip, 32 mm long and 7 mm wide; walls of tube 7 mm thick; filaments numerous, 5-15 mm long, red; style 30 mm long and 4 mm wide, grooved, divided into about 20 pink or greenish brown stigma lobes. FRUIT globular, yellow, about 2.5 cm long and 2 cm wide, or about 4.5 cm long including the persistent perianth. SEED reddish brown, rounded, 1.5 mm long and 1 mm wide, with oval or oblong pits; hilum very small, oval, brown.

Holotype: San Jose Island, Gulf of California, Mexico, *Rose 16570* (US).

Distribution: Hills and coastal plains of southern Lower California, south of the 26th parallel, and San Jose, Margarita and Magalena Islands. Map number five.

Representative specimens: MEXICO. LOWER CALIFORNIA. San Jose Island, Gulf of California, *Rose 16570* (US, holotype), *Johnston 3935* and *4084* (CAS); sandy flats 7 mi. E. La Paz on road to Las Cruces, *Lindsay 1968* (DS,SD); Triunfo, *Jones 27061* (POM);

Fraile Bay, *Remple 318* (AHFH); 7 mi. N. Cape San Lucas, *Lindsay 1919* (DS,SD); granite hills at Cape San Lucas, straight spines and globular body, *Lindsay 2248* (DS,SD); Cape San Lucas, *Lindsay DBG275* (DES); between Queretaro and Pozo Grande, *Wiggins 5711* (DS); Boca de Las Animas, *Brandegee s.n.*, Jan. 29, 1889, (UC); San Gregorio, *Brandegee s.n.* Feb. 3, 1889, (UC).

Ferocactus townsendianus was a name proposed by Britton and Rose in 1922 for a plant which Rose collected on San Jose Island in 1911. It is closely related to *Ferocactus peninsulae*, and formerly had been considered to belong to that taxon. *Ferocactus townsendianus* is a small, conical plant usually less than two feet tall and eight or ten inches in diameter, with about 16 spiralled ribs. Dr. I. M. Johnston collected one specimen (Johnston 4084, CAS) at Amortajada Bay, San Jose Island, which had eighteen ribs and was 42 inches tall and 12 inches in diameter, but the specimen bears the note "infrequent, usually only 1-1-1/2 ft. high." The flowers are large, and of the same general form as those of *F. peninsulae*, but the seeds are smaller, only 1.5 mm long and 1 mm wide. While photographing *F. townsendianus* in flower between La Paz and Las Cruces, in July, 1951, I noticed great variability in the spines of adjacent specimens. The radial spines differed in number and character, and in some plants the upper of the four central spines was rudimentary and nectariferous. Specimens near Cape San Lucas sometimes had all straight spines.

Ferocactus townsendianus grows at lower elevations throughout the Cape region of Lower California, as well as on the Magdalena Plain, Santa Margarita and Magdalena Islands, and on San Jose Island in the Gulf of California. It usually grows on silty or sandy flats, associated with *Opuntia cholla, O. burrageana, Cochemiea poselgeri, Machaerocereus gummosus, Lemaireocereus thurberi, Olneya tesota, Fouquieria peninsularis, Bursera microphylla, Jatropha canescens, Pedilanthus macrocarpus*, etc.

17b. FEROCACTUS TOWNSENDIANUS Britton and Rose var. SANTA-MARIA (Britton and Rose) Lindsay, Cact. and Succ. Journ. 27: 170. 1955.

Ferocactus santa-maria Britton and Rose, Cactaceae 3: 131. 1922.

Echinocactus santa-maria Rose, ex Schick., Monats. Kakteenk. 29: 13. 1919. Nomen subnudum.

STEM simple, cylindric, to 7 dm tall and 2.5 dm wide. RIBS about 13, obtuse, slightly tuberculate, straight. AREOLES large, oval, 2 cm long and 12 mm wide, with tan tomentum. SPINES tending to ascend; central spines 4, rather straight, grayish, annulate, to 4.5 cm long, the lower longest and flattened, sometimes curved at the tip; radial spines about 15, the upper 12 setaceous, lighter colored, radiating, the lower 3 like the centrals and often counted as such, in which case central spines are 7; 12 or more nectariferous, persistent, gland-spines are produced between flower and spine fascicle in flowering areoles. FLOWERS yellow, funnelform, 6 cm long and 7 cm wide; scales on ovary green, imbricate, obtuse, about 6 mm wide and 4 mm long, with yellow, ciliate sclerous margin; scales of tube somewhat longer with brown, apiculate tip; outer perianth segments fleshy, yellow, some with light brown stripe on outer side, spatulate, to 3 cm long and 14 mm wide, tip rounded and margins slightly serrulate; inner perianth segments yellow, linear-oblanceolate with elongate stalk, about 4.5 cm long and 1 mm wide, the thick narrow stalk 15 mm long, 2 mm wide and about 1.5 mm thick, margin of stalk entire and of blade nearly so, tip acute-mucronate; wall of tube to 1 cm thick; stamens very numerous, 1-2 cm long, yellow to pink, attached to inside wall of thickened tube between base of inner perianth segments and a shallow nectary pit which lies between the tube and the base of the style; style yellow, 3.5 cm long and 4 mm wide, the top 1 cm divided into about 16 yellow stigma lobes. FRUIT yellow, fleshy, to 5 cm long and 3.5 cm wide, with the persistent perianth extending 2.5 cm above. SEED dark brown or black, reniform, 2.5 mm long and 1.5 mm wide; testa with fine polygonal reticulations; hilum small, round, about 0.5 mm in diameter.

Holotype: Santa Maria Bay, Lower California, Mexico, *Rose 16279* (US, holotype of *Ferocactus santa-maria*).

Distribution: Known only from the rocky headland which forms Santa Maria Bay. Map number five.

Representative specimens: MEXICO: LOWER CALIFORNIA: Santa Maria Bay, *Rose 16297* (US, holotype); *Lindsay 2160* (DS,SD).

Ferocactus townsendianus var. *santa-maria* was first collected by Dr. Rose in 1911, while he was with the "Albatross" expedition to Lower California. It was briefly mentioned as *Echinocactus santa-maria* Rose in 1919, in *Monatsschrift fur Kakteenkunde* (29: 13. 1919), but valid publication was by Britton and Rose in *The Cactaceae* (3: 131. 1922), as *Ferocactus santa-maria.*

Rose found only small specimens at the one locality. Mr. Howard E. Gates and Wm. Taylor Marshall looked for the plant on Magdalena Island in 1932, and I did also in 1937, but we were able to find only typical *Ferocactus townsendianus* var. *townsendianus.* In 1947 Mr. and Mrs.

Lewis Cavanagh collected barrel cacti for me along the Pacific coast of Lower California, and at Santa Maria Bay found the typical form of *F. townsendianus.* The specimen they brought me flowered at Lakeside, California, in May, 1947. The Sefton Foundation -Stanford University expedition to the Gulf of California stopped at Santa Maria Bay March 31, 1952, and I was able to locate four specimens of *Ferocactus townsendianus* var. *santa - maria* growing on the rocky headland which forms the bay. The largest specimen was about 2.5 feet tall. Two living specimans were collected, one of which was sent to the Museo de la Flora y la Fauna Nacional, Mexico, and the other kept in my study collection, where it blossomed in the summer of 1953, in June 1954, and in August 1955.

Ferocactus townsendianus var. *santa-maria* is close to var. *townsendianus*, with morphologically similar flowers and the same number and arrangement of spines. I feel, however, that the clear yellow flowers of *santa-maria*, its globular rather than conical stem, larger fruit, and larger reniform seed with polygonal recticulations (rather than oval or oblong pits) are sufficient differences to keep it separate as a variety. The straight, ascending central spines mentioned by Britton and Rose in their original description of *F. santa-maria* are not particularly obvious in the holotype specimen or those which I collected. Also, specimens of var. *townsendianus* from near Cape San Lucas with straight or barely curved central spines are not unusual.

Ferocactus townsendianus var. *santa-maria* has been found only on rocky slopes, where it is rare, and growing in association with *Burragea fruiticulosa, Cochemiea halei, Opuntia pycnantha, Wilcoxia diguetii, Fouqueria peninsularis, Agave margaritae, Euphorbia misera*, etc.

Figure 80. *Ferocactus townsendianus* var. *townsendianus*, holotype specimen.

Figure 81. *Ferocactus townsendianus* var. *townsendianus*, (*Lindsay 1968*) seven miles east of La Paz, Lower California.

Figure 82. *Ferocactus townsendianus* var. *townsendianus*, flower detail of *Lindsay 1968*, photographed July 31. 1951.

Figure 83. *Ferocactus townsendianus* var. *townsendianus*, (*Lindsay 1981*), 30 miles south of Santo Domingo, Magdalena Plain, Lower California.

Figure 84. *Ferocactus townsendianus* var. *townsendianus* (*Lindsay 1974*). A straight spined form from five miles south of La Ballena Ranch, southern Magdalena Plain, Lower California.

Figure 85. A straight-spined form of *Ferocactus townsendianus* var. *townsendianus*, (*Lindsay 2248*), from Cape San Lucas, Lower California.

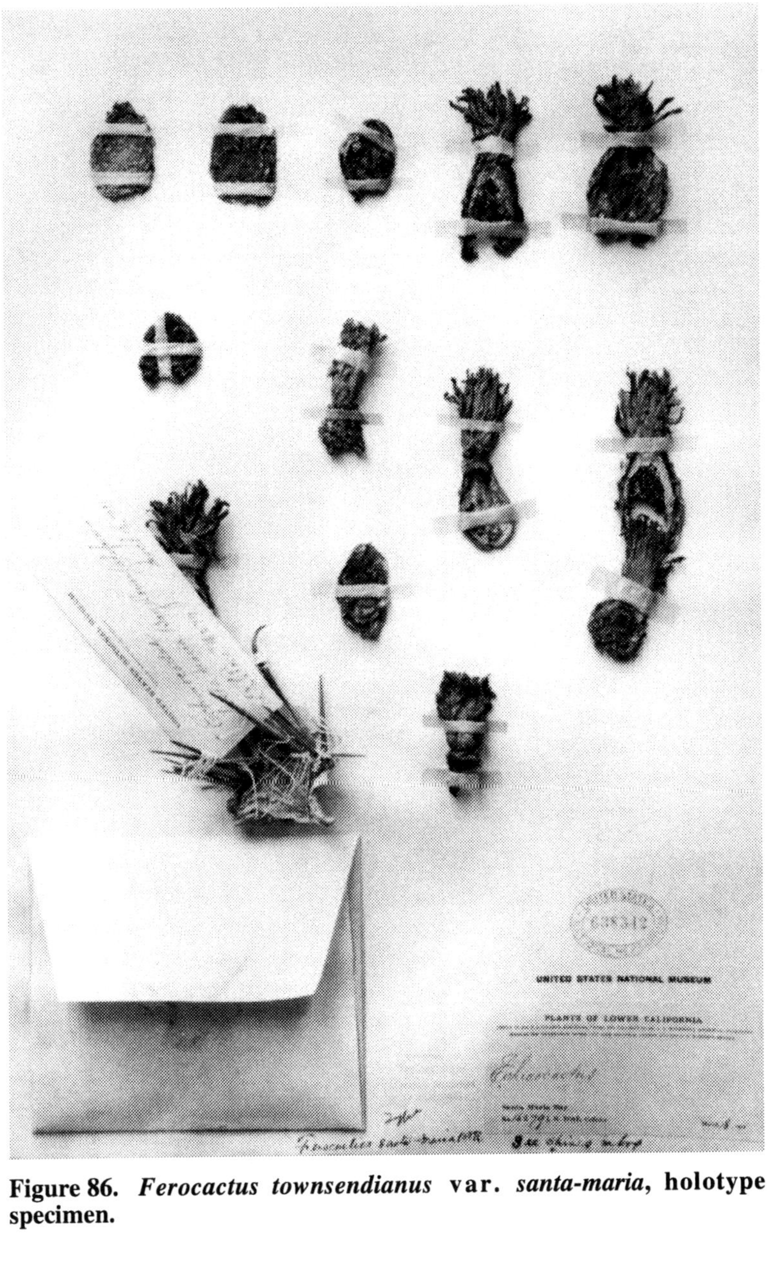

Figure 86. ***Ferocactus townsendianus*** **var.** ***santa-maria*****, holotype specimen.**

Figure 87. *Ferocactus townsendianus* var. *santa-maria*, (*Lindsay 2160*, topotype), at Santa Maria Bay, Lower California.

Figure 88. *Ferocactus townsendianus* var. *santa-maria* in flower, August, 1954.

Figure 89. *Ferocactus townsendianus* var. *santa-maria*, detail of flowers.

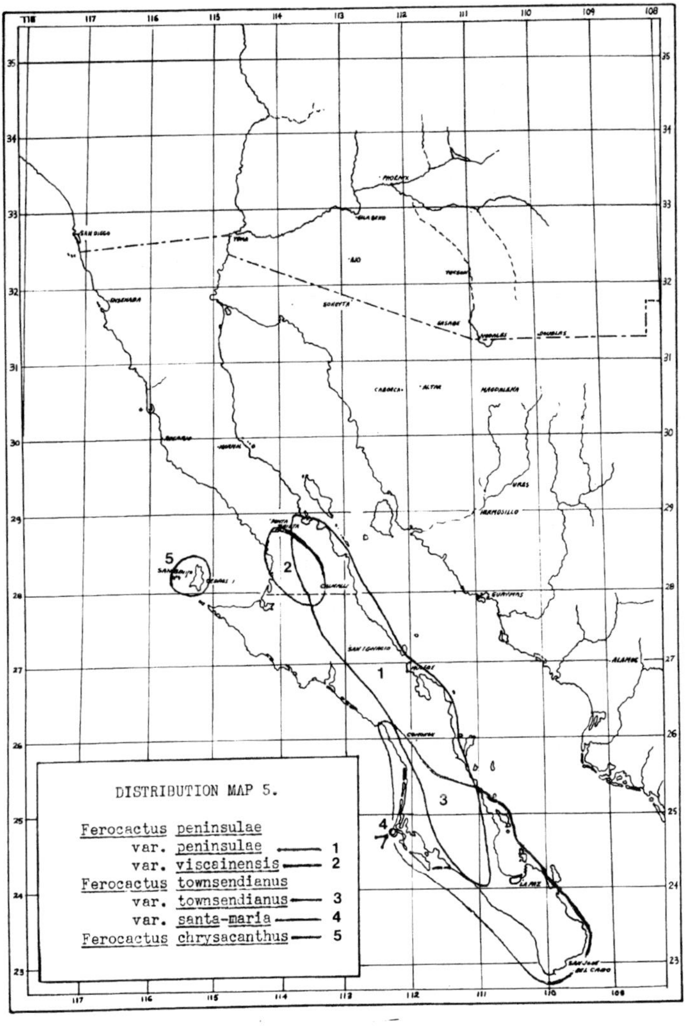

Distribution Map 5

18. FEROCACTUS GRACILIS Gates, Cact. and Succ. Journ. 4: 323. 1933.

Key to the varieties

a. Often over 1 meter tall, the widest central spine usually less than 5 mm wide . . . . *F. gracilis* var. *gracilis*.

b. Less than 1 meter tall, the widest central spine more than 6 mm wide . *F.* gracilis var. *coloratus*.

18a. FEROCACTUS GRACILIS Gates var. GRACILIS

Ferocactus gracilis Gates, Cact. and Succ. Journ. 4: 323. 1933.

STEM simple, globose to cylindric, to 3 m tall and 3 dm wide. RIBS about 24, 2 cm high, slightly tuberculate and expanded under the areoles, deep green. AREOLES oval to elliptic, to 2 cm long and 6 mm wide, with light gray tomentum in youth. SPINES in two series; central spines 7-13, annulate, red with yellow tips, the 4 principal central spines cruciform, the upper and lower of which are flatttened and the lateral 2 subulate, the lower is the largest, to 6 cm long and 5 mm. wide, rather convolute and curved or hooked at the tip; in addition there are usually 2-3 secondary subulate central spines above the principal 4, and also 3 central-like radial spines at the lower side of the areole; radial spines white, flattened setaceous, twisted, the lower 3 acicular to subulate, and annulate. FLOWERS red, funnelform, about 4 cm long and 3.5 cm wide; scales on ovary widely spaced, not overlapping, to 4 mm wide and 3 mm long, green with reddish tip; outer perianth segments to 2 cm long and 6 mm wide, obtuse, red with narrow yellow margin; inner perianth segments linear lanceolate, 25 mm long and 5-7 mm wide, the midstripe lavender red and yellow serrulate margins; filaments 5-15 mm long, fine, appressed against style; style 22 mm long and 2 mm wide, yellow below and red above, the upper 1 cm divided into about 9 stigma lobes which are red on the outside and have an inner yellow stigmatic surface. FRUIT yellow, oblong, about 2.5 cm long, or 4.5 cm long including the persistent withered perianth; scales becoming sclerous; the fruit not opening by basal pore. SEED black, shiny, 1.75-2 mm long and 1.10-1.35 mm wide, rounded and not angled, with small round white hilum and a pit between the hilum and end of the seed.

Holotype: Hills west of Mission San Fernando, Lower California, Mexico, *Gates 22*, July 25, 1932, (DS).

Distribution: Central Lower California, from the southern end of the Sierra San Pedro Martir to below Punta Prieta, including the area between the 29th and 30th parallels. Map number six.

Representative specimens: MEXICO. LOWER CALIFORNIA. Hills west of Mission San Fernando, *Gates 22*, (DS, holotype); 20 mi. inland from Rosario, *Lindsay 1846* (DS,SD).

Ferocactus gracilis is a particularly attractive cactus which was discovered by Mr. Howard E. Gates in 1928. Mr. Gates published the species in 1933. It occurs in northern central Lower California, from Rosario southward to where it intergrades with and is replaced by *Ferocactus peninsulae* var. *viscainensis* in the northern Viscaino desert. The section in which it grows is particularly arid, and the plant seems to have broad edaphic tolerance, from silt flats near the beach to alluvial gravel slopes and benches and rocky slopes. Associated plants include many with unusual forms, among them *Idria columnaris, Fouquieria splendens, Pachycormus discolor, Pachycereus pringlei, Lophocereus schottii, Bursera microphylla, Agave nelsonii*, etc.

Mr. Gates named the species *gracilis* because of its tall, slender form. It is usually less than one foot in diameter, but specimens nine feet tall have been found found. The plants do not ordinarily branch, but if injured may produce a cluster of heads. The red flowers get their color from the strong red midstripe of the perianth segments, which have a narrow yellow margin, and from the mass of bright red stamens. This color pattern is characteristic of most of the Lower California barrel cacti which occur to the south. The flowers appear in the summer in June, July, and August.

Ferocactus gracilis var. *gracilis* appears to be a stable form in the northern portion of its range, but becomes variable farther south. There it apparently intergrades with *Ferocactus gracilis* var. *coloratus*, which may actually represent a hybrid population between F. *gracilis* and *F. peninsulae* or *F. peninsulae* var. *viscainensis.*

18b. FEROCACTUS GRACILIS Gates var. COLORATUS (Gates) Lindsay, Cact. and Succ. Journ. 27: 169. 1955.

Ferocactus coloratus Gates, Cact. and Succ. Journ. 4: 344. 1933.

STEMS simple, globose to subcolumnar, to 1 m tall and 3 dm wide. SPINES like those of the previous variety, except that they are usually somewhat shorter, and the flattened upper and lower of the four principal centrals are always 6 mm, and often over 1 cm wide. FLOWERS similar to var. *gracilis* , but apparently have less red pigment in the corolla segments, which are usually also more obtuse; the flower is not as broadly expanded and scales on the ovary are imbricate. SEEDS are more angular, irregular, and slightly larger than those of var. gracilis, and lack the pit adjacent to the hilum.

Holotype: Southwest of Aguaje San Andres, Lower California, Mexico, *Gates 160* (DS, holotype of *F. coloratus* Gates).

Distribution: Known only from the area between Punta Prieta and Miller's Landing, Lower California, Mexico. Map number six.

Representative specimens: MEXICO: LOWER CALIFORNIA: Southwest of Aguaje San Andres, *Gates 160* (DS, holotype); *Lindsay 2013* (DS,SD); 20 mil S. Punta Prieta, *Harbison s.n.* April 19, 1940 (SD); San Andres, *Lindsay DBG-83* (DES).

This variety was also discovered by Mr. Howard E. Gates, who considered it a distinct species and named it *Ferocactus coloratus* in 1933. It is very near the typical variety of *F. gracilis*, but has differences, already summarized in the above description, which are probably sufficient to segregate it as a varietal form. The population of barrel cacti in which var. *coloratus* occurs is variable, and the specimens which have been collected to represent *coloratus* are usually the extreme examples. It is possible that the population represents a hybrid swarm containing genetic material from *F. gracilis* var. *gracilis, F. peninsulae* var. *peninsulae*, which occurs in the adjacent Sierra San Borjas, and *F. peninsulae* var. *viscainensis*, which occurs in the Vizcaino Desert to the south.

Figure 90. Habitat photograph of *Ferocactus gracilis* var. *gracilis*, near Aguajita, about 20 miles inland from Rosario, Lower California. Associated plants are the large *Idria columnaris*, *Echinocereus engelmannii*, and *Agave nelsonii*. This print is from a kodachrome transparency.

Figure 91. *Ferocactus gracilis* var. *gracilis*, flower of a plant about 12 miles inland from Rosario, Lower California, photographed in July, 1950.

Figure 92. ***Ferocactus gracilis*** **var.** ***gracilis*****, (*****Lindsay 1846*****), from 20 miles inland from Rosario, Lower California, flowering at Stanford University in July, 1955.**

Figure 93. *Ferocactus gracilis* var. *coloratus*, holotype specimen.

Figure 94. *Ferocactus gracilis* var. *coloratus*, (*Lindsay 2301*), topotype specimen from seven miles south of Punta Prieta, Lower California. The plant was photographed when it flowered at Stanford Unlversity, July, 1955.

Figure 95. Flowering specimen of *Ferocactus gracilis* var. *coloratus*, at Agua San Andres, south of Punta Prieta, Lower California.

Figure 96. Flowers of *Ferocactus gracilis* var. *gracilis*, right, and *Ferocactus gracilis* var. *coloratus*, left. The flowers of the two varieties are similar, but var. *gracilis* has more red pigmentation.

19. FEROCACTUS GATESII Lindsay, Cacti. and Succ. Journ. 27: 150. 1955.

STEM simple, gobular to sub-columnar, to 1.5 m tall and 3 dm in diameter. RIBS 30-32, acute, tuberculate, to 2.5 cm deep. AREOLES oval, 1-1.5 cm long, bearing light brown tomentum in youth. SPINES pink, yellow, or horn colored, ageing to gray; central spines usually 4, erect spreading, flattened laterally, annulate, cruciform in arrangement, to 7 cm long and 3 mm wide, the lower the longest and sometimes curved at the tip, but not hooked; radial spines about 16, radiating, the two or three nearest the top and nearest the bottom of the areole heavier, annulate, while the lateral ones are often thinner, twisted and setaceous; short, blunt nectariferous gland-spines produced in flowering areoles, these persisting and drying to spine-like organs in older areoles. FLOWERS large, red, funnelform, to 6 cm long and as broad, produced in circle around apex of plant, in some cases 2 or more areoles on same rib produce flowers simultaneously; short, broad scales of the ovary maroon with yellow, ciliate margins, outer perianth segments to 2 cm long and 1 cm wide, obtuse; inner perianth segments are variable, red with yellow margins, to 3 cm long and 1 cm wide, the tip obtuse to acuminate or apiculate, the innermost series of periath segments narrower, oblong-lanceolate with undulate- cuspidate, ciliate or slightly lacerate margins and apiculate-attenuate tips; stamens very numerous, filaments fine, red, 5-15 mm long, anthers large, yellow, to 2 mm long and 0.7 mm wide; style yellow, 2 cm long and 2.5 mm wide, the upper 1 cm divided into about 16 yellow stigma lobes. FRUIT very large and elongate, the ovary to 7.5 cm long and 2.5 cm wide, including the persistent withered perianth to 10 cm long and extending well above the top of the plant. SEEDS large, black, to 2.5 mm long and 1.75 mm wide, with fine polygonal sculpturing and small hilum.

Holotype: Small islet in Smith Island group at the north side of the entrance of Los Angeles Bay, Lower California, Mexico, 28 59-1/2' N., 113 32-1/2' W., *Moran 4103ul* (DS).

Distribution: Known only from islands and islets in the mouth of Los Angeles Bay, Lower California, Mexico. Map number four.

Representative specimens: MEXICO: LOWER CALIFORNIA. Small islet in Smith Island group, Los Angeles Bay, *Moran 4103* (DS, holotype; MEXU, SD, UC); *Lindsay 2240* (DS,SD).

Ferocactus gatesii was first collected by Mr. Howard E. Gates in 1935, when he stopped on a small islet while enroute from Los Angeles Bay to Angel de la Guardia Island, by dugout canoe. He also discovered *Mammil-*

laria insularis on the same islet. I collected both the *Ferocactus* and *Mammillaria* the following summer, unaware that Mr. Gates had visited the area before me. The barrel cactus very strongly resembled *F. acanthodes*, and I took one or two specimens, assuming it was that species.

In the spring of 1952, and accompanied by Dr. Reid Moran, I again had the opportunity to visit the Smith Island locality with the Sefton Foundation - Stanford University Expedition to the Gulf of California. This time the Ferocacti were in full bloom, with large red flowers and enormous elongated fruit which protruded above the tops of the plants. We knew these could not be of the *Ferocactus acanthodes* complex. Superficially the flowers resembled those of *Ferocactus gracilis* Gates, from the western side of lower California, but the fruit and seeds of *F. gracilis* are very much smaller.

Ferocactus gatesii grows in granite rocks on barren islets, in a region of very limited rainfall. Associated with it is the co-endemic cactus, *Mammillaria insularis*, a small semisubterranean plant which has only its top exposed to the hot, dry environment.

Figure 97. *Ferocactus gatesii*, the plant from which the holotype specimen, (*Moran 4103*, DS), was made.

Figure 98. ***Ferocactus gatesii.*** **Above, habitat at the type locality, a small islet in the Smith Island group at the mouth of Los Angeles Bay, Lower California. Below, flowers photographed May 10, 1952.**

20. FEROCACTUS CHRYSACANTHUS (Orcutt) Britton and Rose, Cactaceae 3: 127. 1922.

Echinocactus chrysacanthus Orcutt, Rev. Cact. 1: 56. 1899.

STEM simple or rarely cespitose with up to 6 heads, to 1 m tall and 3 dm broad. RIBS about 21, tuberculate, 2 cm tall. AREOLES large, oval, to 2 cm long and 1 cm wide, bearing slight gray tomentum, nectariferous gland-spines in area above spine bundle. SPINES bright yellow or red, in some specimens gray; central spines about 10, to 5 cm long, flattened, annulate, more or less twisted, one sometimes curved or hooked at the tip; radial spines 4-12 or more, white, radiating, sometimes bristlelike but usually acicular, intergrading with heavier central type spines at lower side of the areole. FLOWERS yellow or orange, appearing in June from upper areoles in a circle about the top of the plant, 4.5 cm long and 4 cm broad, campanulate; scales on ovary and tube red edged with yellow, intergrading into outer perianth segments, these yellow with red midstripe. Inner perianth segments about 2.5 cm long and 8 mm wide, satiny yellow, sometimes with red midstripe, margin serrate; filaments numerous, 5-15 mm long, red; anthers 1 mm long, yellow; style 15 mm long, pink, with about 11 pink stigma lobes 8 mm long. FRUIT yellow, to 3 cm long and 1.5 cm wide, bearing widely spaced small lunate scales, fleshy, persistent on the plant, sometimes opening by a basal pore. SEEDS large, 2 mm long, 1.5 mm wide and .5 mm thick, dull black, testa sculptured with oval or angular depressions, hilum small, oval, basal.

Neotype: Cedros Island, northwest Mexico. Arroyo behind village at south east side of island, *Lindsay 559* (DS).

Distribution: Cedros Island and West San Benito Island, Baja California. Map number five.

Representative specimens: MEXICO: LOWER CALIFORNIA: Cedros Island; arroyo behind village, *Lindsay 559* (DS); Cedros Island, *Rose 16091* (US); *J. W. Toumey s. n.* July 30, 1896 (US). This specimen is labeled, "*Echinocactus penninsularis* Coult -the plant from islands off coast of Lower California, called by Orcutt var. *Chrysacanthus* of *Emoryi* - from plant in Brandegee's yard type locality"; East side of Cedros, *Rempel 331* (AHFH).

I have been unable to locate type material, and have selected a specimen from the spring area at the south end of the island for a neotype.

Ferocactus chrysacanthus is very common on all the east and south side of Cedros Island, and may also occur on the west side, which is not often visited because of difficult landing conditions. Britton and Rose (1922, p. 127) report it from Cedros Island and the adjacent coast of Lower California. I have looked for it on the coast at Cape San Eugenio, San Bartolome Bay, and southward, but have not found it. A specimen in the U.S. National Herbarium, consisting of a photograph of a cultivated plant and five spine clusters (*J. N. Rose # 249,1911*) was collected at Abreojos Point, Lower California, and probably was the basis for the report that it occurs on the peninsula. This plant however is not *Ferocactus chrysacanthus.* I saw one specimen of *F. chrysacanthus* growing on West San Benito Island in 1948 and 1950. Dr. Moran and I spent some time botanizing the island and no other specimens of this species were seen.

Dr. E. L. Greene collected plants on Cedros Island in 1885, and in a report (Greene 1888, p. 203) mentioned *Echinocactus emoryii* as occurring there. C. R. Orcutt, in the original publication of *Echinocactus chrysacanthus*, stated that it was discovered on Cedros Island in 1894, and distributed under the name of *E. emoryi chrysacanthus*, but that he felt the new species was nearer *E. peninsulae*. He also mentioned that "*E. rubruspinus* is a name proposed by L. M. Ford for the red-spined form, and so distributed." Probably the type collections made by Ford, who then owned a nursery in San Diego and had sent a schooner down the Lower California coast to collect cacti for the European market. *Ferocactus chrysacanthus* is an attractive species, with a short globular or cylindric body covered with a mass of twisted yellow or red spines. Near the beach it grows in loose sand or rocks in arroyo bottoms and sides of canyons, in association with *Opuntia prolifera, Echinocereus maritimus, Cochemiea pondii, Agave sebastiana, Rhus lentii, R. laurina, R. integrifolia, Encelia stenophyllum*, etc. It also grows on the higher slopes of the island, with *Pinus muricata* at over 1,500 feet elevation. There *Ferocactus chrysacanthus* is globular, and the spines are dull, probably because of greater fog moisture at the higher elevations.

Figure 99. *Ferocactus chrysacanthus*, (*Lindsay 559*), on the southeast side of Cedros Island, Lower California.

Figure 100. ***Ferocactus chrysacanthus*, (*Lindsay 2157*), from North Head, Cedros Island, Lower Caiifornia.**

21. FEROCACTUS FORDII (Orcutt) Britton and Rose, Cactaceae 3: 126. 1922.

Key to the varieties

a. Flowers orchid, inner perianth segments spatulate or subovate, to 2 cm long and 6-8 mm wide . . . . *F. f.* var. *fordii*

b. Flowers red or orange, inner perianth segments linear-lanceolate, to 4 cm long and 4-5 mm wide . . . . *F. f.* var. *grandiflorus*

21a. FEROCACTUS FORDII (Orcutt) Britton and Rose var. FORDII

Echinocactus fordii Orcutt, Rev. Cact. 1: 56. 1899.

Ferocactus fordii (Orcutt) Britton and Rose, Cactaceae 3: 126. 1922.

STEM simple or sometimes cespitose, depressed globose to short cylindric, to 5 dm tall and 2.5 dm wide, with a flattened or even invaginated base. RIBS about 21, tuberculate, to 2 cm high. AREOLES tomentose, oval with a truncate floriferous portion extending above. SPINES gray; central spines 4, cruciform, annulate, flattened or angled, to 5 cm long and 3 mm wide, the three upper ones straight and ascending, the lower one porrect and curved or hooked at the tip; radial spines about 17, the two upper ones heavier, erect, and resembling the centrals, the rest radiating, not as heavy, and slightly recurved; short nectariferous gland-spines are produced just about the spine cluster. FLOWERS rose-purple or orchid, funnelform, about 3 cm long and as broad; outer perianth segments obtuse, reddish brown with lighter colored ciliate margins; inner perianth segments about 32, spatulate to subobovate, 2 cm long and 6-8 mm wide, somewhat fringed and more or less aristate, with deep orchid midstripe and lighter orchid margins; stamens numerous, filaments red at top, yellow at base, 1 cm long, anthers orange-yellow; style reddish, 2 cm long, the terminal 4 or 5 mm divided into 9- 11 yellow stigma lobes. FRUIT oval, pink to yellow. SEED black, plump but somewhat angled, with fine reticulate sculpturing, 2 mm long, nearly 2 mm broad, and 1.5 mm thick.

Holotype: Lagoon Head, Baja California, *OrcuttD s.n.*, United States National Herbarium No. 1821079.

Distribution: Coastal area of western Lower California from Rancho San Antonio and San Quintin to Cape San Eugenio, and San Martin Island. Map number six.

Representative specimens: MEXICO: LOWER CALIFORNIA: San Martin Island: *Dawson s.n.*, April 1951 (AHFH); *Moran s.n.* May 5, 1949 (DS); *Lindsay 560* (DS); along coast from El Rosario to Socorro, 1 mi. S. Socorro Beach, *Lindsay 2032* (DS,SD); 10 mi. N. Rosario *Lindsay s.n.* July 22, 1950 (DS); Lagoon Head, Baja Cal. *Orcutt s.n.*, no date, (US), this is sheet number 1821079; a dried plant, from which this was taken, is also preserved at the U.S. National herbarium; Santa Domingo Lagoon, Lower California, *Purpus s.n.*, March 1898 (UC), isotype; just north of Santa Maria Lagoons, near San Quintin, *C. F. Harbison, s.n.* Sept. 8, 1955 (DS,SD); hills of San Simon and about 10 miles east of San Quintin Bay, *C. F. Harbison s.n.*, Sept. 1955 (DS,SD).

21b. FEROCACTUS FORDII (Orcutt) Britton and Rose var. GRANDIFLORUS Lindsay, Cact. and Succ. Journ. 27: 164. 1955.

Differs from var. *fordii* in having a taller habit, to almost 1 m high in exceptional specimens, and in the flowers, which are red or orange rather than purple, and to 6 cm long, with linear-lanceolate inner perianth segments to 4 cm long and only 4 or 5 mm wide.

Holotype: San Bartolome Bay, Baja California, *Lindsay 556*, April 28, 1948, (DS).

Distribution: West coast of Lower California from Cape San Eugenio to below Abreojos Point, and Natividad Island. Map Number six.

Representative specimens: MEXICO: LOWER CALIFORNIA: San Bartolome Bay, *Lindsay 556* (DS), type; *Rose 16188* (US); Natividad Island, *Lindsay 559* (DS); San Roque Point, *Lindsay 555* (DS,SD); San Hipolito Bay, *Dawson 6444* (AHFH); Abreojos Point, *Rose 16249* (US).

The first application of the name *Echinocactus fordii* was made by Orcutt in 1899, when he followed his original description of *E. chrysacanthus* with the brief note "*E. fordii* is a name proposed for an allied form with ashy gray spines," and this reference has been accepted as the valid publication of that species. The following year Orcutt gave a fuller description of the new species in his *Review of the Cactaceae*, 2: 81. 1900.

The plant was named for a San Diego nurseryman, Mr. L. M. Ford, who had imported a large number of cacti from the west coast of Lower California, and from whom Orcutt probably obtained his specimens. Ford distributed various Ferocacti of this relationship under the names *Echinocactus peninsulae*, which is quite a different species, and "E. Santo Domingo", a horticulture name which was never validly published. After *E. fordii* was published that name was applied to the various plants Ford had supplied, and which were not all the same species. In England F. A. Walton reported in *The Cactus Journal* (2: 103) that *E. fordii* "found on one of the small islands in the Pacific Ocean, near the peninsula of California" had flowered in his collection August 1, 1899. Walton's description of the flowers differs from Orcutt's. Karl Schumann illustrated *Echinocactus fordii* with a magnificent colored plate in *Bluhande Kakteen*, plate 8, in 1903, but again the plant illustrated varies greatly from the original description.

Dr. C. A. Purpus was shipwrecked at Santo Domingo Lagoon, the entrance of which is marked by the mountain called Lagoon Head, in March 1898, and collected flowers of *Echinocactus fordii* which are now in the University of California Herbarium. The original dried specimen which Orcutt used as the type of *E. fordii*, which is without flowers, is preserved in the U.S. National Herbarium, as well as several sheets of spines taken from it. The holotype specimen, the Purpus flower specimens, and Orcutt's descriptions in 1900 all agree, and give a conclusive authentic picture of *E. fordii*.

In 1911 Dr. Rose collected Ferocacti at various points along the west coast of Lower California while he was with the "Albatross" expedition. Specimens which he got at San Bartolome Bay flowered in cultivation, and the description of *Ferocactus fordii* in Britton and Rose (1922, p. 126) is partially based on that material. I have had opportunity to observe and collect Ferocacti which grow in the coastal area of central Lower California and believe that more than one taxon is represented. The authentic material of *F. fordii* is quite different from the San Bartolome material which Britton and Rose included in it. It may be that there are two distinct species, but similarities in spine formation, and the numerous distinct but only slightly differing populations represented in the complex seem to indicate that the San Bartolome plants, which are also representative of coastal plants to the south, should be considered a variety of *Ferocactus fordii*. In any case the San Bartolome plants, with flowers which are red or orange with linear-lanceolate perianth segments 4 cm long and 4 mm wide, are not identical with the type of *F. fordii*, which has purple flowers about half the size, with spatulate or subobovate perianth segments only 2 cm long but up to 8 or 10 mm wide.

The isolated population on Natividad Island have red or orange flowers and should be referred to variety *grandiflorus*, although the flowers are not as large as those of typical plants from San Bartolome.

At San Martin Island, to the north near San Quintin, a distinct form is found, in which the plant bodies are decidedly flattened and not globular. The flowers and spines are much like those of *F. fordii* var. *fordii*, and the plants from San Martin Island should be included in that variety.

A very decidedly flattened, disc-shaped *Ferocactus* is common along the coastal mesas between San Quintin and Rosario. This has a rather small orchid flower, and the plants blossom when they are very small. A specimen only three inches in diameter and one inch tall produced three flowers while growing in my study collection. It may be that this plant also deserves varietal distinction, but I do not now have adequate material for a critical comparison, and am referring it to *F. fordii* var. *fordii*.

The plants from San Martin Island and the coastal area between San Quintin and Rosario grow in a coastal chapparal association, and both are very often attacked by the larvae of a lepidopterous insect, which hollows out the inside of the body.

The dried skeleton of the holotype which is preserved at the U.S. National Herbarium also shows evidence of such an attack, which is unusual in the genus *Ferocactus*.

Figure 101. *Ferocactus fordii* var. *fordii*, holotype specimen.

Figure 102. ***Ferocactus fordii*** **var.** ***fordii*****, (*****Lindsay 560*****), blossoming on San Martin Island, Lower California, May 5, 1948.**

Figure 103. *Ferocactus fordii* var. *grandiflorus*, (*Lindsay 556*), from San Bartolome Bay, Lower California. The holotype specimen was made from this Plant.

Figure 104. ***Ferocactus fordii*** **var.** ***grandiflorus*****, (*****Lindsay 559*****), flowering on Natividad Island, Lower California, April 28, 1948. Photograph by Reid Moran.**

22. FEROCACTUS VIRIDESCENS (Nuttall) Britton and Rose, Cactaceae 3: 140. 1922.

Editors' Note: *Since publication of this work, this species has been accorded two varieties: var.* viridescens *and var.* littoralis *G. Lindsay in Cact. Succ. J. (US) 36: 8-10, 1964. Variety* littoralis *is densely spined and found on coastal bluffs in north-west Baja California. From appearances and the collection location, we believe that Figure 109 is for var.* littoralis.

Echinocactus viridescens Nuttall, in Torrey and Grey, Fl. N. Amer. 1: 554. 1840.

Melocactus viridescens Nuttall, in Teschemacher, Bost. Journ. Nat. Hist. 5: 293. 1845.

Echinocactus orcuttii Engelmann, West. Amer. Sci. 2: 46. 1886.

Echinocactus limitus Engelmann, ex Coulter, Contr. U.S. Nat. Herb. 3: 374. 1896.

Ferocactus orcuttii (Engelmann) Britton and Rose, Cactaceae 3: 134. 1922.

Ferocactus viridescens var. *littoralis* Lindsay, Cact. Succ. J. (USA) 45:104. 1973.

Key to the varieties:

a. RIBS 13-25, obtuse, somewhat tuberculate, SPINES 15-24 per areole, ashy red or yellowish, flattened. C. SPINES, 4 principal, cruciform, lower spine heaviest, slightly recurved. FLOWERS have about 18 perianth segments, slightly recurved, 5 cm long x 6 cm wide
. . . . *F. viridescens* var. *viridescens*

b. RIBS about 21-34, not tuberculate. SPINES 21-34, has in addition to four central spines like var. *viridescens*, above these 3-5 additional centrals; spines not flattened; with the increase of ribs and spines per areole, it appears more densely spiny. FLOWERS similar to var. *viridescens* but about one-third smaller, with about 30 perianth segments.
. . . . *F. viridescens* var. *littoralis*

22a. FEROCACTUS VIRIDESCENS var. VIRIDESCENS

STEM simple or cespitose, depressed globose to short cylindric, deep glossy green, usually 1-2 dm tall and broad, but in some localities to 10 dm tall and 4 dm broad. RIBS 13-25, obtuse, somewhat tuberculate with fleshy protuberance below each areole. AREOLES oval in spiniferous portion, 8-12 mm long and 5- 8 mm broad, with narrow floriferous portion extending above, this expanded and truncate at top where appressed against adjacent tubercle; young areoles produce short tan tomentum which soon turns gray. SPINES ashy-red or yellowish, ageing to horn or gray; central spines 4, cruciform, spreading, the lower spine heaviest, slightly recurved, to 5 cm long and 5 mm wide, flattened, annulate; the upper central spine curved upward, terete or flattened, not as strong as the lower; lateral two central spines terete; radial spines about 8-15, subulate, radiating from the margin of areole, in some specimens the upper ones slender and bristle-like; gland-spines produced between floriferous and spiniferous of areole, these reddish, rounded, 2 mm long, persistent and becoming more conspicuous in older areoles after tomentum has eroded away. FLOWERS produced in April or May, usually on youngest mature areole on rib, to 5 cm long and 6 cm wide, broadly campanulate, greenish yellow from above and reddish from side; ovary short, green, with small scales which intergrade with fleshy red scales of tube and thick outer perianth segments; outer perianth segments red with greenish-yellow margin, the upper ones yellow with red midstripe, margins ciliate and tip obtuse, the segments broad in proportion to length, varying from elliptical to obovate; inner perianth segments glistening yellow, sometimes with red midstripe, ciliate to serrulate and sometimes apiculate, to 3 cm long and 8 mm wide; stamens 1-2 cm long; style 2.5 cm long, yellow, the upper half separated into about 15 linear stigma lobes, these spreading during maturation of the flower. FRUIT at first green or reddish, becoming light yellow when mature, to 3.5 cm long and 2.5 cm wide, with scattered lunate fleshy scales which become membranous. SEEDS black, rather angular, 1.5 mm long, 1 mm wide, 0.7 mm thick, testa densely pitted with minute round or oval depressions, hilum minute, white, circular.

Holotype: *Nuttall s.n.*, 1835, San Diego, California, in the herbarium of the British Museum. A. W. Excell, Deputy Keeper of the Department of Botany, found the specimen for me and had it photographed. The photograph of the rather poor specimen is shown on plate 97.

Distribution: Southwestern San Diego County, California, and northwestern Lower California, Mexico. Map number six.

Representative specimens: CALIFORNIA: SAN DIEGO CO.: 10 mi. S. Escondido, *Lindsay 2616* (DS,SD); bluffs over the beach, Torrey Pines, *Peebles S.F. 305* (ARIZ); San Diego: *Parish 375* (DS); *Brandegee s.n.*, no date, (UC); *Setchell s.n.*, Mar. 19, 1901 (UC); *Orcutt 291* (MO); *Snyder s.n.* Apr. 28, 1896 (SD); Sea Beach of San Diego, *Schott s.n.* 1854 (MO); Hills near San Diego, *Pringle 14359* (MO); Mission Hills, *Abrams 3395* (DS,MBG,POM); Hills above San Diego Bay, *Cohen 463* (POM); 15 mi. E. San Diego, *Benson 4281* (POM); 1 mi. S. Otay, *Rush s.n.*, May 30, 1948 (AHFH); dry mesa between Otay and San Ysidro, *Wiggins 3245* (DS); near initial monument of the U.S. and Mexican Boundary line, S. San Diego, *Masson? s.n.* May 1876, (sent by G. M. Hitchcock to Engelmann and the type of *Echinocactus limitus*) (MO); near San Diego, no collector or date, but marked "Type" of *E. limitus* (MO); Boundary Marker 258, on shore of Pacific, *Gander 489* (SD). MEXICO: LOWER CALIFORNIA: Palm Valley, northern Lower Calif., *Orcutt 641 s.n.*, May and June, 1883, (marked type, *E. orcuttii*) (MO); Palm Valley, no collector, April 10, 1885, (marked "part of type" of *E. orcuttii*) (UC); 26 mi. S. Tecate, *Lindsay 2173* (DS,SD); Seaward slopes 37 mi. S. Tijuana, *Wiggins* and *Gillespie 3910* (DS,POM,CAS,MBG,MEXU); 5 mi. N. Ensenada, *Dawson 5129* (AHFH); 7 mi. SW. Ensenada, *Dawson 5140* (AHFH); San Carlos Hot Springs, *Lindsay 1843* (DS,SD); Canyon above San Carlos Hot Springs, *Lindsay 2071* (DS,SD).

Ferocactus viridescens was studied by Thomas Nuttall in 1835, when he found the plant in "arid hills etc., near San Diego." The holotype specimen is labeled *Cactus viridiflorus*, but Nuttall gave the new species the manuscript name of *Melocactus viridescens*, which Torrey and Gray hesitatingly corrected to *Echinocactus* when they published the species in 1840. Dr. C. C. Parry, who botanized for the U. S. Boundary Commission party, collected *E. viridescens* "on dry hills and ridges near San Diego." Mr. Arthur Schott, of the same party, reported them from the sea beach.

In 1876 G. M. Hitchcock sent material from "the boundary line south of San Diego, with *Agave shawii* and *Cereus emoryii*" to George Engelmann in St. Louis. Engelmann prepared a manuscript description under the tentative name of *Echinocactus limitus,* but did not publish it. John M. Coulter, who was preparing a revision of the North American Cactaceae after Engelmann's death, published a number of species from the Engelmann manuscripts preserved at the Missouri Botanical Gardens, among them *Echinocactus limitus* (Coulter 1896: 374). I believe that Engelmann had intentionally withheld that name because the plant is not distinct from *E. viridescens.*

On May 29, 1883, H. C. and C. R. Orcutt collected a large cespitose *Ferocactus* at Palm Valley, Lower California, which is in the Tijuana River watershed about forty-five miles southeast of San Diego. The plants found by the Orcutts were robust, to over three feet tall, and material was sent to Engelmann, who prepared a manuscript description with the proposed name of *Echinocactus orcuttii.* The manuscript is preserved in the Engelmann notes at the Missouri Botanical Garden, number 1504. C. R. Orcutt published the species from Engelmann's description, adding that it was "occasionally found with *E. viridescens* at San Diego."

Britton and Rose (1922, pp. 134-35) retained *Echinocactus orcuttii*, combining it in *Ferocactus*, but included the following note:

> We know this plant only from descriptions and illustrations. After our manuscript was in type Mr. C. R. Orcutt wrote us as follows: "you know, I suppose, that I consider *Echinocactus orcuttii* only a luxuriant development of *E. viridescens*? At Palm Valley, Lower California, I have seen it very large and one cluster contained 25 heads, forming quite a large mass. I found one large cristate." The published illustrations do not indicate close relationship with *F. viridescens.*

I have observed and collected the robust *Ferocactus* from the Palm Valley area, as well as south of Tecate, Lower California, and the hills between Lakeside and Bostonia, California. The principal difference between it and *F. viridescens* is size, although *F. orcuttii* is described as having a darker colored flower. This may have been because the original description was drawn from dried material in which the maroon midstripe and scales are particularly conspicuous. Plants from near Tecate blossomed at Stanford and while the maroon midstripe was present it was within the variation found in normal-sized *F. viridescens.* I do not believe that *Ferocactus orcuttii* can be retained as a species or even a variety, because the material at hand indicates it is no more than a large inland form of *F. viridescens.* There are also other more or less distinct forms, one of which is a population of cylindrical plants growing at about 1200 feet elevation on the walls of a narrow canyon above San Carlos Hot Springs, behind and south of Ensenada, Lower California. The plants are about 3 feet tall and 14 inches in diameter, and resemble *F. acanthodes.* A similar type, with bright yellow and red spines, occurs in the canyon which leads from the Ensenada plain towards San Tomas. Another cylindrical form grows along the beach near Hamilton Ranch, Lower California. This has appeared in the trade as *Ferocactus viridescens* var. *littoralis*, but has not been validly published. Both of these types deserve critical study during the flowering period.

Ferocactus viridescens occurs in the coastal and semi-coastal chaparral area from near Escondido, California, to below San Quintin, Lower California. This region averages between six and twelve inches of rain annually, most of which falls during the winter and early spring. *Ferocactus viridescens* is not a desert species. In the northern portion of this range it grows in well drained areas, often on rocky outcrops on south slopes. Associated chaparral species are *Eriogonum fasciculatum, Dudleya pulverulenta, Photonia arbutifolia, Cercocarpus minutiflorus, Xylococcus bicolor, Rhus laurina, R. integrifolia, Adenostoma fasciculatum, etc. In the southern portion of its range associated plants include Opuntia prolifera, O. occidentalis, Myrtillocactus cochal, Machaerocereus gummosus, Bergerocactus emoryii, Mammillaria dioica, Agave shawii, Euphorbia misera, Dudleya spp., Aesculus parryi*, etc., in addition to some of the chaparral shrubs which also occur farther north.

Fire is an ecological factor of little importance to the genus *Ferocactus*, but it does affect *F. viridescens*. The chaparral brush and grass areas are subject to recurrent fires, which burn the spines from the little barrel cacti and sometimes destroy the tissues at the edges of their ribs. The plants usually survive, producing a thick corky scar tissue over the injured areas. The spines do not regenerate.

Higgins (1931, p. 68) reports that seeds of *Ferocactus viridescens* were harvested and used for food by the San Diego Indians, who parched and ground them into a meal.

22b. FEROCACTUS VIRIDESCENS var. LITTORALIS

STEM depressed globular to sub-cylindric, to 3 dm tall x 18 cm wide, simple or rarely branched at base. RIBS about 21-34, vertical, not tuberculate, about mm high and 15 mm wide. AREOLES elliptical, 10-12 mm long, 4-5 mm wide, bearing tan tomentum. C. SPINES 7-9, yellowish or pinkish, terete or slightly flattened, annulate, usually slightly recurved, 2-4 cm long and about 1.5 mm wide, the four principal ones cruciform, usually with 3-5 additional ones above. R. SPINES 15-24, acicular to bristle-like, yellowish to white. FLOWERS funnelform, about 3 cm long x 25 mm wide; scales of pericarp and tube reddish with yellow margins, obtuse, intergrading with sublinear, reddish outer perianth segments; inner perianth segments about 30, yellow, oblanceolate, 8-10 mm long and 5mm wide; filaments numerous, yellow, to 10 mm long; style red, 15 mm long, 2 mm thick, with longitudinal furrows separating at tip into about 14 red or yellow stigma lobes about 5 mm long. FRUIT shiny red or yellow, globular, about 15 mm thick, with broad scales about 2 mm long and 3 mm wide; perianth persistent. SEEDS black, pitted or finely reticulate, 1.5 mm long and 1 mm wide.

Type: Collected by Reid Moran, no. 8277, 15 May 1960, on the seacoast bluffs at Puerto Santo Thomas, Baja California, Mexico, near 31° 33' N, 116° 41' W, and deposited in the herbarium of the San Diego Natural History Museum. Isotopes are deposited in the herbaria of the Instituto de Biologia of Mexico, the California Academy of Sciences, Stanford University, the University of California at Berkeley, and in the United States National Herbarium.

Distribution: Coastal zone from north of Ensenada to Mission Santo Domingo, Baja California, Mexico. I have collected this variety at Punta Salsipuedes, Punta Banda, Puerto Santa Tomas, Punta Calavaras, 3.7 miles south of San Isidro Erendira, 9.5 miles south of the same village, and 1.3 miles west of Mission Santo Domingo.

Mr Howard E. Gates discovered this cactus in the early 1930's between Camalu and the Hamilton Ranch. Though he listed it as *Ferocactus viridescens* var. *littoralis* in his 1934 catalog, the name was not formally published. *Ferocactus viridescens* var. *littoralis* is taller, in comparison with its diameter, than var. *viridescens*; it has about half again as many ribs, these being lower and narrower; it has more spines, averaging 22-33, compared with 15-25 in var. *viridescens*; it has, like var. *viridescens*, four principal central spines, but above these are three to five additional centrals; the spines are not flattened as they are in var. *viridescens*; flowers of var. *littoralis* are about one third smaller, although there are about 30 inner perianth segments compared with about 18 in var. *viridescens*. Fruits too are smaller, but the seeds of the two varieties look alike. Since the ribs of var. *littoralis* are closer together and the spines are more numerous in each areole, the plant is much more densely spiny. The spines are all fine and usually bright chestnut or yellow. It is an attractive plant, growing on rocks and cliffs over the sea, often associated with *Bergerocactus emoryii, Agave shawii, Dudleya brittonii, D. attenuata ssp. orcuttii, Opuntia prolifera, Mammillaria dioica*, and other coastal species.

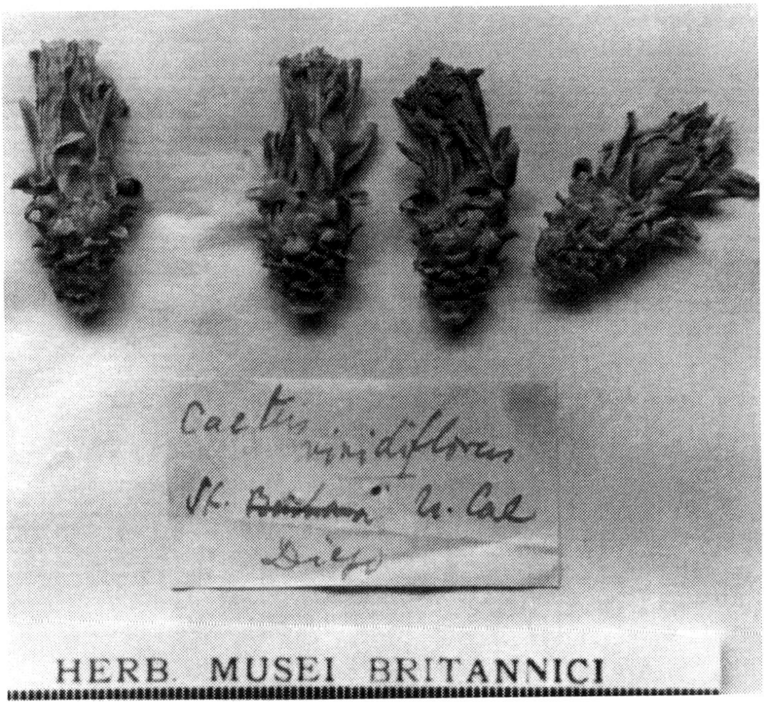

Figure 105. Holotype specimen of *Ferocactus viridescens,* collected by Thomas Nutall in 1835, and now preserved in the British Museum.

Figure 106. ***Ferocactus viridescens.*** **Above, a colony ten miles south of Escondido, California Below, a large specimen photographed at Palm Valley, Lower California, the type locality of** ***Echinocactus orcuttii.***

Figure 107. *Ferocactus viridescens*, (*Lindsay 2616*), from ten miles south of Escondido, California, flowering at Stanford University.

Figure 108. *Ferocactus viridescens* collected 26 miles south of Tecate, Lower California (*Lindsay 2173*) and blossoming at Stanford University.

Figure 109. *Ferocactus viridescens*, collected at San Carlos Hot Springs, about 15 miles southeast of Ensenada, Lower California (*Lindsay 1843*), in flower at Stanford University.

Figure 110. ***Ferocactus viridescens*** **in fruit, photographed at the Rancho Santa Ana Botanic Garden in January, 1955.**

Figure 111. *Ferocactus viridescens* var. *littoralis*, type collected by Reid Moran, May 15, 1960 near Puerto Santo Tomas, Baja California Norte.

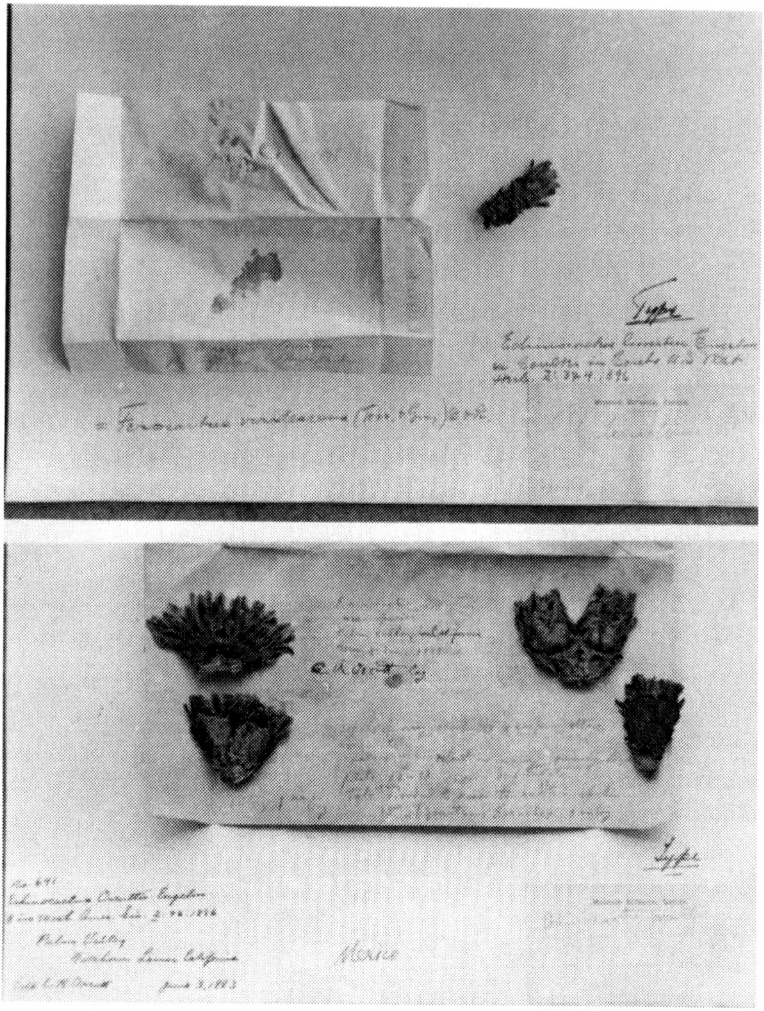

Figure 112. Holotype specimens of *Echinocactus limitus* Englemann in Coulter and *Echinocactus orcuttii* Engleman, perserved at the Missouri botanical Garden.

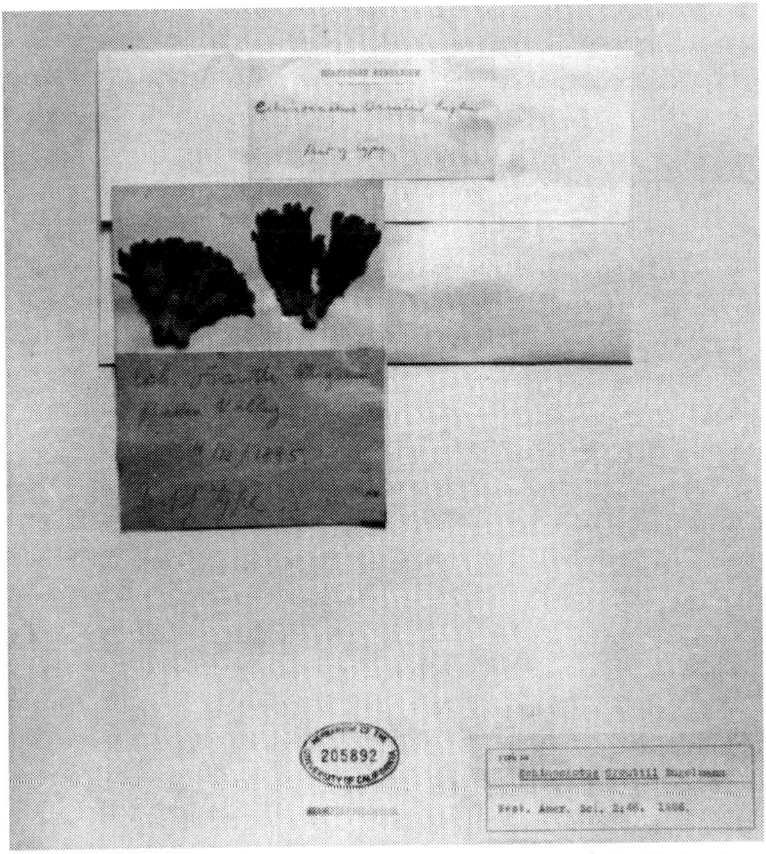

Figure 113. Isotype specimen of *Echinocactus orcuttii* at the Herbarium of the University of California.

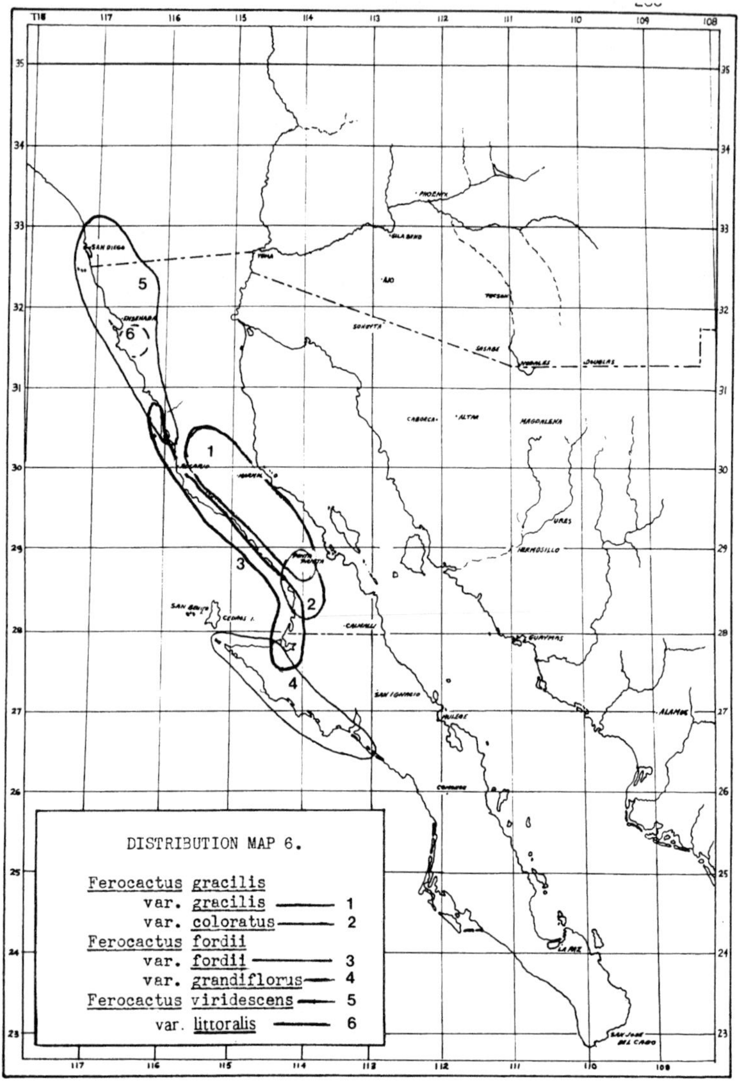

Distribution Map 6

23. FEROCACTUS ACANTHODES (Lemaire) Britton and Rose, Cactaceae 3: 129. 1922.

Editors' Note: *Lindsay recognized three varieties of this* Ferocactus: acanthodes, lecontei, *and* tortulispinus. *Current opinion by others, including Lyman Benson, Nigel Taylor, and Frank Thrombley , adds a fourth variety,* eastwoodiae. *A discussion of these varieties by Frank Thrombley closes this section.* F acanthodes *var.* eastwoodiae *has been seen with binoculars by some of the editors perched high up on cliffside ledges in Arizona, its typical habitation. As Lyman Benson related, "Var.* eastwoodiae *is a cliffhanger - one species in little danger of extinction, since the huge, yellow-spined stems are mostly perched on ledges far out of reach of man and other large mammals."*

Key to the varieties

a. Central spines more or less tortuous and spreading

b. Plants often over 6 dm tall, spines ususally yellow, red, or brown . *F. a.* var. *acanthodes*

bb. Plants under 6 dm tall, body broad with flat apex, spines gray . . . . *F. a.* var. *tortulispinus*

aa. Central spines more or less appressed and recurved back against the plant, usually not twisted . . . . *F. a.* var. *lecontei*

23a. FEROCACTUS ACANTHODES (Lemaire) Britton and Rose var. ACANTHODES

Echinocactus acanthodes Lemaire, Cact. Gen. Nov. Sp. 106. 1839.

Echinocactus viridescens cylindraceus Engelmann, Amer. Journ. Sci. II. 14: 338. 1852.

Echinocactus cylindraceus Engelmann, Proc. Amer. Acad. 3: 274. 1856.

Ferocactus rostii Britton and Rose, Cactaceae 3: 146. 1922.

Ferocactus cylindraceus Orcutt, Cactography 5. 1926.

Echinocactus rostii Berger, Kakteen 238. 1929.

Echinocactus acanthodes var. *rostii* Munz, Man. South. Cal. Bot. 328. 1935.

Echinocactus acanthodes var. *rostii* Marshall and Bock, Cactaceae 148. 1941.

STEM simple or cespitose, globose to cylindric, to 3 m tall and 4 dm wide. RIBS 20-30, vertical, about 2 cm high, usually tuberculate and marked with transverse creases between areoles, occasionally somewhat undulate. AREOLES large, oval, 15 mm long and 10 mm broad, closely spaced, becoming contiguous, the youngest bearing conspicuous brown wool to 15 mm long. SPINES variable but typically flexuous, spreading, annulate, from white to red or often yellow or brown; central spines usually 4, 5-15 cm long, flattened, twisted, the lower broader and longer, sometimes curved or hooked at the tip; radial spines variable, usually several larger ones above and below the centrals, and in addition there is usually a series of radiating lateral setaceous spines which intergrade with the heavier acicular ones, the total number of radial spines usually 15-25, including bristles and heavier types; persistent nectariferous gland-spines are produced in the floriferous section of areole between the spine bundle and flower. FLOWERS yellow or sometimes slightly tinged with red, broad funnelform, 4-6 cm long and wide; scales of ovary deltoid to ovate, imbricate, the margins ciliate, tip acute; outer perianth segments 3 cm long and 8 mm wide, oblanceolate, yellow with darker yellow or pinkish midstripe, the margins serrate; filaments pink or yellow, 5-15 mm long, anthers yellow; style about 25 mm long and 2.5 mm thick, ridged, the upper end of style divided into about 17 stigma lobes. FRUIT globular, yellow, to 3 cm long and 2 cm wide, to 5 cm long, including the withered perianth, and opening by basal pore. SEEDS dark reddish brown or black, plump, round angular, about 2.5 mm long and 1.5 mm thick; testa reticulate; hilum small, round, tan.

Neotype: San Felipe, eastern declevity of California Mountains, *C. C. Parry s. n.* (MBG, holotype of *Echinocactus cylindraceus* Engelmann). Apparently there was no holotype material preserved for *Echinocactus acanthodes*, and I am unable to select a satisfactory neotype. The species was described from a sterile, dead plant which had been raised from seed obtained from “California,” and cannot be certainly identified with any taxon within *Ferocactus*. Weber (1898, p. 104) compared Engelmann’s *Echinocactus cylindraceus* with what was considered authentic material of *E. acanthodes* then preserved at Cels, a cactus nursery firm in Paris, and his decision that they were exactly the same is actually the only basis for placing *E. cylindraceus* in the synonomy of *E. acanthodes*. For this reason I have selected the holotype of *E. cylindraceus* to serve also as the neotype of *Ferocactus acanthodes*.

Distribution: Desert areas in San Diego, Imperial, Riverside and San Bernardino Counties of California, northeastern Baja California, Mexico, Yuma County, Arizona, and northwestern Sonora, Mexico. Map number seven.

Representative specimens: CALIFORNIA: SAN DIEGO CO.: San Felipe, eastern declevity of California Mts., *Parry s.n.* (MBG, holotype of *E. cylindraceus*); intersection of Vallecitos road and highway between Julian and Borrego Valley, *Lindsay 2063* (DS,SD); Borrego Valley, *Wolf 8491* (DS,RSA); Agua Caliente, *Parish 163* (MBG); *Dubber, Harbison* and *Higgins 44.131* (SD); W. end Sentenac Canyon, *Gander 5299* (SD). IMPERIAL CO. Mountain Springs, 2,500 ft., *Benson 10365* (POM); U. S. Highway 80, grade to Mountain Springs, 1,500 ft., *Benson 4235* (POM); RIVERSIDE CO. Rocky slopes, Keyes Ranch, *Munz* and *Johnston 5291* (DS), *5292* (UC), *5293* (DS,POM); Borders of the Colorado Desert, *Parish 163* (DS); Cottonwood Spring, *Evermann s.n.* April 1924 (CAS) *Hall 6013* (UC); 22 mi. E. Indio along Highway 60-70, *Wiggins 8760* (DS); among rocks on steep hillsides, Chuckawalla Springs, *Wiggins 8748* (DS). ARIZONA. YUMA CO. Basaltic slopes 14 mi. NW. Tyson on old road from Yuma to Quartzsite, ribs 19-22, *Wiggins 8629* (DS); Petrified Forest, Yuma Co., *Peebles s.n.*, 1935 (ARIZ). MEXICO. SONORA. 12.7 mi. SW. Sonoyta on road to Punta Penasco, *Wiggins 8358* (DS). LOWER CALIFORNIA. 40 mi. SE. Jacumba, *Rost 327* (US, holotype of *F. rostii*); San Rafael, *Orcutt s.n.* July 29, 1883 (MBG); E. face Sierra Juarez, 33 mi. W. Mexicali on Tijuana Highway, 1,250 ft., *Lindsay 2064*(DS,SD).

Echinocactus acanthodes was described by Lemaire in 1839, and was based on a dead juvenile specimen which had been raised from seed from California. Apparently other plants from the same source survived, one of which blossomed in Monville's collection in 1846. In 1852 Dr. Engelmann described *Echinocactus viridescens cylindraceus* from specimens which Dr. C. C. Parry collected at: "San Felipe, eastern declevity of the California Mountains" in 1850.

I retain Lemaire's *acanthodes* as the legitimate name for this taxon on the bases of Weber's observations and their acceptance by subsequent authors. It is unfortunate that holotype material of *acanthodes* cannot be located for positive proof of its identity, because there is reason to doubt it represents the species which has been assigned to it. *Echinocactus acanthodes* was described from a dead juvenile specimen which had been raised from seed brought from Lower or Upper California. It is improbable that the seed was from plants which are now designated *F. acanthodes*, which grow in inland desert areas far from the coast, and which were inaccessible in the 1830s. It is more likely that seed brought from California would have been obtained from one of the coastal species. For example, the spines and habit of *F. fordii* var. *grandiflorus* from San Bartolome Bay and vicinity fit the original description of *acanthodes*, as do those of *F. chrysacanthus* from Cedros Island. It is doubtful if the name *acanthodes* is properly applied.

Ferocactus acanthodes is a plastic polymorphic complex with several distinct, though intergrading, geographical types. The more important of these have been described as separate species, but the characters upon which they were based are not constant and most recent workers have recognized only the one species. I think that the distinct variants within a species deserve recognition in infraspecific categories, particularly if those variants occupy diverse geographical ranges. The recognition of varieties within a species complex does not deny the close relationships which exist within a polymorphic group. Rather they recognize that there are incipient species within that complex which have not yet evolved far enough to have attained genetic independence. A variety is very often a geographically isolated or semi-isolated population which has developed morphological uniqueness, but is still capable of gene exchange with at least some of the other varieties within its species. For that reason intermediate forms which cannot be positively placed in one particular variety can be expected. The fact that variant forms show intergradation is not sufficient reason to refuse them recognition as varieties.

Three taxa, *Ferocactus rostii, F. lecontei*, and *F. tortulispinus*, which were once considered to be distinct species, have recently been combined in *Ferocactus acanthodes*. I consider *lecontei* and *tortulospinus* to be varieties of *F. acanthodes*, but the holotype specimen of *F. rostii* appears to be inseparable from the typical variety.

The original material of *Ferocactus rostii* was collected in northern Lower California by Mr. E. C. Rost in 1921, and the species was described the following year by Britton and Rose. Their assumption that it differed from *F. acanthodes* was based on its having more slender stems and appressed, straw-colored spines, but the photograph on the type sheet shows a specimen which is heavier than normal for *acanthodes*, and the spines with specimens are within the normal variation of that species. Easily accessible examples of the "rostii" form are found along U. S. Highway 80, in San Diego and Imperial Counties, California, just east of Jacumba. Specimens in the Borrego Valley area of San Diego County are similar. Mr. Wm. Taylor Marshall told me that plants meeting the description of *F. rostii* are to be found on the Cave Creek road in northern Maticopa County, Arizona. The barrel cacti along the Apache Trail, in the Superstition Mountains, and between Superior and Miami, in the adjacent corners of Maricopa, Gila, and Pinal Counties, Arizona, resemble the "rostii" form.

In November, 1937, I collected and photographed a number of barrel cacti in the lower section of Cantillas Canyon, Sierra Juarez, which is near the cited type locality of F. rostii. I sent photographs to Mr. Rost, and asked him if they were the species he had discovered. I also asked where he had collected the holotype specimen. Mr. Rost said that the photographs which I sent were not of *F. rostii*, but did not indicate where he had collected his specimens. In conversation, Mr. Rost said one had to look through a large number of plants in order to find *F. rostii*, all of which suggest that "species" was founded on a minor variation of *F. acanthodes*.

While the type specimen of *F. rostii* shows no important differences from typical *acanthodes*, certain trends in characters are displayed by the Lower California plants of this complex. Mr. Charles F. Harbison, of the San Diego Natural History Museum, sent me photographs and herbarium samples which he took in the central section of Cantillas Canyon in 1951 and 1955. Some of the plants he found were abundantly cespitose, and one specimen about one meter tall had 39 heads, some of which were well up on the stem. The colored photographs taken by Mr. Harbison, one of which is reproduced in Plate 111, seem to show a beautiful and apparently distinct species, but the areoles and spines of his specimens appear to be *F. acanthodes* var. *acanthodes*. The areoles were oval, 15 mm long and 8 mm wide. Central spines were four, golden yellow, cruciform, annulate, with the upper and lower flattened and recurved. Radial spines numbered 14-16, with the upper ones more robust and possibly should also be counted as centrals. Some radial spines were setaceous. The fruit was yellow, ovate, and about 2 cm long and wide when dry. Seeds were very strongly angled, 2-2.25 mm long and 1.5 mm wide, with a deep maroon or black pyriform testa.

Dr. Kenton Chambers collected flowers and an areole from a red-spined *Ferocactus* at the mouth of the Canon Diablo, in the Sierra San Pedro Martir, in June, 1954. Flowers of his specimen have an elongated tube, and resemble those of *F. diguetii*. The one spine cluster with the specimen had four annulated red central spines, and only six acicular annulate radial spines, these from the lower part of the areole and not strongly differentiated from the centrals. This lack of difference between central and radial series also suggests the type of spines found in *Ferocactus diguetii*, which is endemic to the islands of the Gulf of California.

Dr. Philip Munz (1935, p. 328) proposed that *rostii* be given varietal status under *acanthodes*, but most authors agree with Baxter (1935, p. 73), who first suggested that *Ferocactus rostii* can be considered only as a very slight variant of, and taxonomically synonymus with, *F. acanthodes*. I think that some of the Lower California forms which have been associated with the name *F. rostii* may be distinct, but the type specimen of that species shows that name is synonymous with *F. acanthodes*.

23b. FEROCACTUS ACANTHODES (Lemaire) Britton and Rose var. TORTULOSPINUS (Gates) Lindsay, Cact. and Succ. Journ. 27: 168. 1955.

Ferocactus tortulispinus Gates, Cact. and Succ. Journ. 4: 343. 1933.

Differs from the typical variety in its depressed, stout shape and the constant dull grayish red color of its spines. Always simple, and not over 6 dm tall and 4 dm wide.

Holotype: Low hills 10 miles north of Laguna Seca Chapala, Lower California, Mexico, *Gates 161*, July 24, 1932 (DS).

Distribution: Apparently limited to a small section in the arid interior of northern central Lower California, near 29 35' N, 114 40' W. Map number seven.

Representative Specimens: MEXICO: LOWER CALIFORNIA: Low hills 10 mi. N. Laguna Seca Chapala, *Gates 161* (DS, holotype); 6.5 km W. dry lake 13 km N. Laguna Chapala, *Moran and Lindsay 2064* (DS,SD).

This southernmost representative of the *Ferocactus acanthodes* complex is a short, broad form from the arid interior of north central Lower California. It has long, grayish red spines with yellow tips, the lower central of which is twisted and sometimes 13 cm long. The plant was first collected by Mr. Howard E. Gates in July, 1932, and he described it as *Ferocactus tortulispinus* in 1933. Flowers and fruit were unknown at that time, and the consistent characters of spine color and squat habit seemed to separate it from *F. acanthodes*, although Mr. Gates indicated that the two were closely related. Marshall and Bock (1941, p. 149) stated that *tortulispinus* was a form of *F. acanthodes*. On April 23, 1946, Dr. Reid Moran and I found *tortulispinus* in flower (*Moran and Lindsay 2010*, DS) and the flowers and fruits were indistinguishable from those of *F. acanthodes*.

I feel that the unusual habit, consistent color type and type of armament, and disjunct range of *tortulispinus* are sufficient to maintain it as a separate variety of *F. acanthodes*. It is recognizably different from the typical variety, although the two are closely related. According to Mr. Wm. Taylor Marshall plants very similar to *Ferocactus acanthodes* var. *tortulispinus* occur also in Arizona, south of Needles, and in the Mountain range behind the headquarters building in Organ Pipe National Monument.

23c. FEROCACTUS ACANTHODES (Lemaire) Britton and Rose var. *LECONTEI* (Engelmann) Lindsay, Cact. and Succ. Journ. 27: 169. 1955.

Echinocactus lecontei Engelmann, Proc. Amer. Acad. 3: 274. 1856.

Echinocactus wislizeni lecontei Engelmann, in Rothrock, Rep. U. S. Geogr. Surv. 6: 128. 1878.

Ferocactus lecontei (Engelmann) Britton and Rose, Cactaceae 3: 129. 1922.

Ferocactus acanthodes var. *lecontei* differs from var. *acanthodes* in having more appressed spines, more clavate body, and smaller seeds. Features of this plant are shown in Figure LBH725. The spines are not as twisted, and the upper and lower of the principal central spines are usually wider and recurved against the body of the plant. None of the characters which separate the two varieties is absolutely constant.

Holotype: Bill Williams Fork of the Colorado River, *Bigelow s.n.* 1854, (MBG, from the George Engelmann herbarium).

Distribution: Eastern Riverside and San Bernardino Counties of California, southern Nevada, and all of Arizona except the northeastern section. Map number seven.

Representative specimens: CALIFORNIA: SAN BERNARDINO CO.:

E. slope Providence Mts., open desert slope, 3000 ft., *Munz, Johnston & Harwood 4298* (POM,UC); Cedar Canyon, between New York Mts. and Providence Mts., *Munz* and *Everett 17454* (RSA); E. range of Whipple Mts., Alexander 1939 (UC); rock crevices high on S. slope cliffs, W. end Sheep Hole Mts., *Fosberg 8183* (POM). NEVADA. Rocky ridge E. Wilson's ranch, 1300 m, *Clokey 8428* (DS,RSA); Limestone ledges, S. Indian Springs, *Clokey 7539* (UC); Rock benches, Larrea belt, 1,200 m, S. Indian Springs, *Clokey 7212* (UC). ARIZONA. MOJAVE CO. 14 mi. SE. Hoover Dam, Black Mountain Range, 2,000 ft., *Benson 10114* (POM); Colorado Canyon, Arizona Territory, *Rusby 3445* (UC); 4 mi. NE. Kingman, 3500 ft., *Benson 10160* (POM). COCONINO CO. Havasu Canyon, 2 ft. tall, 19 ribs, *Howell s.n.* May 26, 1950 (CAS). YUMA CO. Bill Williams fork of Colorado River, *Bigelow s.n.* 1854 (MBG, holotype of *E. lecontei*); 3/4 mi. above Parker Dam on well drained rocky hillside, *Lindsay 2061* (DS,SD); basaltic slopes 14 mi. NW. Tyson on old road from Yuma to Quartzsite, ribs 19-22, *Wiggins 8629* (DS); Cabeza Prieta Mts., *Benson* and *Darrow 10809* (POM); Petrified Forest, Yuma Co., *Peebles s.n.*, 1935 (ARIZ). MARICOPA CO. 10 mi. N. Hassayampa, 900 ft., *Benson 9998* (POM); Aguila, *Dawson 6669* (AHFH); Papago Park, Tempe, *Blakley H2103* (DES), *Blakley B504* (DES). PIMA CO. 6 mi. E. Papago Well, Agua Dulce Mts., *Benson* and *Darrow 10707* (POM,ARIZ); Baboquivara Mts., (flowers 6.5 cm long) *Jones 24954, 24955* (POM).

Ferocactus acanthodes var. *lecontei* was considered to be a distinct species until recently. It occupies the northern and eastern portions of the range of *F. acanthodes*, often at high altitudes, particularly in the Mojave Desert in California and the Charleston Mountain region of Nevada. It is common along the Colorado River and its major Arizona tributaries. The plant usually differs from var. *acanthodes* in having wider, recurved central spines, with all the spines less twisted and more appressed. In some regions the stems are rather clavate, in other columnar and heavy. Seeds of var. *lecontei* are usually smaller than those of var. *acanthodes*.

Dr. George Engelmann described *Echinocactus lecontei* in the *Proceedings of the American Academy of Sciences* (3, p. 274) in 1856. In his discussion of the Cactaceae in the *Pacific Railway Report* (4, p. 29, 1856) he gave the following account of the discovery of the plant:

This gigantic species was first noticed by Dr. John L. Le Conte, on the lower Gila, where also Dr. C. C. Parry saw it. Both took it for the New Mexican *E. wislizeni*, to which, indeed, it bears a great resemblance in habit as well as in botanical characters, but the seed that I received from the first-named gentleman at once satisfied me that I had a distinct species before me. Subsequently Dr. Bigelow met with this remarkable plant, abundantly, from the Cactus Pass, at the head waters of William's River, down this stream to the Colorado, and west of it till *E. polycephalus* took its place.

Engelmann later treated *lecontei* as a variety of *Echinocactus wislizeni*, but Britton and Rose (1922, p. 129) maintained *lecontei* as a distinct species in their new genus *Ferocactus.* Benson, et al. (1940, p. 102) retained *lecontei*, but stated it was "probably merely a form of *Echinocactus acanthodes*." Marshall and Bock (1941, p. 148) included *Ferocactus lecontei* as a synonym of *F. acanthodes.* Kearney and Peebles (1942, p. 601) stated of *Echinocactus lecontei* "this species appears to intergrade with, or simulate, *E. acanthodes*," and the same authors in *Arizona Flora* (1951, p. 674) said "*Ferocactus lecontei* should perhaps be treated as a variety of *F. acanthodes*, but there are several points of difference in the spine characters." Benson (1944, p. 261) stated "the common barrel cactus in western and central Arizona does not seem to have any points of consistent difference from the type common in the California deserts," and placed *lecontei* in the synonym of *acanthodes.*

Ferocactus wislizeni and *F. acanthodes* var. *lecontei* share habitats in some parts of Arizona, and in those areas plants which appear to be morphologically intermediate between the two species are sometimes found. The regular flowering period of *F. acanthodes* var. *lecontei* is in April and May, and that of *F. wislizeni* is midsummer. Under these circumstances it seemed impossible that the intermediates were hybrids, but Mr. Wm. Taylor Marshall found a possible explanation when he observed an unusual sequence of summer rains which induced a second crop of blossoms in var. *lecontei* which were produced simultaneously with those of *F. wislizeni.* I have no information concerning the fecundity of the hybrid plants. A good example of a typical colony of the apparent hybrids is located in the Pinnacle Peak area north of Scottsdale, Maricopa County, Arizona.

Both *Ferocactus wislizeni* and *F. acanthodes* var. *lecontei* occasionally produce monstrose individuals in which the ribs are broken up into irregular tubercules and the apical meristerm divides irregularly. In 1929 Weinberg described *Echinocactus hertrichii* based on a monstrose plant of one or the other of the species. Several authors have considered it to be a monstrose form of *F. acanthodes*, but I have treated it as *F. wislizeni.*

The principal range of *F. acanthodes* is in the Lower Colorado Valley of the Sonoran Desert, with extensions into the Arizona Upland section as well as the southern Mojave and Great Basin deserts. Over much of this area annual rainfall averages less than five inches, most of which comes during the winter, but in the eastern sections, where var. *lecontei* occurs, the rainfall may reach fifteen inches, a large part of which comes in summer. *Ferocactus acanthodes* is found on well drained alluvial valleys and rocky mountain sides near sea level to about 4000 feet elevation. On the western side of the Imperial Valley, in California and northern Lower California, var. *acanthodes* is most common between 1000 and 2000 feet. The same variety grows into the oak belt at Sangre de Cristo and San Rafael, behind Ensenada in Lower California. In the Mojave Desert and in Nevada var. *lecontei* grows at higher elevations. Clokey collected one specimen at 1300 meters near Wilson's Ranch, Clark County, Nevada.

Associated plants vary greatly from one locality to another, but among the more common are *Yucca schidigera, Opuntia echinocarpa, Mammillaria tetrancistra, Echinocereus engelmannii, Larrea tridentata, Franseria dumosa, Olneya tesota*, and *Dalea spinosa*.

Observations on Ferocactus Acanthodes and its Varieties

Frank Thrombley

The name *Ferocactus acanthodes* is used by nurseries and a majority of botanists, with a few taxonomists using *F. cylindriceus* for this species. The root Fero = bold or fierce in Latin, and some of the plants are indeed ferocious to handle. *Ferocactus* varieties range from the southwest corner of Utah at its northern limit to Calamajue mission site, Baja California Norte, a straight line distance of about 845 km (525 miles). They are most prominent in the Mojave and Sonoran deserts but probably reach the limits of the Great Basin and Chihuahuan deserts as well.

There are four varieties currently recognized and in my opinion there is a fifth one, yet to be determined. They are: *Ferocactus acanthodes* varieties *acanthodes, lecontei, tortulispinus, eastwoodiae*, and a form from Calamajue Canyon. The taxon *Ferocactus rostii,* which was considered to be a distinct species, has been combined with *Ferocactus acanthodes* var. *acanthodes* and could possibly be called the 'rostii' form.

All of these plants have yellow flowers with a little red along the basal portions of the veins. Their size is atypical in that full grown plants can range from 0.6 to 2.75 m (2 to 9 ft) tall. The majority are columnar or barrel-shaped solitary stems. They are fascinating for their variable spination. Spine colors vary from white, gray, yellow to orange, and to a brilliant red; spine lengths go up to 18 cm (7 inches) and can be shaped oval to elliptical, flat to twisting, stiff to flexible, and in some cases having a hook on one or more of the centrals (Central Spines).

The greatest concentration of these barrel cacti are in the Riverside and San Diego Counties of California, which is the southern part. This very large population is divided into 75% var. *acanthodes* and 25% var. *lecontei.*

Ferocactus acanthodes var. *lecontei* has the greatest distribution. It is found in all areas of this vast range, with the exception of the Laguna Chapel Seca and Calamajue site in Baja California. It can grow to 1.8 to 2.3 m (6 to 7 ft) in length with a columnar stem completely covered with red or dull-red spines. The diameter can grow to 0.66 m (2 ft). It is an impressive sight, standing as a sentinel in its habitat, its stem covered completely with its broad, curving but not twisting central spines and its narrow, flexible, undulating radial spines.

Ferocactus acanthodes var. *eastwoodiae* is distributed over a very limited range, in small areas of Organ Pipe National Monument and the Dripping Springs and Mescal Mountains of Arizona. This plant grows to 2 m (6 ft) tall and the spine color is from straw-yellow to bright yellow. The spines are also comparatively short (not covering the plant body), with stout centrals and stiff radials which are a little shorter than the centrals. This is an impressive plant, growing on rocky cliff faces in habitat.

Ferocactus acanthodes var. *tortulispinus* is found in a very local area near Laguna Chapala Seca, Baja California, approximately 350 km (200 miles) south of its closest relatives, which are in northern Baja California. The colony seems to be located on two rocky hillsides with a relatively small population. A paved road, Mexican Highway 1, passes through the lower range of these plants. They grow to 66 cm (2 ft) tall and about 41 cm (16 in) in diameter (although this is not common). The spines are its most outstanding feature. The radials are grayish-white, acicular, and number about 20; the centrals are grayish-red, yellow-tipped, banded , and about 11 in number, and spreading. The lower central is usually very contorted, hooked, and up to 15 cm (6 in) long. A very fierce looking plant! They 'blend in' with their reddish and rocky hillside surroundings. A colony of *Ferocactus* growing at the Calamajue site about 14 to 17 km (8 to 10 miles) directly southeast of Laguna Chapela Seca have been assigned to var. *tortulispinus* by Nigel Taylor. He wrote that this disjunct variety is very similar to var. *acanthodes* and is maintained here as var. *tortulispius* more for proximity than for morphological differences (N. Taylor in Bradleya 2/1984). George Lindsay wrote me that he passed through the region and the colony looked to him like var. *acanthodes*, but he didn't have a chance to analyze them. The colony however is very variable in all aspects. The plants on the mesa can grow in excess of 200 cm (6 ft) in height. I measured a plant 216 cm (6.5 ft) tall, 33 cm (1 ft) in diameter, with all yellow spines, and no contorted central spines. In the same location there is a *Ferocactus* 126 cm (3 ft 10 in) tall, yellow spined, with 11.4-12.7 cm (4.5-5 in) contorted central spines. All of these plants were photographed. They had yellow flowers, and were growing at about a 600 m (1,800 ft) elevation. As one travels down into the canyon they look less and less like var. *acanthodes*. You would find the Ferocacti becoming much smaller, (up to 100 cm or 3 ft high), with spination colors of orange, yellow, red, and dull grayish-red. The spines vary in length and description from short straight to hooked, and of course many contorted centrals, but only in the canyon. This is a much larger colony than the one at Laguna Chapala Seca and certainly deserves to be studied further.

And last of this series, *Ferocactus acanthodes* var. *acanthodes* is certainly the most variable and colorful. The Anza-Borrego State Park of California in San Diego County is an ideal location to study this variety. Some colonies with thousands of these plants appear to be at a maximum height at 100 cm (3 ft). Other colonies, in different habitats within the park grow to 200 cm (6 ft), with an occasional 265 cm (8 ft) plant. I measured a plant 234 cm (7 ft 1 in) tall and I know of a 300 cm (9 ft) tall sighting. They are primarily growing on the rocky hillsides at elevations between 165 and 825 m (500 to 2,500 ft) and into every canyon and arroyo. Within the Park's 500,000 plus acres there must be 50,000 to 100,000 Ferocacti. The spine colors include all those previously described, with some plants having both orange and red on each spines.

Ferocactus spination varies from the symmetrical form on var. *eastwoodiae* to the long twisted spines of var. *tortulispinus*, with some growing to a length of 18 cm (7 in). Their shapes range from barrel to columnar, with occasional clumping, and pups or offsets on older stems. A few plants divide dichotomously. I believe that I have found both *lecontei* and *eastwoodiae* growing in the park, but further study is needed to confirm this. The Calamajue site needs further study by a taxonomist/morphologist, one versed in the science of form and structure of organisms. The *Ferocactus* growing at Calamajue are very much the same as the var. *acanthodes* growing in Anza-Borrego Park, and I would guess that they are of this variety.

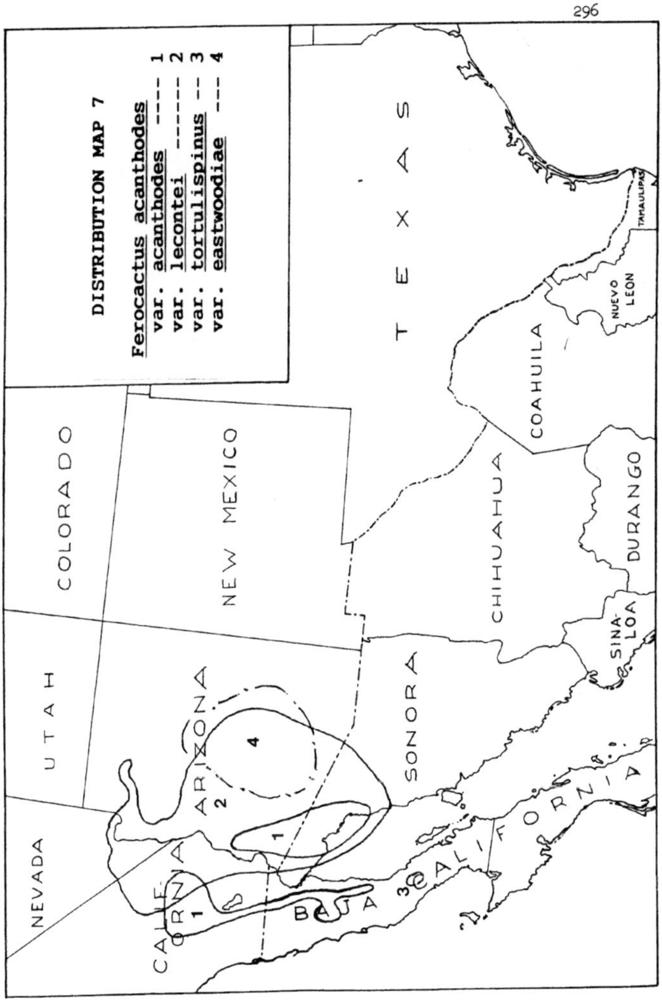

Distribution Map 7

Figure 114. Holotype specimen of *Echinocactus cylindraceus*, which has been selected to serve also as the neotype of *Ferocactus acanthodes*.

Figure 115. *Ferocactus acanthodes* var. *acanthodes* from the approximate type locality of *Echinocactus cylindraceus*, in San Felipe Wash, San Diego County, Californla.

Figure 116. Flowers of *Ferocactus acanthodes* var. *acanthodes*, (*Lindsay 2063*), shown in figure 115, from San Diego County, California.

Figure 117. *Ferocactus acanthodes* var. in the Anza Desert State Park, San Diego County, California.

Figure 118. Holotype specimen of *Ferocactus rostii,* preserved in the U.S. National Herbarium.The photograph does not indicate it is a particularly slender species.

Figure 119. *Ferocactus acanthodes* var. *acanthodes*, of the "*rostii*" form, in the lower section of Cantillas Canyon, Sierra Juarez, Lower California.

Figure 120. *Ferocactus acanthodes* var. *acanthodes*, a beautiful golden yellow form in Cantillas Canyon. This print is from a kodachrome transparency by Mr. Charles F. Harbison, of the San Diego Natural History Museum.

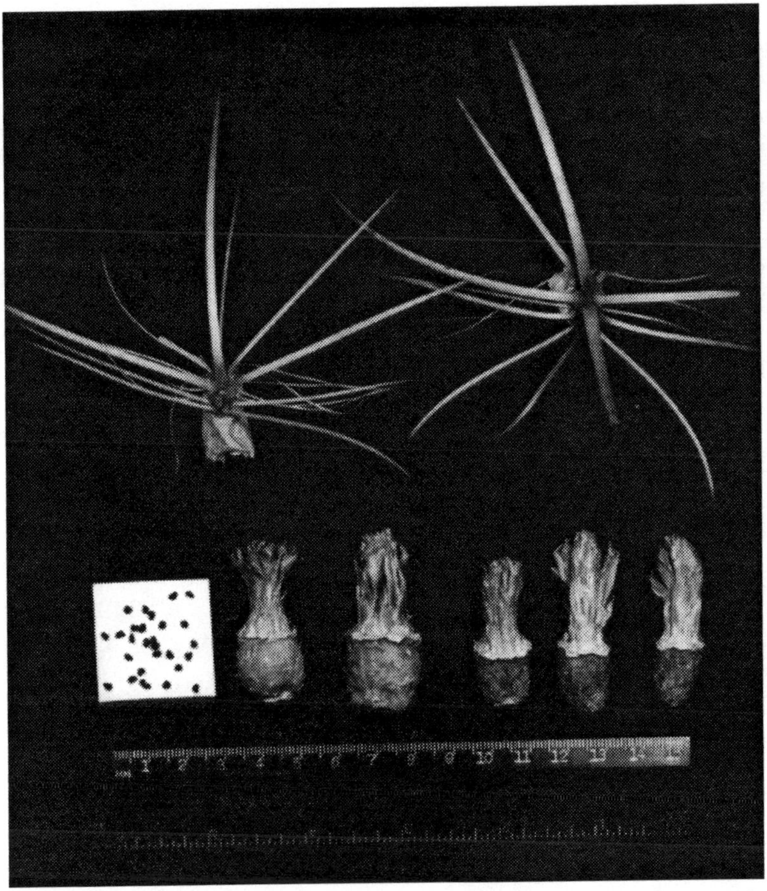

Figure 121. Preserved material from the plants shown in figure 120, collected by Charles F. Harbison in Cantillas Canyon, Lower California.

Figure 122. *Ferocactus acanthodes* var. *acanthodes*, (*Lindsay 2064*), from 33 miles west of Mexicali, Lower California, at an elevation of 1,250 feet on the east slopes of the Sierra Juarez.

Figure 123. Holotype specimen of *Ferocactus tortulospinus* Gates, preserved in the Dudley Herbarium, Stanford University.

Figure 124. *Ferocactus acanthodes* var. *tortulospinus* growing a few miles north of Laguna Seca Chapala, Lowrer California.

Figure 125 *Ferocactus acanthodes* var. *tortulospinus*, (*Moran 2010*), photographed April 23, 1946, 13 km. north of Laguna Seca Chapala, Lower California.

Figure 126. ***Ferocactus acanthodes*** **var.** ***lecontei*****, from near the probably type locality of** ***Echinocactus lecontei*** **Engelmann, at the mouth of the Bill Williams River, Arizona.**

Figure 127. Specimen of Ferocactus which may be a hybrid of *Ferocactus wislizenii* var. *wislizenii* and *F. acanthodes* var. *lecontei.* Photographed at Pinnacle Peak, Maricopa County,

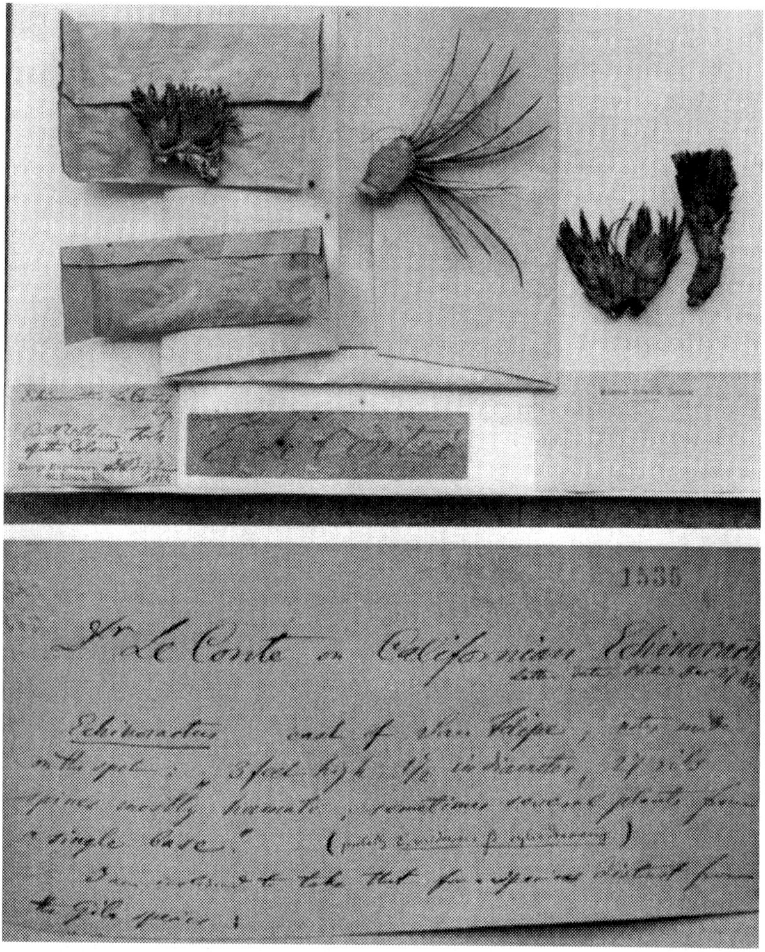

Figure 128. Holotype specimen of *Echinocactus lecontei* and notes concerning *E. cylindraceus* in the George Engelmann material at the Missouri Botanical Carden.

24. FEROCACTUS JOHNSTONIANUS Britton and Rose, Cactaceae 4: 287. 1923.

Echinocactus johnstonianus (Britton and Rose) Fosberg, Am. Mid. Nat. 27: 257. 1942.

STEM simple, globular to short-cylindric, to over 1 m tall and 3.5 dm broad. RIBS 24-31, slightly tuberculate, 2 cm tall. Areoles elliptic, 2 cm long and 7 mm wide, closely set. SPINES golden yellow aging brown, about 22-25, to 6 cm long and 1.2 mm thick, all about the same and not differentiated into central and radial series, sublate, slightly recurved outward and sometimes slightly annulate; nectariferous gland-spines in flowering areoles are small, conical, and persistent. FLOWERS yellow, funnelform, to 5 cm long and 3.5 cm wide; broad orbicular imbricate scales of ovary intergrading with the outer perianth segments which are yellow tinged with red, to 2 cm long and 1 cm wide with ciliate margin and obtuse tip; inner perianth segments yellowish, 2 cm long and 7 mm wide, margins slightly errose, tip short acuminate; filaments yellow below, reddish above, anthers yellow; style 2 cm long, the upper 1 cm divided into 8-13 flesh-colored stigma lobes. FRUIT when dried 3 cm long and 1.5 wide, of 5-6 cm long including the withered perianth; fruit sometimes opens by basal pore. SEEDS shining black, irregularly angled, averaging 2.5 mm long, 1.5 mm wide, and 1.25 mm thick, covered with rather regular oval depressions.

Holotype: Wash behind lagoon on east side of Angel de la Guardia Island, Gulf of California, Mexico, *Ivan M. Johnston 3394*, May 2, 1921, (US).

Distribution: Angel de la Guardia Island. Known only from the type locality behind the lagoon on the eastern side, and from slopes and bluffs on the southwestern side opposite Los Angeles Bay. Map number eight

Representative Specimens: MEXICO: GULF OF CALIFORNIA: Angel de la Guardia Island, wash behind the lagoon, *Johnston 3394* (US, type, and CAS); *Lindsay 539* (DS,SD).

Ferocactus johnstonianus was named for its discoverer, Ivan M. Johnston, botanist on the California Academy of Sciences Expedition to the Gulf of California in 1921. It is known to occur only on Angel de la Guardia Island, and is rare there. Johnston reported a "few plants in wash" at the lagoon on the eastern side of the island in 1935, and I got three plants from the rugged cliffs in the same area in 1936. On April 6, 1947 I collected herbarium material and two small living plants at the type locality, one of which flowered in my garden on July 3, 1947. The type specimen was in bloom at the time it was collected on May 2, 1921.

Ferocactus johnstonianus is very attractive, with intermeshed golden yellow spines almost hiding the stem. It is always unbranched, and sometimes grows to more than three feet tall. The original description erred in giving 6 dm as the maximum height it attains.

While this plant was first referred to *Ferocactus diguetii*, it is probably not very closely related to that species, having three times as many spines, a much smaller habit, and very different seeds. On the other hand it seems to be close to *Ferocactus acanthodes* of the "rostii" form. The two species possess in common a large number of unspecialized yellow spines, similar yellow flowers, and occasional juvenile plants with reddish spines.

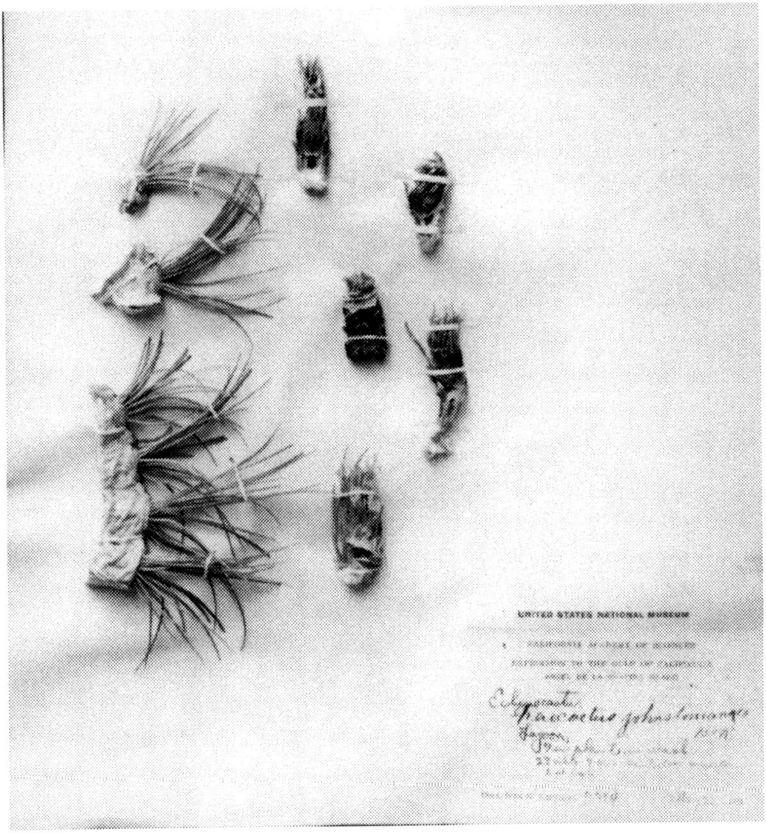

Figure 129. ***Ferocactus johnstonianus*****, holotype specimen in the United States National Herbarium.**

Figure 130. ***Ferocactus johnstonianus,*** **(*Lindsay 539*), growing at the type locality behind the lagoon on the northeast side of Angel de la Guardia Island, Gulf of Callfornia, Mexico.**

Figure 131. *Ferocactus johnstonianus* on the southwest side of Angel de la Guardia Island, an exceptionally large specimen.

25. FEROCACTUS DIGUETII (Weber) Britton and Rose, Cactaceae 3: 131. 1922.

Key to the varieties

a. Stem massive colmnar, mature specimens over 1 m tall and 5 dm in diameter, juvenile specimens usually depressed globular, broader than tall . . . . *F. d.* var. *diguetii*

b. Stem sub-columnar, mature specimens less than 1 m tall and 5 dm in diameter, juvenile specimens globular and not flattened . . . . *F. d.* var. *carmenensis*

25a. FEROCACTUS DIGUETII (Weber) Britton and Rose var. DIGUETII

Echinocactus diguetii Weber, Bull. Mus. Hist. Nat. Paris 4: 100.1898.
Ferocactus diguetii (Weber) Britton and Rose, Cactaceae 3: 131. 1922.

STEM simple, massive colmnar, to 4 m tall and 6 dm thick. RIBS 25-35, to 3 cm tall, vertical becoming sinuate in old specimens. AREOLES elliptic, to 2 cm long and 1 cm wide, bearing tan tomentum which turns gray and erodes away. SPINES clear yellow or occasionally reddish brown, usually 7-8, but sometimes only 4 and in some juvenile specimens to 10, not differentiated into central and radial series, sublate, very slightly, if at all, annulate, to 5 cm long and 1.5 thick, ere+ct spreading, slightly curved outward. FLOWERS red, funnelform, 4 cm long and 4 cm wide; floral tube V-shaped in long section, the walls about 8 mm thick; scales on ovary imbricate, fimbriate, semi-orbicular, 4-5 mm wide, intergrading with outer perianth segments, these dark red with cream margins, spatulate, about 1-1.5 cm long, 8-10 mm wide; inner perianth segments 2 cm long and 8 mm wide dark red with yellow margin, oblanceolate, tip obtuse or acuminate; stamens very numerous, erect, inserted in dense band in the perianth tube extending from the base of style; filaments 10-13 mm long, tapering upwards, yellowish below tinged with red above; anthers yellow; nectary pit about 4 mm wide, with a glandular ring around the base of the style; style red or orange, 17 mm long, with longitudinal ridges each of which continues into one of the stigma lobes; stigma lobes 12, 5-10 mm long, yellow. FRUIT when dry 3 cm long and 2 cm wide, 5 cm long including the withered perianth, covered with lunate scales, usually dehiscing through basal pore. SEEDS glossy brown, irregular in shape, 1.5 mm long, 1 mm wide, with small oval pits rather than the usual polygonal sculpturing, the testa smooth in a collar around the hilum, the hilum very large and deep, 0.5 mm long.

Neotype: Santa Catalina Island, Gulf of California, Mexico, *Moran 3883* (DS). Weber described this species from photographs and a dried carcass of a small plant. None of the holotype material is preserved at the Paris Museum, and is presumed lost. A representative specimen from the type locality has been chosen as a neotype.

Distribution: Restricted to the islands of the Gulf of California, including Santa Catalina, Monserrate, Dansante, San Diego, and Ceralbo. Also reported from Coronados Island, near Loreto, but probably now extinct there. Map number eight.

Representative specimens: MEXICO: GULF OF CALIFORNIA: Santa Catalina Island, southwest corner, *Johnston 4098* (CAS), *Lindsay 525* (DS,SD); northeast side, *Moran 3883* (DS, neotype), *Lindsay 2200* (DS,SD); San Diego Island, *Lindsay 2187* (DS,SD); Ceralbo Island, one half mile N. Gordas Point, *Johnston 4037* (CAS); middle of south coast, *Moran 3581* (DS), *Lindsay* 2170 (DS,SD).

This species is the largest and most spectacular of the Ferocacti. It was discovered by Leon Diguet on Santa Catalina Island while he was making natural history collections for the Museum d'Histoire Naturelle in Paris, and was described by Albert Weber, the Director of the Museum, in 1898. *Ferocactus diguetii* var. *diguetii* has a wide distribution on the islands of the Gulf of California, but has not often been collected and is rare in cultivation because it is endemic to that infrequently visited region.

On Catalina Island the plants are particularly large, some even twelve feet tall. They never branch. The red flowers are almost hidden among the golden colored spines at the tops of the plants. Young specimens are flattened globular in shape, and could be mistaken for mature *Echinocactus grusonii*. The ribs are acute and straight on most specimens, but the bodies of some of the older individuals seem to buckle and sag, and the ribs become sinuously twisted and contorted, or even monstrose. This phenomenon is characteristic of some of the larger central Mexican Echinocacti, particularly *Echinocactus grandis* from near Tehuacan, Puebla.

Dr. Ivan M. Johnston reported finding *Ferocactus diguetii* on Coronados Island, near Loreto, in 1921, but I failed to find it when I looked there in 1938 and 1952. The inhabitants of Loreto said that in the years of drought they collected the "visnagas" from Coronados and Carmen Islands, to use as stock food, and this practice may have eliminated the plants on Coronados.

Ferocactus diguetii var. *diguetii* and *Pachycereus pringlei* form the dominant elements of the vegetation on Santa Catalina Islands, where they grow from the gravel flats just behind the beach to the tops of the precipitous rocky mountains. Another cactus, *Machaerocereus gummosus*, forms impenetrable thickets in the arroyo bottoms. Also associated with *Ferocactus diguetii* are *Bursera microphylla, B. rhoifolia, Esenbeckia flava, Castela peninsularis, Viscainoa geniculata, Atriplex barclayana, Haplopappus spinulosus*, var. *incisifolius, Cercidium peninsulare, Hofmeistera fasciculata, Porophyllum gracile, Euphorbia carmenensis, Dalea parryi*, etc.

25b. FEROCACTUS DIGUETII (Weber) Britton and Rose var. CARMENENSIS Lindsay, Cact. and Succ. Journ. 27: 167. 1955.

Differs from the var. *diguetii* in size, never over 1 m tall and 4 dm in diameter, usually much smaller. Juvenile plants tend to be globular rather than flattened, with somewhat heavier spines than the typical variety.

Holotype: Balandera Bay, Carmen Island, Gulf of California, Mexico, *Lindsay 2204* (DS).

Distribution: Carmen Island, Gulf of California, Mexico. Map number eight.

Representative specimens: MEXICO: GULF OF CALIFORNIA: Balandera Bay, Carmen Island, *Lindsay 2204* (DS, holotype, with cotypes at MEXU,SD), *Lindsay 518* (DS).

Ferocactus diguetii var. *carmenensis* was collected by Dr. Rose in 1911, and noted by Johnston in 1921. I first visited Carmen Island in 1947, looking for the giant *Ferocactus diguetii*, but was able to find only small specimens, the largest about three feet tall and 15 inches in diameter. The habit of the juvenile plants also was noticeably different. Instead of being flattened with a depressed apex they were short-cylindric, with rounded tops, and the spines seemed heavier and browner. The small size of the obviously mature plants on Carmen Island was particularly puzzling because a plate in Britton and Rose (1922: plate 11, facing p. 122) showed two huge barrel cacti, captioned *Ferocactus diguetii* and reportedly taken by Dr. Rose on Carmen Island. However, the same photograph had been used by Townsend (1916, p. 429) in his general account of the "Albatross" voyage, where it was captioned as having been taken at Santa Catalina Island, which undoubtedly is correct.

I suspected that the Carmen Island barrel cacti deserved varietal recognition at the time of my first visit (*Lindsay 1948*, p. 22) in spite of the similarity of spines and flowers to those of the typical population. Dr. Reid Moran and I had opportunity to examine the Carmen Island plants in 1952, just after studying them on Catalina and Ceralbo Islands. I am convinced that the uniformly small size and different habit of the Ferocacti on Carmen Island indicate they are a distinct variety.

Ferocactus diguetii var. *carmenensis* is known only from the one island, although the population formerly on nearby Coronados Island may have been the same variety. It forms only a minor element of the vegetation of Carmen Island, because the small plants are rare and scattered. This is in marked contrast to the typical variety on Catalina Island.

Figure 132. *Ferocactus diguetti* var. *diguetii* at the type locality, Santa Catalina Island, Gulf of California, Mexico.

Figure 133. An old specimen of *Ferocactus diguetti* var. *diguetii* on Santa Catalina Island, showing the sinuate ribs which result from sagging of the stem.

Figure 134. Above: *Ferocactus diguetti* var. *diguetii* blossoming on Ceralbo Island April 3, 1952. Below: Flower of *F. diguetii* var *carmenensis*.

Figure 135. *Ferocactus diguetti* var. *carmenensis* photographed at Marquer Bay, Carmen Island, Gulf of California. This was the largest specimen seen.

Figure 136. *Ferocactus diguetti* var. *carmenensis* at Balandera Bay, Carmen Island.

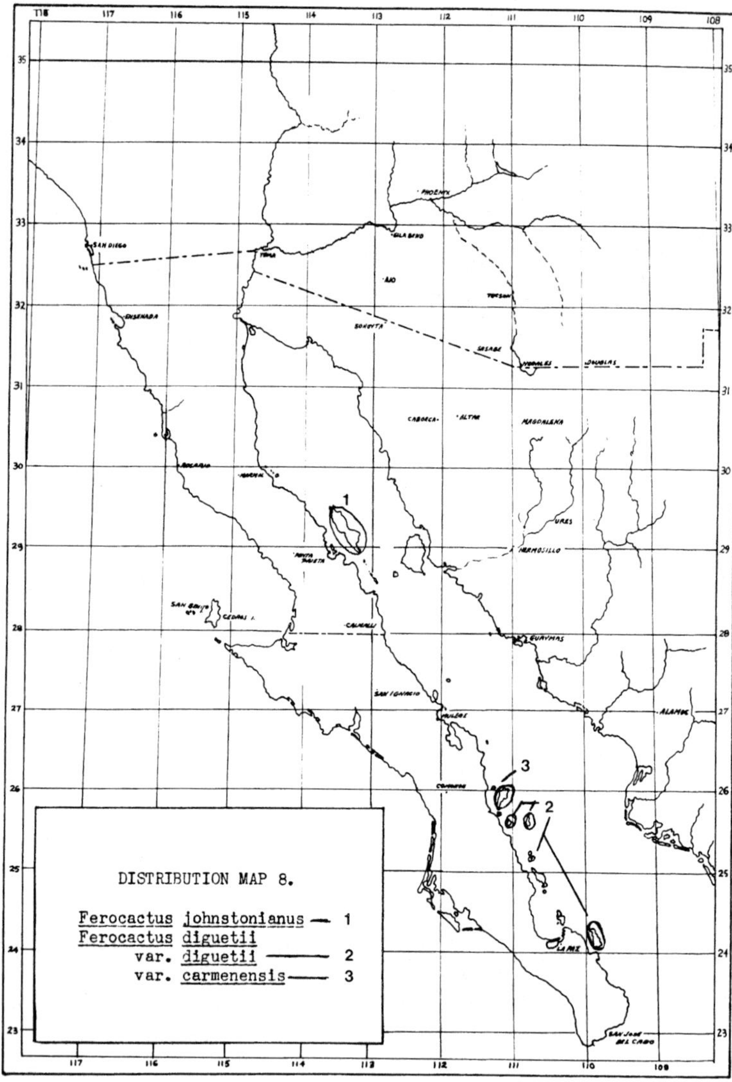

Distribution Map 8

26. FEROCACTUS REPPENHAGENII G. Unger, Kakt. and Sukk. 25: 50-54. 1974.

Editors' Note: *This is a recently named species. There are 3 adult specimens in the ground at the San Diego Zoo Wild Animal Park (the WAP). They were sprouted from seed collected by Gordon Tekleberg in the field. They flowered in early May, and we have just collected a couple of seed pods.*

Some have placed Ferocactus reppenhagenii *within* F. schwarzii *as a variety, i.e.,* F. schwarzii *var.* reppenhagenii. *Nigel Taylor recognizes it as a species, although he mentions that "Juvenile plants suggest a close afinity with [*F.schwarzii*], but the adults retain their round-edged ribs and long spines (Bradleya 2/84)." We have accepted Taylor's view.*

STEM solitary, depressed-globose, columnar to 80 cm (*the flowering WAP plants are about 30 cm high after 20 years, and are becoming columnar*), 9-24 cm diameter. RIBS 12-18, edge rounded. AREOLES confluent on old plants. RADIAL SPINES (6-)7-9(-11) to 4 cm. CENTRAL SPINE 1, 2.8-8 cm. FLOWERS 2-3 x 2-3 cm, yellow to orange; stigmas 7. FRUIT ovoid, 1.5-2.2 x 0.8-1.7 cm, bright to dark red; seed to 2.3 mm, reddish brown to black, very smooth.

Range: Reportedly Colima and Michoacan; Oaxaca; SE and SW facing slopes; 1900-2500 m. Note: Colima and Michoacan are adjacent states and are about 200 miles from the Oaxaca border, across Guerrero State.

27. FEROCACTUS LINDSAYI (H.Bravo-Hollis) Cact. Succ. Mex. 11: 9-12. 1966; Cact. Succ. J. (US) 45: 104, figures 3 and 4. 1973.

Editors' Note: *This species was identified and named in 1966, 11 years after the George Lindsay text was submitted as his Ph.D. dissertation. The following information is supplied by the Editors.*

Ferocactus lindsayi was named for George Lindsay. Nigel Taylor suggested in Bradleya 5/1987, 95-96 that *F. lindsayi* could fit into what he terms the *Ferocactus pottsii* Group. This is one of four *Ferocactus* Groups that Dr. Taylor has assembled, based on his field work, and on his examinations of fruit and seeds. However, members of the Taylor *Pottsii* Group are located along the Gulf of California in the Mexican states of Baja California, Sonora, and Sinaloa. The southern-most state, Sinaloa, is about 500 miles north of the *F. lindsayi* type locale in the state of Michoacan along the lower course of the Rio Balsas, which empties into the Pacific. Dr. Taylor suggests that it could be the southern Mexico representative of the Group. This would place representatives of all four Groups in southern Mexico, which could be a center of radiation, with allopatric speciation. An interesting viewpoint, but there is no convincing evidence for this. Dr. Taylor related to us that he expects that the *Ferocactus* molecular studies of Hugo Cota could, and probably would, modify his groupings. Dr. Taylor examined *F. lindsayi* in Michoacan, Cuenca del Balsas, Hwy. 37, Paso de Chivo, 250-300 m, on 19 July 1986 (Bradleya 5/1987: 95-96) and observed that it inhabited bare rocky cliffs (hopefully out of reach of man and large plant eating mammals).

STEM globose to short cylindric, to 60 x 40 cm, gray- glaucous green. RIBS 13-18. AREOLES 10-18 mm apart, elliptic, gray-felty. RADIAL SPINES 5-6, round or more or less flattened, 2.5-3 cm large. CENTRAL SPINE 1, 4.5 cm, terete, straight. FLOWER 5 x 3-4 cm, subapical, bell-shaped, glossy yellow, style and 12 stigmas yellow. Fruit bright red, ovoid, dry interior, basal pore. Seeds small, dark-brown to black, boomerang shaped.

Figure 137. ***Ferocactus lindsayi*** **Bravo, La Presa del Infienillo, Michocan, Mexico. Arthur Bridge in the upper photo.**

28. FEROCACTUS HAEMATACANTHUS (Salm-Dyck)

***Editors' Note:** This section has been interpolated from several sources, including Taylor and Backeberg.* F. haematanthus *is currently believed to be a species. It has been named with profusion and confusion since its probable first description as* Echinocactus electracanthus *back in 1853.* E. electracanthus *was also believed to be a* Ferocactus histrix *synonym (as discussed in Section 8). It was once identified as a variety of* Ferocactus pilosus *or as previously known,* stainesii *(Backeberg, 1961). The 1973 Backeberg states "Not a variety of* F. stainesii *."*

Echinocactus haematacanthus, Cact. Hort.Dyck 1849, 150 (1850).

Ferocactus haematacanthus, Sanchez-Mejorada, in Cact. Succ. Mex. 9:41 (1964) and 11:31-40, 51-52 (1966); also Hirao in Kakt. and Sukk. 31:14-16 (1980).

STEM globose to cylindrical, 30-120 h.x 26-36 cm diameter., green with a white wooly crown, glaucous when young. RIBS 13-27, narrow, slightly wavy. AREOLES 16-23 mm apart, silky-yellow at first, later graying. RADIAL SPINES 6, upper 2 flattened, 25-35 mm large., deep-blood red tipped with yellow. CENTRAL SPINE 4, directed downwards, similarly colored, straight or slightly curving, 40-80 mm large. FLOWERS purplish pink, 6-7 x 5.8-6.8 cm, in a ring around the crown; style whitish-yellow; stigmas 9-10, intense yellow. FRUIT ovoid, deep purple, 2.2-3.5 x 1.4-2.7 cm; seed 1.8 mm, black.

Neotype: Puebla-Veracruz border, road between Tehuacan and Cumbres de Acultzingo, 1966, *Sanchez-Mejorada 10786* (MEXU).

29. FEROCACTUS HAMATACANTHUS (Muhlenpfordt) Britton & Rose, Cact. 3:144. 1922.

Editors' Note: *Placing* Ferocactus hamatocanthus *in the genus* Ferocactus *has been a struggle, having been in* Echinocactus, Ancistrocactus, *and* Hamatocanthus . *Some place it in* Echinocactus. *The Ferocacti of the Texas Big Bend region and Rio Grande Plain, which includes* F. setispinus *as well as* F. hamatacanthus,, *are considered to be Ferocacti by Benson and Nigel Taylor. Their observations have been blended in the following text.*

Key to the varieties

a. STEM solitary, rarely cespitose, hemispheric to cylindric, to 60 x 30 cm. RIBS 12-17, rounded, not compressed, strongly tuberculate. RADIAL SPINES 8-20, 1.5-4 cm. CENTRAL SPINES 4-8 to 10 cm, terete or somewhat flattened, twisting but not flexuous. FLOWER usually 6.5-7.5 cm diameter, 6-7 cm long with a funnel shaped tube; petaloids yellow except for red in the throat; stigmas 11-14, yellow; sepaloids with green and red midribs. FRUIT ovoid to oblong, about 5 x 2.5 cm, pinkish red. SEEDS black, finely pitted, asymetrically obovoid, to 1.6 mm long, 1 mm broad.
.... *F. hamatacanthus* var. *hamatacanthus*

b. STEM 30 x 20 cm. RIBS about 13, strongly compressed, more acute, well-defined. RADIAL SPINES 8-12, some markedly flattened. CENTRAL SPINES 4, lowermost strongly flattened and markedly flexuous. FLOWER 6.5-7.5 cm dia., entirely yellow; stigmas 8-10. FRUIT to 2.5 cm, dark greenish to dark brownish-red, sometimes globose. SEED about 1 mm.
.... *F. hamatacanthus* var. *sinuatus*

Juvenile plants have shorter and slenderer central and radial spines.

29a FEROCACTUS HAMATACANTHUS variety HAMATACANTHUS

Echinocactus hamatacanthus Muhlenpfordt, Allg. Gartenz 14:371. 1846
Echinocactus longihamatus Galeotti var. *brevispinus* Engelmann, Rept. U.S.and Mex. Boundary Surv. 2: Cactaceae 22. 1859.
Ferocactus hamatacanthus subg. *hamatacanthus* H Bravo-Hollis, Cact. Succ. Mex. 21:66. 1976.

Neotype: Coahuila, Saltillo, Mexico, 1880, *Palmer 374(K)* .
Distribution: See Map 9. Chihuahuan Desert from SE New Mexico through the Texas Desert Grassland and Rio Grande Plain into S Chihuahua and E Durango, Mexico.
See also Figure 143.

29b FEROCACTUS HAMATACANTHUS variety SINUATUS

A. Dietrich, Allg. Gartenz. 19: 345. 1851.

Echinocactus sinuatus A. Dietrich, Allg. Gartenz, 19: 345. 1851.
Ferocactus hamatacanthus var. *sinuatus*, L. Benson, Cact. Succ. J. (USA), 41: 128. 1969; also G. Unger, Kakt. and Sukk. 31:289-291. 1981.

Neotype: Collected in W Texas, probably on the Pecos or San Pedro [Rivers], 1852, C. Wright.
Distribution: See Map 9. From SE Texas and the Rio Grande Plain southwards into NE Mexico, on the eastern side of the Sierra Madre, into the states of Tamaulipas and Nuevo Leon, occupying brushland, mostly at low altitudes.

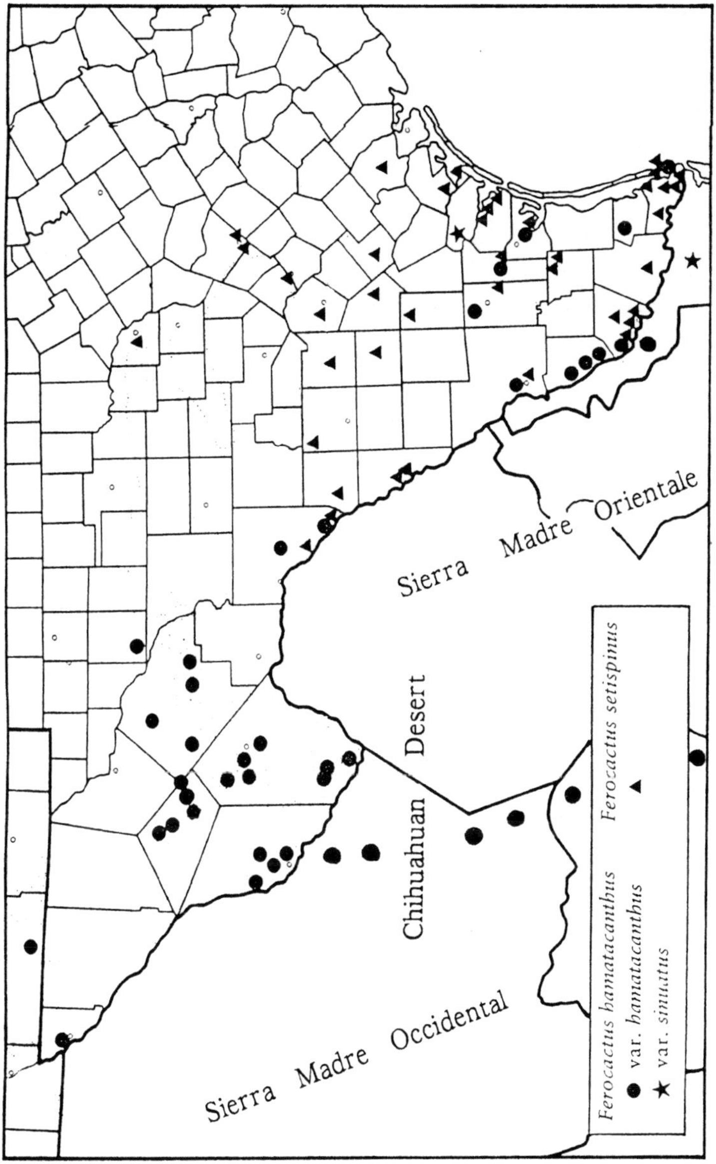

Distribution Map 9

30. FEROCACTUS SETISPINUS (Engelmann) L. Benson

Editors' Note: *Neither George Lindsay nor Nigel Taylor nor Hugo Cota includes this as a* Ferocactus *species. Some may consider it to be an* Echinocactus. *Lindsay wrote, "... in my opinion flower, fruit, stem, and spine morphology place* hamatacanthus *and* setispinus *in the same genus, and that genus is not* Ferocactus *(see Taxa Excluded From* Ferocactus*)." At present, both Taylor and Cota recognize* hamatacanthus *as a* Ferocactus, *but not* setispinus. *Britton and Rose proposed placing* setispinus *in a new genus,* Hamatacanthus, *because of its narrow funnelform floral tube. Lyman Benson was of the view that it was a* Ferocactus, *and that in its sectional view (see Plate LBH748) it resembles other Ferocacti. He related that "The often slender ovary gives the false impression of a narrow tube." He recognized that it was different looking. He wrote, [It] "is a miniature barrel cactus, and its slender hooked spines and its tendency to branch are not reminiscent of its gigantic western relatives."*

George Lindsay commented "Many species of Ferocactus *are actually actively evolving complexes of distinct populations which are quite different from each other" and "some are possibly incipient species which have not yet evolved genetic isolation (see the section "Taxonomic treatment")." As we trace the genus* Ferocactus *northward into the Baja California and the USA, we find an increasing tendency to actively evolve. Some species remain isolated from others by geographical isolation and different flowering times. However, occasional late year rains may bring a second flowering which overlaps with normal flowerings of other species, producing hybrid intergrades.* Ferocactus setispinus *occurs in Texas and nearby Mexico, around the Rio Grande Plain, sharing much of the area with* Ferocactus hamatacanthus . *This is a head scratching region for us. We doubt that this plant is a* Ferocactus. *But Benson could be proved correct, so we have included it here, but not elsewhere in this book.*

Ferocactus setispinus *is depicted in Figure 144, and its habitat is shown in Map 9.*

Description (from Benson)

STEMS green, solitary to numerous, ovoid or cylindroid, 3.8-10 (20) cm long, 3.8 cm diameter RIBS +/- 13, narrow. AREOLES 1.5 mm diameter, typically 9-12 cm apart. SPINES rather dense, but not obscuring stem. PRINCIPAL CENTRAL SPINE straw colored to reddish-brown with lighter tip, strongly hooked (sometimes with 2 or 3 additional smaller straight upper centrioles per areole), perpendicular to stem, finely scaberulous-canescent, 1-3.8 cm long, basally 0.5 (0.7) mm diameter or breadth, usually acicular but rarely flattened, nearly circular to sometimes narrowly elliptic in cross section. R. SPINES 12-15 per areole, straw colored or white to brown, varying within the areole, spreading, nearly straight, the longer mostly to 12 mm, upperradials sometimes mmuch longer, basally 0.25 mm diameter, acicular, nearly circular in section. FLOWER 4-5.5 cm diameter, 3.8-5 cm long; sepaloids with the midribs and adjacent areas green, margins red, the largest cuneate-oblanceolate, to 20 mm long, to 6 (9) broad, the lower obtuse, uppermost acute and fimbriolate; petaloids clear yellow with red bases, largest oblanceolate, 20-25 mm long, 6-9 mm broad, acute, cuspidulate, the margins entire; filaments pale yellow to white, +/- 6 mm long, very slender; anthers yellow, narrowly oblong, length about 3 times breadth, 0.7 mm long. FRUIT red, fleshy at maturity, with +/- 10-15 scales, globular, 9-12 mm long and diameter; seed minutely papillate, obovoid, but base flaring around micropyle, usually 1-1.4 mm long, 0.8-1 mm broad, +/-0.5 mm thick; hilum obviously basal.

Ferocactus setispinus lives in black or clay soils and leaf mold on hills and flats in grasslands, usually in mesquite thickets at or below 300 m (1,000 ft) in the Rio Grande Plain and Edwards Plateau. See Map 9.

IMPERFECTLY KNOWN SPECIES

1. ECHINOCACTUS CALIFORNICUS in Monville's Catalogue, 1846.

Echinocactus californicus Cels ex Labouret, Monogr. Cact. 199. 1853.
Echinocactus californicus Hort. ex Forester, Handb. Cact. ed. 2, 472. 1885.

Echinocactus californicus was a name applied to a plant, probably of the *Ferocactus acanthodes* relationship, which was raised from seed in France about 1840. The species was first mentioned in a catalogue of the Monville collection in 1846, where it was placed between *Echinocactus spiralis* and *E. acanthodes*. The plant was said to have been raised by a M. Dumesnil, of Harve, from seeds which a Navy Captain brought from Lower California.

Engelmann (1852, p. 338) was aware of the name in 1852, but said that it was applied to young plants raised from seed in Europe, and that he was informed that neither the identity nor native country of the seedlings was satisfactorily known. Engelmann (in Brewer and Watson, 1876, p. 245) later considered it to be a synonym of *Echinocactus viridescens*, which he said was"cultivated in Europe under the name *E. Californicus*." Weber (1898, p. 103) discussed *Echinocactus californicus* in some detail. He apparently had seen the specimens of Dumesnil in flower, in which case the plants would have been about fifty years old. Weber described the plants as subglobose, 30 cm in diameter and 21 cm tall, with 20 ribs. The spines were all stiff, round and not flattened, and annulate. Radial spines were 7-9, 4 long, straight, and yellow with purple spots. The four central spines were cruciform, the upper ones straight, the lower one sturdier, annulate, hooked, and about 6 cm long. The flowers were yellow, 5 cm long and 6 cm wide, with carmine filaments.

Weber felt that Engelmann was wrong in assigning *E. californicus* to *E. viridescens*. Possibly more than one taxon was raised in Europe under the name *E. californicus*, because Schumann (1898, pp. 346, 356) referred *E. californicus* hort. to *E. viridescens*, and *E. californicus* Monville to *E. Emoryi*.

In vicw of the lack of a type specimen, uncertainty about the locality from which the original seeds were obtained, and the wide divergence of opinions expressed by different taxonomists in applying the name during the past century, precise assignment of this name to a currently known taxon seems impossible. It probably will remain a "nomen ambiguum" indefinitely, and as in accordance with the provisions of Article 75 of the International Rules of Botanical Nomenclature, the name *Echinocactus californicus* must be rejected

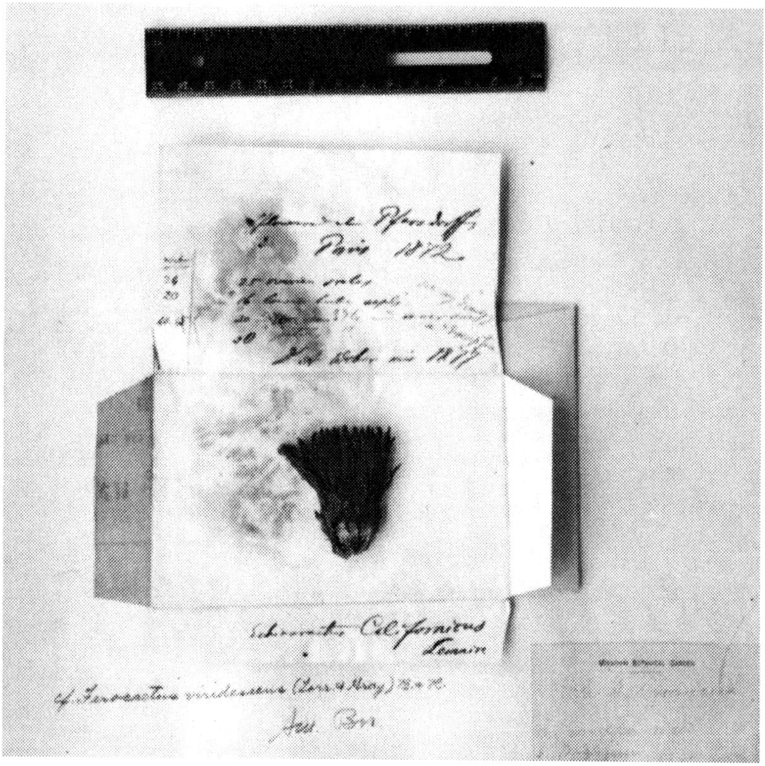

Figure 138. Specimen of *Echinocactus californicus* Lemaire in the George Engelman collection, Missouri Botanical Garden.

2. FEROCACTUS RAFAELENSIS (J. A. Purpus) Britton and Rose, in Borg, Cacti 236. 1937

Echinocactus rafaelensis J. A. Purpus, Monatsschr. Kakteenk. 12: 163. 1912

Bisnaga rafaelensis (Purpus) Orcutt, Cactography 1: 1. 1926.

In 1912 Dr. J. A. Purpus described *Echinocactus rafaelensis* from plants and photographs which C. A. Purpus took at Minas de San Rafael, San Luis Potosi, Mexico, in 1910. I do not know this species, nor have I been able to locate Minas de San Rafael, although there is a town called San Rafael about 30 km. north of the city of San Luis Potosi. Mr. Fritz Schwartz, a cactus dealer who lives in San Luis Potosi does not know the species or the locality. The original description is good, and is accompanied by a habitat photograph of a large plant. the following description is taken from that of Purpus.

STEMS cespitose from the base, globose to globose-cylindrical, with depressed top bearing slight dark tomentum. RIBS 13-20, undulating, 2.5-3 cm. high, acute. AREOLES widely separated, elliptical, somewhat elongated above the spine fascicle, covered with white or light gray tomentum. SPINES 7-10, acicular, amber flecked with red or brown, becoming gray; radical spines about 8, the upper ones longer, to 3 cm. long; central spine 1, sometimes 4-6 cm. long, usually directed downward, lighter colored and stronger than the racials. FLOWER and FRUIT unknown. SEED shining black, very small, about 1 mm. long, somewhat twisted ovoid.

Dr. Purpus, in the original description of this species, said that C. A. Purpus found the attractive plants near Minas de San Rafael in the autumn of 1910. The plants formed large polycephalic clusters which resembled the clumps of *Ferocactus flavovirens*. The number of ribs and number and length of the spines were variable.

Under *Ferocactus echidne* var. *victoriensis* I have discussed the application of the name *Ferocactus rafaelensis* to plants of that relationship, and pointed out that if they are the same, the name victoriensis would have priority, having been published three years earlier. There is a good possibility that intensive field work will bring recognizable specimens of *F. rafaelensis* to light and the question concerning its relationship to *F. echidne* settled. Therefore, I prefer to postpone final disposal of this name and its application to a separate taxon or relegated to synonymy.

Figure 139. Copy of the illustration which accompanied the original description of *Echinocactus rafaelensis* J. A. Purpus in - 22: 163, 1912.

TAXA EXCLUDED FROM FEROCACTUS IN THIS TREATMENT

Britton and Rose included four taxa in their new genus *Ferocactus* which have since been transferred to other genera. I feel that all four should be excluded from *Ferocactus*, and will indicate their disposition by the various authors who have treated them.

1. *Echinocactus johnsonii* Parry, in Engelmann, Bot. King's Surv. 117. 187.

Echinocactus johnsonii octocentrus Coulter, Contr. U. S. Nat. Herb. 3: 371. 1896.

Ferocactus johnsonii (Parry) Britton and Rose, Cactaceae 3: 141. 1922.

Echinomastus johnsonii (Parry) Baxter, Calif. Cact. 75. 1935.

This small globular cactus is found in eastern California, southern Nevada, southern Utah, and western Arizona. There is no question that it belongs in *Echinomastus* rather than *Ferocactus*, as was first pointed out by J. P. Hester (1934, p. 504), although the actual combination was made by Edgar Baxter in 1935. The flowering portion of the areole is situated on the axil of a rather distinct tubercle and separated from the spiniferous portion of the areole by a groove. Catherine Cole (1854, p. 37) found that the seeds of *johnsonii* differ from those of the Ferocacti, and belong with the Echinomasti.

2. *Echinocactus uncinatus* Galeotti in Pfeiffer, Abbild. Beschr. Cact. 2: pl. 18. 1848.

Echinocactus ancylacanthus Monville in Labouret, Monogr. Cact. 201. 1853.

Echinocactus uncinatus wrightii Engelmann, Proc. Amer. Acad. 3: 273. 1856.

Echinocactus wrightii Coulter, Cycl. Amer. Hort. Bailey 2: 513: 1900.

Ferocactus uncinatus (Galeotti) Britton and Rose, Cactaceae 3: 146. 1922.

Echinomastus uncinatus Knuth, in Backeberg and Knuth, Cactus ABC 358. 1935.

Glandulicactus uncinatus (Galeotti, in Pfeiffer) Backeberg, Beitr. Sukkulenk.-pflege, 1940 7. 1940. (Without basonym.)

Thelocactus uncinatus (Galeotti) Marshall, in Marshall and Bock, Cactaceae 170. 1941.

Glandulicactus uncinatus (Galeotii, in Pfeiffer) Backeberg, Cactac., Jahr. Deuts. Kakt. Gesellsch. 1941, pt. 2, 59. 1942. (First valid publication.)

Echinocactus uncinatus is a rather small globular or sub-columnar species from southern Texas and northern Mexico. It has tubercles which are grooved on the upper side by an elongated areole, and flowers appear in the axils of the tubercles, some distance from the spine fascicle. Nectariferous gland-spines are scattered along the furrow which connects the flowering and spine-bearing portions of the areole.

Mr. J. P. Hester (1934, 504) suggested that *Ferocactus uncinatus* belonged in *Echinomastus*, but did not make the formal combination. Count F. M. Knuth, in Cactus ABC (1935, p. 358), did treat the taxon as *Echinomastus uncinatus* Knuth. In 1940 Curt Backeberg proposed a new genus, *Glandulicactus*, which was characterized by tubercular ribs, areolar grooves with several glands, and flowers which arose at the end of a groove. Backeberg combined two species, *Ferocactus uncinatus* and *F. crassihamatus*, in his new genus.

Marshall, in 1941 (Cactaceae p. 170), referred the species which Backeberg had placed in his genus *Glandulicactus* to *Thelocactus*, listing them as *Thelocactus uncinatus* (Galeotti) Marshall and *T. crassihamatus* (Weber) Marshall. Catherine Cole (1954, p. 21) found the seeds of *Thelocactus bicolor* and *T. uncinatus* alike, and that seeds of *T. uncinatus* are quite different from those of *Echinomastus*.

3. *Echinocactus crassihamatus* Weber, Dict. Hort. Bois 468. 1896.

Echinocactus mathssonii Berge, Monatsschr. Kakteenk. 7: 76. 1897.

Ferocactus crassihamatus (Weber) Britton and Rose, Cactaceae 3: 144. 1922.

Bisnaga crassihamatus (Weber) Orcutt, Cactography 1: 1. 1926.

Glandulicactus crassihamatus (Weber) Backeberg, Betir. Sukkulenk.-pflege, 1940 6. 1940.

Thelocactus crassihamatus (Weber) Marshall, Cactaceae 169. 1941.

This little central Mexican plant has yet to be satisfactorily placed in a genus. It is characterized by an elongated areole which forms a groove along top of the tubercle, with the flowering portion in the axil of the tubercle and widely separated from the spine fascicle at the opposite end. The grooved tubercle has led several workers to consider *crassihamatus* to be very close to *Thelocactus uncinatus*, and both Backeberg and Marshall have treated the two species as cogeneric. Britton and Rose knew *crassihamatus* only through inadequate description and one illustration. They had no idea about the size of the plant or details of its structure, which probably explains why they included it in *Ferocactus*. Backeberg included it with *uncinatus* in his *Glandulicactus*, and Marshall combined both *uncinatus* and *crassihamatus* in *Thelocactus*.

Catherine Cole (1954, p. 39) pointed out that grooved tubercles are characteristic of *Echinomastus*, *Sclerocactus*, and *Thelocactus* and that character alone is of little taxonomic significance. The habit and armament of *crassihamatus* and *uncinatus* are quite different, and Cole (ibid, p. 69) thinks that evidence from seed characters indicates *crassihamatus* does not belong in either *Ferocactus* or *Thelocactus*, but she was unable to suggest a satisfactory position for the species.

4. *Echinocactus hamatacanthus* Muhlenpfordt, Allg. Gartenz. 14: 371. 1848. (as hamatocanthus)

Echinocactus flexispinus Engelmann in Wislizenus, Mem. Tour North. Mex. 111. 1848.

Echinocactus sinuatus Dietrich, Allg. Gartenz. 19: 345. 1851.

Echinocactus setispinus sinuatus Poselger, Allg. Gartenz. 21:119. 1853.

Echinocactus setispinus robustus Poselger, loc. cit.

Echinocactus setispinus longihamatus Poselger, loc. cit.

Echinocatus longihamatus hamatacanthus Labouret, Monogr. Cact. 201. 1853.

Echinocactus treculianus Labouret, op. cit. p. 202.

Echinocactus longihamatus gracilispinus Engelmann, Proc. Amer. Acad. 3: 273. 1856.

Echinocactus longihamatus crassispinus Engelmann, loc. cit.

Echinocactus longihamatus brevispinus Engelmann, op. cit. p. 274.

Echinocactus flavispinus Meinshausen, Wochenshr. Gartn. Pflanz. 1:28. 1856.

Echinocactus haematochroanthus Hemsley, Biol. Centr. Amer. Bot. 1: 532. 1858.

Echinocactus hamatacanthus longihamatus Coulter, Contr. U. S. Nat. Herb. 3: 365. 1896.

Echinocactus hamatacanthus brevispinus Coulter, op. cit. p. 366.

Echinocactus longihamatus sinuatus Weber in Schumann, Gesamtb. Kakteen 342. 1898.

Ferocactus hamatacanthus (Muhlenpfordt) Britton and Rose, Cactaceae 3: 144. 1922.

Hamatocactus hamatacanthus Knuth, Kaktus ABC 353. 1935.

Hamatocactus hamatacanthus var. *papyracantha* Knuth, loc. cit.

Brittonia davisii Hort., not Houghton.

Hamatocactus hamatocanthus var. *davisii* Marshall, Cactaceae 145. 1941.

Hamatocactus hamatacantus var. *crassispinus* (Engelmann) Marshall, Cact. and Succ. Journ. 16: 80. 1944.

Hamatocactus hamatacanthus var. gracilispinus (Engelmann) Marshall, loc. cit.

Hamatocactus hamatacanthus var. *brevispinus* (Engelmann) Marshall, loc. cit.

This polymorphic species occurs in southern Texas and northern and central Mexico. It is extremely variable in form, as evidenced by its huge synonymy. Without doubt some infraspecific taxa deserve recognition.

The flabby, tuberculate nature of the stems, unique character of the spines, long tubular flowers, thin-skinned fruits with fleshy pulp, and seeds with large basal hila are all characters separating *hamatacanthus* from *Ferocactus*. Backeberg and Knuth (1935, p. 353), Borg. (1937, p. 218), and Marshall (1944, p. 80) combined *hamatacanthus* in the genus *Hamatocactus* which Britton and Rose erected for the single species, *setispinus*.

Recent studies of seed characters apparently suggest a closer relationship between *hamatacanthus* and *Ferocactus* than the gross morphology of plants indicates. Buxbaum (1951a, p. 196) gives the following review of the complex:

> *Hamatocactus* now contains the three species, *H. setispinus*, *H. crassispinus*, and *H. uncinatus* (formerly *Ferocactus*). Thus Backeberg's *Glandulicactus* is a synonym of *Hamatocactus*. Contrary to W. T. Marshall's opinion, *Echinocactus hamatacanthus* is a true species of *Ferocactus* because it has the same structure, a type which never occurs in Ramus I. Also it has the same succession of spine development and a very solid, short receptacle ("tube") which bears areole hairs within the throat. This is as it occurs in *Brasiliopuntia*, *Pereskia sacharosa*, *Tacinga*, and also, as I have found, in *Leuchtenbergia*.

Catherine Cole, (1954, p. 67), also on the basis of a seed study, indicated "the transfer of *Ferocactus hamatacanthus* to *Hamatocactus* cannot be justified on any basis. Certainly the fruit and seed of this species cannot be linked with the type species of the genus, *Hamatocactus setispinus*." In this conclusion Cole agrees with Buxbaum, but their interpretation of seed data led to quite diverse opinions concerning other taxa. Buxbaum said that *Hamatocatus* contains three species, *H. setispinus*, *H. crassispinus* (*crassihamatus*!) and *H. uncinatus*. Cole (ibid, p. 126) says "*Hamatocactus setispinus* rightly belongs in the genus *Thelocactus*," on page 69 indicates *crassihamatus* belongs in neither *Ferocactus* nor *Thelocactus*, but on page 38 says that *uncinatus* is a *Thelocactus*.

In spite of the evidence based on seed characters I cannot agree with Dr. Cole that morphological differences are not sufficient grounds for separating *hamatacanthus* from *Ferocactus*, and in my opinion flower, fruit, stem, and spine morphology place *hamatacanthus* and *setispinus* in the same genus, and that genus is not *Ferocactus*. Dr. Buxbaum's quoted article may have suffered in translation, but my impression is that the areole hairs which he observed in *hamatacanthus* and a number of very primitive genera, but which do not occur in *Ferocactus*, is additional reason for separating that species.

BIBLIOGRAPHY

Anthony, H. E. 1948. *Rhipsalis* in the rain forest of Nyasaland. Desert Plant Life 20: 52-54.

Backeberg, Curt. 1944a. Die verbreitung der Cactaceae in den landern der Neuen Welt. Cactaceae, Jahr. Deuts. Kakteen-Gesells. 5: 7-35.

___________. 1944b. Die vorkommen der einzelnen verwandtschftsgruppen und die Typ-Standorte. Cactaceae, Jahr. Deuts. Kakteen-Gesells. 5: 36-105.

___________ and F. M. Knuth. 1935. *Kaktus-ABC.* Copenhagen. 432 pp.

___________. 1976. *Cactus Lexicon*, 3rd. ed. England: Blandford Press, 828 pp.

Baxter, E. M. 1935. *California Cactus.* Los Angeles: Abbey Garden Press. 93 pp.

Benson, Lyman. 1943. The goal and methods of systematic botany. Cact. and Succ. Journ. 15: 99-111.

___________. 1944. A revision of some Arizona Cactaceae. Proc. Calif. Acad. Sci., 4th ser., 25: 245-268.

___________. 1950. *The cacti of Arizona.* Tucson: Univ. Ariz. Press. 135 pp.

___________, J. J. Thornber and A. A. Nichol. 1940. *The cacti of Arizona.* Univ. Ariz. Biol. Sci. Bull. 4: 1-134.

___________. 1982. *The Cactus of the United States and Canada.* Stanford University Press. 1,040 pp.

Berger, Alwin. 1926. *Die entwicklungslinien der kakteen.* Jena: Gustav Fischer. 105 pp.

___________. 1929. *Kakteen.* Stuttgart: Eugen Ulmer. 346 pp.

Besler, Basil. 1613. *Hortus eystettensis.* Eichstatt. 366 plates and additional unnumbered pages.

Boke, Norman. 1953. Tubercle development in *Mammillaria heyderi.* Am. Journ. Bot. 40: 239-247.

___________. 1955. Development of the vegetative shoot in *Rhipsalis cassytha.* Am. Journ. Bot. 42: 1-10.

Borg, J. 1937. *Cacti.* London: Macmillan. 419 pp.

Brandegee, T. S. 1905. Plants from Sinaloa. Zoe 5: 196-226.

Bravo, Heila, (Helia Bravo Hollis), 1937. *Las Cactaceas de Mexico.* Mexico: Univ. Mex. Press. 755 pp.

___________. 1953. Cactaceas del suroeste de Tamaulipas. An. Inst. Biol. 23: 502-557.

___________. 1954. Cactaceae de las Mixtecas Altas. An. Inst. Biol. 25: 473-552.

Brewer, W. H., S. Watson and Asa Gray. 1876. *Botany of California*, vol. I. Cambridge, Mass.: Welch, Bigelow and Co. 628 pp.

Britton, N. L. and J. N. Rose. 1919-23. *The Cactaceae.* Carnegie Inst. Wash. Pub. 248. Four vols., vol 1, 1919; vol. 2, 1920; vol. 3, 1922; vol. 4, 1923.

Brown, J. G. 1915. The effect of desiccation on the structure of *Echinocactus wislizenii.* Phyiol. Research. 1: 216-325.

Buxbaum, Franz. 1950. *Morphology of cacti*, sect. one, pp. 1-87. Pasadena: Abbey Garden Press.

___________. 1951a. Stages and lines of evolution of the tribe Euechinocactineae. Cact. and Succ. Journ. 23: 193-197.

___________. 1951b. Entwicklungstufen und entwicklungslinien der tribus Euechinocactineae. Kakt. And. Sukk. 2: 31-38.

___________. 1951c. Die phylogenie der Nordamerikanischen Echinocacteen. Oster. Bot. Zeitschr. 98: 44-104.

___________. 1953. *Morphology of cacti*, sect. two, pp. 89-170. Pasadena: Abbey Garden Press.

___________. 1955. *Morphology of cacti*, sect. three, pp. 172-223. Pasadena: Abbey Garden Press.

Candolle, A. P. de. 1828. *Prodromus systematis naturalis* etc. 3: 457-476. Paris: Fortin, Masson et Socicrum.

___________. 1834. *Memoire sur quelques especes de cactees nouvelles ou peu connues.* Paris. 27 pp., 12 pl.

Cannon, W. A. 1906. Biological relations of certain cacti. Am. Nat. 40: 27-46.

___________. 1911. *The root habits of desert plants.* Carnegie Inst. Wash. Pub. 131. 96 pp.

Cole, Catherine A. 1954. Cactus seeds and their value as an aid in generic segregation. Doctoral thesis manuscript, University of Michigan. University Microfilms. 143 pp.

Coulter, John M. 1894. Preliminary revision of the North American species of Cactus, *Anhalonium,* and *Lophophora*. Cont. U. S. Nat. Herb. 3: 91-134.

__________. 1896. Preliminary revision of the North American species of *Echinocactus, Cereus*, and *Opuntia*. Cont. U. S. Nat. Herb. 3: 355-466.

Croizat, Leon. 1943a. The cactus and its body. Cact. and Succ. Journ. 15: 37-42.

__________. 1943b. Notes on the Cactaceae. The typification of *Echinocactus*. Lilloa 9: 179-198.

Delf, M. 1912. Transpiration in succulent plants. Am. Bot. 24: 409-441.

Dodonaeus, Rembertus. 1583. *Strirpium historiae pemptades sex, sive libri XXX*. Antwerp. 860 pp.

Emory, W. H. 1848. *Notes of a military reconnoissance, from Fort Leavenworth, in Missouri, to San Diego, in California.* Washington. 416 pp.

Engelmann, George. 1852. Notes on the *Cereus giganteus* of south-eastern California, and some other Californian Cactaceae. Amer. Journ. Sci. ser. 2, 14: 335-339.

__________. 1856. Synopsis of the Cactaceae of the United States. Proc. Am. Acad. Sci. 3: 259-314.

__________. 1859. Cactaceae of the boundary. In: Emory, W. H., *Report of the United States and Mexican boundary survey*, vol. 2, pt. 1, pp. 1-78, 76 pl. Washington.

__________. and J. M. Bigelow. 1856. Description of the Cactaceae. In: *Rep. Explor. Surv. Mississippi Pacific Oc.*, 4: 27-58, 24 pl. Washington.

Erdtman, G. 1952. *Pollen morphology and plant taxonomy.* Waltham, Mass.: Chronica Botanica Co. 539 pp.

Forster, C. F. 1846. *Handbuch der cacteenkunde in ihrem gangen unfange, etc. Leipzig*. 543 pp.

__________. 1885. Revised edition. Leipzig. 1029 pp.

Gates, Howard E. 1931. *Ferocactus rectispinus*. Cact. and Succ. Journ. 2: 390-391.

Gerarde, John. 1597. *The herball, or general histoire of plants*. London. 1392 pp.

Greene, E. L. 1888. The botany of Cedros Island. Pittonia 1: 194-208.

Haworth, Adrian H. 1812. *Synopsis plantarum succulentarum cum descriptionibus, synonymis, etc.* London: Taylor. 334 pp.

Hester, J. P. 1934. Neglected *Echinomastus*. Cact. and Succ. Journ. 5: 503-504.

Higgins, Ethel B. 1931. *Our native cacti*. New York: De La Mare. 170 pp.

Hollis, Helia Bravo. See Bravo.

Johnston, I. M. 1924. The botany of the expedition of the California Academy of Sciences to the Gulf of California. Proc. Cal. Acad. Sci. 4th ser., 12: 951-1218.

Kearney, T. H. and R. H. Peebles. 1942. *Flowering plants and ferns of Arizona*. Washington : U. S. Govt. Print. Office. 1069 pp.

____________. 1951. *Arizona flora*. Berkeley: Univ. Calif. Press. 1032 pp.

Lanjouw, J., and F. A. Stafleu. 1954. *Index herbariorum. I.* The herbaria of the world. ed. 2. 179 pp. International Bureau for Plant Taxonomy and Nomenclature, Utrecht.

Lawrence, G. 1841. Catalogue of the cacti in the collection of Rev. Theodore Williams. London Gardener's Magazine 17: 313-321.

Lemaire, Charles. 1838. *Cactearum aliquot novarum ac insuetarum in horto Monvilliano cultarum accurata descripto*. Paris. 40 pp.

____________. 1839. *Cactearum genera nova speciesque novae etominium in horto Monvilliano cultarum ex affinitatibus naturalibus ordinato nova, indexque methodicus*. Paris. 115 pp.

____________. 1863. *Les cactees*. Paris. 140 pp.

Linke, H. F. and F. Otto. 1827. Ueber die gattungen *Melocactus* und *Echinocactus* etc. Verh. Ver. Beford. Gartenb. 3: 412-433, 28 pl.

Lindsay, George. 1948. *Ferocactus diguetii*. Desert Plant Life 20: 20-23.

____________. 1964. *Ferocactus littoralis*. Cact. and Succ. Journ. 36: 8-10.

Linnaeus, Carolus. 1753. *Species plantarum*. Stockholm. 2 vols.

__________. 1767-1771. *Mantissa.* Pp. 1-142, 1767; pp. 143-588,1771. Stockholm.

Livingston, B. E. 1907. Relative transpiration in cacti. Plant World 10: 110-114.

Lobelius, Mathias. 1576. *Iconis stirpium seus plantarum tan exoticarum quam indigenarum.* Antwerp.

Lobelius, Mathias, and Petrus Pena. 1570. *Stirpium adversaria nova.* London. 455 pp.

Lowry, W. E. Sr. 1936. West coast Ferocacti. Cact. and Succ. Journ. 7: 189-191.

MacDougal, D. T. and E. S. Spalding. 1910. The water balance of succulent plants. Carnegie Inst. Wash. Pub. 141. 77 pp.

MacDougal, D. T. and E. R. Long and J. G. Brown. 1915. End results of desiccation and respiration in succulent plants. Physiol. Research. 1: 289-325.

Maheshwari, P. 1950. *An introduction to the embryology of angiosperms.* New York: McGraw-Hill. 453 pp.

Marshall, Wm. T. 1944. *Hamatocactus.* Cact. and Succ. Journ. 16: 79-80.

__________. 1950. *Arizona's cactuses.* Tempe, Arizona. 111 pp.

__________, and T. M. Bock. 1941. *Cactaceae.* Pasadena: Abbey Garden Press. 206 pp.

Maximov, N. A. 1929. *The plant in relation to water.* London: George Allen. 451 pp.

Miller, Philip. 1768. *The gardeners dictionary,* 8th ed. London.

Moran, Reid. 1953. Taxonomic studies in the Cactaceae. Gentes Herbarum 8: 316-327.

__________. 1954. On Buxbaum's phylogeny of the "Euechinocactineae." Cact. and Succ. Journ. 26: 45-48.

Mortensen, E. 1930. Cactus caterpillars. Cact. and Succ. Journ. 1: 171-173.

Orcutt, C. R. 1926. Cactography 1: 1-48. San Diego.

Oviedo y Valdez, Gonzalo Fernandez de. 1526. *Sumario de la natural historia de las Indias.* (First published in Toledo in 1526, now available in recent edition edited by Jose Miranda)

Mexico, 1950. Mexico: Fondo de Cultura Economica. 279 pp.

Pfeiffer, Ludwig. 1837a. *Beschreibung und synonymik der Deutschen garten lebend vorkommenden kakteen.* Berlin: Oehmigke. 231 pp.

____________. 1837b. *Enumeratio diagnostica cactearum hucusque cognitarum.* Berlin: Oehmigke. 192 pp.

____________ and Friedrich Otto. 1843-50. *Abbildung und beschreibung bluhender kakteen.* Kassel: Fischer. 2 vols., 60 colored plates.

Preston, C. E. 1900. Observations on the root sytems of certain Cactaceae. Bot. Gaz. 30: 348-351.

Roland-Gosselin, R. 1913. Are the species of *Rhipsalis* discovered in Africa indigenous? Torreya 13: 151-156.

Rose, J. N. 1906. A new species of *Opuntia* and *Echinocactus*. Contr. U. S. Nat. Herb. 10: 126-127.

____________. 1909. Studies of Mexican and Central American plants, no. 6a. Contr. U. S. Nat. Herb. 12: 259-302.

Runyon, E. H. 1934. The organization of the creosote bush with respect to drought. Ecology 15: 128-138.

Salm-Reifferscheid-Dyck, J. 1822. *Index plantarum succulentarum in horto Dyckensi notatae*. Aquisgrani. 60 pp.

____________. 1841. *Cacteae in horto Dyckensi cultae anno 1841, additistribuum gererumque characteribus emendatis*. Dusseldorf. 48 pp.

____________. 1845. *Cacteae in horto Dyckensi cultae anno 1844, additistribuum gererumque characteribus emendatis*. Dusseldorf: Arnz et. Co. 51 pp.

____________. 1850. *Cacteae in horto Dyckensi cultae anno 1849 secundum tribus et genera digestae additis adnotatt etc*. Bonn: Henry Cohen. 267 pp.

Schumann, Karl. 1898. *Gesamtbeschreibung der Kakteen. Neudamm: J. Neumann*. 832 pp.

____________. 1899. *Die verbreitung der Cactaceae im verhaltniss zu ihrer systematischen gleidering*. Berlin. 114 pp.

____________. 1903. *Gesamtbeschreibung der Kakteen nachtrage 1898 bis 1902*. Neudamm: J. Neumann. 171 pp.

Scott, Flora M. 1950. Internal suberization of tissues. Bot. Gaz. 3rd, ser., 4: 369-394.

Shields, Lora M. 1950. Leaf xeromorphy as related to physiological structural influence. Bot. Rev. 16: 399-477.

Shreve, Edith B. 1916. An analysis of the causes of variations in transpiring power of cacti. Physiol. Research. 2: 73-127.

Shreve, Forrest. 1935. The longevity of cacti. Cact. and Succ. Journ. 7: 66-68.

Skene, Macgregor. 1924. *The biology of flowering plants.* New York: MacMillan. 523 pp.

Sweert, Emanuel. 1612. *Florilegium, tractans de variis floribus et aliis indicus plantis, etc.* Frankfurt-am-Main. 110 plates.

Taylor, Nigel. 1984. A Review of *Ferocactus* Britton & Rose. Bradleya 2/1984: 19-38.

___________. 1987. Additional Notes on some *Ferocactus* Species. Bradleya 5/1987: 95-96.

Toumey, J. W. 1895. New or little-known plants, *Echinocactus wislizenii* and some related species. Gard. and For. 8: 154-155.

Tournefort, J. P. de. 1700. *Istitutiones rei herbariae*. Paris. 3 vols.

Townsend, Charles H. 1916. Voyage of the "Albatross" to the Gulf of California in 1911. Bull. Am. Mus. Nat. Hist. 35: 399-476.

Weber, Dr. 1895. Les cactees de la Basse-Californie. Bull. Mus. Hist. Nat. 1: 316-326.

___________. 1898. Les *Echinocactus* de Basse-Californie. Bull. Mus. Hist. Nat. 4: 98-105.

Went, Frits W. 1955. The ecology of desert plants. Scient. Amer. 192: 68-75.

Wislizenus, A. 1848. *Memoir of a tour to northern Mexico, connected with Col. Donephan's expedition in 1846 and 1847.* Washington: Tippin and Streeper. 141 pp.

Walton, F. A. 1899. Cacti we have flowered. Cact. Journ. 2: 103.

Glossary of Terms

TERM	FOR	DEFINITION
acicular	spines	Needlelike; elongate or tapering.
acuminate	flowers	Abruptly narrowed into a long, pointing apex.
acute	ribs	Straight sided and tapering to a point.
annulate	spines	With encircling, ringlike, projecting bands.
apiculate	fruit/flwrs	With an abrupt, short, flexible terminal point.
areoles	stem	For cacti, a speciallized area in which spines are produced.
aristate	flowers	A slender terminal point, drawn out into a bristle.
auriculate	fruit	An appendage with the shape of an ear lobe.
biscuit	stem	Depressed globular shape.
campanulate	flowers	Bell shaped.
cespitose	stems	With numerous stems that form a low tuft or mat.
ciliate	flowers	Having marginal, eyelash-like hairs.
clavate	stem	Club-shaped.
cordate	spines	Heart-shaped.
cruciform	spines	In the shape of a cross.
cuspidate	flowers	Ending in a sharp, firm, point.
cylindric	stem	In the form of a cylinder.
decumbent	flowers	Lying flat on the ground, but with the tips turned upwards.
dehiscing	fruit	Opening lengthwise by splitting along precise lines.
dichotomous	flowers	Forking, with the two branches at each level being equal.
dorsiventral	spines	Broadest faces on front or back, not sides.
fascicle	spines	A cluster or a bundle.
fimbriate	flowers	With a marginal fringe.
floriferous	flwr/areol	Bearing flowers.
funicular	fruit	The stalk supporting the ovule, later the seed.
glaucous	stem	With a bluish powdered surface wax.
globular	stem	Spheroidal.
hilum	seed	A scar on the seed from the funicular attachment.
hyaline	flwr/sd/frt	Thin, translucent, resembling glass.
hypanthium	flowers	A floral tube extension of the receptacle.
imbricate	frut/flw/sp	To overlap, like shingles.
incurved	flowers	Curved, or bent inwards.
intergrade	flowers	A gradual change, such as the suffusion of two colors.
lanceolate	flowers	Lance shaped, 4 - 6 times longer than broad, end tapered.
lateral	spines	Broadest faces on side.
locule	fruit	Compartment or cell in an ovary.

TERM	FOR	DEFINITION
lunate	fruit	The shape of a half moon or crescent.
mammilate	spines	Nipple shaped.
mucronate	flowers	Having a short, sharp terminal point of tissue.
nectariferous	spines	Bearing nectar.
oblanceolate	flowers	Lanceolate, but attached at the narrow end.
obovate	areole	Ovate, but attached at the narrow end.
obovoid	stem	Ovoid, but attached at the narrow end.
orbicular	flowers	Nearly spherical.
ovate-deltoid	fruit	Between egg-shaped (ovoid) and triangular (deltoid).
perianth	flowers	Sepals and petals of a flower, of different origin for cacti.
persistent	fruit	Remaining attached.
porrect	spines	Directed outwards and forward.
reniform	seed	In the shape of a kidney or bean.
reticulate	seed	In a meshwork, or netlike.
sclerous	flowers	Hardened, stiff, unyielding.
serrate	flowers	With marginal teeth like a saw, forward projecting and acute.
serrulate	flowers	Minute teeth.
setaceous	spines	Bristlelike.
spatulate	flowers	Narrowly oblong with rounded corners, base tapering.
spiniferous	areole	Bearing spines.
striated	flowers	Having longitudinal ridges and grooves.
subovate	stem	Nearly egg shaped.
subulate	spines	Narrow ellipse, flat and tapering to a point.
terete	spines	Slender cylindroid, circular cross section, varying diameter.
testa	seed	Seed coat.
tomentose	areoles	Wooly.
tomentum	areoles	Wool.
tuberculate	ribs	In cactus, a stem projection bearing an areole.

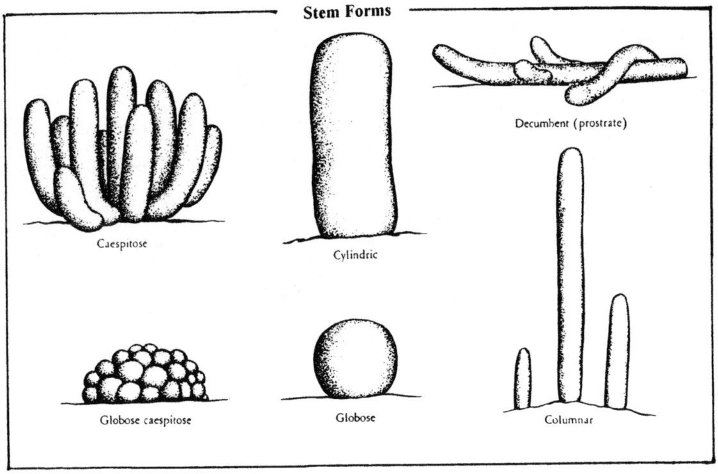

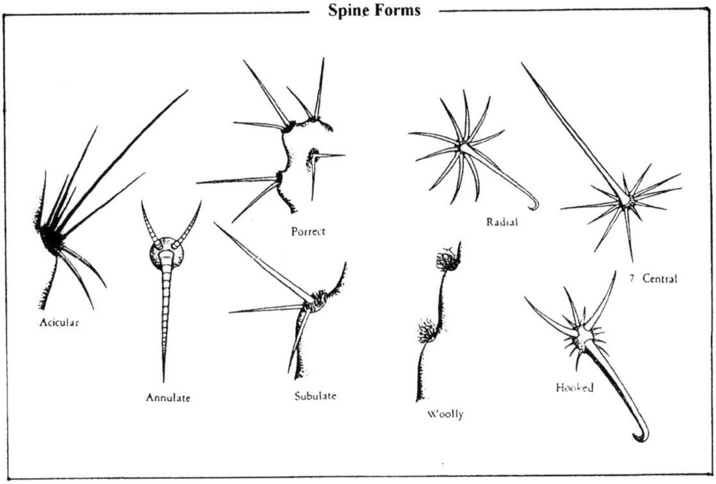

Glossary Illustration 1.

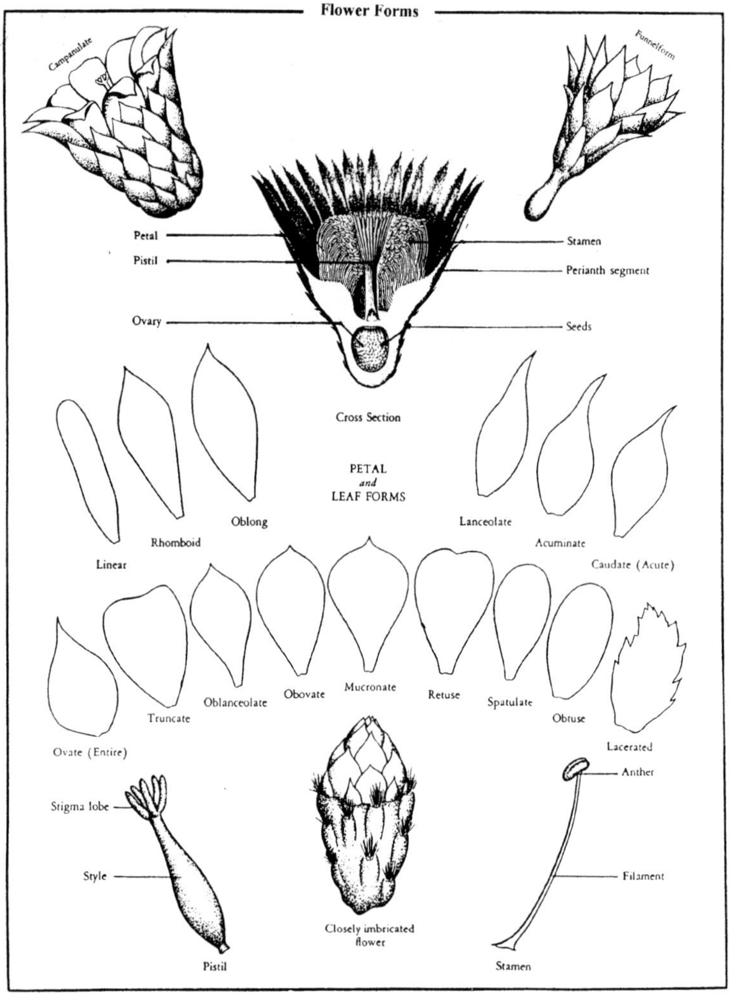

Glossary Illustration 2

GEORGE E. LINDSAY— EXPLORER AND PLANTSMAN

LARRY W. MITICH

Department of Botany, University of California, Davis, CA 95616

George Edmund Lindsay was born at Pomona, California,17 August 1916. He was the youngest of three children, following a sister, Elizabeth Anne, and a brother, Lester Burke.

His parents, Charles William Lindsay and Alice Horton Foster Lindsay, also native Califor nians, were orchardists, and George was raised in the country on citrus orchards. He lived in Pomona until he was 6 years old, and there attended kindergarten. When he was 7, his parents moved to Corning, California, to raise and pro cess olives, and he attended the first through third grades at Corning Grammar School. The family returned to Pomona when George was 10, and he graduated from Pomona High School in 1934.

His college education, interrupted by many adventures, was sporadic and prolonged. He joined friends at Chaffey Junior College in Ontario, California, for his freshman year in college, 19351936, then lived with his parents on their Lemon Crest Ranch at Lakeside while spending his sophomore and junior years at San Diego State College, 1936-1938. He did not return to schooluntil after World War II, when he completed his senior year at Stanford University in 1949-1950. In 1955 he received his Ph.D. degree from Stanford under Ira L. Wiggins. The title of his doctoral dissertation was The Taxonomy and Ecology of the Genus *Ferocactus*.

George was interested in desert plants before he was 10 years old. He remembers planting a pad of"Burbank spineless cactus" when his mother explained that it would put out roots and grow; another time he saw a neighbor with a flower stalk of Yucca whipplei in a bucket of water, and was told it was illegal to collect them. But it was legal to remove the flower stalks of dead plants; he made these into pincushions for his aunts by sawing the stalks into sections and gilding them.

Opuntias, probably *O. littoralis* var. *vaseyi*, grew in a dry arroyo behind an uncle's orange orchard, and George was entranced with their yellow-orange flowers. His mother suggested the flowers could be preserved by dipping them in melted paraffin wax, which he tried with some temporary success; in the process he learned about glochids.

George cannot explain his early fascination with cacti and succulents. He remembers reading about barrel cacti, which he had never seen, in an article in Touring Topics, the magazine of the Automobile Club of southern California, and he recalls his first sight of Joshua trees in the Mojave Desert.

One afternoon when he was in the seventh grade, he happened to walk by a Pomona garden filled with hundreds of cacti and succulents. Mrs. Morton Emerson, a white-haired lady who was tending the plants, noticed George's interest and invited him in. She had just received a shipment of little cacti from A. R. Davis of Marathon Texas, and gave him a few of the duplicated species. His latent interest was aroused and six decades later it is yet to be satisfied.

When he and his family visited the village of Palm Springs, he saw his first barrel cacti and the glistening *Opuntia bigelovi*, the soft-looking teddy bear cactus. He touched one which became impaled on his fingers. When he tried to shake it off, it flipped to the back of his hand. His father removed the joint with pliers, and he took it home to plant! On the same trip, he stepped barefooted on an ocotillo branch which punctured his foot, but again he took the offending piece home and planted it. His tenth grade botany teacher recommended him to the San Bernardino County forester, who issued George a permit to collect two specimens of each cactus species from public property at least 100 yards from the road. Riverside County did the same.

Through Mrs. Emerson he met a group of Pomona Valley Cactus and Succulent Club mem bers, who held meetings, potluck suppers, and frequent field trips to the desert. The Mojave Desert was a favorite destination, particularly the Ord Copper Mine in the Ord Mountains south of Daggett, reached by driving up roadless sand washes. The mine was closed, but its hospitable and lonely old caretaker let the club members use the bunkhouse and collect beautiful blue and green azurite and malachite from the mine dumps to decorate their cactus gardens. Grizzly bear cacti (*Opuntia erinacea* var. *ursina*) were beautiful, and there were beaver tail cacti (*O. basilaris*), diamond chollas (*O. ramosissima*), hedgehog cacti (*Echinocereus engelmannii* and *E. triglochidiatus* var. *mojavensis*), and many-headed barrel cacti (*Echinocactus polycephalus*). More difficult to find were small fishhook cacti (*Mammillaria tetrancistra*). There were many desert tortoises then.

In the 1930's, drivers' licenses were issued to 14-year-olds, making it possible

Figure 1. George at age 3 with his dog Flui at the Lindsay family home in Pomona, California. (All pictures are courtesy of George Lindsay.)

for George to make many exploring and collecting trips as a young teenager. Once he journeyed to Arizona with his father's truck to get a saguaro. A collecting permit allowed him to remove a nice specimen. On a weekend trip to Ajo, Arizona with a permit from the manager of the New Cor nelia Mine, he collected organ pipe cacti (then *Lemaireocereus thurberi*), barrel cacti (*Ferocactus wislizenii* and *F. covellei*), and other plants from the corporation's property. Returning from that trip, he stopped at John Hilton's trading post at Thermal, California. He traded an organ pipe cactus seedling for a large blue geode Hilton had collected near the Colorado River, and another lifelong friendship started. Hilton's

Figure 2. George's first cactus garden in Pomona in 1932

later paintings of smoke trees hang in George's living room, and Hilton's huge collection of meteorites is now at the California Academy of Sciences.

George's parents purchased a lemon orchard at Lakeside, San Diego County, and moved there while he was in high school. He remained in Pomona to finish high school with his class friends. An early visit to Point Loma in San Diego, with the son of the commanding officer of the military reservation, resulted in the unexpected discovery of plants new to him: *Bergerocactus emoryi, Ferocactus viridescens, Agave shawii, Mammillaria dioica, Euphorbia misera, Opuntia prolifera, O. serpentina, O.*

oricola, Dudleya spp., and chaparral growing in a natural botanical garden overlooking the sea.

In 1931 there were several cactus nurseries in San Diego—Helen McCabe's Cactus Gardens on Imperial Avenue, Neff K. Bakkers' Knickerbocker Nursery, Charles Cass Nursery in Pacific Beach, and some nurseries in Encinitas. Those were exciting days for a teenage cactophile.

Figure 3. In 1934, George graduated from Pomona High School at age 1 7

Helen McCabe and Neff Bakkers were rivals and competitors. Mrs. McCabe was quite deaf and had a wooden leg. She raised cocker spaniels as well as cacti, and used the dung of the former to fertilize the beds of the latter. Her nursery was not a pleasant place to be on hot days. And when hobbyists went from the McCabe Cactus Gardens to the nearby Knickerbocker Nursery they were conditioned to shouting to be understood. The irreverent and indomitable Neff Bakkers would say, "I am not deaf and you better pick that sliver out of your finger."

George's cactus garden in Pomona continued to grow. Every September the Los Angeles County Fair was held in Pomona, and horticultural exhibits included desert gardens. Sometime during high school (probably in 1932 or 1933) George decided to enter the desert garden com petition and won first place, with a $25 prize! But getting the blue ribbon was a bittersweet achievement because all the competitors were his friends, and Mrs. Emerson, who usually received the highest award, was hurt. George felt bad about Mrs. Emerson's disappointment. Their friendship survived but they never discussed the show.

He made his first trip to Baja California in 1932 with George McLain, whose lumberyard in Glendora, California, was planted largely to cacti. They drove as far south as the Maneadero below Ensenada, and saw *Machaerocereus gummosus, Myrtillocactus cochal,* and *Echinocereus maritimus.*

In summer of 1934, Theodore Hutchison, then secretary of the Cactus and Succulent Society and his mother Louisa, introduced George Lindsay and George Aschenbrener to the beautiful deserts of north central Baja California. Ted had accompanied Howard Gates on an earlier expedition, so he served as their guide. They stayed at Don Carlos Verdugo's ranch at the palm-filled arroyo oasis of Catavinia, and drove as far south as Laguna Seca Chapala. On the return up the coast, Louisa purchased roasting ears of corn at El Rosario, and they stopped to cook them on the beach at Socorro. There she observed a miniature mammillaria completely covered with flowers. Twenty-two years later, in November 1954, Helia Bravo and Mr. and Mrs. Charles Mieg found the plants in flower and fruit at Socorro, as well as at Punta Baja near El Rosario. In December 1960, George described and named the plant *Mammillaria louisae* in honor of Louisa Hutchison.

In February and March 1935, George, armed with a USDA plant importation permit, made a solo trip to Baja California, driving to Punta Priete. From there he went by muleback to Mission San Borjas, where he found the long-lost Cochemiea setispina, and to Punta Blanca on the Pacific Coast, where he collected a new Cochemiea which he named C. maritima two years later. That lonely trip,53 years ago when George was 18, was one of his greatest experiences.

Howard E. Gates, the pioneer collector and nurseryman, had started exploring Baja

Figure 4. In July 1 938, George (left) and Robert S. Hoardmade an overland trip the length of the Baja California peninsula.

Califor nia in 1928, and continued through 1951. Howard's first nursery in Anaheim, and the later, larger one near Corona, were actually botanical gardens of Baja California plants. In 1934-1935, Howard made a botanical garden for the World's Fair in Balboa Park, San Diego. While Gates and Lindsay never made a trip together, Howard was a generous friend and teacher who whetted George's interest in the peninsula's flora.

From 3 to 24 August 1936, George drove to El Arco, in mid Baja California, with college classmates Arthur Bridge, Robert Davis, and William Davenport, Bridge's 13-year-old friend. They were caught by a chubasco (a violent thundersquall), and the normally dry roads to the south became impassable with water and mud. That turned out to be a blessing, because they drove eastward across the peninsula to Bahia de los Angeles, seeing enroute a magnificent bighorn sheep up close and a gold rush in progress at the bay. Mexican prospectors were placer mining the dry arroyos, and patient burrows powered primitive mills grinding hard rock gold ore from the mines. Seri Indian turtle fishermen took the boys by dugout canoe to Angel de la Guarda Island. Since there was no breeze, they could not sail and it was very hot. But they saw numerous sharks, turtles, orcas, dolphins, and finback whales. The crossing took 30 hours, but the return a few days later, with a brisk breeze, was one-fifth as long.

On Angel de la Guarda, they found *Ferocactus johnstonianus*, and a flowering mammillaria that Dr. Robert Craig named *M. angelensis* in 1945. In the summer of 1937, Arthur Bridge and George again drove to El Arco. Lindsay does not recall finding any unusual plants, but they collected *Lophocereus schottii* var. *monstrosus* forma *obesus* along the road between El Arco and Calmalli. Years later George collected forma mieckleyanus at Rancho Union, a few miles further east.

From 22 June to 11 August 1938, George drove the full length of the peninsula after shipping his Model A Ford panel truck from Ensenada to Cape San Lucas by sea. His companion was Robert S. Hoard, an instructor at Pomona College, who collected reptiles. They visited Cedros Island while the ship unloaded supplies there, and later took a mail boat to Magdalena Island. On Cedros they collected *Cochemiea pondii* and *Ferocactus chrysacanthus*, and on Magdalena they found *Cochemiea halei* and

Figure 5. George's first boss was Mrs. Gertrude D. Webster, president of the Arizona Cactus and Native Flora Society, here breaking ground for the Desert Botanical Garden administration building, May 1939

Echinocereus barthelowanus. On the long drive back to San Diego they collected many cacti for the first time, having permits issued by the forestry departments of the state of Baja California Norte and the territory of Baja California Sur.

In late August and September of 1938, George made a plant collecting trip through

Figure 6. The adobe administration building was completed in the fall of 1939.

Figure 7. The dedication of the Desert Botanical Garden, 22 January 1940.

central Mexico as far as Oaxaca, which in those days could be reached only by narrow-gauge railroad train from Tehuacan, Puebla. In Mexico City, Salvado Guerrero, General Secretary of the Forestry Department, received George and issued him a collecting permit for all of Mexico.

George frequently visited Guirocoba ranch in southern Sonora, which William Taylor Mar shall, Robert T. Craig, Howard Scott Gentry, John Hilton, and others had used as a base for plant exploration. The arid thorn forest wilderness surrounding Guirocoba at the junction of Sonora, Sinaloa, and Chihuahua was of great bi ological and historical interest; scientists and his torians from many countries visited there. The beautiful hacienda extended as far as the eye could see.

In March 1939, George and Dr. Robert T. Craig prepared for a pack trip from Guirocoba into the Sierra Tarahumara and the Barranca de Cobre, Chihuahua. Before they left, Scott Haselton, editor ofthe Cactus and Succulent Journal visited George in San Diego to discuss a new botanical garden proposed for Papago Park in Phoenix. Mrs. Gertrude D. Webster, president of the Arizona Cactus and Native Flora Society the sponsoring organization, had enlisted Scott's help in her search for a director, and he recommended George. But George,22 years old and not graduated from college, had never worked for an employer, was unprepared in many ways, and was not interested in applying for the job. Scott asked George to stop by Phoenix on his way to Sonora, in order to meet Mrs. Webster. He remembers driving up the gravel driveway to her large New Mexican style winter home on Camelback Mountain, to be met by her Filipino butler and ushered into her grand, antique-filled living room.

Gracious Mrs. Webster described her dream of the Desert Botanical Garden. After lunch her chauffeur drove them to the garden site, with its red buttes, saguaros, Palo Verde trees, and other native plants. Later that afternoon Mrs. Webster saw him offas he continued his journey to Guirocoba. She was amused by his Model A Ford coupe, which was piled high with camping equipment and supplies for the pack trip.

At Guirocoba, preparations were completed. The animals were shod, a young steer had been converted into carne seca, toasted corn and brown sugar were ground and combined into pinole (a staple concentrated food), and shoes and clothing were purchased for their guides, two men and two boys. George picked up Dr. Craig at the train station in Navajoa, and they were off on a fine, productive venture.

When George returned home to Lemon Crest Ranch 6 weeks later, he found urgent letters, telegrams, and telephone messages from Mrs. Webster concerning the directorship of the Desert Botanical Garden. He accepted the position on 1 May 1939. It was a marvelous experience working with outstanding philanthropists, who were trustees of the new garden, and with architects, contractors, gardeners, and young Hispanic and black men from the National Youth Administration.

Fred Gibson, Director of the Boyce Thompson Arboretum; Forest Shreve, Director of the Desert Laboratory of the Carnegie Institution of Washington in Tucson; and Robert Peebles, who with Thomas Kearney wrote Arizona Flora, became

Figure 8. During WWII, George served as a combat cinematographer with the Fourth Combat Camera Unit of the 9th Army Air Force. This picture was taken Christmas Day 1944 at Melun, France.

Figure 9. George was surprised and pleased to find potted cacti for sale in Pans in the spnng of 1945.

George's friends and advisors. The socially prominent trustees of the garden introduced him to an interesting new life style. William Hertrich of the Huntington Botanical Gardens and nurserymen Howard Gates, Gilbert Tegelberg, Harry Johnson, and many others provided truck loads of rare plants. During his one year in Phoenix the Administration Building (now called Webster Auditorium) was built, gardens were laid out, and a dedication was held 21 January 1940.

In August 1939, George made a collecting trip through Baja California Norte to get a large truckload of *Pachycereus pringlei, Fouquieria columnaris*, and other peninsula plants for the garden; they are now magnificant specimens.

His job at the Desert Botanical Garden completed on 1 June 1940, George returned to Lemon Crest Ranch. Neff Bakkers became a good friend, and George was at her nursery photographing plants for Bakkers' catalog on Sunday morning 7 December 1941, when the radio program was interrupted with startling news—Pearl Harbor had been bombed.

During World War II, George was a combat cinematographer with the Army Air Force. He went through basic training at Jefferson Barracks Missouri; Ladislaus Cutak, cactus specialist at the Missouri Botanical Garden and author for many years of the CSSA Journal column Spine Chats, made him welcome. In 1943 his overseas staging area was again Jefferson Barracks, and he renewed friendship with the Cutak family.

In England, collector George Turner, to whom Lindsay had sent cacti before the war, first showed him the cactus collections at Kew Gardens. The Turners were brave people. Their only child, a son, was an invalid as a result of his military evacuation at Dunkirk. The Turners' home, garage, and two fine automobiles were obliterated in a bombing raid. Their conservatory took a direct hit and Turner was unable to find a single spine remaining from his fine cactus collection.

Later, on the continent, George was surprised to find cacti for sale in Paris, and was amazed by the number of succulent collections in window gardens. Finally in 1945 the war was over, and George was home for Christmas, intending to be a lemon orchardist for the rest of his life.

In February 1947, Herbert Bool and George returned to Sonora, chartered a small boat at Guaymas and visited San Pedro and San Pedro Nolasco Island. On the headlands of San Pedro Bay, Bool found a miniature *Mammillaria* which Lindsay later named *Mammillaria boolii*. On San Pedro Nolasco Island they collected an *Echino cereus* which George named *E. websterianus*, and a *Mammillaria* which he called *M. multidigitata*.

George had an opportunity to make his first of many long cruises in the Gulf of California with Bill and Lynne Wilson on their yacht "Adventurous." They sailed north from Guaymas to Tiburon Island and on and around Angel de la Guarda Island to Bahia de los Angeles, then south to Cerralvo Island and across the Gulf to Mazatlan. The Sea of Cortez was almost deserted then. They passed only one vessel during their weeks of exploration. Every island was a new adventure, and most of them had cacti which George had never seen before.

Figure 10. On the 23 March 1964 television program "Science in Action," George (right) lectured on cacti.

In April 1948, Reid Moran and George chartered a small ketch and with its owners, Louis and Marcho Cavanagh, as a crew, visited Todos Santos, Guadalupe, San Benitos, Cedros, Natividad, San Roque, San Geronimo, and San Martin islands. Moran made extensive general collections on that cruise, and later returned to Guadalupe Island many times. Moran also rode a mule the length of Baja California, spent years exploring the peninsula and its adjacent islands and is the authority on its flora as well as the genus *Dudleya* in the Crassulaceae.

After his return from military service in WWII George was a trustee of the San Diego Natural History Museum. The museum's board included professional and business men and scientists from the Scripps Institution of Oceanography and San Diego State University. His association with the museum and Scripps Institution was so interesting he finally changed his avocation, scientific pursuits, to his vocation. He sold Lemon Crest Ranch in 1949 and went to Stanford University to work under Ira L. Wiggins and to complete at last his undergraduate work in 1951; he received his Ph.D. in 1955. Field work for his thesis on the taxonomy and ecology of the genus *Ferocactus* was extensive and prolonged.

The Cactus and Succulent Society of America awarded George a Fellowship in July 1949 for his botanical explorations, descriptions of new taxa, and his many publications. He served on the CSSA Board of Directors during 1949-1950 when Robert Craig was the society's president. George has given programs at CSSA conventions.

From 6 July to 15 August 1951, George collected the length of Baja California and then went to central and southern Mexico. Dr. Helia Bravo Hollis and her students,

Figure 11. He was Scientific Director on the Sefton Stanford Gulf of California Expedition in 1952.

including young Her nando Sanchez-Mejorada, took him to classic cactus areas.

In spring of 1952, George's friend J. W. Sefton sponsored the Sefton-Stanford Gulf of California Expedition; George was Scientific Director. "Orca," the fine research ship ofthe Sefton Foundation, sailed from San Diego 26 March 1952, was out 61 days, and traveled over 5,000 miles. They cruised down the west coast of Baja California and

Figure 12. .George admiring an ancient specimen of *Ferocactus diguetii* on Isla Catalina, 1965.

north in the Gulf of California to the northern end of Angel de la Guarda Island. They made collecting stops on 26 islands, 23 of them in the Gulf. Reid Moran, then at Bailey Hortorium, Cornell University, was botanist, Professor William C. Steere of Stanford was bryologist, and seven Stanford graduate students were the scientific investigators in entomology, herpetology, and ichthyology. It was a productive trip.

While a graduate student at Stanford,

Figure 13. With a marine iguana on the Galapagos Islands, July 1970.

Figure 14. Wedding reception at the Academy, July 1972. Geraldine (Gerry), her son Charles, and George.

George continued field work in central and southern Mexico, with the cooperation of Dr. Bravo, Hernando Sanchez-Mejorada, Dudley Gold, Dr. Jorge Meyran, and Dr. Faustino Miranda, of the Instituto de Biologia. Professor Wiggins and George collected in western and central Mexico and with Faustino Miranda visited Thomas MacDougal in Tehuantepec. George worked with Professors Steere and Wiggins in Arizona and northern and Baja California on the Ferocactus lecontei complex.

There were many field trips, not all to the desert for cacti. For two summers, George served as an administrative assistant and botanical collector for the Arctic Research Laboratory of the Office of Naval Research at Point Barrow, Alaska, which was under the directorship of Dr. Wig gins.

Lindsay's Stanford work was concluded in 1956, and he became Director of the San Diego Natural History Museum in 1957, after taking a cruise to the Revilla Gigedo Islands with Walter and Katie Maertins aboard their schooner "Evening Star." Reid Moran was invited to be Curator of Botany, a position held previously by Ethel Bailey Higgins. Reid continued his very active field work in Baja California

Figure 15. The California Academy of Sciences dedicated its new herbarium facility on 15 May 1975. George (right), Director of the Academy, showed the facility to Dr. Peter Raven Director of the Missouri Botanical Garden.

and mainland Mexico, and assembled a large living plant collection which was housed on the roof of the museum. Under his direction the museum's herbarium became the most important repository for Baja California plants.

With National Science Foundation support, George established the Vermilion Sea Field Station at Bahia de los Angeles, which was given further support by the Belvedere Scientific Fund of San Francisco. Transportation was provided mainly by Francisco Munoz and his Baja Flying Service. The Station was used by numerous scientists and was visited by cactus specialists from many places.

On 1 October 1963, George left San Diego to become Director of the California Academy of Sciences in San Francisco; he was succeeded in San Diego by Dr. E. Yale Dawson. In January 1964, the Academy, the University of California, and the National Science Foundation sponsored an international expedition to the Galapagos Is lands. Yale Dawson and George collected cacti; this was his last serious cactus collecting trip. On trips since then, he has observed, photographed, and otherwise enjoyed his surroundings.

The 14th of July 1972, was a red letter day for George. He married Geraldine

Figure 16. On a trip to Namibia in 1981, George and Gerry saw *Welwitschia mirabilis* in habitat.

(Gerry) Kendrick Morris of San Francisco, a widow with five children. He now has 10 grandchildren.

In 1981, Sven-Olof Lindblad, George, and Gerry Lindsay visited South West Africa (Namibia) and saw *Welwitchia mirabilis* and *Lithops* spp. in habitat. In August and September 1986, George spent several weeks with Myron Kimnach of Huntington Botanical Gardens and Dr. and Mrs. Frank Almeda (he is Curator of Botany at the Academy) looking at the wonderful succulent flora of South West Africa and South Africa.

A prolific author, George has written over 120 articles and co-authored many others during the 51 years between 1936 and 1987. He also wrote annual reports for the

Figure 17. A portrait of George painted by Diffenderfer in 1981 hangs in the Trustees' Room, California Academy of Sciences.

Figure 18. Dr. Lindsay at his job in 1980 as Director of the California Academy of Sciences.

San Diego National History Museum from 1957 to 1963 and for the California Academy of Sciences from 1963 to 1982. His publications cover diverse subjects— descriptions of new taxa, travelogues, biographies, expeditions, ecology, geography, whales, and bristlecone pines. Most of his papers were published in the Cactus and Succulent Journal, Desert Plant Life (ceased publication in 1952), and Pacifc Discovery.

George described 18 taxa, all cacti, between 1937 and 1967. With one exception, all were published in the Cactus and Succulent Journal (see Table 1). Many noted botanists—Craig, Moran, Wiggins, Bravo, Walther, and Meyran— named seven taxa, chiefly succulents, in Lindsay's honor (see

Figure 19. George still enjoys exploring and he is stillfascinated by cacti, especially huge specimens like this one of *Pachycereus pringlei* on Isla Catalina, Gulf of California, March 1986.

Table 1. Taxa described by George Lindsay

Taxon	Year	Publication
Cochemiea maritima	1937	Cactus and Succulent Journal 8:143-144
Opuntia rosarica	1942	CSJ 14:56-57
Mammillaria craigii	1942	CSJ 14:107-109
Ferocactus alamosanus var. *platygonus*	1942	CSJ 14:139-143
Mammillaria radiaissima	1945	in R. T. Craig, *Mammillaria* Handbook, pp. 292-293
Mammillaria multidigitata	1947	CSJ 19: 151-154
Echinocereus websterianus	1947	CSJ 19:151-154
Mammillaria boolii	1953	CSJ 25:48-49
Ferocactus schwarzii	1955	CSJ 27:70-71
Ferocactus gatesii	1955	CSJ 27: 150-151
Ferocactus wislizeni var. *tiburonensis*	1955	CSJ 27: 163-175
Ferocactus diguetii var. *carmenensis*	1955	CSJ 27: 163-175
Mammillaria louisae	1960	CSJ 32: 169
Lophocereus schottii forma *mieckleyanus*	1963	CSJ 35: 184
Lophocereusschottii var. *tenuis*	1963	CSJ 35:187
Ferocactus viridescens var. *littoralis*	1964	CSJ 36:8-10
Mammillaria tegelbergiana	1966	CSJ 38:196-197

Table 2. Taxa named for George Lindsay

Taxon	Year	Publication
Mammillaria lindsayi Craig	1940	Cactus and Succulent Journal 12: 182
Lavatera lindsayi Moran	1951	Madrono I 1: 158
Cuscuta lindsayi Wiggins	1959	Contrib. Dudley Herb. 5: 133
Myrtgerocactus lindsayi Moran	1962	CSJ 34:186
Ferocactus lindsayi H. Bravo	1966	Cact. y Sucul. Mex. 11 :9
Echeveria lindsayana E. Walther	1972	Walther, Echeveria, p. 90
Echinocereus lindsayi Meyran	1975	Cact. y Sucul. Mex. 20:79

****

Vaejovis lindsayi Gertsch and Soleglad = *Uroctonus lindsayi* Williams, a scorpion from Sierra Laguna, Baja California.

Leptotvphlops humilis lindsayi Murphy, Lindsay's Blind Snake or Lindsay's Blind Worm Snake, from Isla Carmen, Gulf of California, 4 April 1962.

Table 2). A scorpion and a blind snake also have been named for him!

George worked under Professor Ira Wiggins and received most of his botanical training at Stanford University's Dudley Herbarium. There has long been a close association between the California Academy of Sciences and Stanford University: David Starr Jordan, Stanford's first president, was also president of the Academy. During George's tenure as Director of the Academy, research collection facilities were built to house the large natural history collection of the University which, while enormously important, was too expensive for the University to maintain. On 15 May 1975, Dudley Herbarium was combined with the California Academy of Sciences Herbarium in a beautiful new Botany Department. The Academy's herbarium now houses more than 1.5 million plant specimens, including many cacti. This is where George has his retirement office.

George retired in the spring of 1982. Mrs. Lindsay died in December 1983. While his active collecting days are long past, he enjoys occasional visits with friends like Dave Grigsby. George still admires beautiful plants and enjoys reading the Cactus and Succulent Journal from cover to cover, a habit of half a century. He spoke at the celebration of the 50th anniversary of the incor poration of the Arizona Cactus and Native Flora Society in January 1987, and found friends from those exciting days 50 years ago.

May 1996 Update

George Lindsay

The editors decided to include the 1987 biographical sketch by Dr. Larry Mitich and requested that I bring it current with the following epilogue. I don't deserve this complimentary treatment, but I am nonetheless flattered.

Picking up from where Larry left off, I retired in 1982, and my wife Gerry died in 1983. She is enormously missed. I have continued to travel. Most years I returned to Baja California aboard ships of Special Expeditions, owned by Sven-Olof Lindblad, and once again I drove the length of the peninsula by road. And on Sven's ship the Polaris I crossed the Atlantic three times, went to coastal Europe and to Spitsbergen, sailed the Baltic to St. Petersberg, and made a seven weeks cruise to West Africa and Brazil and up and down the Amazon and the Orinoco in Venezuela. Another time we crossed the isthmus of Panama to the Pacific and up the coast to Costa Rica and Mexico. Another year saw us off to Honduras, Belize, and Yucatan. On the chartered sailing vessel Sea Cloud we sailed from Easter Island to Tahiti. On other years we flew to Australia and New Guinea, to China, and to Rajasthan in India. The ship Iliria took me to Indonesia and again to the Mediterranean.

For some time I was a trustee of the L. S. B. Leakey Foundation, which supports palentological research and studies of the origins of human behavior. Gerry and I had known Mary Leakey in Kenya and Tanzania and she and her sons Richard and Phillip had all lectured at the Academy. Subsequently, we showed Mary the Grand Canyon and the Southwest, Yosemite, and Baja California on her annual visits. I was president of the Leakey foundation until 1988, when I resigned because of medical problems. I remain an honorary trustee.

Following surgeries for knee replacements with prosthesis joints I required assistance and a student, Marcos Ballesteros, accompanied me on trips to Baja California and Mexico and to Europe and Africa. A stroke and further complications made his assistance invaluable since then.

The fiftieth anniversary of the founding of the Desert Botanical Garden in Phoenix brought great satisfaction in seeing the dreams of its founders realized. And in April 1992, it was the scene of the meetings of the International Organization of Succulent Plant Studies which attracted botanists from around the world. Gertrude Webster's memory was honored. I received a sculpture, Cactus D'Or, from the Principality of Monaco. I appreciate it, although other Americans are far more deserving of this award.

On May 31, 1996, Dr. Michael Hager announced the Inauguration of the Biodiversity Research Center of the Californias and the Mary and Dallas Clark endowed Chair of Botany at the San Diego Natural History Museum. Dr. Jon Rebman was appointed Curator. Dr. Rebman has done much field work in Baja California, studying particularly the puzzling phylogenetics of the cylindropuntias. He proposes to continue his research on the cacti and Baja California flora at the museum. Dr. Reid Moran's lifetime of studies and his accumulated herbarium collections at the museum will be utilized. This is all gratifying.

This is my eightieth year. I appreciate the luck and good fortune I have enjoyed. I worked for three institutions, the Desert Botanical Gardens, the San Diego Natural History Museum, and the California Academy of Sciences, under the direction of outstanding trustees who always were my friends. My professional colleagues have been stimulating and interesting and capable. Working with them has been a pleasure.

Interest in cacti has been my avocation since I was a boy. My permissive parents did not assign me to psychiatric therapy; on the contrary they tolerated and encouraged my interest in cacti and deserts and natural history. That, in turn, led to a full and gratifying life. I appreciate my blessings.

I am indebted to many who have been associated with my hobby. Among the pioneers were Mrs. Morton Emerson, Scott Haselton, William Hertrich, Howard Gates, Ethel Bailey Higgins, William Taylor Marshall, Harry Johnson, Gilbert Tagelburg, Yale Dawson, Robert and John Poindexter, Neff Bakkers, Howard Bullard, Reid Moran, Ted and Louisa Hutchison, Philip Munz, Lyman Benson, Dorothy Harvey, L. H. Bailey, Forest Shreve, Robert Peebles, Fred Gibson, Dean Thornbur, Gertrude Webster, Herbert Bool, Robert Craig, Fritz Schwarz, Helia Bravo Hollis, Hernando Sanchez-Mejorada, Dudley Gold, Jorge Meyran, Ira Wiggins, William Steere, Salvadore Guerrero, Enrique Beltran, Hernandez Corzo, Bernardo Villa, Bob Diehl, Halum and Mary Koons, Joseph Sefton, Robert Foster and Charles Glass, Virginia Martin, Curt Backeberg, Count F. M. Knuth, George Turner, Myron Kimnach, Sir Oliver and Lady Leese, T. Kaku, Alan White, John Hilton, students John Sloan, Chris Parrish, and Marcos Ballesteros, Larry Mitich, Lad Cutak, Arthur Bridge, David Grigsby, Madelyn Lee, Luis Baptista, and many others. What an incredible galaxy of friendships and associations; and what memories! And now I add Hugo Cota, Reese Brown, Mark Raptis, and Stan Yalof, whose idea it was to publish this book. I am grateful that you thought it worthwhile. Thank you all.

Acknowledgments

The Editors thank Larry Mitich for permission to use his fine biography of George Lindsay, which first appeared in the CSSA Journal. In the biography, Larry expressed his appreciation to George and to Guy

Kyser, University of California, for reviewing the manuscript. We are relative newcomers to the genus *Ferocactus* and Cactaceae, and our knowledge and appreciation arise from the works of George Lindsay and his associates. Our interest in *Ferocactus* was kindled by Frank Thrombley, who introduced us to this fascinating genus, and to Dr. Lindsay's work. This manuscript is stored in computer memory and is available for periodic updates.

Growing Ferocactus Seedlings

Stan Yalof

Introduction

There is great satisfaction in watching seedlings break through the soil crust, appearing as little green nubs with small leaves, quickly shed in favor of fine spines. Fero seeds are comparatively large (1-3 mm, 0.040-0.120 in), hence easily handled. There are several favored propagation methods, selection depending on the number of seeds sown and available equipment. To give a broad view on how to go about propagation, I have talked to Phyllis Flechsig, a grower in Encinitas, and to Carl Volkers, co-owner of C&J Cactus Nursery, Vista, to my knowledge the best of all cactus seedling nurseries. To the opinions of these experts, I have added my own amateur experiences.

Seed Collection

One must have seeds before having seedlings. Some Feros can cross-pollinate, and unless care is taken may hybridize in your garden. In habitat, there is usually both geographic and flowering time separation to preventing hybridization. To be safe, transfer pollen from plant to plant, with a fine brush, and then cover the flower with gauze to prevent subsequent pollination by outsiders. After ripening, split the fruit, remove the seeds, rinse them several times until any loose or sticky material is removed, then dry them. I have used 5 percent bleach in warm-to-the-touch water (120-130º F) as my first and second rinses in order to sterilize the surface and to remove any natural sprouting inhibitors. Phyllis and Carl use Physan 20 (Maril Products, Inc.) as a seedbed sterilant. The Physan manufacturer recommends that seeds be soaked for 5 minutes in a Physan solution as a seed surface sterilant. This probably does as well, perhaps better, than my bleach wash. I also clean up any old pots that I intend to use by soaking them in a 10 percent bleach solution for a few hours. I usually rinse seeds several times through a paper coffee filter. Some Fero seeds are dry, some are covered with a sticky, hard to remove, mucous. When dried, the mucous tends to adhere to the filter paper more than to the seeds. After rubbing the seeds loose, you can rewash them in a fresh filter to further clean them. The object is to separate the seeds from the goo, wash away most clinging residue, dry them, and then store them. Some loose residue is acceptable.

Materials Needed

Seedbed vessels come in so many forms that I'll stick to the usual for now and cover some others in a closing section. You will need pot **labels**.

Small 2-2.5 inch plastic **pots** or foil trays (with drain holes) within **plastic** bags will do fine for small batches. A 2 inch pot will support about 50 seeds. C & J Nursery works in plastic flats, seeding about 10-20 per square inch, per my observation. The seedbed soil preferred by both Phyllis and Carl is a mixture of a modified and steam **sterilized soil** (such as Supersoil, a tradename of the Rod McLellan Co.) mixed with an equal part of medium-fine graded **perlite**. This perlite has its dust and large lumpy particles removed since dust limits drainage and large lumps won't support seedlings. A local supplier calls this Grade 1. A kitchen sieve or shaking a load in a pot to settle out the dust works well. Big stuff grades toward the top and can be scraped aside. I have mixed up my own soil, warming it in a pot till steam appeared and holding it at temperature for 20 minutes, or until thoroughly steamed. My soil mix was 20-30% topsoil + 10-15% peat moss + perlite for the balance. I then store the sterilized soil in a plastic bag. Dave Grigsby used oak leaf mold in lieu of peat and soil and a fellow editor of this book, Reese Brown, swears by this combination. He has performed difficult germinations with this mix. I've tried it with Fero seeds, and from my limited experience it seems to work better than the Supersoil mix (SM). One such seedling batch is shown in Figure 140A, where oak leaf mold mix (OLMM) with fungicide was better than OLMM without fungicide, which was better than SM with fungicide, which was better than SM mix alone. My limited experience with OLMM should be substantiated by the reader. C&J and Phyllis Flechsig do well with Supersoil. Oak leaf mold which is packaged by Kellogg and is not carried by many nurseries. You could dig your own beneath oaks, but you'd have to screen out leaves and twigs. The apparent superiority of oak leaf mold might be due to its acidity or to some friendly biological substance.

You must use **good water**. The salts in hard water will dehydrate the seedlings. Use either soft water, softened water, rain water, or water saved from a refrigerator defrost. Joe Kratz uses distilled water (see Adventurous Methods, below).

To prevent damping-off of the seedlings, **fungicides** are applied by Phyllis and Carl. Both use Physan 20. I have used Benomyl (E. I. duPont de Nemours, Inc. tradename, but blended into specialty products). Alternatively, the soil can be heat sterilized in an oven, pot, or microwave oven or by pouring boiling water over it. The objective is to hold its temperature for at least 30 minutes in the 46 to 56 deg. C (140 to 160 F) range. If you don't use soil as a seed bed, as for "Adventurous Methods" described below, damping off doesn't seem to occur. One explanation is that the rootlets are better aerated, limiting the growth of pernicious anaerobes.

Carl uses fine gritty chicken grit as a **topping;** Phyllis uses #10 coarse sand; I use coarse decomposed granite, which I have aplenty at my home. A water mist applicator completes the needed supplies.

Seeding

Fill your containers near to the top with seedbed soil. Either immerse the seedbed container in a pan of water/fungicide solution (1 tablespoon per gallon or manufacturer's recommendation) or immerse the seedbed in water and spray the surface with the solution. The first method is preferred. The pan can be covered, topped off with fresh solution, and reused. Before sowing, Carl lightly presses the soil with a board to remove surface indentations, lightly compressing the surface, which brings dampness to the top. Before seeding, label the batch with traceable information such as sowing date, seed name, and source. Sow the seeds 10-20 per inch, 50 or so in a 2-2.5 inch pot, as evenly as you can. Glancing at a low level across the seedbed will make the seeds stand out and you can sprinkle into the missed areas. A light misting will settle the seeds into the bed. Both Phyllis and Carl mist with Physan solution. A single layer of grit, just enough to cover the seeded soil, finishes the seeding. Too much grit is not disastrous, but does put a strain on the seedling and could block out the needed light for germination.

Cultivation

Seedlings ideally need a balance of constant moisture and avoidance of drowning, temperatures of 75-80 degrees, and shading protection against UV. The preceding soaking of the seedbed will have taken care of initial moisture requirements. Small pots can be placed in plastic bags, subsequently tied closed. Large flats can be covered with empty upturned flats. After seedlings sprout and lose their seed caps, the bags can be cracked open. When the seedlings become small cacti, they can be set out. They sunburn easily, so keep them screened. Carl's experience has taught him that seedlings can take some excess heat or some excess light, but not the two together.

Fero seedlings do best when temperatures are kept within range. Carl is fairly sure that night growth is greater than day, and he tries to maintain constant seedling temperatures. Phyllis also uses heaters. I grow only in warm weather and get by with ambient temperatures. One year I successfully used the refrigerator exhaust as a warm bed until the seeds sprouted, then moved them into diffused light. Most Fero species will sprout under reasonable conditions the year around in about 1 week to 10 days.

When seedlings are out of the bag and show distress due to dehydration (puckering, shrinking), give them a light mist. I mist them every few days when exposed to air, particularly if the soil feels too warm or dry. They have enough mineral sustenance in the soil to carry them until pot transfer. Too much watering and not enough drainage time will cause damping-off.

Cactus seedlings do better when clumped together. When they get to a handleable size, perhaps 0.25 inch each, Carl's workers remove them by hand in clumps of 5 to 10 plantlings, to be planted in checkerboard arrays in new flats.

Adventurous Methods of Cultivation

Rudy Lime is well known throughout the CSSA (Cactus & Succulent Society of America) as a consistent winner of plant show competitions. His stock plants are often raised from seed. A method that he favors and that I've tried at his suggestion is to lay the cleaned seeds between the folds of a moist paper towel. The towel is sealed within a sandwich bag and kept warm. Every few days the seeds are inspected. He removes the seeds after the skin has cracked and plants them. I'm now raising a batch which I started between toweling and have rooted into the top toweling sheet (see Figure140B). To adapt them to soil without harming their roots, I have moved their sheet to a thin bed of soil and sprinkled some grit around them for their support and to weight the toweling against the underlying soil. So far, the seedlings are doing well on the modified Rudy Lime regimen. They'll get a dilute feeding when (and if) they become established. No fungicide is required.

A related method employs modified hydroponics. The seedbed is a ventilator air filter, about 1 inch thick, fiber filled, and available in a variety of sizes. After seeds are dispersed on the surface, the filter is saturated from below for some minutes, then allowed to drain. This is repeated daily, or more often. As the plantlets grow, nutrients are added to the water. Mechanization with some hose, a pump, a bucket, and a timer would be easy and soil would not be initially required. Subsequent transfer into soil could be a problem. Maybe not. The rootlets would grow into the fiber medium. The idea behind this method is that providing superior aeration to the roots would aid plantlet respiration and growth without introducing harmful organisms. Nutrients supplied would also have to include micro as well as macro nutrients. The usual micro nutrients are boron, chlorine, iron, magnesium, manganese, molybdenum, and nickel, which are usually in sufficient supply within soil. Nutrient mixtures can be obtained from hydroponic materials suppliers.

I have sterilized a wet soil mix and seed within a jar by microwave heating. The jar was capped with plastic and then screw capped and set aside for germination. I picked up this method from a report in the CSSA journal. One could vary this method, e.g., with agar as the medium and by sterilizing within a hot water bath. These jars can apparently remain closed for years.

Joe Kratz, a local grower succulent and palm grower, grows on a thin bed of sphagnum moss/perlite mix atop a floral foam layer, the kind used by floral arrangers. He waters from below, by absorption, with distilled water and reports no damping-off. He transfers to soil after slight growth. Hydroponic feeding would allow one to carry growth on foam to almost any size. Joe chops the moss in a food processor.

Summary

Ferocactus propagation methods would work for most cacti. Fero seeds will come up at any time of the year. Damping-off is the major problem. A closed bag is the most forgiving for climate control. Phyllis offers the advice, "Don't sow all your seeds at once." Please also remember that as seedlings grow and get repotted, their space requirements swell mightly. Sow only what you can nurture. Most of the advice within this article is based upon the practice of several individuals. Different methods work better for different people. A study of the relative benefits of these methods and the parameters that control them would be useful.

Figure 140. Ferocactus latispinus. top Photo; SM mix above, OLMM mix below: first three rows from right were treated with fungicide. Bottom Photo: seedlings on toweling, no fungicide used.

About Our Illustrators

Ars Longa, Vita Brevis

Nature illustration goes back to human prehistory, preceding writing, possibly even speech. This artistry ranged from realistic to impressionistic to sybolic.

Even in this time of photography, graphic illustration is prospering, depicting the essentials of the living kingdom. The plant kingdom has had a full share of gifted illustrators. This book contains a sampling.

The *Ferocactus* line drawings shown in the following pages were prepared for Lyman Benson by Lucretia Breazeale Hamilton, with the exception of Figure 141 by Paulus Roetter for George Engelmann.

There is art distributed through the book. The front cover was done by our art director, Sandra Reed. She wanted a cover that did justice to the idea of *Ferocactus*, rather than the specifics of a particular varity. Taking the impressionistic road, she created the books imaginative front cover, Ferocactus Fantasy.

The end papers are patterns of drawings by Lucretia Breazeale Hamilton and others.

The glossary illustrations were by T. M. Bock, slightly modified. They were published back in 1941, but our editors have found none better for their task.

The back cover of George Lindsay (right) and Reid Moran by Gerhard Marx is reproduced with his kind permission. It makes me smile every time I look at it.

Our appreciation for permission to use the preceeding art is given in the Acknowledgments page.

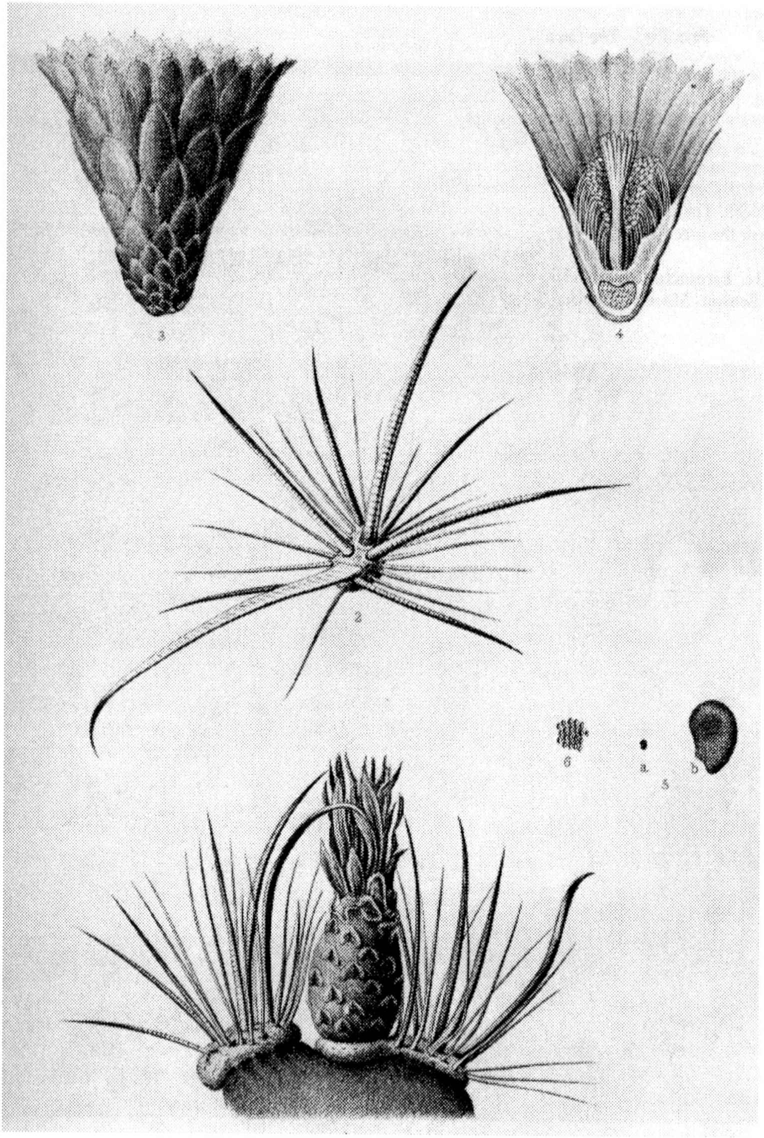

Figure 141. ***Ferocactus acanthodes*** **var.** ***lecontei***

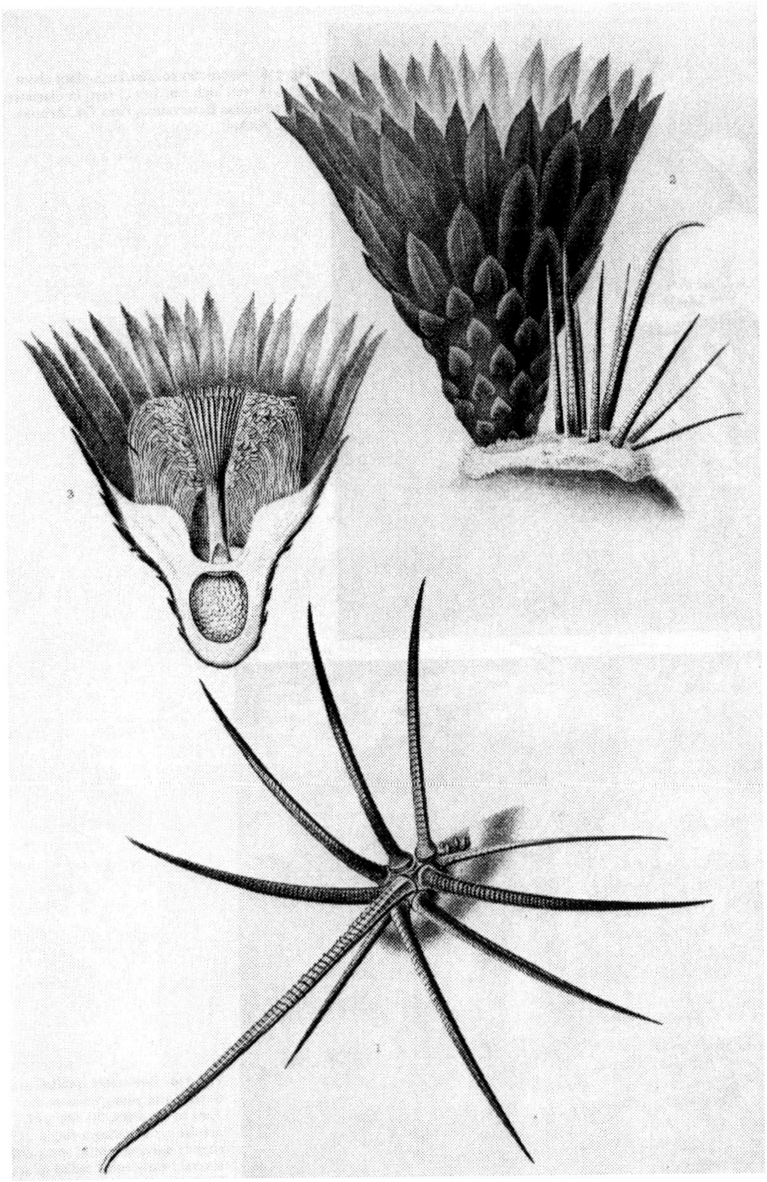

Figure 142. *Ferocactus covillei*

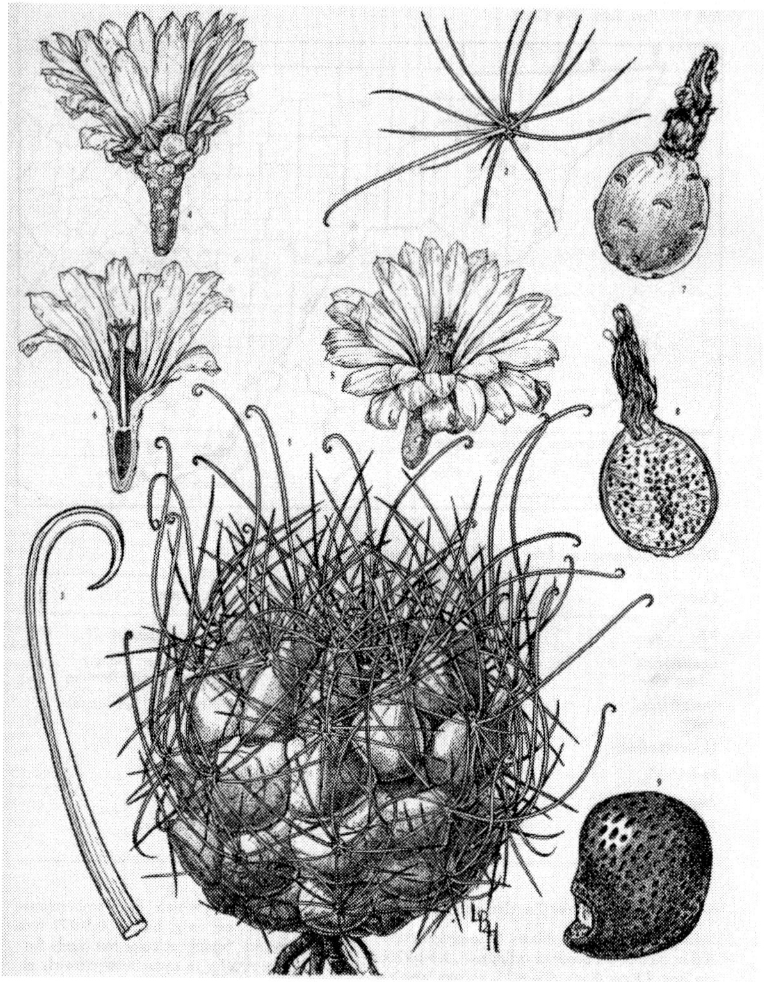

Figure 143. ***Ferocactus hamatacanthus*** **var.** ***hamatacanthus***

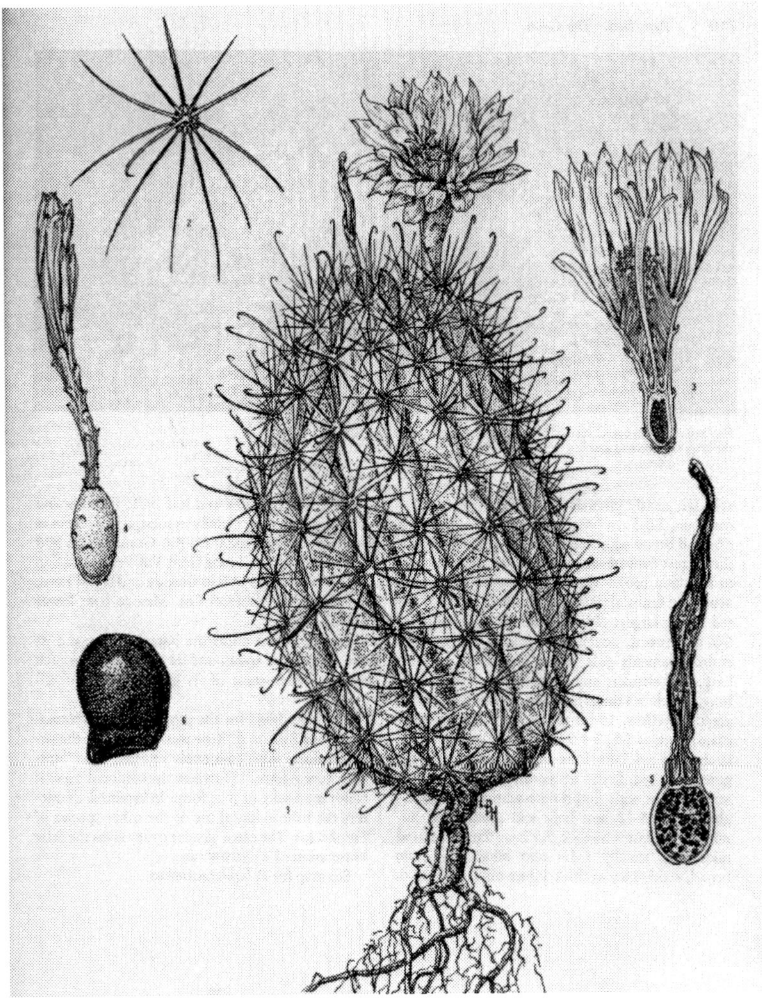

Figure 144. ***Ferocactus setispinus***

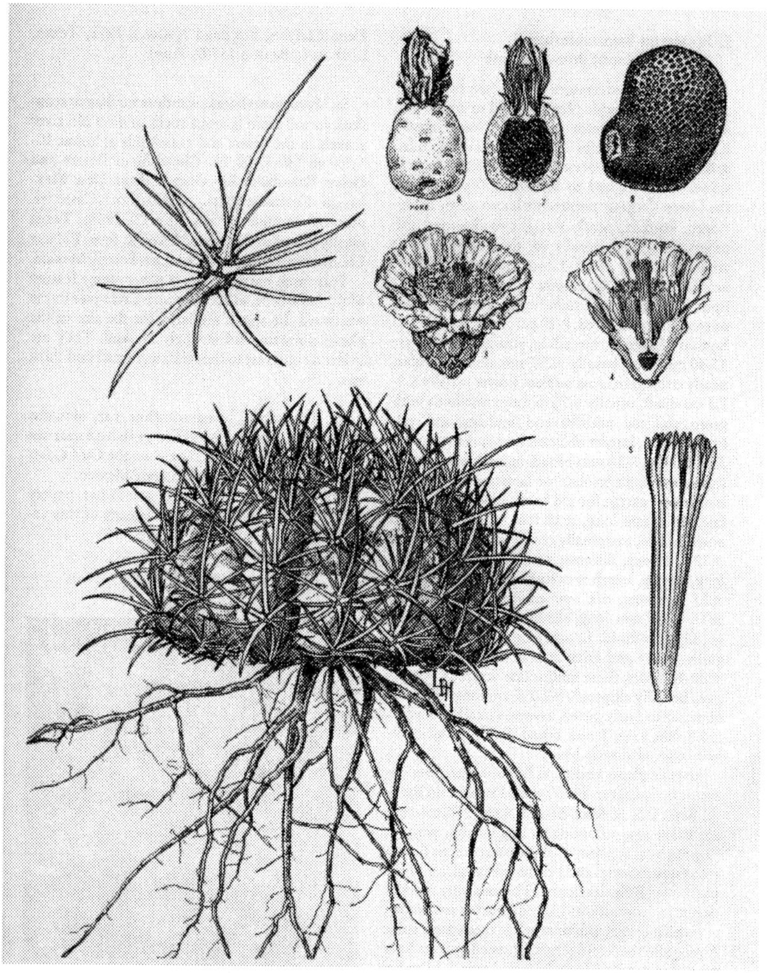

Figure 145. ***Ferocactus viridescens***

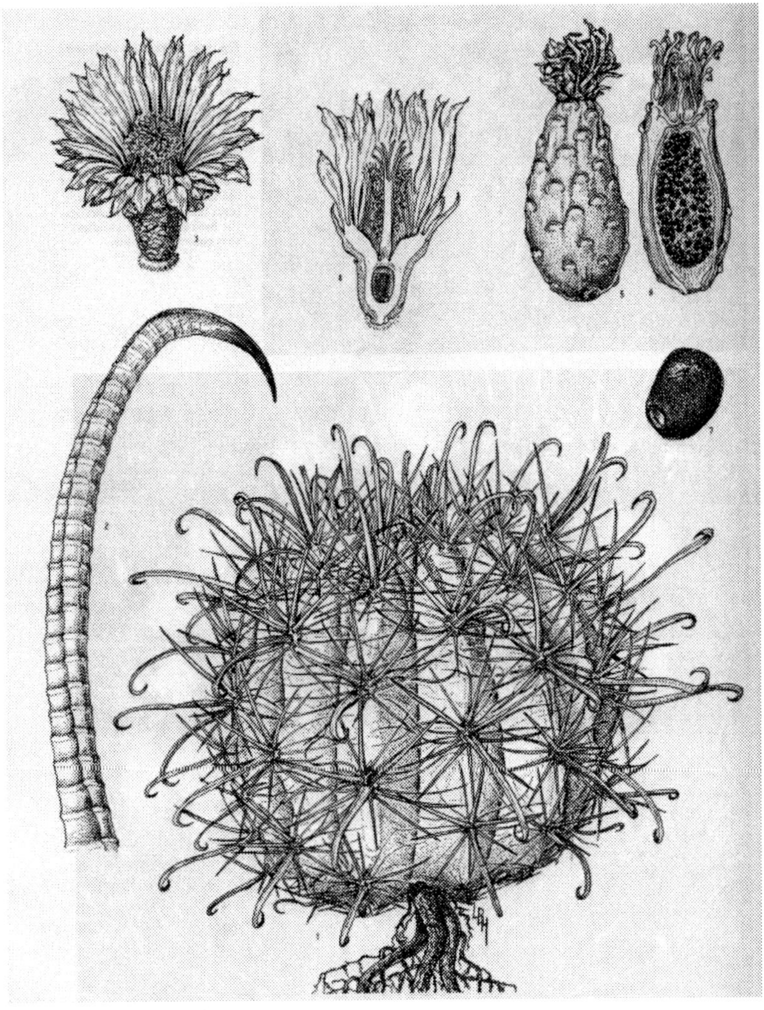

Figure 146. *Ferocactus wislizenii*

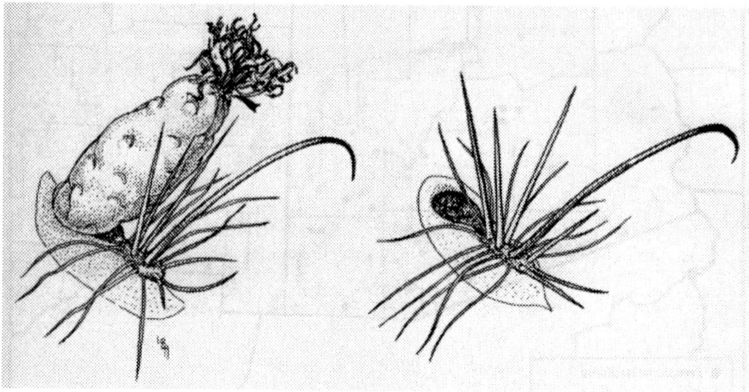

Figure 147. ***Ferocactus wislizenii*** **var.** ***wislizenii***

The Hanna Portfolio

The Story Behind These Color Plates

George Lindsay

In 1963, after joining the California Academy, Dr. G. Dallas Hanna surmised that I might publish something about Ferocactus. He volunteered to make the color plates. Working as a team with Mrs. Hanna and Maurice Giles, the Academy scientific photographer, they developed an inexpensive color printing process, using an office multilith machine. The following sixteen remarkable color plates are the result, printed many years ago. It was intended that this process be used for low cost scientific illustration.

Dr. Hanna was a remarkable, versatile man, a genius, and a great friend. He was a scientist, inventor, engineer, and field geologist. He joined the Academy in 1919 and was there for 51 years. He was an authority on fossils and recent diatoms and perfected optical instruments for their microscopic analysis and illustration. He published many papers about living as well as fossil shells and many other subjects. During World War II, Dr. Hanna developed an optical shop for the armed forces. With that equipment he and a team of instrument makers and astronomers invented and built a projector for the new Morrison Planetarium at the Academy. From that experience the color printing plate process was developed.

I first met him when he was Director of the Arctic Research Laboratory at Point Barrow, Alaska. He took a leave in 1964 to head a group investigating the Alaska earthquake under the auspices of the US Geological Survey and then the National Science Foundation. Doc was then seventy-seven years old. He died on November 20, 1970. His wife Margaret is pleased that at long last the Ferocactus book is going to be published. So am I. Having these plates in storage after all these years had weighted my conscience. At last they are going to be used.

Figure 148: *Ferocactus acanthodes* var. *acanthodes*. San Felipe desert, northern Baja California.

Figure 149: *Ferocactus covillei*. Above: flowers. Below: a straight-spined specimen (*Lindsay 2251*) photographed 4.8 miles north of Magdalena, Sonora. Its flowers range from mahogany through red to clear yellow in color.

Figure 150: *Ferocactus diguetii* var. *diguetii* with Dr. William Emerson at the type locality, Isla Santa Catalina, Gulf of California.

Figure 151: Above: *Ferocactus echidne* var. *echidne* from Venados, Hidalgo, flowering at Stanford 1 May 1955. Below: *Ferocactus echidne* var. *victoriensis*.

Figure 152: *Ferocactus flavovirens* at Zapotitlan de Salinas, Puebla.

FIGURE 153: *Ferocactus gatesii.* Above: Habitat at the type locality, a small islet in the Smith Island group, at the mouth of Bahia de los Angeles, Baja California. Below: Flowers photographed 10 May 1952.

Figure 154: *Ferocactus glaucescens.* Above: The waxy glaucous blue-green color is unique. Below: a cespitose plant at Canon de Venado, near Meztitlan, Hidalgo.

Figure 155: *Ferocactus gracilis* var. *gracilis*, 20 miles east of El Rosario, Baja California.

Figure 156: *Ferocactus herrerae* photographed near Culican, Sinaloa.

Figure 157: *Ferocactus histrix* (De Candole) Lindsay, Cact. Succ. J, 27:171, 1955.

Figure 158: ***Ferocactus macrodiscus*** **from San Juan de Teposcula, Oaxaca, (*Lindsay 2607*).**

Figure 159: *Ferocactus peninsulae* var. *viscainensis*, near Mesquital, Baja California.

Figure 160: *Ferocactus rectispinus* from 5 miles west of Canipole, Baja California.

Figure 161: *Ferocactus robustus* near Tehuacan, Puebla.

Figure 162: Above: *Ferocactus townsendianus* var. *santa-maria* in flower at Stanford August 1954. Below: *F. townsendianus* var. *townsendianus* (*Lindsay 1968*), 7 miles east of La Paz on the road to Las Cruces, Baja California, 31 August 1951.

Figure 163: *Ferocactus wislizeni* var. *wislizenii* photographed 10 miles **east of Coolidge Dam, Arizona, 23 August 1951. The first blossoms of the season had just opened. The blossoming period runs through September.**

Editors' Photo Gallery

Stan Yalof

The following *Ferocactus* photos supplement those preceding. Unless otherwise noted, they were taken at the San Diego Wild Animal park (WAP). I am a volunteer at the WAP, sharing responsibility for the planting and upkeep of several large desert gardens. The WAP has a good collection of Ferocacti, about 30 species and varieties, some planted in the gardens, others in its succulent collection greenhouse. The Baja California plants were collected with Mexican permission by WAP volunteers. The entire Ferocactus collection has been largely assembled and nurtured by fellow volunteer Frank Thrombley. In taking these photos, I merely had to wait until the cacti flowered and fruited. This requires patience as some skip a year or two or don't flower until their mature years. My fellow editors and I picked some favorites for this section.

Figure 164. ***F.acanthodes* var. *acanthodes*. Plant and flowers.**

Figure 165. *F. acanthodes* var. *tortulispinus*. Plant and flowers.

Figure 166. ***F. covillei*. Plant and flowers.**

Figure 167. ***F. chrysacanthus*. Plant and flowers.**

Figure 168. ***F. echidne*** **var.** ***victoriensis*****. Variegated plant with flower.**

Figure 169. ***F. fordii*** **var.** ***fordii*****. Plant and flowers.**

Figure 170. ***F. glaucescens*****. Plant and flowers.**

Figure 171. *F. gracilis* var. *gracilis*. Catavina, Baja California (H. Cota)

Figure 172. ***F. gracilis*** **var.** ***gracilis*****. Plant and flowers.**

Figure 173. ***F. gracilis*** **var.** ***gracilis*****. Plant and flowers, yellow spined.**

Figure 174. ***F. gracilis var. coloratus*. Plant and flowers.**

Figure 175. *F. haematacanthus*. From Puebla, Mexico (S. Arias).

Figure 176. Above: *F. histrix*. (S. Yalof). Below: F. recurvis var. greenwoodii, (S. Yalof)

Figure 177. *F. johnstonianus*. **Angel de la Guarda Island (R. Moran, 8/83).**

Figure 178. *F. latispinus*. Plants and flowers: (above) white flower form, (below) violet flower form.

Figure 179. ***F. peninsulae*** **var.** ***viscainensis*****. Plant and flowers.**

Figure 180 *F. pilosus*. Plant and flowers

Figure 181. *F. pottsii* var. *alamosanus.* Plant and flowers.

Figure 182. *F. rectispinus*. Plant and flowers.

Figure 183. ***F. recurvus*** **var.** ***recurvus*** **(*latispinus var. recurvus*). Oaxaca (S. Arias).**

Figure 184. ***F. reppenhagenni*****. Plant and flowers.**

Figure 185. ***F. schwarzii*****. Plant and flowers.**

Figure 186. ***F. townsendianus var. townsendianus*** **and** ***townsendianus*** **var.** ***santa-maria*****. Flowers.**

Figure 187. Above: *F. townsendianus* var. *townsendianus* and *townsendianus* var. *santa-maria*. Plants. Below: *F. wislizenii* Flowers.

RAPTIS